MORE THAN A
CONQUEROR

CONFESSIONS OF A TRUE TESTIMONY

TANISHA CARTER

ISBN 978-1-64079-552-5 (paperback)
ISBN 978-1-64079-553-2 (digital)

Christian Faith Publishing, Inc.
832 Park Avenue
Meadville, PA 16335
www.christianfaithpublishing.com

Cover photo and design:
Photographer SikatHeart @sikatheart

Makeup Artist:
Jacen Bowman @Shadesofjacen

Hair stylist:
Erica Felder @ericabellahairbox

Printed in the United States of America

CONTENTS

FOREWORD

THEY SAY THAT IF you concentrate really hard, you will notice that angels walk amongst us in plain sight. If this is the case, then we are witnessing an angel right before us, in Tanisha D. Carter. Tanisha has the ability to captivate the soul. Her inspirational words echo in your mind's ear; the conviction that she speaks with shakes your core being, and her story is beyond miraculous. Upon reading the first few pages, I was moved to tears. The book is a true testimony, and I am a personal witness to its validity.

As little brother (literally), it is an honor to speak on behalf of my amazing sister Tanisha D. Carter. Growing up, Tanisha was my model for success. I didn't have my father around. Instead, I watched how Tanisha succeeded through school. I saw the praise that she received and wanted that same acclaim. Tanisha and I used to compete as to who could bring home the most awards, as siblings. We never determined who won, so on my big sister's debut book, I'll admit it—Tanisha, you won.

You won because you convinced a little boy to dream. You showed a young black man that there was hope, when he was surrounded by dismay. The truth is "Neesh," the countless times I thought about giving up, I had you to think about. The many mental and emotional battles you've dealt with. The physical ridicule you've endured. The many tears you've cried on my shoulder, but somehow mustered strength to continue on with life. To defy literally every odd stacked up against you with such *Sh*eroism; Tanisha D. Carter, you are the ultimate winner. I tell you all the time; without you, there is no me. You have been, and always will be, the greatest winner in my life.

Many people ask me all the time about my success. I have over twelve books published to my name, two of which I've personally authored. I have been recognized by both the City of Philadelphia and United Way of Greater Philadelphia as a leader and mentor to my community. I am one of the youngest recipients of the Department of Navy's Community Award, and I have been named one of the Department of Defense's Emerging Leaders. None of this is possible without Tanisha.

This book will challenge you. It will cause you to think deeply about the excuses many of us come up with that prevents us from succeeding. It will challenge your definition of success. For a moment, it will force you to look beyond the surface of social media culture and surface-level concerns and you will delve into a story of true perseverance. Ladies and gentleman, if you have not witnessed an angel in the flesh, I assure that you are about to read about one.

It is my sincere pleasure to introduce you to my best friend, big sister, psychologist, teacher, coach, mentor, and my personal angel… Tanisha D. Carter.

Go Get Em, Neesh!

—Joshua J. Rivers

Mom : Thank you for being an example of strength amidst great suffering. It is because of your love, faith, and strength that has always inspired, encouraged, and motivated me. You had the courage to fight for me, and because of this I was able to learn to fight for myself.

Thank you for instilling the love and word of God in me, I would have never made it without knowing Him. It is the greatest gift a parent can give a child.

You are one of the most beautiful souls I have ever encountered. I am beyond proud to be your daughter, and am so very blessed to have received your love. I tell these truths with no shame but, as proof of God's infinite power. To show the nature of the human spirit, which I have witnessed through your adversity, can never die when it is manifested in strong faith.

I know you have gone through your life feeling invalidated, rejected, and alone. Like me, so many have not had the compassion to see you past your scars. Please know that you are beautifully and wonderfully made. Your heart is pure and loving, and your generosity is no match to even the wealthiest giver. You are successful because so many who have known you have experienced the love of God, and that is the greatest purpose for our lives. Be proud of yourself because many of those who have not had the challenges you faced, will never be able to accomplish the same.

I love you. Thank you for always believing in me.

Dad: Thank you for all you have done for me. I know you have always honored me through your thirty years as a firefighter. I especially thank you for helping to raise Keyan. It is because of you Keyan has the chance to reach his fullest potential.

Rasheen: Thank you for being my hero, for your protection and loyalty. My love for you is special because we faced death together and survived together, therefore without you I am incomplete.

Hakiem: Thank you for being my eyes and ears to the relentless streets, your wisdom saved me from heading down even darker paths. I have been convicted many times by your humbleness, through your suffering I have learned not to complain and to be patient just a little longer.

Erica: Thank you for being my sister, my confidant. With loss there is always a gain, because of you I experienced sisterhood. You are the true definition of beauty inside and out. When I look at your beauty, I do not know if you ever notice, but I always get emotional. When I look at you, I know all that you have gone through that tried to conceal that beauty, but you did not allow it. I see how your confidence has grown from the adversity you faced. You are like the beautiful lotus flower that grows from the murkiest waters. You truly embody everything it represents (look it up I am not doing the work for you). Your determination, perseverance, and drive have always impressed me. Keep going, you're almost there.

Josh: Through you I have experienced true love from a man. Your tenderness, unconditional love, patience, and compassion have helped me through some of the most painful times that only you have witnessed. I am most blessed that my sons have a true definition of a man to model after. Since we were little we had a special bond and today it's even stronger. I am so grateful to have had a partner through all of the difficult times we faced that have only made us love harder and give more. Through your success I am successful. Thank you for always showing me my truth when I could not see it. Love you more than you will ever know!

Keyan, Caiden, Kiye: My three kings. Mommy loves you all and have always told you more times than I can count, so you will never ever doubt that you were truly loved.

Mark: You have been through so much, and to see the positive man you have become shows true character. I love you!

To my nephews and nieces: Quadir, Symir, Skylar, Alyna, and Nasheen: I am so proud to be your aunt, you all have blessed me with your love and I truly can't wait to see the greatness God has planned for each of you.

Rose Mary Worthy Washington: I could not have made it this far without your guidance, truth, and compassion. No matter what I deal with, you always meet me where I am with comfort and understanding. You have always been the role model I have looked up to, because you look like me. It is because of you, I carry myself with poise, style and my head held high. I love you!

Michele Wise: During one of the most difficult and painful experiences in my life, you entered with your cheerful spirit, spiritual wisdom and willingness to assist me as I sought out to go deeper inside myself to learn how to finally take care of me. A few years later, you continue to be a part of my journey. You have given me such a remarkable gift, a deeper understanding and awareness for my internal conflict that once kept me victimized, but now I have the power to manage. Your presence in my life has been a true blessing and because of our unique bond, I will always hold you close to my heart.

To everyone one else I wish I can name, but there are so many. Thank you! I would not have a story to tell were it not for your support and role in my life.

Fight the good fight of the faith. Take hold of the eternal life to which you were called when you made your good confession in the presence of many witnesses. 1 Timothy 6:12 (NIV)

PRELUDE

IN MY WRITING OF *More Than a Conqueror: Confessions of a True Testimony*, I write with truth, conviction, meaning, and purpose. The nature, tone, and perspective in which I share about persons depicted are only to illustrate pertinent and significant roles, impacts, impressions, and effects those have had on my life. The intentions of this book, emphasizing on the word *Confession*, is not to be misconstrued as a "tell all" with the intentions to criticize, judge, slander, belittle, talk down, offend, cause trouble, or harm. This is not written in anger, resentment, nor is it a personal need or desire to "getting back" at the depicted.

The purpose is to tell my complete story as it happened, and how I struggled, felt, handled, embraced, learned, and accepted the things I went through with the people I experienced. With any truth, there are always two sides, both good and bad. The reality of my story is that I have had bad, horrible, cruel, unjust, and painful experiences with people, but these experiences are the critical components that have shaped me into the woman I am today. My intentions are not to make anyone look bad or be depicted in a negative light. To further demonstrate this, I have changed the names of many depicted. With this being said, I do not assume the responsibility of how my experiences come across to those depicted.

My sharing of experiences in their rawness is intended to do two things: to share how these experiences affected me and my life, and (more importantly) to show the power of forgiveness. Personal growth is contingent upon many facets, one of them being interpersonal relationships with others. Those mentioned are mentioned because they honestly have had a profound impact on my life in some way—whether they were briefly in my life or in my life for a long time. Those depicted have affected my life whether positively or negatively, but in ways I believe are important to the contribution of telling this story. I am grateful and blessed for the wonderful experiences from the loving, supportive, and kind people in my life along the way. I am evenly grateful for the most difficult experiences and the painful ways I have been treated by people.

Were it not for those experiences, I would not have felt the emotions associated, or have had the experiences that expanded my human capacity to love, feel, understand, and forgive. These experiences have given me a greater perspective of the human experience and a depth for which my faith flows. No one is perfect, even me. There is someone reading this book who can identify specifically with the writer. There is someone reading this book who can identify with someone depicted. The goal of writing what I experienced in its truth is to connect with those readers.

The purpose of this book is to inform and inspire all who have taken the time to read what life has been like for me. I have been on an interesting journey full of twists and turns, but the beauty is that I know the destination that awaits my arrival will be worth the travel. It is an honor and privilege that you have allowed me to share my experience thus far with you. My hope is that you will take something profound from this reading. That you are touched and are changed in some way. That you learn to look at life and people a little differently than you would normally, and that your heart will become more sensitive to the plight and suffering of others. Finally, that you will get in touch with your inner truths—but above all, that you will be blessed!

CHAPTER 1

Tragedy

"NO, THERE'S A BABY in there"! I can imagine the frantic screams of someone shouting from amongst the crowd of witnesses. I think about that day when raging flames engulfed the house where I had been welcomed six months prior. I imagine how I laid as my fate began to change, alter, and unfold. The screams, the terror, the cries, as I laid in peace unknowingly unsecure.

On a cold winter's day in January of 1983, I imagine that not even the arctic chill of the early morning was enough to contain the powerful inferno that would claim our home. I imagine the flames grew stronger despite the contrast of the blustery weather. I am sure this sudden attraction disrupted the quiet morning routine of the residents living on Garfield Street, a small but lively block tucked behind the main historic streets of Germantown Avenue. I picture a large crowd conjuring at the sight of bright rays of flickering red, yellow, and orange flames illuminating the block against the pale morning's natural light. The loud sound of windows combusting as a silent giant made its presence known. The smell of smog polluting the fresh breathable air, causing onlookers to cover their airways.

People were probably more concerned with the fact that there may have been occupants trapped inside and if so, they were right to suspect as such. I am sure they were all mortified to learn that the occupants were two small children and an infant.

According to my older brother, Rasheen, one of the two children inside, my mom had found it urgent to leave us alone to go to the corner store for pancake mix. I imagine the look of bewilderment on my mother's face upon returning from her trip with the box of powder. I can imagine the horror and sheer shock of disbelief when she discovered that it was her house on fire. She probably became instantly paralyzed with grief and guilt for making what then appeared to be a foolish decision, irrationally thinking that it was somehow okay to leave only for a moment, two young children to tend to themselves and a baby. I am sure that a sense of fear gripped her tight and for a second, her breathing was probably cut short from the strangulation of that surreal moment. Realizing she was outside, safe and unharmed, while her babies were inside helplessly vulnerable to the forceful flames that would not subside.

I wonder if it was then that shock turned into panic at the thought of the severe consequences of having a critical lapse of judgment, a thoughtless decision that seemed so harmless. Amongst the screams and shrieks outside, someone's voice could be heard shouting "There's a baby in there!" The voice was that of my aunt Evelyn. According to her version, the fire happened in the early evening as she was returning from work, and upon hearing this terrifying news, tried going into the house, but had been restrained by those knowing there was absolutely nothing she nor anyone could do alone. I am sure the couple of minutes waiting for rescue to arrive felt like an eternity. I am sure all everyone could do was cling on to hope and pray.

My illustration is how I always pictured the scenario to have played out in my head. Like reading a book with no pictures, my mind used words to create visuals. Not having remembered anything that took place that day, because I was so young, my premature memory saved me from ever having to relive or remember aspects of my trauma. My developing psyche served as protection, shielding me from being psychologically traumatized.

I do not remember specifically at what age I was told the story of my tragedy, but I do remember Rasheen being the only narrator. Throughout my life, he had always been the keeper of this painful truth. As painful as it was for him to relive the trauma, Rasheen believed it was important I knew the details of the experience he and I suffered through together. This event created a unique bond between the both of us, because we were the only two who survived. Not only did Rasheen live to tell the story, but he was in part the cause of the fire.

According to Rasheen, the fire started as a result of him playing with matches. He lit one, then when that one blew out, he lit another. Enjoying the instant light of the flame, my older sister Nakisha, who was only three, then decided to light her own match. Nakisha's lit match dropped and instantly the carpet caught fire. In a panic, Rasheen tried frantically to put the fire out, but in that moment, there was a hard knock on the door that struck them both with instant fear. Terrified, my brother did what any five-year-old would have probably done, he took his sister and ran. At once they darted upstairs to their rooms. Slamming the door behind them, they quickly hid under the bed in fear that they would soon be exposed for playing with matches.

The fire furiously began to grow life, spreading up the steps and into the hallway following the carpet trail. My mother's room door was open, where I laid in my crib wrapped in a blanket, peaceful and unaware of how my life was rapidly changing without my consent.

At the other end of the hallway, the fire met the closed door where Rasheen and Nakisha hid silently under the bed. When smoke was spotted filtering through the slit under the door, Nakisha began to cry. Rasheen's first reaction was to go to the door and try to open it.

But Nakisha cried and exclaimed "Oooh, you're going to get a beatin'!"

They had not realized their danger had switched from getting in trouble by mom to life threatening. He voiced his frustration quickly. "You did it!" They fussed about who should open the door. That was when Rasheen ran to the door to open it, but the doorknob broke and fell to the floor while profusely burning his hand. Hopelessly they were frozen from fear.

They continued to wait until Nakisha yelled, "Look! There is someone at the window!"

Rasheen and Nakisha clutched onto each other desperately, as the firefighter shattered the window with his axe, causing them to tremble with fright. Rasheen emerged from under the bed and made his way through the smoke toward the window, where a firefighter called out and signaled for Rasheen to come toward him. The firefighter brought Rasheen out from the burning house and after he was safe, he looked and asked for his sisters. He would learn later that Nakisha did not make it. She died from smoke inhalation, and I had been gravely injured.

When it came to retelling the story, Rasheen appeared to be the only person in my family who freely gave me information—his version is the one I tell when asked what happened. It is the only version that has remained consistent every time he told it to me. Rasheen would retell it as if we were characters in a story. Although Rasheen was deeply affected emotionally, he always managed to conceal his pain and sorrow as he told the story.

Rasheen never let on that retelling was too painful for him, it was something I always sensed. After realizing just how painful talking about the fire was for many in my family, I became conscious and careful not to make anyone experience unwanted feelings, including my brother.

I felt a sense of obligation to protect Rasheen from feeling guilty, because he was the one who struck the first match, inspiring the curiosity that led to Nakisha's match that hit the floor, starting the blaze. I thought of what it must have been like for Rasheen to carry around such heavy guilt, and I did not want to give off any impressions that I had ill feelings toward him, fearing any inclinations might just be that added weight that would tip him over. I wanted to heal his broken heart with love and forgiveness. Although Rasheen had taken responsibility for starting the fire, I never wanted my brother to think that I blamed him in any way, but I'm sure whether I blamed him or not, he must have blamed himself.

I believe because I was so young and have no recollection of what happened, it was effortless for me to forgive Rasheen. I instinctively never faulted my brother because he was a child himself. I have searched my heart many times over when it came to whether or not I carried ill feelings toward him, but there were none.

I believe I loved Rasheen more for demonstrating such bravery and acting in my defense. How many five-year-olds would have had the courage to think as fast as he had to assure that his sisters were safe. Despite being frightened, as expected a child would be, he showed great courage. Rasheen was my hero then, and I continued to see him in the same light growing up.

Maybe it was because Rasheen was my older brother that I just looked up to him. I saw Rasheen as being big, strong, and fearless. Nothing appeared to bother him. The way he carried himself and protected me, gave the impression that he was tough and in control. I felt special that I had a brother like him to watch over me. Rasheen may not have fully understood the dangers in what appeared to be as harmless as lighting a match, but when he eventually grasped the severity of the danger we were in, he immediately became my protector, and has made it his responsibility to protect me, even still.

Not just Rasheen, I did not want anyone close to me to believe I blamed them for what happened. I felt I was the dealer of the blame card, and I wanted to be careful not to issue it out to anyone. I did not want anyone in my family to think I had in any way judged them.

I learned early on the topic of the house fire was taboo, and because of the significance of guilt, over time it was barely discussed. As I got older, I became more and more inquisitive about what happened to me. Why and how this horrible situation occurred that negatively set me apart from everyone else. Although I felt a sense of entitlement to my truth, my history, I realized it was not easy for members of my family to disclose without being made to relive that painful day. I felt guilty for causing someone to relive something that seemed evident they were trying very hard to leave in their past. No one was more traumatically affected than my mother. The pain, guilt, and shame she felt when the topic was brought up were so obvious through her eyes and in her tone, that I felt the discomfort in my heart, body, and soul. It was way too painful. As with my brother, I felt the same obligation to protect my mother.

Knowing the emotional effects on loved ones, I never out-right asked anyone, "What happened?" The information was always obtained voluntarily. Therefore, I would just sit and listen; allowing for whoever was sharing their perspective to disclose what parts of their version they wanted me to know. As much as I craved the truth, in knowing the complete story, I realized I would not get it, and would have to settle on the bits and pieces others were comfortable to add.

If and when my mom, dad, or aunt made reference to the fire, I listened carefully, and looked for opportunities to solicit more infor-mation. My aunt lived across the street from us with my two cousins Aisha and Naeem. She told me on that day when she saw what was going on, she frantically tried getting in to save us. It was my aunt knocking for Rasheen to open the door, but he could not, because the doors locked from the outside. Another account given by my cousin Aisha, was that my mother was out with my aunt. My dad stated that he had been informed while working, by the neighbor who was good friends to both him and my mom. At first he did not grasp the concept when she repeatedly said, "Tony, your house is on fire and the kids are inside!" My dad stated that he immediately got up and ran out of the door. Another friend of his saw him running in the frigid winter without a coat, and said that my dad struggled to utter the words "My house is on fire." She told my dad to get inside of the car, as she then drove him to the house.

My dad stated just the day before the fire, he was furious with my mother, that they argued about her being irresponsible and hanging with the wrong people. According to my father's version, my mother left us unattended several times before. She would leave us to go next door to hang out with her girlfriend, which corresponded with my aunt's account, although according to my aunt my mom was play-ing cards. My aunt however denied my father's account of being at work that day. Hearing this made me angry and confused—confused because it differed from the version I was most familiar with, and angry at the thought of my mom being deliberately irresponsible.

My dad stated that he angrily confronted my mom about her lack of parental supervision. Speaking with caution, he warned her the next time might hold dire consequences. According to my dad, his epiphany came true the very next morning. I wonder if on that day, realizing what had happened, my mom ever regretted calling his bluff. I would like to believe it was in that very moment she probably wished she had heeded his warning.

I remember feeling angry in the disruption of the version I had become familiar with. My dad stated the store was a cover-up to save my mom from the repercussions of the truth. I remember thinking it is so much easier to accept the accident happened because she left us alone to go to the store for an urgent need, rather than for something as asinine as hanging with friends. For a long time after he told me, it was difficult to fathom that truth, and I struggled to accept it. Living in denial makes coping so much easier. One does not have to unpack and neatly put pain in its rightful position, just shove it anywhere and keep moving. Accepting that my mother was intentionally negligent would have meant seeing my mother in an uncomfortable truth. My immediate thought was, *My mother would never do that, she would not be intentionally irresponsible.*

When I think of how I experienced my mother in my early childhood, it contradicted the person my father described her to be. I then felt this need to defend her against his allegations, thinking maybe my dad resented my mom so deeply for the fire that he wanted to portray her as the villain. My mother always stuck to her version that she was at the store, why would she lie to me?

Then the sheer horror of reality set in as I began to think harder of the possibility that maybe my dad was telling the truth, knowing how my mother struggled with addiction most of my life. I then felt embarrassed and ashamed, having to explain I was injured to this degree because my mother neglected us. I think I liked the store version better. It sound more like an accident, and an accident usually does not hold anyone to blame. I preferred to just toss that pain in a corner, because it required too much work to unpack.

Despite my feelings or what I thought, I never wanted anyone to ever hold more pain or personal responsibility than I am sure they already held for themselves. I loved my mom and my brother so much, and because many looked to both as the culprits of this tragedy, I wanted them to know I did not share the same view of them.

I believed all that mattered was the fact that I had survived! I was here and everything would be okay. In my mind, since I was the dealer of blame, I chose to discard that card! I believed if I determined that all was well with me, then my comfort and acceptance should have been enough for others to shed their guilt. I was hoping the avoidance of painful feelings and not talking about what happened meant that everything would be okay, and everyone could move on and be happy. It hurt me to see people unhappy. Pleasing and caring for those around me, at the expense of denying and neglecting my thoughts, feelings, and wellbeing, would become a major theme in my life, later having many adverse effects.

Despite the attempted act of heroism by my brother, neither his attempts nor the attempts of any other could prevent the inevitable. After the worst came and went, not even the fate of something so vicious could predict what God already determined. Badly injured and forever scarred, but not lost, my brother and I survived! I was only six months old, and my tiny infant body was in grave condition. Time was of the essence, I was barely able to hold on. Every second became more critical than the last, as we both were rushed to the hospital.

CHAPTER 2

Damage Done

RASHEEN AND I WERE treated at St. Christopher's Hospital (when it was located on Lehigh Avenue) of Philadelphia. For many months, it would become home to my brother, mother, and I as we endured our arduous, painful, and uncertain recovery. God spared my life, and as it thinly hung in the unforeseen balance, He would play a pivotal role in the long road that laid ahead of me. He took my place acting as the strength my fragile, mangled body needed to endure the torture it was not equipped to handle.

I would come to know my older sister Nakisha only through other people's memories of her; which made me wish I could remember even the smallest detail about her—the sound of her voice, or the smile on her face when she looked at me. Hearing my brother retell the story, I somehow had hope in the way the events played out, that they both would have made it out alive. I then became deeply saddened to learn that in the end, Nakisha could not escape the ugly, powerful monster, it devoured her. I get emotional just thinking how she was so young, so afraid and alone. I was even more heartbroken by the fact that I would never know Nakisha, but I always believed her spirit watched over and protected me as an older sister does. I like to think that she encouraged my spirit to live on.

Rasheen and I sustained thermal burn injuries. This type of burn is typical of being in contact with hot objects, fire, hot liquids, or hot metals. When describing the types of burns, the severity of burn injuries is measured in six degrees. The most widely known burns are first-, second-, and third-degree burns. Someone can suffer one type, a combination of two, or a variation of all three. In rare cases, it is possible for someone to survive fourth-degree burns, but not with fifth- and sixth-degree burn trauma. Fifth and sixth degrees are what medical examiners determine in situations where a body is charred or burnt to the skeleton.

We both suffered from first-, second-, and third-degree thermal burns. However, Rasheen's injuries were less severe than mine, and did not cover as much of the body, a term referred to in the medical field as Total Surface Body Area (TSBA). Rasheen suffered first-, second-, and third-degree burns on his arms, back, face, and hands. The scars on his arms and back looked like strong, thick tree branches. Just as branches are the strength of a tree, Rasheen bore proof from each scar, just how strong he was.

I, however, was not as fortunate. I suffered first-, second-, third-, and some fourth-degree (when the damage of the burn passes the skin and goes to the bone) burns over about eighty-nine percent of my TSBA from head to toe. In layman's terms, most of my body was burned, with the exception of my back and the back of my legs. These were the only areas of my body not exposed while lying on my back in the crib. This served as a crucial benefit for my healing. While performing plastic surgery, doctors were able to take the unaffected "good" skin from my back and the back of my legs to "graft," allowing my body to regenerate its own skin cells in the place of damaged and severely scarred skin.

In such little time, I had made tremendous progress, but not enough to convince doctors that I would survive. During the critical time of my convalescent state, as doctors began to exhaust their options, their skepticism grew more and more, that the trauma would prove to be too grave. I am sure they were thinking, although it looked as though I was making progress, it was superficial and I would not survive. I am sure it is never easy for a medical professional to tell a loved one, "Sorry, we have done all we could do, but your loved one won't make it."

I am sure delivering such tragic news has to be disheartening just as much for the messenger. For my mother, a doctor must have sat her down, explained to her that it would be in my best interest to end my suffering, because to prolong death would only be harder on her and more agonizing for me. My mother told me she was given a consent form to terminate the morsel of hope that lay hidden inside a charred, bloated, lifeless, tiny body; a document of just cause giving permission to end the lifelong suffering I would be forced to live with if she did not sign. Signing would be her way of showing that she loved me enough to end my suffering.

While being resuscitated, my heart stopped twice, doctors had already pronounced me dead, but just needed my mother's signature to seal my fate. However, it was my mother's reluctance to sign the consent forms changing that fate. On whatever day that was, my mother would find her courage, strength, and faith through that ultimatum; the same strength my mother would lend to me in order to face and cope with what had become of me post tragedy.

My entire face was gone. The flames melted away my identity, erasing all of my humanistic features. Just like that, my image disappeared and I instantly became unrecognizable to those who knew me as the pretty baby doll with a head full of hair. Hearing stories of how I looked as a baby made me feel the deepest sense of grief over my physical loss, because of the thought of what that beauty could have developed into today.

I wanted to know what it was like to be "normal," grieving over what could have been. It was the sadness of never knowing my former image and wanting desperately to have seen for myself what beauty I possessed; at the same time not knowing was a blessing. Not knowing saved me from myself, from comparing myself to that lost image and not being able to embrace the new.

The inherited distinctions that connected me to both my parents were gone, leaving nothing but a blank, tattered canvas for doctors to try to repair and re-sculpt as best they could. They worked hard to give me a face that was functional enough to get by in life. The doctors' main objective was to save my life. I am sure, however, being the skeptics their profession taught them to be, in the back of their minds was the belief that any efforts would eventually fall short due to the severity of my physical circumstances. The odds of an infant surviving the trauma my body sustained, were technically unheard of. I am sure none of those plastic surgeons ever had a case like mine. In the eyes of medical professionals, I was a casualty, but their ethical principle taught them to exhaust all options to protect life, so doctors did what they were professionally mandated to do, work hard to save mine. However, little did they know, through their hands, God worked. Doctors were sure they had exhausted all options and there was nothing more they could do for me. Whatever they were able to do to save my life would still create deeper concerns regarding long-term functioning and quality of life. I was beyond bad shape.

I was unable to use my hands. All five digits on my left hand had to be amputated down to the knuckles, leaving me with a paw-like limb as a hand. The disfigurement to my hands resulted in the loss of dexterity; therefore, I was unable to do simple things such as write, eat, and bawl a fist to hold small objects such as coins. I had no nails to pick up objects, just hardened calluses in the place of them. I could not manipulate buttons to clothe and unclothe myself, and tying shoestrings was too sophisticated. I was basically helpless, relying on constant help from others. The fingers on my right hand were deformed and shortened.

One arm is shorter than the other, the scarring on my arms restrict range of motion, causing my arms to easily tire when extending outward, and I am unable to fully raise both above my head. The weak muscle tone, because of the new formation of my upper skeletal makes lifting and holding anything heavy, tiresome and painful.

My legs and feet were so severely burned that my mother was told I would not be able to walk without the use of permanent apparatuses, such as leg braces. My left leg is longer than my right, creating a visual imbalance when I walk. Both of my feet turn inward as a result of the reformation. I do not have flat soles; therefore, I actually walk on the sides of my feet. Good supportive shoes help to conceal this defect.

On each foot both pinky toes were either amputated or burnt off, resulting in four disfigured toes on each foot. My feet only grew to be a size three and a half in a children's shoe. I was always told having small feet was a good thing. Women often joked about being envious over my small feet, because all the cute shoes came in smaller sizes. I did not find my feet cute at all. I was always ashamed to expose them, because they were hideous and useless to me. I could not walk without feeling pain with every step.

The severity of injuries to my feet affects walking, standing, and my balance. Most pressure is applied to my right foot to sustain good balance. On the backs of both feet is thick, hard, dead skin (callus) that form at the heels. When dead skin accumulates it creates thick, hardened layers which makes walking dreadfully painful. It is a maintenance that must be maintained for the rest of my life. In order to relieve the pain caused by the pressure from the callus, my mother shaved the dead skin routinely with sharp razor blades. As a child, I dreaded the procedure, always scared that she would cut me. To decrease the pain, she had me soak both my feet in warm water mixed with Dr. Scholl's foot soaking solution to soften the callus, making cutting the growth easier and less painful. When my mom chiseled away, I always had to watch, to be sure she did not make any mistakes, and to let her know when I felt pain as she cut closer to my actual heel.

One time my fear came true, my mother made a mistake and cut too deep, creating a huge gash in the heel of my left foot. I remember the cut being so deep that my mother had to stuff bundles of gauze in my heel to prevent the bleeding. The pain was excruciating! I went to school limping for weeks. The dead skin acted as a level of support. I do not have range of motion or arches in either foot. When I was younger, I had to wear hard and heavy custom-made supportive shoes to give me the support I needed to walk. I remember my mother taking me to Buster Brown shoe store where my shoes were constructed. I also needed to wear leg braces that extended from my knees to my feet.

I have perfect hearing in my right ear, and good hearing in my left. This may be because the helix (the outer cup of the ear) melted, but left the parts of the inner ear intact. Doctors feared I would encounter respiratory complications such as the inability to breathe on my own because my nose and mouth were so badly burned. The holes in my nostrils and mouth had been sealed shut by the melting of my flesh. Even if they were successful in correcting the damage with plastic surgery, the remaining concern was whether I would continue to exhibit difficulty breathing, and have serious issues with congestion throughout the course of my life.

My eyelids were burned off exposing my eyes to the elements. Not having lids prevented my eyes from moistening. One of my first major surgeries was having lids constructed. Doctors had to pull the skin from my brow area to make lids. Evidence of this is that the hair from my brow, grows in the crease of my right eyelid.

Even when I am in the deepest of sleep, the left lid remains open. As I got older, lashes grew on my right lid but not on my left. My left eye was slightly delayed and I was slightly cross-eyed for much of my childhood. I struggled for a long time finding focal points when staring at objects.

I had no nose, as it had been melted completely off. The end result after surgery was a bridgeless hump with two carved holes to serve as nostrils. With no structure to my nose, I continued to encounter problems with congestion in my passageways, allowing air to easily get in, causing mucus to build up. It was always difficult dealing with the embarrassment of constantly having a runny nose and hardened mucus that was visibly noticeable.

I have had to learn to keep pristine maintenance, carrying tissue with me at all times. I remember being in school and my nose leaked so frequently that it became nearly impossible to maintain, to the point where I started forgetting and walked around looking like a two-year old with a snotty nose. I always felt extremely self-conscious when in front of people, not looking in their faces fearful mucus had accumulated, even after I repeatedly cleaned it. Worse, I noticed how people never brought it to my attention. I could be face -to -face in a deep conversation with someone and unsuspecting of my nose. It would not be until I looked in the mirror and saw crust literally hanging from my nose.

I could understand how someone might feel uncomfortable, thinking that I would be embarrassed if they confronted me. What was hard to understand though was how those closest to me never said anything. "Neesh, go clean your nose." I mean, they were the ones I trusted to bring things to my attention to prevent public humiliation, but that lead me to realize it was just as uncomfortable for them too. Always having to consciously be aware of this nuisance contributed to my lack of self-esteem.

My mouth had been sealed shut by the tightness of my face, which required intensive surgery to reconstruct. The procedure was to expand my mouth, because the tiny opening made it incapable to pass anything larger than a pea. The formation of my mouth made it difficult not only to eat, but to breathe and talk. After the procedure, my lips were sown shut at each corner. They were huge from the swelling. I could not talk and had to be fed liquids through a straw. When I gained use of my mouth, the sensations were weird. Afterward, I remember drinking out of cups and the fluid spilling from the new slits that expanded my mouth. I grew frustrated every time I drunk from a cup, because majority of the fluids ended up all over my clothes.

I still could not open my mouth wide, so certain foods were difficult for me to eat. Those that were gritty and hard, requiring excessive chewing, caused my jaws to easily tire. I especially have difficulty eating large foods such as hamburgers. Anytime I go out to eat, I am always conscious of making sure foods I order do not create messes when putting it into my mouth; also choosing foods that do not require having to be cut up into the appropriate size.

Not having fingers on my left hand makes it difficult to hold a fork firmly, obstructing my ability to secure food as I cut it with my right hand; therefore, I make sure food is easy to cut through with a fork. If not, then I pass on ordering it, even if it is something I really crave. For a very long time I never felt safe to expose myself to people who could not understand my way of being. For much of my life I felt humiliated and ashamed because of my defects. I was more concerned with not making people uncomfortable, so I found ways to hide who I was and my adaptations.

My entire chest was covered with thick scars that became more painful and problematic as I hit puberty, experiencing the maturation of breast. I had to undergo several plastic surgeries to reconstruct the extensive scar tissue surrounding my breast. As a young girl, I held hope after every procedure, that my chest would look more like a normal woman's, which was important because having breasts symbolized femininity. After each procedure, I anticipated the revealing of my chest, hoping to feel more like a woman. I had what are known as keloids, which are thick, raised scars.

I remember feeling disappointed after each surgery, to see that not much had changed. They were still grotesque and deformed. The left one was smaller and flatter than the right, which resembled a normal breast.

Doctors were always pleased with their work, as they hovered over me during their rounds (when a team of doctors visit the patients, either outside their hospital room's door or with the patient's consent at their bedside discussing the case and latest condition of the patient). I allowed the team to make their rounds at my bedside because I wanted to know what was going on, have any questions answered and have an understanding of the terminology used. This was my reality and I needed to be educated.

When they stood before me speaking of the surgery being successful and describing what they had done, I would sit and curse them in my head. *This does not look good, it looks gross!* It looked as if my chest had been mutilated, like a victim in a slasher film who met their demise by a chainsaw or butcher knife. I could not burst the bubble they were riding high on, so I waited until the doctors left the room to cry, grieving over the loss of my womanhood that I would never fully grow into.

Every procedure allowed for my breast to grow to some degree. Despite the success, in my eyes, the procedures were a failure because they did not make me look or feel feminine. Doctors were successful in eliminating the unbearable pain I lived with when the scars were so tight. Before the surgeries, I always slept wearing a bra to keep my breast in place, and with my arms crossed because they were very painful to lie on without the support.

I had many expectations of doctors. I felt their craft to reshape and correct flaws of my body would be the magic wand to make me look normal after I came to from the anesthesia. Every time I awoke, I was disappointed again and again. Little had changed, no magic, nothing attractive or normal that the typical eye could notice. I was devastated to still be stuck in the same uncomfortable and mangled body.

The fire transformed me into a monster, it took away everything that made me human. As if there was nothing else on my body that could be eradicated, I no longer had hair. All of my beautiful, soft curls were scorched, revealing a bare, burnt, patchy scalp with only the remnants of what once was a head full of chestnut brown-colored locks.

The major concern with incurring burn injuries is developing infections, as a result of damage to the largest organ of the body, the skin. The skin is the body's natural protective barrier against infection, so when it's destroyed, the body is exposed and more susceptible to infections. Infections are the leading cause of death from burn injuries. Luckily for me, I did not experience many setbacks in my healing related to infections. My immune system was strong and my body did what it was supposed to do so that I could heal. In many cases of burn injuries as acute as mine, the immune system can slow down allowing for the onset of other infections. The body can reject the new skin whether manufactured from an animal or the donor's own. Considering the extent of my burns, the fact that I was so young gave my body the advantage to heal.

The brain is an amazing organ. When affected by trauma, it is astonishing all that the brain is able to recall, even at an age before memory forms.

Trauma has a way of preserving moments in time. Like a time traveler, one can relive through all five senses trauma. I do not remember the fire, or even that small window of time when I was first admitted into the hospital, but my memory begins shortly after that crucial time at the age of two. I was out of the woods, but far from a full recovery. Everything is distinctly clear and familiar to me. I have a precise recollection of what I went through as a child living in the intensive care unit of St. Christopher's Hospital for Children, and all of the horrors I would endure there throughout my childhood.

A picture of my mother, brother, and I was taken around the time I was two or three. I do not remember sitting for the picture, but I do remember the experience of having the plastic mask mounted on my face and wearing the pressure garments that suffocated my entire body. In the picture, my mother wore a striped fuchsia and white polo shirt, with her lips slightly outlined in black liner and filled with clear lip gloss (a makeup trend during that time). Her lightly teased curls formed into a moderate afro which seemed to take up the entire backdrop. She wore a pair of dark blue denim jeans, while holding me securely on her lap. My brother stood closely behind her, dressed in a tan and white striped polo shirt with a white ace band around his head that looked more like a fashion statement than what it was intended for (to suppress and smooth the scarring on his forehead).

We both wore matching tan-colored therapeutic pressure garments called Jobes that fit the body snug and tight like an ace bandage. We had to wear them over the areas of our bodies that were scarred, to reduce swelling, and to deflate the keloids. When scars form and set in, they become thick and tight. Wearing the garments helped preserve elasticity to the skin, allowing for more range of motion. My brother wore one on both arms. They looked like two long gloves beginning at the top of his shoulder, extending down his entire arm and hand, and cutting off to expose the tips of his fingers. In the picture they are both smiling as if signifying happiness and hope, a testament that we had weathered a hell storm. The fact remained, I was still caught in a category 5 and my storm had just picked up tremendous speed.

I am pictured sitting on my mother's lap in a light dusty pink shirt, giving a glimpse of the tiny, customized, form-fitted pressure vest that held my little chest snuggly. I am wearing tiny gloves that were custom made to precisely fit my deformed small fingers on my right hand and my fingerless stubs on my left hand. On my head I wore a cute little white sailor's hat, with a thin built-in strap that went under my chin to secure the hat, to keep my fragile scalp covered. The mask I wore resembled the hockey mask of the classic horror villain, Michael Myers. The mask served the same purpose as the pressure garments, to smooth out the scarring on my face. My skin was so tight that the tightness pulled the flaps from under my eyes, exposing the pink flesh underneath. The tightness also pulled and stretched the corners of my mouth, making it difficult and painful to make facial expressions such as a smile.

So even if the person behind the camera made funny faces to get a perfect smile from me, I was unable to produce a Kodak moment. In the picture, I was in the early stages of wearing the mask, so it revealed a very bloated, featureless face. The scarred, sad, still face staring into the lens was one that showed the pain and fear I was experiencing at the time. I was a child who was frightened and who lived in constant shock from such a horrific trauma. For me there were no reasons to smile and be happy. Up until that part of my life all I knew was fear and pain from my trauma. I did not know safety, happiness and laughter. I would look at the picture and wonder what was going through my little mind at that very moment. Having been stripped of my innocence and security, I was always sad because I lived in excruciating pain that I could never escape.

A child at such a cherub age is eager to explore the world in front of her, and is mesmerized by its wonders. Instead, my world consisted of pain and uncertainty of the grueling physical challenges I faced every day. At about three or four years old, I can remember being mummified in white gauze that needed to be changed periodically in one day. I had to undergo a process called "tanking," also known as hydrotherapy.

The burned patient is taken into a sterilized room where the affected areas are cleaned by submerging the body in a "hydrotub" to wash away dead skin and prevent infection. It was a procedure that took hours depending on the areas affected, and the pain threshold of the patient. Something so soothing and relaxing as bathing, can be painful and uncomfortable for someone who has been burned, because of the sensitivity to the affected area. Hydrotherapy is the first medical procedure that happens when a person is severely burned. It is used to prevent loss of fluid within the skin that can result in dehydration. Dehydration can cause the body to go into septic shock, which is another common cause of death in burn-related injuries. It also helps wounds heal and protects tissue. A mixture of water and chlorine is used to disinfect the wounds.

I can vividly remember the pain. The distinct sensation of pain is something I will never forget. When the flesh is exposed, pain becomes intense as nerve sensations become extremely heightened. I felt the pain even before the water hit my body. I had to be held down for short intervals of time to allow water to cleanse the wounds. The best way to describe the pain was that my body burned and stung at the same time, like a thousand hot needles stabbing me all at once. Regardless of water being warm and soothing, the pain was agonizing.

I remember the different types of procedures I underwent. I never got use to the pain. I remember feeling very fearful and anxious, acting hypervigilant and suspicious of everyone and my surroundings. I was fearful of falling asleep, waking up to being in pain, or some unfamiliar masked individual tugging and pulling at me. I needed to observe everything, as if witnessing would lessen the pain.

As a child I lived in a very terrified world, where everyone walked around in pale yellow or sky blue, thin, cotton smocks with matching hair nets, latex gloves, and blue masks that only exposed their eyes. Not being able to see their facial expressions scared me. Doctors and nurses looked like scary, possessed, masked monsters reaching for me, hurting me as I laid on the table helpless and unable to fight them off.

The hospital became my new home, I remember living every moment in constant imminent fear. I became very afraid when I heard the voices of doctors, calling my name as they entered the ward and grabbed my chart from the nurse's station. My heart skipped beats, my stomach would drop, and everything around me stopped. Inside myself I was trying to escape. The fight or flight reaction always kicked in, but there was nowhere for me to run to and no way for me to fight off who I considered to be the enemy.

There was always that uneasy anticipation seeing and listening to doctors and nurses prepping for my arrival in the sterilized treatment room. In their pleasant and soft voices, the nurse announced,

"Tanisha, we are ready for you now." She would walk over to my bed, releasing the steel railings of the isolated cage where I spent most of my time to remain sterile, to escort me into the surgical room.

My fright was heightened by the piercing brightness of the florescent, strobe lights that aligned the ceiling. The room was large and voices bounced off the walls as they echoed. Once on the gurney, the doctor would then adjust several huge round lights that looked like photographer lights, blinding me as they pointed directly into my face. I remember growing cold. The room was always set to a cooler temperature to keep it sterilized, but I believe my nerves were rattled from being so scared, that it was the fright that chilled my body.

What made the procedures so frightening was that I could not see what was going on as doctors and nurses huddled over me with their masked faces, poking, prodding, pulling, and yanking simultaneously in different areas of my body. It was awful, especially when there was an area in which a piece of gauze or dressing crusted over by the saturation of blood and other bodily fluids. To avoid infections, the doctor or nurse would have to apply force to remove it. At times it was very difficult for doctors and nurses to deal with me when changing my dressings. I was intolerable to the pain; therefore, treatments sometimes had to be completed in shifts. It had gotten to the point where I had to be strapped down, because I kicked, screamed, and tried biting, in hopes my feistiness would make them flee. The pain was never-ending, the procedures became a routine; eventually I learned to tolerate the pain, but never became immune to it.

The room was cluttered with machines, tables large and small, layered with baby blue disposable cloths and all kinds of medical stuff, both plastic and metal utensils, such as scalpels, scissors, and other sharp surgical instruments. There were opened packs of square shaped, white cotton gauzes, and packs of thin fluorescent yellow adhesive-type gauze called xeroform covered with bacitracin, an antibiotic ointment that protects against infections and helped the skin to heal. The instruments and bandages were neatly and systematically laid out, according to when they were used. The large room was absent of any windows, which made me feel even more scared, because it meant that my cries went unheard. In the middle was a surgical flat gurney covered with a white thin sheet. I observed everything. It was my way of believing I had some kind of control. My heart raced as I watched them prep the room; I was beyond afraid.

When the doctor finally came in, he tried to create a comfortable atmosphere by talking to me. He and the nurses made jokes, asked questions about things I liked and what my plans were when I returned home. I remember attempting to demonstrate my bravery by joking around, but nothing ever took away the fear of the pain I was about to endure. When the torture began, I kicked and screamed as loud as my little lungs would allow. A nurse usually had to intervene as I tried clenching onto one of their arms with the best grip I could get with my bandaged hands in protest, screaming out for my mother, hoping she would prevent them from hurting me.

The head reconstructive surgeon who performed my surgeries name was Dr. Stuart J. Hulnick. I remember him as being very gentle, always smiling and funny. He was a high-spirited man full of life and cared very much about his patients, especially me. After many years as my surgeon, his presence became very assuring to me. When he entered, I felt safe. He cut the tension in the air with a smile and jokes that always did the trick of calming me down. Dr. Hulnick was very familiar with my fears and would just talk to me. He somehow understood my pain. What I loved most about him was his compassion and sympathy for me. Well aware of my tantrums, defiant antics to defend myself, and the unease of having multiple nurses approaching me at once, Dr. Hulnick began seeing me in private and personally changing my bandages.

Dr. Hulnick began seeing me one on one and this became a time of bonding. He made special accommodations such as staying late just to change my evening bandages. During our time together, he would come in, turn the radio on, make jokes and interact with me in ways that took the edge off. It was just him and me alone together, laughing and talking about whatever came to mind.

Dr. Hulnick was a big kid, which was a plus for me because I was one myself. He slowly and carefully removed my bandages, stopping at the sight or sound of my discomfort, telling me stories in between when he saw that I needed a break. Dr. Hulnick always allowed me to watch, describing and explaining everything he did and what he was about to do. I would become reliant on this form of interaction with future doctors, telling them how important it was that everything be explained in order for me to relax. Dr. Hulnick was my calming escape from all the pain I endured.

I remember distinctly one major plastic surgery Dr. Hulnick performed to my nose. It was the most uncomfortable and painful procedure I underwent. What made it so uncomfortable was the constant feeling of pressure from the heavy packing of dressings (bandages) and the tightness from the stitching. Eventually the sign of healing came with intense itching that was unbearably irritating. I experienced the most pain the day the stent (bundle of dressings wrapped and held together by stitches) came down. The feeling of the packaging being pulled from the depths of my nose was indescribable. The clipping and pulling felt as if my brain was being pulled out from my nose.

Another major surgery was to correct the crookedness of my feet and legs. When my feet and legs were not in long metal braces, they were put in place with metal rods and then casted in attempts to straighten them. This would be a reoccurring procedure, where I would go to meet with the orthopedic surgeon who applied the casts named Dr. Alburger.

When having a cast applied or removed, Dr. Alburger walked me through the process. He took a white chalky roll of material, rough in texture, but instantly became soft and mushy when wet, resembling the texture of plaster. Dr. Alburger first fitted my leg with a protective thin garment, pretty much like a thin sock with the bottom cut out. He then applied several layers of the wet cast, which harden to become a thick, heavy, solid molding of my leg and foot. This part of the procedure was without pain or anxiety. More so it was fun, because Dr. Alburger allowed me to participate in the molding process. I actually enjoyed the feeling of having the cast molded to my body. The material was soaked in a basin of hot water, the heat and pressure from the cast being applied and secured felt relaxing.

It was not until the cast hardened when the heaviness and tightness made the cast uncomfortable. It was so tight that I tried putting my fingers inside to loosen its grip. Eventually as the cast aged, it loosen up enough, to where I was able to slip my leg out, but never enough to where I could get it completely off. When my leg healed, the worse part of wearing a cast was that it itched so bad. I stuck long, thin objects such as pens, pencils, and butter knives inside to relieve the discomfort of the itching by scratching until I felt pain.

After weeks or months of wearing the casts, I dreaded the day of having it removed. The next time I saw Dr. Alburger, I was never as calm and playful as when he applied the cast. I was petrified of the thin blade used to cut the cast off. He attempted to calm me by assuring there was nothing to worry about, that the blade would not cut through my flesh. To prove his point, he ran the blade across his hand, and, although it did not cut him, I was not convinced. I jumped in extreme fear at the loud chainsaw sound coming toward me. Dr. Alburger went a step further and ran it across my arm. I only felt a tickling sensation with a small amount of pressure as it pressed against my skin, but nothing piercing or sharp.

Having convinced me that there was nothing to fear, I allowed him to proceed, but as soon as I heard the loudness and felt the blade nearing closer to my leg as it cut through the hard plaster, I could never get my nerves in order. When the pressure of the heavy cast was removed, my leg or foot felt so light that I believed it would break once I stood up.

Then there were the tissue expanders. This procedure was to stretch and expand skin that was needed to cover a larger area surrounding healthy skin. I had to make weekly visits to the hospital to receive injections of saline, which caused my skin to inflate like a balloon. I remember every week visiting the clinic, where I met with the nurse assisting Dr. Hulnick. Her name was Sharon, and I remember Sharon always welcomed me with ice cold hands. No matter how much she tried to warm them before touching me, they were always freezing cold.

When seen by the doctor, he would inject small amounts of saline into a thin plastic device positioned under my skin, gradually inflating the bubble each week, from the size of a pea to the size of a tennis ball. When the balloon was at the intended size, I would undergo surgery where the balloon was deflated and the skin used as needed. I remember having the expansions on the back of my right leg. I could only wear skirts or dresses to prevent the balloon from rupturing, so it was exposed for all to see. I felt embarrassed, like a monster because of the additional attention. I was subjected to harsh criticism from onlookers because of my scars and deformities. The staring, the pointing, and the gawking were all too overwhelming. I was just a child who did not understand what happened to me, let alone the evil by others I experienced every single day.

A major procedure in burn treatment is known as skin grafting. The purpose of skin grafting is to correct scars that are obvious in shape, size, and location and are unattractive, painful, and compromises functionality. The process consists of literally carving good, healthy skin from an area on the body not damaged, called "the donor site," and applying it to an affected area needing skin. The donor site is good transplanted skin. In burn injuries, the grafted skin is applied to an area with augmented scarring to reduce the size of the scar or make it obsolete.

Scars that become extremely tight eventually need to be released to provide relief and allow for range of motion and other functions.

There are different types of skin grafting, with burns the most common used is called a split-thickness graft; the thickness of the graft depends on the area being treated. Smaller areas with minor scarring may only require small thin strips of skin, whereas larger, and more severe areas require larger and thicker layers of skin.

The process of skin grafting includes cutting, skinning, or shaving healthy skin using a surgical instrument called a dermatome. The instrument resembles the one used in the deli section of a supermarket to slice lunch meat. The skin is then processed through a surgical instrument called a skin mesher that makes tiny holes called apertures into the layer of skin. This causes the skin to expand several sizes larger than the original size, which allows the skin graft to cover larger affected areas. Conventional methods used animal skin as a substitute for tissue, especially if the donor's tissue was rejected by its own body, or if there was not enough tissue to cover the grafted area. Once the graft took (showing signs of producing new skin) the punctured graft created a polka dot-like design in the skin, evident of the grafting.

Earlier skin grafts on my arms and legs display the intricate spotted designs. Living in an era where tattooing has become the ultimate form of artistic expression, where nearly everyone walks around with meaningful or meaningless works of art, I have been asked many times if I have any tattoos. My response is always with humor, "What do you mean? Look at all of the intricate artwork tapering my body. I think I stand out enough artistically." Lastly, the graft is then put into place using surgical staples, not that different from the staples used for paper, or sewn with stitches. The donor site is extremely painful, and susceptible to infections.

I have had more skin grafting procedures than reconstructive surgeries. In counting, I have undergone over fifty in my lifetime. I needed major skin grafting pretty much all over my body, mainly to release the tightness of the scars. The process of "releasing" is cutting the scar, in the form of the letter Z, known as a "Z-plasty." It expands a scar that is contracted and tight, increasing the expansion of the scarred skin.

Luckily for me, because I was lying on my back while in the crib when burned, the skin on my entire backside from neck to calves was unaffected. With every grafting, skin was taken from the backs of my legs, thighs, and back. I was very fortunate that every skin graft procedure I underwent was successful. I was fortunate that my immune system was strong to ward off infections, accepting grafts and expediting the healing process.

I had been under the knife so many times that the entire experience became very familiar. The familiarity of the process, procedures, and post-op helped me to prepare mentally, emotionally, and physically for the expectation of pain. Waiting to get everything over and done with was the frightening part. Eventually as I got older, I was able to shed the fear of being hospitalized.

The greatest fear other than the pain was the method used to sedate me. Being put to sleep always gave me great anxiety, to the point where I became physically sick to my stomach hours and then minutes leading up to surgery. Reason for my inordinate fear was because of the breathing mask. The mask was a thick, hard rubber apparatus that covered both my nose and mouth. I remember it being placed over my face, and as the anesthesia was administered through the mask, the anesthesiologist would tell me in a soothing voice to think pleasant thoughts and to count backward from ten. Never actually making it through the countdown, I would be sedated within seconds.

I instantly became nauseous at the smell and taste of the gas. I remember feeling stuck in a fog that was cloudy and disorienting. I hated that I fell for the same trick in every procedure by being asked to choose a flavor for the gas, knowing that when I went under, the taste and smell were always the same - horrible. I was always left feeling violently sick hours after post-op, and the taste lingered in my mouth for days.

I remember the experience being as such: In the seconds it takes for me to fall asleep, I feel the air grow colder, voices become distant echoes, and the space around me closes in as everything fades to black. I am now under. The torture worsens as a thick, long tube is inserted down my throat to assist with breathing since I am in an unconscious state and unable to breathe on my own. I gag, I can't breathe. I feel myself suffocating. I feel I'm choking to death. I'm screaming, crying, yelling, but I'm under so no one can hear me. My eyes are sealed shut and my body temporarily dead, so no one can see me fighting. I am aware of the loud muffled sounds. I feel my body twitching and my head constantly moving from side to side trying to shake the tube from deep inside my chest. No luck. I'm tired. I succumb and pray that I do not choke to death.

Next thing I know, I am awakened by a strong obnoxious smell that is used to bring me to from the anesthesia. The first sign that I survived the torture is a gentle voice calling my name, bringing me out of the comatose state. "Tanisha, wake up, honey, you're all done, everything went well in surgery." I open my eyes and feel at ease to see my mother's face, as she leans over with her comforting smile that always assured me everything was alright and that I was safe.

Awakened from being heavily sedated, I would inspect the areas that had been operated on, to see the extent of what had been done.

Sedated by large dosages of the strongest pain medication, my body would be numb to the piercing pain for at least the first day. The donor site was always tightly wrapped in gauze, then after a few days, the bandages were removed. As always, anything that caused me great pain, I had to try to control. Donor sites were taken from either the outer, back, or inner parts of my thigh. There are rectangular patched scars in those areas where skin had been taken multiple times.

Through the course of my surgeries, my doctors and nurses had become familiar with my need to be a part of my treatment and eventually allowed me to call the shots. Being somewhat in control of my treatment, whether it was telling doctors or nurses when to start and stop, or participating in the changing of my bandages, helped me to become less anxious and manage pain better.

The treatment procedure I was given most control over was that of removing the initial bandages from the donor site. Removing bandages from the donor site was a very tedious process. After about four or five days, the bandages were removed to allow air to the site for healing. If left moist too long, infection was likely to set in. I knew my tolerance level and managed pain best when it became intolerable.

The nurse and I worked simultaneously. I peeled away at the bandages while the nurse cut the stitches. Unraveling the gauze that wrapped around the area several times was effortless and without pain. Underneath the heavy layers of gauze revealed a plastic bandage covering, resembling clear adhesive tape. This bandage was used to seal in the draining fluids. Under the bandage was a patch of yellow gauze fused to the wound with stitches at each corner to secure the gauze with antibiotic ointment in place.

The most painful part of the process was having to remove both the adhesive clear bandage and then the stitched gauze. Taking my time and with careful precision determined by my threshold of pain, I sometimes had to force myself through the pain to rip the materials off from my pink, raw flesh. Sometimes the process went smoothly, and I was able to tolerate the pain enough to get the entire bandage off in small segments. Maybe going for five to ten minutes, resting for a while, then finishing the process. Then there were times I would press straight through with no breaks, just to get everything done and over with. Donor sites were extremely painful, more painful than the grafted site. After having so many surgeries, I eventually became familiar with the pain, and learned to manage it, but I never got used to it.

I cried long and hard because the pain was so agonizing. It seemed that time stopped during nights spent in the hospital. The middle of the night was when the pain appeared to be at its worse. I could not sleep and became even more uncomfortable because I was so restless. I would cry out and call on God to save me, especially after being denied medication because it was too early before my next dosage. "Please, Jesus, help me with this pain. Please take it away, God, it hurts so bad." I cried until I felt my prayers were answered when my tears stopped and the pain temporarily subsided.

It typically took two weeks for the donor site to heal. When the site healed, revealing fresh pink skin free from signs of infections, I was released to go home. The graft usually required an additional two weeks to heal. My mom would resume nurturing my grafts at home. Nurses demonstrated for my mom and gave us instructions for proper cleansing and rewrapping. My insurance would only cover my hospital stay usually no more than two weeks, so my stays in the hospital were always shorter or no more than the insurance allowed.

If there was an indication that the site had become infected, or when the bandages were too stubborn to remove, an emergency procedure was required. The nurse would have to apply a liquid solution called silver nitrate. There was one time a donor site did show signs of infection and required the emergency procedure, in which I had to uncomfortably endure every six hours. When applied, the area had to be soaked then re-soaked at the next scheduled time. Cultures were then taken to the lab for observation of any signs of infections.

On average it took twenty-four hours to complete the treatment. The site had to be doused with the solution, soaking the bed and my hospital gown. The liquid was clear, but after application, the liquid turned everything it touched tar black. Not only was it messy and uncomfortable, it made everything it came in contact with look nasty. The discomfort came when I had to lie in the cold liquid throughout the night. My sheets were changed periodically and the nurse placed padding underneath me to keep my lower body dry. Nevertheless, the padding was of no use, and the bed and I would be completely drenched by the next time the solution was applied.

If there were no signs of infection after treatment, I would be forced out of bed to walk. This task always seemed impossible with the amount of pain standing caused. Just the sensation of air or the thought of me moving sent a stream of pain shooting straight to the area. It was more painful standing up than lying down. Walking and standing meant that I had to stretch my leg, which made the pain even more unbearable. Every step, every movement took insurmountable effort. It always took so much out of me, and I hated being pushed beyond limits I felt I was incapable of. However, I pushed forward with my recovery in mind, knowing that I would be doing a disservice to myself by hindering my own recovery.

The plastic surgeries Dr. Hulnick performed were highly successful. He gave me a face that was highly functional. A face that I learned to grow into, accept, and eventually love. If I ever considered additional surgery, the only corrective work would be to reconstruct my nose to give it a more natural look, adding a bridge that would give it definition. Having my nose reconstructed would also eliminate the maintenance issues.

Ironically, after performing the major surgeries that were vital to functionality, Dr. Hulnick died from leukemia. It was with purpose that he was in my life when he was, because he gave me the most precious gift: a future. I miss him very much and attribute in part the woman I have become to his hard work and vision. He is the man that sculpted beauty out of tragedy, the very beauty that I would learn to accept with the same pride and admiration. Although I was very young I remember him vividly and keep him dear to my heart; and by the way he took care of me, I know he kept me close to his. I think of him every time I look at my face. God anointed his hands, which makes me feel even more blessed to have the face he crafted. I wish Dr. Hulnick could have witnessed my physical evolution. I'm certain he would have been proud of the woman I have become.

Along with the surgeries was constant therapy. My recovery consisted of vigorous physical and orthopedic therapy that was very daunting. I was stubborn and difficult because of how painful and tiresome therapy was. I was even more disturbed by the high enthusiasm of the therapists I worked with, so cheerful and excited to make my life miserable. They did not have to go through the grueling exercises and deal with the pain. They were not in the position of having to push, run, stretch, lift, and so forth, sometimes days after having surgery. Therapy recommended before the body healed completely was to prevent restriction of limbs, joints, muscles, and skin, which could become tauter than before surgery. I understood therapy was imperative to my recovery; however, I still hated having to go through it.

All in all, the surgeries and therapy proved to be significant successes, helping me reach important milestones in my recovery, and also gave doctors newfound hope that I might beat the odds of their earlier presumptions. They began to welcome the thought of possibility that I might be able to gain mobility and function sufficiently to live somewhat of a normal life.

The battles fought as a child prepared me for later battles that would follow throughout my life. God showed me favor and promise at such an uncertain time, under unfavorable conditions. He saw to it that in the beginning I would not be defeated, and equipped me with the tools needed then and later in life. He favored me for reasons at that time were unknown. He strengthened my mother to raise me up for his greatness. Who knew such fight and persistence lived in such a fragile child? It would be these experiences that gave me the will to cope with future pains and uncomfortable situations.

As if being injured in a horrifying fire would be the only trauma I would experience in my lifetime, much more trauma, pain, and uncertainties would follow me throughout the course of my life. God had a powerful purpose for me, but He also knew that in order to come into it, I would have to fight, suffer, and struggle. Therefore, He equipped me with a unique, unbreakable armor not only to overcome and claim victory, but to be more than a conqueror! To give honor and glory to His name and serve as an example of His infinite power, love, and mercy. Through the pain and suffering, I learned and gained understanding of life's profound meanings and how to identify with human suffering.

Through constant suffering, I learned to embrace adversity with love, empathy, and compassion, which gave me strength, courage, and resiliency, later developing the character that has made me into a conqueror. God's favor over my life allowed me to survive all of the traps of failure and death. It was predestined on that fateful day, in that fateful fire, that I be reborn with the will to live and the audacity not to give up, despite many times desperately wanting to. This is my story, this is who I am. More Than a Conqueror!

CHAPTER 3

Healing Hands

AS DISTINCTLY AS I can remember the pain, I also clearly remember the nurturing, love, and support that helped me through my recovery. Every memory includes my mother loyally by my bedside every day of every hour. I do not ever remember her leaving to go home to tend to my other siblings, or taking time for herself to regroup. My mother was present for every operation. She was by my side when I was sedated, as if she never left when I awoke post-op. As hospital stays became the norm, her presence was my medication, my assurance. She was a comfort amidst the discomfort. No matter the circumstances, I felt I was her number one priority. I wondered if that loyalty in part was a way of coping with the overwhelming guilt she felt, or an unconscious effort to rectify the wrong of leaving me alone for those few minutes, by vowing to never leave my side again.

My impression of my mother when I was very young was that she exuded the most incredible strength. Knowing that she in her own way grieved, was filled with fear, apprehension, and internal pain, she never exhibited any signs of being in distress. I remember my mom always being high spirited. Unaware of the cross she carried, those who came in contact with her would never know the hell she was enduring by looks alone, because she appeared peaceful, positive, with a worry-free presence.

My mother was and still is one of the most physically beautiful women I will ever know. The color of her chocolate skin made me proud that mine was the same color. She was built and toned, the muscles in her legs were sculpted as those of an athlete. Her legs are an asset that she is most proud of. My mom bragged that her legs were formed from her years of running track in high school. My mother wore the most beautiful smile, one that I hoped to inherit, she was always smiling. Every time I looked at her no matter the situation, she was smiling. My mother's smile dimmed the sun and was the constant nourishment my soul needed. Her touch and embraces were soothing and comforting. I looked up to my mom and wanted to do everything like her when I grew up. I loved my mother's scent, her style, the way she talked, and her mannerisms. As a child I thought of my mother as a goddess.

I never saw her in any way other than as a beautiful, strong, and confident woman; however, her confidence and strength birthed the feistiness and bold woman she is known to be. Maybe her nonchalant and don't-take-no-stuff attitude was her way of fighting and protecting herself. The adversities my mother faced as a child, including internalized racism within her family, that made her feel she was the "black sheep," created a deeply rooted inferiority complex that grew large throughout her life, with branches that bore many rotted fruits of insecurity, worthlessness, and low self-esteem. None of which were easily detected in my mother. She was the life of the party, the popular girl, especially among the men. Women spoke of her infinite beauty and her poise. Men could not get enough of her sultriness that kept them coming back. No matter what divided them apart, they wanted more of her. She was a God-fearing woman raised in the church and her soul was committed. My entire life revolved around God, church, and spirituality. She built that foundation in all of us.

What I would come to admire most about my mom was her faith. No matter what was going on or where we were, she sought the opportunity to preach to people whether they were interested in what she had to say or not. She allowed no interruptions or denial of the Most High God she served. While we waited at the hospital to be called for my apportionment, she would lean over and encourage another grieving mother or father, by telling them there was nothing to fear as long as they put their faith in God. "If He can do it for me and spare my child, He will do the same for you." Even nonbelievers found hope when my mother spoke. Before and after every surgery, my mother would pray over me. She prayed with an anointed power that resonated from the depths of her. My mother's faith is what strengthened and gave her the courage to stand tall, and confront the cruelties of society she experienced while boldly wearing her Scarlett letter. Caring for a child with physical imperfections and or limitations is difficult enough, but facing the world every day and revealing that child requires impeccable resilience of the parent.

Whatever her method was for keeping sane, my mother saw to it that I was never burdened by her struggles, only comforted and assured that all would be fine, with her constant love, affection, and support. Having my mother there for everything I went through eventually gave me the strength and courage to endure. Although the fire was the first defining moment in my life that disrupted my sense of security in the world, my mother's presence during the pain partially returned to me that sense of security. As long as she was with me, I always felt safe.

My memories also include nurturing and love from others. The host of nurses, doctors, therapists, social workers, extended family, and close friends of my mom are included in that support. Recovering under the auspices of so many involved with my care and those who showed me compassion, was what I needed most at the time. Having been shown so much, love, attention, affection, and sympathy during my early childhood, taught me that just because bad things happen, there are genuine people who will love you through it. All my life, I have come in contact with many members of my family whom I do not remember, but who remember me as a baby or child, and who were amazed at how far I had come. Many shared stories of visiting me in the hospital, holding and caring for me, loving and going above for me as though I was their child. These experiences influenced the love, affection, and sensitivity I show toward others. Touch is a basic need of survival, it has the power to heal. It did for me in my recovery.

My mother and I formed close and tight bonds with many responsible for my care. Aside from Dr. Hulnick, I remember the bond I had with a RN named Janice, an Italian woman with pale skin, jet black short cut hair, thin in stature and she wore glasses. What I distinctly remember most about Janice was that she spoke loud with a thick Italian accent, similar to Fran Dresser's character from *The Nanny*. When I had appointments at the outpatient clinic, Janice was there to greet me with candy, which is another great memory I have of her. Janice was one of my favorite nurses. I loved her because she made me laugh by telling the funniest jokes. She completed the usual procedures with me before seeing the doctor: checking my blood pressure, height, and weight. She then consulted with my mom and me about any questions and concerns, before checking in with my mom about home care with regards to changing my dressings. We somehow got off tangent by talking and laughing about anything random. Sometimes while my mom and I waited to be seen, if Janice knew I was there, she joined me in the play area.

Another person we formed a great relationship with was the hospital social worker, Bernice Macintyre, an African American woman, somewhere in her thirties. Whenever I had inpatient procedures, Bernice arranged for my mother to stay close beside me. She arranged for my mother to have meals and transportation to and from the hospital as well as cab service to get me to and from appointments. Bernice went above and beyond to make our stays as comfortable as possible. She was more than just a social worker arranging assistance and providing outside resources, she was someone who truly cared about how our family was coping with this tragedy. Bernice would sit and talk with my mother, lending that ear to listen and that shoulder to cry on, when she had no one to talk to. Bernice was a good confidant. Although she had no personal experiences to relate, she knew how to provide comfort from her experience working with families experiencing trauma in the ways our family had. Bernice brought me stuffed teddy bears and coloring books to occupy my time. When she was able to spare moments in her schedule, she watched cartoons with me or took me to the recreation room and played a game or two. Bernice was special in the sense that we saw her more as a friend than as a professional. She was a dedicated worker whose outpouring of love and affection for my mother, brother, and me helped us all get through those trying times.

It was these kinds of relationships that have had an everlasting impact on my life. Many times through the years, I came in contact with Bernice during my frequent visits to St. Christopher's. When I attended summer camp for burn survivors, buses that transported campers to the camp met and departed from the hospital. Every year I would go into the hospital and ask for Bernice. It felt as if time only changed by a day. She still looked as she did when I was a child. Her voice, smile, and mannerisms were all familiar and took me back to those great memories.

We got to know many generous, sincere, and caring people associated with my stays in the hospital and during my trips to the clinic. From the medical professionals, receptionists who greeted us by our names and cared to get to know us, the driver who transported us to weekly visits, to the environmental staff who provided great conversations and laughter throughout the days, while I was stuck in bed.

Not all of my memories are ones filled with fear and pain; many are of fun, laughter, and special moments. I have nothing but happy memories of a lot of good people who showed me the utmost love, attention and affection, and who admired my will to fight and live. I was constantly told how so many people held me, prayed for me, and loved me. I was told by many nurses how they were inspired by my recovery, and discovered the reasons for becoming nurses by being a part of my healing. From seeing me through the worse, when it was predicted that I would not make it, to seeing me flourish into a child full of life, hopping and running around the burn unit.

When our stays were long (for several months), we were housed at a patient residential facility called the Children's Seashore House in New Jersey. This facility was an extension of St. Christopher's rehabilitation care, offering extensive variations of therapy. I remember it being a house of fun, with children who had different afflictions, gentle nurses and vibrant recreational attendants. My time was spent playing every game and toy made for children, enjoying story time, listening to music, playing instruments, making art, having movie nights, eating big ice cream sundaes, just living the high life of a kid. Something exciting was always happening.

On special occasions, the staff took us out on trips to fun places along the shore, but what I loved the most, was that the facility was on the beach. We would go down to the beach when permitted and played in the sand, building huge castles out of plastic buckets and sand stencils, then went out into the ocean with a chaperon. I loved being at the Seashore House because it was a definite escape from the constant reminder of the state of pain I was in. I wanted to engage in everything, forgetting that I was confined to a wheelchair, or bandaged from head to toe.

I do not have memories of my father visiting in the earlier years while in the hospital; however, I do remember when he came to visit me at the Seashore House. He pushed me up and down the halls in my wheelchair, racing with other kids. I remember a nurse at the Seashore House who became my second mother, when my mother was not around. During the day and night if she was working, she would find me, take me to the recreational room where there was a big wooden rocking chair, sit me on her lap and rock me. She sang to me in a soft, motherly voice, rocked and held me, sometimes for hours, just the two of us. I felt safe, secure, and through her gentle affection—loved. They were very special moments.

During the holidays, I remember Santa coming to the hospital to grant our wishes. The patients, nurses, and families partook in decorating the ward for Christmas, with a big, brightly lit tree, stuffed with wrapped gifts underneath for the children on the unit. I remember receiving gifts from nurses for my birthdays and even when there were no reasons to celebrate. Receiving gifts was always something that got me excited. There was something about seeing big, bright balloons and gift-wrapped packages with my name on them that compensated for having to be in the hospital. Being the center of attention made me feel special, and that I was special because something so awful happened to me. I think every child should experience moments when they are celebrated and validated because they survived something traumatic. Terrible things should never happen to children, and when they do, extra efforts should be made to honor their resilience.

Receiving gifts became the upside of having to be in the hospital. My mother began what evolved into a tradition that became a part of the healing process for me. My favorite color is purple (cutest story to follow later of how this became), therefore, after every surgery I awoke to a bundle of shiny, aluminum purple balloons with the words "Get Well Soon" and other appropriate slogans, held in my mother's hand. I became excited at the sight of balloons bouncing as she came around the closed curtain (that divided my bed from the other patient sharing the room) peeking her head through and whispering, "Neesha, hey, baby girl," with her big, beautiful smile. She also had in her possession a mega box of Crayola crayons and a jumbo coloring book. Once the anesthesia wore off and I was feeling better, we sat together coloring the pages. She outlined the pictures in black, then colored neatly within the lines. My mother's coloring was perfect, not leaving any trace of white in the background. I always tried concentrating hard to emulate her neat coloring. This became a part of my hospital experience that I most looked forward to, a special bond shared with my mommy.

As my body healed and I got older, hospital stays became fewer and fewer, because I no longer needed to have major surgeries. I would have to continue to undergo skin grafts because of the stretching as my body grew. As I got older and able to walk, I underwent several procedures attempting to correct my crooked feet, followed by intensive outpatient Orthopedic Therapy (OT); Because of my crooked feet, I had to walk with the assistance of leg braces.

They were made of metal bars that extended from my knees down to my feet, attached to two plastic foot holders securing my tiny feet. Each brace had three thick Velcro straps, one across the foot, another across the middle of my legs, and the third across my knee. I then had to wear custom-made shoes that gave me additional support to walk with and without the brace. The sales people at Buster Brown shoe store came to know us personally and made shoes affordable for my mom based on the close relationship. The shoes were much like toddler training shoes, thick with hard wooden bottoms. I had a pair in white, black, navy blue, and light pink. Each had a leather flap buckle in the front. The white and pink pairs had flower designs on the sides of them. My mom dressed me in the cutest outfits, complete with leotards and ruffle socks in every color to match my skirts and dresses. I am known to be very stylish, even as a child I was. My mother always had me looking my best.

I absolutely hated wearing braces, they were extremely uncomfortable. The metal pinched and scraped my skin and the hardness of the plastic hurt my feet. They were also annoying because they constantly had to be manually adjusted anytime I sat down or stood up. On the sides were tiny metal bars that slid up and down to lock and unlock the brace. When sitting, the bar unlocked to allow my legs to bend, and locked straightening my legs to walk. As my walking improved, and I no longer needed to walk with the metal braces, I graduated to just wearing plastic braces, conformed to the fit of my feet. My feet slid into the braces, secured by two Velcro straps, and my shoes or sneakers slipped on over them. The plastic braces were no more comfortable than the metal ones, but were lighter and less painful to wear, and I could easily walk in them.

I had to wear leg braces until the time I was in kindergarten, at which point my mother decided her method of teaching me how to walk was better than medical rehabilitation. After years of learning how to take care of me, my mother believed she had become just as much of a medical expert regarding my recovery as any doctor. She believed everything was in its rightful place and time. Doctors had done their due diligence and had gotten me thus far, but it was God's turn to do the rest, to show up and show out as He does in times of uncertainty.

My mom somehow knew my capabilities, during a time when my future was still unknown. Through her own expertise, she had determined that I no longer needed to wear braces. My mom constantly worked with me, following through with my daily exercises, pushing me to go the extra mile by encouraging me to push past the tears.

Gradually I learned to walk on my own confidently, by becoming conscious of keeping my feet straight while walking. My feet had the tendency to turn inward into its new formed position, causing me to easily trip and fall. My mother was not insensitive, but led by determination to get me to walk on my own. Her trust was solely in God and not in man, especially doctors, because their skepticism refuted faith, and faith was all she had and needed to believe that God would have me walk.

Her eagerness to do things herself was putting that faith into action. Her persistence and tough love were all with good intentions and assurance that God would have me do the things that man said I would not be able to. In my mother's eyes, she was doing God's work by proving with faith, prayer, and her motherly guidance I would be just fine. My mother had already proven doctors wrong, believing I would live by refusing to sign papers to terminate my life. I believe with that same faith she also had the determination to prove those same doctors wrong, who years earlier had given me the prognosis of never being able to function efficiently on my own. My mother was determined to prove that I could learn to do for myself. She was a constant motivator in my life. She pushed and pushed me with both sensitivity and understanding, but also with toughness.

My mom never saw me as a victim. She saw me the same as God did, a conqueror. She would say to me, when I stumbled and fell, "Girl, there is nothing wrong with you, you don't need them things, walk, go ahead and walk. Straighten out your feet, your legs, you can do it!" I wanted my mommy to be proud of me, so I made the conscious effort to try my best and give this task my all. Over time, my legs grew stronger. My feet never straightened completely and is something I have to be aware of even now.

With this consciousness, it was not long before I no longer needed the support of braces. However, I was still prone, to stumbling over my feet and tripping when tired or in pain from walking long distances, standing for long periods of time or walking on uneven surfaces, such as pavements and hills. While walking, I have to slowly and sometimes pay close attention to the ground for potential shifts in the pavements. In inclement weather such as snow and rain, I find it easier to walk in the street because pavements can be too slippery and difficult to see.

Throughout grade school and high school, I was more prone to tripping and falling. This was because I had to rely on public transportation as my primary means of getting around. I was obsessed with keeping focus on every step I took. In doing so, I walked around with my head held down. Many people looking at what happened to me instantly made the assumption that I held my head down to avoid people's stares. It was a fact that I felt shameful of my appearance, but it was not always as it appeared. I walked with my head down to prevent from falling. Every time I fell, I always landed on the same side of my body, which was to the left. My left foot always caught on to my crooked right foot causing me to fall over, landing on my side. My entire left side would become scuffed and bruised.

I remember one particular day walking home from school, I had one of the most embarrassing experiences while attempting to keep up with my friends. I never told anyone about my difficulties because I did not want anyone to feel sorry for me or treat me differently. I tried proving that I could do what others could, in efforts to be accepted.

On this particular day, I was walking with my clique of girlfriends and some other kids we hung out with. I tried my hardest to keep up, because they were walking at a fast pace. I was doing less talking, focused on catching my breath, and not falling. Everyone was rushing to catch the 36 trolley that connected to the G bus near Woodland Avenue. I wanted to tell everyone, "Please slow down I can't keep up," but I felt embarrassed to bring that kind of attention to myself. I told myself, *Dummy, shut up!* I was fearful of the thought that I would be laughed at, made fun of, talked about, or rejected. I also felt unimportant, thinking why would anyone slow down on account of me.

It was a cold day and I wanted to make the trolley so I would not have to stand for a half hour or so, waiting for another. Most kids took the route behind the school because it was much quicker. We walked through a small field and then down a short block. The pavements on the side of the street we walked on were horrible. There were a few trees that were slightly uprooted, lifting the pavement a few inches. I dreaded walking the path, but instead of confidently speaking up, I ended up falling. I always wore Timberland boots, because again I was trying to fit in, and they were the trend back then. I was engaged in a conversation and took my attention away from the steps I was taking. I came across the uprooted pavement near one of the trees and down I went. I had fallen many times before, usually with no one in sight to witness, so I was able to recover by getting up and walking off as if nothing happened. This time there were plenty of people around, those I hung with, in addition to some popular kids, who all witnessed my embarrassment. I hurt myself badly, I was bleeding on my leg and corner of my hand. In an attempt to evade further humiliation I tried quickly getting up and playing it off, but it was too bad of a fall to pretend it did not happen.

Everyone around me asked if I was okay, several people appeared concerned. I heard a few chuckles, as a couple of guys ran off laughing. Someone yelled out the names of those who laughed, as a way of calling them out for being insensitive and disrespectful. Many came to my aide, but I shrugged it off and dismissed their help. I stood up and continued walking. As everyone continued to walk on, inside myself, I was crying in sheer embarrassment. Other times included tripping while walking up subway stairs, down stairs, in the middle of large crowds. Each time I wished I could disappear from the feelings of humiliation I brought upon myself.

I do not know what happened, but as I got older I fell less and less to where I barely fell at all. I like to think it is because I do not do as much traveling as I did back then, and I have mostly maintained a car since getting my license at the age of seventeen. I remain aware of my surroundings, but not with the same constant focus, and surely no longer with my head down.

Teaching me independence so early on was my mother planting the seed that would grow to become my trademark. She told me throughout my childhood that I was capable beyond my physical capacities. My mother looked at me with a firm face and spoke in a stern voice. "Baby girl, you can do all things through Christ who strengthens you. You are fearfully and wonderfully made. You can do anything, probably better than most. The word 'can't' is not in your vocabulary."

Not just with learning to walk on my own, my mother refused to enable me in any way. I remember being five or six years old, sitting at the kitchen table trying to eat. When I ate, my mom placed a fork and spoon in front of me and left me alone to figure out the rest. I sat at the table with Rasheen and the latest addition, my toddler brother Joshua (my mother had also just given birth to my youngest brother Hakiem) and my mom gave them the instructions that I was not allowed to receive any assistance from either of them.

I dropped my utensils numerous times and would get extremely frustrated. I tried picking up a fork with one hand, then with both, however, it was really hard to put the fork up to my mouth with both. With my right hand, which was the "good" hand, I struggled to figure between which fingers to hold the fork in order to get a good grip, to raise it towards my mouth. Not only did I have a hard time, but I was always the last one seated at the table, because my brothers always finished before me. There I sat, trying, food cold, and everywhere from my failed attempts, but my hunger made me even more determined. Eventually I figured it out, even if I only managed to get a few spoonfuls into my mouth, I had succeeded! Only after I made an attempt would my mom assist or allow Rasheen to assist with feeding me. I felt a sense of pride and happiness because of my efforts, and then my mom would kiss, hug, and praise me for a job well done, telling me how proud she was of my determination.

She then explained her reasons for refusing to do for me. Explaining that I had to learn to do for myself, to be independent, because she would not always be around to tend to my every need. I was beginning to gain confidence in myself and in my capabilities that no one but my mother first noticed. I had mastered many of the skills that others said I would not be able to perform. As I learned to do more and more for myself, I became more independent; gaining a newfound sense of confidence and pride.

The intuition and belief my mother had in my capabilities nurtured in me a desire to become even more independent. My independence would later become an essential tool to navigating the many winding roads that lay ahead of my life. Independence was the best skill my mother could have ever taught me. A tool that, despite my physical limitations, gave me the audacity to push beyond those barriers to discover that with effort and tenacity, those limitations did not exist.

Retrospectively, when I think of the pain and suffering I experienced throughout my life from the cruelty, iniquities, rejection, discrimination, and prejudice of the world, I have gained a profound sense of gratitude and love for my mother; knowing that she shared the same experiences while exposing me to the world as a child. I inherited my strength, courage, and dignity from her.

Looking back now, and having an understanding of how insensitive and ignorant people can be when they do not understand the differences in people, I imagine the amount of courage it must have taken for my mother not to hide me. I admire her boldness and strength to face those disgusted reactions and ridicule from people while out in public with me; and the insurmountable strength demonstrated day after day, as she dragged her heavy cross with dignity and pride.

My mother demonstrated such determination and resilience. Being knocked down, but quickly getting right back up, despite the many times I am sure she wanted to run as fast as she could away from it all. There was no escaping the pointed finger of blame. She was subjected to horrendous treatment from outsiders, people believing it was their right to pass judgment, knowing nothing about what we had gone through. Not only did random people condemn her, but she received harsher criticism and resentment from members within our family. I could only imagine that the constant criticism and bigotry from pretty much every one she came in contact with, made it that much easier for my mother to punish and hate herself. However, as a child, I never saw how the pain she felt affected her. Maybe that was why she worked hard to maintain that strength and courage, to create a hardened shell to protect the fragility that laid beneath.

Looking back, I now understand the reason for the hostility my mother often had toward people. Constantly being looked down and frowned upon, and critically judged by many who lacked any sympathy or compassion for a child who was visually in pain, her stance was a protective one. I remember many times witnessing confrontations between her and strangers where she constantly defended my condition and she never edited what she had to say, which most of the time was heated and explicit. I felt embarrassed and protected at the same time. Embarrassed that she would cuss someone out, and did not care where she was or who was around. If they were bold enough to say something about her child, then they were brave enough to face her wrath. We could be in a confined space such as a bus, she did not care. I felt protected that my mom never allowed people to use words to hurt me.

She knew just how easy it was for her to "get outside of herself." My mother was extremely protective of me; therefore, it took absolutely little to set her off. As my mom had taught me to do for myself, she also taught me how to take up for myself. She gave me responses to say when someone stared or made fun of me, such as, "Excuse me, is there a problem that you have to stare so hard?" and "I am different because I am special."

She was not only teaching me how to use words as a powerful sword to fight back against the cruelty of others, she was also trying to make me as fierce and tough as she was. I think my mom wanted me to learn how to stand up for myself, because she knew I would eventually have to do so. She knew that defending myself would become a lifelong battle for me.

My mother loved me and did anything to lessen my pain, so in her defense, confronting ignorance the way she knew how to was necessary, when she felt I was being attacked. Although my mother showed endurance, she did not and would not tolerate malicious scrutiny from anyone! She could put on a performance if anyone antagonized it, especially if she felt someone was just outright disrespectful and insensitive. If pushed to the brink, my mother would tell whomever it applied to, what was on her mind. If she felt I was being attacked or threatened, she was going to make that person wish they had kept their ignorance to themselves. In her tone you could hear the anger, frustration, exhaustion, and hurt she carried. At times that anger and rage could be a frightening sight to see as a child. For my mother, I believe it was cathartic.

I imagined that she wanted people to see just how difficult life was for her raising a disfigured child, and how society made it even more arduous by the lack of sympathy and compassion. Their ignorance put them in the position of receiving my mother's explicit confrontation. No matter how bold and courageous my mother was, her vigor never seemed to dissipate because of the constant brutalities brought on by society's relentless brutes.

Although my mother was quick to get heated, she cooled off just as quickly. She often apologized to me for someone else's ignorance, assuring me that everything was all right because she would never allow anyone to hurt me. In my mother's eyes, I was her little girl. Despite my physical condition she took pride in keeping up my appearance. She dressed me in the cutest outfits and shoes, the same any mother would with their daughter. My mother was not ashamed of me, she never tried hiding me in any way. She showed me off in public and dared anyone to have a problem with it.

In school and around loved ones, I was completely exposed. Only while out in public would she cover my head with hats that matched my outfits. My mother always dressed me in hats with straps to protect my head from the sun's beaming rays. My scalp was still very sensitive to the elements, especially when it was hot. The patch of hair that remained, my mother styled and maintained it as if I had a full head of hair. I remember her taking time in the mornings preparing me for the day's adventure. Whether it be going to school or on an outing, she sat me on the stool at her bar, and proceed to style my hair.

In front of me she sat the brush, comb, purple hair grease, and the suede purple and gold stitched sack that encased the popular alcoholic beverage Crown Royal. After the alcohol was gone, she found use of the case to keep all of my hair barrettes. She gave me the job of picking out the ones that matched the colors in my outfit. However, I only picked out the purple ones, no matter what color

I wore. My mom chose the Crown Royal casing because purple was my favorite color. She combed and divided the patch of hair on the right side of my head into two sectioned braids secured with elastic barrettes called "ballies" and matching purple clasped barrettes that held the braid in place.

My favorite story to tell is about how my obsession with the color purple came to be. I was attending John B. Kelly Elementary School and was in kindergarten.

I remember having my class pictures taken. My mom dressed me in a lavender-colored frilly dress with purple tulips printed all over. It had puffy shoulders with lace at the trimmings of each arm and the hem of the dress, and a satin ribbon synching the waist that tied into a bow in the back. My mom accented my dress with violet- and lavender-colored barrettes. I was in love with the dress and wanted to wear it every day. It was a fancy dress that could be worn on Easter Sunday or for church. There were a couple of times when my mother gave in and let me wear the dress on uneventful days to school. I could imagine people wondering what she was thinking, sending me to school in the dress repeatedly. I did not care, it was my favorite dress and all I wanted was to wear it every day.

My mother did not care about what anyone thought about her or me. No one knew what she endured or the trauma I experienced. No one knew how beautiful I still was, and that her love for me never changed even though my appearance had. No one knew the countless sleepless nights my mother stayed awake, praying to God to save me and make me whole. No one could imagine her pain, so she defended it by defending me.

The advocating my mother did for me was her fighting so that I could be myself. I believe the acceptance from those who did not try hiding me is what allowed me to feel comfortable in my own skin. I was learning that I had a right to live and be just as anyone else. I had the right to be seen, heard, and respected despite the discomfort from those who did not understand. "You don't like what you see and have something disrespectful to say, then keep it to yourself" is what my mother would say. She included that she hoped God made them suffer his eternal wrath for not recognizing I was a child they were laughing at.

Recovery from my burns monopolized most of my life, and restricted me from exploring the world hands on as a child. Although I endured many hurdles, my early childhood memories were full of love, affection, and doing many of the things kids do.

Whatever my mother was dealing with, whatever she did to cope, and however she came across to those who knew her best, I was shielded from experiencing that version of her. I remember my mom as being lively, popular, loving, caring, providing for my brothers and me, beautiful, and happy. My early childhood was a time when I felt most safe and secure with my mom. Those years meant more to me than any other times in my childhood, because of those wonderful, calm, and loving moments. It was a time full of the 80's culture, an area that still to this day gives me a sense of nostalgia. There is not a song from that decade that does not send me back to when everything and everyone was good!

CHAPTER 4

A Normal Girl

AROUND THE AGE OF five or six, I began to recognize that something was wrong with me. My skin looked and felt different than everyone else's. I had to miss a day out of the week from school to see the doctor. Sometimes I had to stay in the hospital, and when I came home some part of my body was wrapped and I was told I could not do this or that. At nights my mom gave me treatments, I was always in pain. I was aware of everything that was happening to me, but I did not fully comprehend or understand what happened to me. I assumed all those things were normal. No one around me brought to my attention my differences, and my experiences had yet to punish me or make me suffer the consequences of being different.

I had come a long way in the years of my healing, and was not much different than any child my age. The exception was that my fragile state allowed me more leverage, consideration, and privileges. Bottom line, I was spoiled rotten, and got away with any and everything.

There was nothing, I could have ever done wrong, even when my hand was caught dead in the cookie jar, and my face was stained with chocolate, I never got in trouble. I honestly think because of my trauma, in my mother's eyes, I was the child who never could do any wrong, even when I participated equally in mischief and purposefully misbehaved; nothing I could have ever done warranted her to chastise me. In my mother's eyes, I was perfect. Unsuspectingly, I got into all sorts of things, even things she knew I should have been punished for were ignored. As a result, I cleverly used my mother's obliviousness and my physical condition to my advantage.

Rasheen's recovery did not require living in the hospital as mine had. However, he underwent a few surgeries for skin graphing and had to go through the same physical therapy as me. Rasheen's recovery was swift, and he was able to resume a life of normalcy way before I could. My brother was very much like any young boy, very adventurous, inquisitive, and wild. I looked up to Rasheen and wanted to do the things he did. I wanted to be everywhere he was and wanted his friends to be my friends. For a while, it was just he and I. Rasheen's twin, younger by a few minutes, lived in a facility that cared for children with intellectual disabilities. There were complications during birth, which caused his disability. Tysheen was still very much a part of the family, visiting on special occasions every year. My younger brother Joshua was a baby, so it was just me and Rasheen.

When not in the hospital or visiting the clinic for checkups with my mom, my brother was responsible for watching me. Anything he did I was usually a part of, everywhere he went, so was I. We moved around a lot as children, mostly within the Germantown section, Topohocken, Rittenhouse, Pastorious, and then Manheim Street.

Most of my fondest memories were living in a two-story apartment above a storefront on the corner of Manheim Street. Every morning, my brother and I awoke and sat in front of the television in the living room, turning the dials from channel to channel watching our favorite Saturday morning cartoons. *Pee-wee's Playhouse* was our must see show, followed by *ThunderCats*, *The Smurfs*, *Heathcliff*, and *Transformers*.

My brother and I sat in front of the TV with our big bowls, filled with Captain Crunch cereal watching cartoon after cartoon, until it was time for wrestling. WWF (formally known as The World Wrestling Federation) came on, where the original pioneers, the legends of wrestling—Hulk Hogan, Macho Man Randy Savage, The Bull Dog, and Lex Luger—were the dominant competitors of the masculine slam down.

Rasheen never watched as a spectator, but took on the role of his favorites. In his reenactments I was always casted as the opponent. He imitated his favorite moves such as the DDT and the Jackhammer, some of the signature moves of his favorite wrestlers. My brother was a hard core devoted fan. He marveled the sport by assuming the voices of the characters. His impression of Macho Man was precise and my favorite. Rasheen really used his imagination; he carved championship belts out of cardboard and wrapped the bulky center buckle with aluminum foil, making it look very much like the ones the characters wore on TV.

Rasheen paraded around the house wearing replica bandanas of the characters he portrayed. He paced around the small living room space in search of his opponent, helpless little me. When he found me, he gently performed wrestling moves, such as pining, stumping, swinging me around, and securing me in headlocks. I had so much fun playing with my big brother, but I was happier that he enjoyed playing with me. I loved all the attention I got from Rasheen, and by the way he protected me. Rasheen often got in trouble with our mom because she thought he was being rough with me, which he never was, we had so much fun.

I knew all of Rasheen's friends. If they had sisters my age, I was most likely friends with them. Everyone in our neighborhood knew my mom and knew about what happened to me and my brother. Therefore, my brother's friends became my additional brothers. They saw how overprotective my brother was of me, and they too became my protectors.

My mom was great friends with a woman named Angie who lived very close to us. My mom allowed me to spend the night with her two daughters, and they stayed over at our house. Angie's two daughters were close in age to me, and a son who was around my brother's age, so they hung out together. I loved playing with her daughters, they were pretty and had lots of fun toys to play with. They loved coming over my house because I had lots of Barbie dolls. After losing my sister, I grew close to the girls wishing they were my sisters.

There was another of my mother's friends who had a total of like ten children, nine girls and one boy, whose name I remember was Sean. I could never forget Sean because I had the biggest crush on him. I was about six years old and Sean was my brother's age, about ten or so. I remember him being tall and slender, with caramel complexion, and cute. My brother and I had a great bond with all the kids whose ages ranged from toddler to teenager.

My family grew very close to their family. The girls closest to my age were very overprotective of me. Anyone who had anything negative to say were confronted by an angry mob of sisters, ready to fight. I can imagine they felt a sense of sorrow, that something so horrible happened to me, and that it was not fair. I am sure, because they were too young to process and understand how something so grave could happen to anyone, they must have felt helpless and unsure of how to be my friend. I am sure what they did understand was that no one should take advantage or hurt someone who was helpless and could not defend themselves. One of the codes of the hard streets stated that one "takes up" for the defenseless, by fighting for them, not just physically, but verbally as well.

My friends would say, "Don't worry, Tanisha, I got your back, let anybody try to mess with you, I'll step to them." If ever I was made fun of or teased by other kids in the neighborhood who did not know about what happened to me, the entire clan, along with my brother, came to my defense. I knew the sisters had my back because they really cared and saw that I could not stand up for myself. I also wondered if they did so because they liked my brother, wanting to win his attention and for him to like them back.

Whatever the reason being, again I felt protected by people who cared for me. I began feeling a sense of entitlement, deserving of special treatment because this bad thing happened to me. I had grown accustomed to people taking care of me, showing me ample affection, and pitying me, that I began to expect special treatment from any and everyone. For people to instantly be kind, friendly, and easy upon realizing that I had gone through something that warranted the deepest sympathy and compassion.

Some of the girls my age would come sit on my front steps to hang out with me, or I walked to their house with my brother to sit on their porch. We played in front of their house running up and down the streets. Several times throughout the day, many of us ambushed the corner store to buy brown paper bags full of penny candies, little fruit juices in plastic cylinder-shaped containers called "hugs," and bags and bags of junk food. I loved junk food, probably more than I loved real food. My favorite was the brand of chips called Golden. They came in a variety of plain, BBQ, and sour cream and onion, all in golden-colored aluminum bags; my favorite was the BBQ.

We would race back up the block, playing rope, hopscotch, singing and dancing to the latest jams played on the popular hip-hop and R&B radio station Power 99 FM. The music filled the entire block, coming from a boom box propped up in the window of their house. On some days we just sat on either's steps, enjoying the summer's fresh air, watching the traffic and people passing by. We randomly talked about the cute male celebrities we were going to marry, the cars we were going to drive, and the extravagant lifestyle painted by our young imaginations.

I have no recollection of being teased or harassed by my peers during this time in my life. Those days in my early childhood were full of fun and having lots of friends who did not care about what I had been through, but saw me as their equal. Aside from my brother were my two favorite cousins Naeem and Aisha, who I loved spending time with. Aisha was close in age with my brother, pretty, very popular, and took absolutely no mess. The looks alone she gave anyone who fixed their face to look at me wrong were enough to indicate that she was not the person anyone wanted to mess with. Naeem and I were the same age, and were extremely close, because we spent a lot of time together. He was equally as protective of me as my brother. I was always excited to go over my aunt's house to play with Neem. I especially loved traveling together around the city with our grandmother. I adored Neem so much; He was always so gentle and attentive to me.

Like any sibling relationship, my brother and I had times when we yelled and bickered with one another, mostly when Rasheen refused to include me in whatever he was doing that did not involve me tagging along. I was spoiled, had tantrums and acted sassy just like any ordinary kid. Everything was about me and had to be about me, when I did not get my way, I found ways to demand it.

I knew how to manipulate people, especially my mom and brother. My mom already had a soft heart for me. I used her vulnerability to my full advantage. If my brother refused to give me what I wanted or did what I wanted him to do, I simply found ways to get him in trouble. My brother and mom's relationship was not like the one I had with my mom. Rasheen got in trouble what seemed to be all of the time. He was either being yelled at for not coming home when told to by our mom, hanging around kids she told him not to, acting up in school, or just being defiant. I think my brother behaved badly because any attention from our mom meant he was being noticed.

I am sure it was difficult for my brother, being as though our mom's focus was so much on me. My brother always appeared to me older than he was. I think in part it was because he was considered and expected to be the man of the house; neither of our fathers were present. Rasheen was also made responsible to care for me, looking after me when my mom was not around. I am sure the level of stress and responsibility he had at the age of ten or eleven put immense pressure on his young, underdeveloped psyche.

Rasheen had never gone to therapy to process his grief, or to learn how to cope with the trauma, so I am sure his acting out was in many ways vying for attention and affection from our mother. Maybe he wanted her attention to make sure she still loved him. I wondered what were my mother's feelings toward my brother after? I wonder how Rasheen felt, seeing how our mom treated me versus him. I can imagine he experienced feelings of abandonment and felt unloved. I wonder if my mother held deep resentment toward Rasheen for not keeping a better eye on Nakisha and being a kid allowing his curiosity to allure him into what he should have known was danger. I wonder if my mother ever had a sit down with Rasheen teaching him about the dangers of playing with matches, or if she just expected him to know better. Was the sight of him uncomfortable to her, serving as a daily reminder of her guilt? Did she feel less guilt by transferring it to Rasheen? Did she show favoritism toward me because I was the victim, and disdain toward him for being the reason I was a victim? Rasheen was just as much a victim, but I never saw my mom look at him as she did me. The focus was always on my pain and recovery.

My brother was the causality of my mother's wrath whenever a tear looked as if it was about to fall from my face. There were times when I plotted revenge on Rasheen, if he went out with his friends and did not allow me to tag along. I remember one time I demanded that I go with my brother to the park to ride his brand new huffy bike with his friends. Rasheen yelled "no" because they would be riding in and out of the park and he would not be able to keep an eye on me. I wanted to ride with him, as he had always allowed me to do when riding his bike from one end of the block to the other. Again Rasheen said "no", so I went and told my mom that Rasheen would not take me with him. My mom's response was, "Rasheen, why can't you take your sister with you?" subliminally she was also saying, "Boy, you better take your sister with you!" Rasheen knew better than to reply, so it was off to the park we went.

We walked instead of riding on his bike, it was his way of making me pay for having to tag along.

At the park Rasheen and all of his friends were found admiring their bikes' features, talking about the latest add-ons they got, or bragging about getting a new bike. When all members of their bike crew assembled, they rode around the park together, doing tricks, seeing whose bike was the fastest and who could jump off of railings and platforms the highest.

On our way home I begged Rasheen to let me ride with him on his bike, which he gave in and allowed me to. Rasheen sat me on the seat and rode his bike standing on the pedals. He told me to wrap my arms around his waist as tightly as I could, but my arms were too short, so I could only latch on to the back of his pants. I wanted to go fast as Rasheen had done with his friends. "Go faster, Sheen," so my brother picked up speed.

We then got to a street with graveled pavement, causing him to flip the bike still going at full speed, resulting in both of us falling off. I was not badly injured, just a few scrapes and cuts, but my brother hit his leg on some debris and badly wounded it. I was scared because there was blood everywhere. He was more scared to return me home crying from the fall. He knew my mother would not care to hear an explanation, for her, seeing that I was hurt told the entire story.

Sure enough, that night Rasheen got his butt whipped and could not ride his bike for a while. I remember spitefully getting my brother in trouble whenever he made me mad. All I had to do was say, "Mommy, Rasheen…" and without finishing she instantly reacted. My mom would spank him and I sometimes stood close by, listening and quietly laughing while he was suffering, later finding Rasheen still upset asking him if he was okay with a smirk on my face.

Knowing just how gullible my mom was, I used the fact as leverage to bribe my brother into giving me what I wanted. I would say to him, "If you don't let me go to the store with you, I'm going to tell Mommy." or "If you don't take me to the basketball courts with you, I'ma tell Mommy."

Despite our on again-off again debacles, we genuinely got along. No matter whether we were having fun, yelling and screaming or mad at the other, it never changed the way my brother took up for me. We could be bickering one minute and the next minute he would be in another kid's face letting him know not to talk about his sister. No matter where we lived, Rasheen was well respected by kids in the neighborhood and they knew he did not play when it came to his sister.

My mom was a single mother, who loved her children and did everything she could to make us happy. Maybe giving us our hearts' desires was her way of telling us she was sorry for what we had gone through and made it her goal to see that we remained happy and content. One of the reasons we were well liked was because we were the kids on the block who had everything: toys, toys and more toys.

The newest toys advertised on TV, we had them. We had more clothing than we needed. The apartment we lived in above the storefront looked more like a house on the inside.

When entering, there was a staircase leading to the kitchen at the top of the stairs, then a bedroom to the left of the staircase and the living room in front of the bedroom, facing the front of the house. Behind the first staircase was a second staircase that led to three bedrooms on the upper level, and at the foot of the stairs was the bathroom. My brother's room was the first to the left of the staircase, my room was in the middle. My mom had the biggest room, with a doorway connecting both our rooms together.

My room was more so used as a storage place for all of my toys and clothes, because every night I slept with my mom. It made sense that my room served the purpose of storing my stuff, because I had more than a child my age should have had. I had every Barbie doll in the company's collection, several large plastic bins of Barbie dolls, along with accessories, lots of clothes, cars, and about three town houses. Barbie lived extravagantly in my room. I also had life-size dolls. My favorites were My Kid Sister, and my pillow friends, squared shaped plush pillows with windows as its big eyes and big fun colorful faces with long floppy arms and legs. All of my friends loved coming over to play with my toys, we got lost for hours in play.

The weekends were the most anticipated time of the week, because there was no school, which meant we were able to stay up as late as we wanted. Best of all, our friends often stayed over, and we roamed free all hours of the night. As a child the weekends appeared to be a party, every weekend seemed like one big, loud, endless party. My mom entertained her friends, who gathered at our house where she bartended from behind her personal bar, a chocolate wooden bar stand she bought that sat in the corner of our living room. It looked like an expensive miniature bar counter, that held an excessive amount of alcohol.

I remember my mother yelling at Rasheen and me to get from behind the bar before we broke any of her bottles. There was a collection of glass. Tall bottles, short ones, skinny ones, huge ones, all filled with an assortment of colors. My mom was always entertaining someone at our house. When her girlfriends came over, they often brought their children so Rasheen and I could have company. Playing upstairs with our friends, the women could be heard in their loudness, over the interchanging sounds of hip-hop and smooth R&B.

After some serious and exhausting play, all of us kids would race down the stairs toward the kitchen for a snack. All of us jolting down the stairs at once sounded like a stampede of a wild herd. I was always the last one behind, trying to keep up. As soon as I finally made it down the last step, my mom greeted me, whisking me away in her arms as she sung to a song that was one she really liked. She would say, "Oh this is my jam. Here's my baby girl." She danced with me and then prompted me to dance for everyone by saying, "Go, Neesha, go, Neesha!" I was very shy for being put on the spot in front of others; however, after much encouragement, I performed with the cuteness of a child. After I performed for my mom and her company, she bragged about me to her friends.

As a child I spoke as a child and did childish things, I stayed in a child's place with no level of knowledge or understanding of what was actually going on. In hindsight, as an adult I have clear knowledge and understanding, that every weekend was the time when my mom would drink until drunk, I am sure she was dabbling in drugs as well, and I remember my mother always having a man around. Whether it was a male friend who knew my mom well offering their support in times of need, or a man with whom she was romantically involved with, there was always a man around.

Nice men too, I might add. Men who appeared to genuinely care for us and my mom, and who were deeply in love with her. My brother Joshua's father, Jay Jay, was one of the good men. What I significantly remember most about Jay Jay was his height, he was very tall, slender with thick, dark eyebrows that made him look serious and angry all of the time. When Jay Jay came around, he would stand in front of me staring, no expression to tell the mood he was in, just a blank and intimidating stare. Seconds later, he would grip me up, give me a bear hug and say, "How is my lil girl?" with a kiss on the cheek. He was the most gentle and loving man who treated me like I was his biological daughter.

Despite my mother's many faults and flaws, that at the time to me were unknown and unseen, she was my foundation. She appeared to be strong, confident, radiantly beautiful, and unwavering. My early memories of my mom were of her possessing these qualities. The admiration that I felt for my mom made me want to be just like her. I believe my view of my mother as she was then, developed from seeing her dedication and commitment. She was always there for me. She was patient and supportive with the protracted steps toward a full recovery, all to which she did alone.

I was too young to fathom anything different about the woman who I idolized. My mom appeared to have it all together. All the while there was an internal whirlpool that was slowly forming into a catastrophic storm. Everything seemed copacetic with her, because she showed the ability to provide the childhood I enjoyed. From my perspective as a child my mom was pleasant, nurturing, and involved. What I did not know or see was that she was also a hurting, lonely, angry, grieving woman, riddled with guilt and shame.

A picture speaks a thousand words. In the family portrait of her, my brother, and me, she looked very much like the intact woman I described. However, my mother told me once that although she was smiling and all looked well, she was hurting immensely. My mother shared with me that the picture had been taken after my father abandoned her, leaving my mother with nothing but all the burdens of caring for two sick children alone. For my mom life was difficult and she sustained the best she could.

Eventually all of her baggage became too heavy, and getting by became too cumbersome, so much so that the pressure and lack of coping skills, led her down several dead-ends with my brothers and I in tow for the ride. Careening head on into the arms of the wrong men, stuck in the gutters that resulted from drugs and alcohol, rest stops of sobriety, and the dark back roads of abuse and violence.

Throughout her trials and tribulations my mother resiliently would reemerge and start over again (another trait that I would inherit). My mother's charismatic personality and determination allowed her to regain her composure and will power to press forward and attempt to reconcile for those setbacks. Demons harbored, stemming from insecurities as a child, and the suppression of the family's tragedy, a festering wound still freshly raw and sensitive under the thin scab that protected it. The scab represented the avoidance of not talking about the tragedy because it was too harrowing. When the scab was picked or fell off, it was always an ugly sight to see and a mess to clean up.

My mother dealt with what she was given throughout her life as best she could, alone with two physically injured children, two toddlers, and another baby on the way. Handling so much with no support and resources, she found comfort, acceptance, and temporary relief in the outlet of drugs, alcohol, and repeated failed, dysfunctional relationships with men whose false promises and dense validations never were enough to fill my mother's emptiness.

That smile I had come to depend on to make me feel safe, loved, and assured had wilted. It subsided deep beneath her sorrow, pain, and misery. My mother's luster became dull. Her current paramour, during that time, was said to have introduced her to crack cocaine. This was the beginning of the end to the life I had known thus far. Addiction took hold of my mother and was the catalyst for the dysfunction which lead to the breakup of our family.

Suddenly I found myself ejected from what was my world and interjected into a new world, known as the foster care system. Without my brothers, without my mommy, without anything familiar. My brothers and I had become wards of the state, in the care of the Department of Human Services, also known as DHS. I had been placed several times with strangers who I did not know, and was given a new life that I was forced to adjust to. My childhood as I knew it was gone, things would never be the same. Foster care was only the beginning of many unexpected changes to come.

CHAPTER 5

Another Trauma

EVERYTHING CHANGED SO FAST and without warning. My perspective of my family was happy, content, full of love and being well taken care of. My brother's perspective was completely different. Rasheen's perspective of our mother was the antithesis of my experience of our mother. Instead of being the happy, loving, and protective mother I knew her to be, to him, she was emotionally unavailable, neglectful, and irresponsible. My mother and brother had a volatile relationship.

I can imagine how abandoned he must have felt as a child and probably was envious and jealous that most of our mother's attention and affection had been given to me. How does the heart thrive without a mother's love and constant affection? Somehow Rasheen's did, enough to still love, care, and feel the need to protect others at such a young age. It goes to show how powerful the resilience of a child is. Children are the best example of how the soul in no way can never be defeated. A person is evident in their resilience. It is not just the ability to bounce back from whatever life throws one way, but resilience proves that the spirit is designed to endure what the self is unable to. One's spirit always lives in truth and can never deviate far from it.

They clashed, from an early age. The threads from the fabric of their relationship slowly began to unravel. For my brother, his anger brewed from the maltreatment of my mother because of her active drinking and according to him, our mother's uncontrollable using.

For a child to witness his mother drunk or high evokes many emotions. The resentment of having their world disrupted and forced to take on responsibilities they are not prepared to handle. The anger felt from the parent choosing drugs over the child, the feelings of abandonment created as that parent's focus moves away from their child and primarily on using. Fear from the violence, abuse, and dysfunction caused by the altered state of mind of that parent, while under the influence. Shame the child feels that their parent is not like others, and is dealing with something considered to be very "bad." The embarrassment of the possibility that the child's reputation will be ruined if the family's "secret" has been exposed, therefore, causing disdain to the family's image. Also the helplessness in knowing that no matter how much the child acts out or how hard they love that parent, these approaches often become meaningless efforts in convincing that parent to end the addiction. I would later come to understand, as I would experience these same emotions in the same context dealing with my mother's monstrous addiction.

Rasheen's experience of my mother's addiction had gotten to the point that he went to school one day and asked his teacher if he could go home with her. He stated he went to school previously, telling his teacher that his mom used drugs and was not taking care of him. According to Rasheen, our mom found out what he told his teacher and she threatened him to keep his mouth closed. That day when he sobbed to his teacher, she drove him home to talk to our mom. When Rasheen spotted her, he begged his teacher not to leave him with her, because he noticed that she was exhibiting symptoms of being under the influence of using drugs. According to Rasheen, this incident is how DHS entered into our lives.

My memory of when my life abruptly changed was when my mother got involved with a man who allegedly introduced her to crack cocaine. Instantly she became hooked. They took a trip to the mountains, and my mom said sometime during their trip, she tried to leave him after he became abusive, to the point that she feared for her life. She finally found the opportunity to leave and returned back to Philly without him. I believe the weight of her addiction, plus the reasons she turned to drugs to numb the pain, just became too much for her to bear. My mom decided that she needed an extended vacation away from the world and escape the confines of her addiction. She said making the decision to "put her children away" (voluntarily placing us into the care of DHS) was the most difficult, but selfless thing to do, while she took the time to seek much needed help.

Devastatingly, we all were separated and without one another. Initially, Rasheen and I were placed together at a group facility called St. Joseph's Home for Children located in Bensalem, Pennsylvania. My toddler brother Joshua and baby brother Hakiem were placed together with an older couple who fostered them the year or two we were in placement. I did not see my baby brothers for the entire time we were in foster care. Rasheen was placed in the group home's boys housing. Although we were in the same program, we did not often see each other, but when we did, I clung on to him for dear life. My brother was all I had and being there together solidified our bond, because yet again it was another trauma we experienced together.

St. Josephs was a Catholic facility that housed many displaced children. What I remember about my time at St. Josephs was attending Catholic school, which was conveniently on the same campus, and having to dress in a uniform every day. The attire was a light yellow color shirt, short sleeve when it was warm and long sleeve with a cardigan when the weather was cold. The skirts were a dark army green, with a checkered pattern of yellow and red lines. I wore dark green leggings and black and white uniform shoes. I remember there being kids of all ages, but we were grouped with peers in the same age range. I got along with the other children and made friends. I remember having to do everything with the group of kids I was sectioned with, such as having to eat together, and share a large room.

St. Josephs attempted to create a home-like environment, and provided things familiar to a child, such as favorite foods, toys and special events on weekends. There were so many toys. I selected the ones I was interested in, found a quiet corner, and played alone. Playing was very comforting, pretending allowed me to escape.

Movie nights were on weekends. We got dressed in our favorite pajamas and all of the children in the house united to watch *The Little Mermaid* or *The Jungle Book*. Staff created the atmosphere of being in a theater by popping popcorn and turning out the lights. I enjoyed and looked forward to movie nights.

Although I was stimulated with fun food and toys, I was home-sick, I still did not understand why I had to live with strangers and children who came and went, who were of different colors, ages and sizes. I did not understand where my mom had gone, and why I could not be with her. I missed my mom, I thought about her every day; at night I laid in my bed and cried to be with her. I cried silently so that none of the other kids heard me. I cried until my pillow was drenched from tears.

What calmed me down was closing my eyes until I saw noth-ing but black, and if I squeezed them hard enough, focusing on the blackness, I began to see images, small specks of white. Like stars in the open galaxy, that is where I imagined myself to be. Far away in a distant land with no one around, just me, away from the strangers, the feelings of hurt and the betrayal of being abandoned. I was in a place where I felt safe and at peace. Once I fell into a deep sleep, every dream was about being with my mom, back in our home, back to the way things were. Then the lights came on and I awoke to the ugly sight of reality, the disappointment that it was all a dream and I was not with my mom.

DHS appointed our family with a case worker named Pat McMillan, a Caucasian woman who appeared to be in her forties. She was a nice woman, who really cared about our family. One of her tasks was to assist my mother with applying for Section 8 housing. Section 8 was a government housing assistant program for low- to no-income residents in need of suitable and affordable housing. Ms. Pat wore many hats, not just being solely responsible for connecting all of the pieces to reunify our family, but she had a heavy case load of other DHS-involved families that she juggled simultaneously. Unlike the horror stories of many case workers, Ms. Pat made our family feel we were her only client. She was passionate and dedicated to getting our family back together. We all felt that she cared about each of us. Rasheen and my mom, to this day still talk about the ways she touched them individually.

My memories of Ms. Pat were that she was a generous, soft-spoken, and kind woman. She came to the group home to take me to my appointments, and to see my mom for our bi-weekly scheduled visits. After the visits, on our way back to the group home, Ms. Pat sometimes took me out to lunch. She allowed me to choose, and I always chose to go to McDonalds. I loved the Happy Meal boxes that came with a special gift, usually a toy from the latest Disney movie. When Disney's *Rescuers from Down Under* came out, Ms. Pat took me to see it.

McDonald's had been advertising the movie by offering collectible ornaments of the characters from the movie. Ms. Pat knew I loved the movie, so she took me to McDonald's after visits with my mom until I collected the three main characters, Bianca, Bernard, and Jake the Kangaroo. Mrs. Pat had also taken me to see Disney's *The Little Mermaid*. I am unsure if the outing was for a special occasion such as my birthday, but it meant so much that she made time for me in such ways. I felt important to her and that helped me get through such a difficult time when my trust for adults had become insecure.

In my twenties, I had been approached by a guy who was friends with my brother, and who also resided at St. Josephs during the same time as us. The guy's name was Jose, we both were exiting a gas station several blocks from where I lived. He grew excited when he saw me.

"Hey, how are you doing! Don't you have a brother named Rasheen and didn't you both stay at St. Josephs?" He exclaimed.

"Yes," I replied, a bit confused. I had no idea who he was, but Jose had immediately recognized me.

We talked, his eyes filled with tears as Jose hugged me repeatedly. Jose became emotional as he shared how inspired he was by me then. Jose went on about how good God was and how he thought about us often growing up. Jose's facial expression showed that of awe, as he told me how beautiful I had become. Jose asked about my brother, while reminiscing over when they both were best friends, how he held a sense of obligation to look out for me as my brother had done. Jose shared how he had the upmost respect for Rasheen, therefore I was just as much his sister. I told Jose how touched I was by his remarks and apologized for not remembering him and everything we all experienced together as friends.

Just as I had gotten acclimated at St. Josephs, I was told I had to say good bye to my brother, because I was moving to another foster home. My life was crumbling brick by brick, first my mother left, and then I was taken away from my brother, the person who always looked after me. My biggest fear was that I would never see him again. With all that I had gone through physically, not having the support system I had come to rely solely on, made me feel lost and even more alone. I had no idea where I was going or who I was going with. Were they nice people, mean people? Would they like me? Would I like them? How many children did they have? Would I be treated good? Would they notice me, love me? I was placed in a temporary/permanent home. It was temporary until my mother got back on her feet and permanent in the sense that I would not be moving again.

My new home was with the Jones family. They were a middle class nuclear, African American family, who reminded me of the Huxtables from *The Cosby Show*. My experience with the Jones was all so different for me coming from a single parent household. Both parents were present in their children's lives and had very good careers, which afforded them to live a content lifestyle. Anita and her husband Michael had three children. The oldest, Michael Jr., was in his early twenties and went by the nickname Mike Mike. Mike Mike did not live with the family, but was always around as if he did. They also had a teenage son Darren, who was about fifteen or sixteen years old as well as their only daughter, Nikki, who was about my age, seven or eight years old. They also had another foster child, a little girl, Shanika, five years old, whom they had fostered since she was a baby.

Whenever Mike Mike came around, he spoke, but always struck me as a man of few words. I remember feeling a bit timid around him, because he always appeared to be in a bad mood. Most of the times when I saw Mike Mike, he was either coming in to grab something to eat or he was leaving. He sometimes stayed and had dinner with the family. Eating together as a family most nights out of the week, was different for me. Mrs. Jones cooked full-course meals, meals that my mother would only prepare on holidays or special occasions.

On my mother's budget, my brothers and I ate meals that were quick and inexpensive, such as hotdogs and baked beans, oodles-and-noodles with grilled cheese and lunchmeat and cheese sandwiches. We rotated those selections at least once a week. Sometimes my mom would throw down! making fried chicken, rice and gravy with greens, corn bread and every now and then she may have baked a cake or chocolate cookies for dessert.

When she went out of her way to cook big meals, it felt like a special holiday. We got so excited, savoring the foods, wishing we could have such a luxury every day. Until seeing all that the Jones's had, it made me realized that my family really did not have as much as other people did. I came to learn we were considered impoverished. I do not remember my mother going to work every day, I do not ever think I thought about how my mother made her living. As a child, those were things I did not think about, I just knew we were well taken care of and never wanted for anything.

My mother relied on food stamps to feed us. They were governmental assistance that subsidized the cost of food for those who otherwise could not afford a month's worth of groceries. Food stamps looked like counterfeit money designed to replicate the same amounts as real money.

Each amount was a different color. A one-dollar bill was brown, a five was blue, ten was green, twenty was blue, and fifty was red. They were given as a booklet, with the value printed on the cover that depended on a household's monthly amount. My mom had several booklets that added to her month's amount. I had always believed all people used food stamps. Money was used for everything else other than food. I do not know if I ever saw my mom pay for food with real cash. Anytime she sent us to the store, it was with stamps. The change returned after a purchase was always in stamps, except for the coin currency.

Everyone in the neighborhood mostly used food stamps. My friends and I could be outside playing or walking around and find a dollar or five-dollar stamp on the ground, and believed we won the lottery. When I moved into the Jones's house, it was a culture shock to see that they paid for food with real money. I had never heard of, much less ever tasted rye and wheat breads until living with the Jones. There were many foods that I had to learn to acquire a taste for, like Brussels sprouts and asparagus. To this day I have been unsuccessful in acquiring a taste for them, because the first time was my last.

Mr. and Mrs. Jones had a beautiful home filled with antiques and nice expensive furniture. They had a furnished basement that functioned as the common area for watching TV and entertaining company. There were four bedrooms, Nikki and I shared a room, their middle son Darren had his own room and the younger foster child had Mike's old room. It was a comfortable and nice place to live, but it took me a while to get acclimated. I felt a sense of discomfort because I did not know what the family thought of me at first, whether they liked me. I felt fearful and intimidated with Anita, I was unsure why, she appeared stern and I could not read her emotionally. I felt Anita did not like me or wanted me around, therefore, I tried to stay out of her way. I did not tell Anita when I was hungry, I just waited for her to call me for meals. Sometimes, I would sit for hours starving, but felt afraid to tell Mrs. Jones. I felt I was an inconvenience and thought she resented having to care for me. I convinced myself to stay out of sight and not be heard, to make the family happy.

I do not remember if I went to school, but do remember spending lots of time during school days with Anita, running errands and being home with her most days. I remember feeling really anxious and just out of place.

Months went by and I began to feel more comfortable, I started to feel acknowledged, but I never felt as though I was a part of the Jone's family. I envied the way they lived, and wished I belonged with them. They seemed to have it all, and I had nothing, not a home, my mother or my brothers. It was to no fault of the family, they were great and cared for me, I just wanted to be where I felt I belonged and nothing could fill that void. Nothing else in the world mattered.

As more time passed, I eventually began to form bonds. Initially, I thought Mike Mike despised me, let alone by the looks he gave. When I was around, Mike Mike did not say much, and when he did say more than a few words, such as engage in a conversation with me, I not only was surprised, but enjoyed talking with Mike Mike and saw that he was actually nice. Mr. Jones was very cool to be around, a very kind-hearted man, he wore glasses with a warm smile. Mr. Jones was also a man of few words, but had a strength and boldness that made those around him feel protected.

My favorite person was Darren. It was love at first sight. Darren was tall, slender, and handsome, but what I admired most about him was that he was a great performer. Darren was funny and very theatrical. Darren's greatest talent was dancing, he knew every popular dance move. The '80s was the booming of pop and hip-hop music. Darren was the reason I developed a passion and love for hip-hop.

A close bond was established through our common love for hip-hop and R&B music. We both knew everything there was to know about the most popular artists. We rapped and sung along to the biggest hits, as Darren showcased all the dance moves from our favorite videos. For hours, we would watch one video show after another, MTV's *Yo! MTV Raps*, The Box, *The Basement* with Big Tigger, and *Video Soul*. We watched the shows' countdowns, featuring the top ten latest and most requested videos of artists from the '80s such as MC Hammer, LL Cool J, Kwamane, Salt n' Pepper, Slick Rick, and Big Daddy Kane, just to name a few. I anticipated Darren's arrival from school just to share this part of the day with him. I loved watching him dance, and debate over who was the hottest rapper of the week.

Darren's favorite artist was Janet Jackson. Favorite really was an understatement, he idolized and worshiped her. Darren wore black to honor Janet, and had all of her pictures plastered over the walls of his room. Anything that had to do with Janet, Darren knew it all. He knew every move from her videos to the "T", and mirrored them with precision and perfection.

It was 1989, the *Rhythm Nation 1814* album had just dropped, and was the most important event in Darren's life at the time, as it was a big moment in music history. As soon as the album hit store shelves, he had his copy. When the video first premiered on MTV, Darren watched it over and over until he knew all of the words and moves. Janet was his everything. Experiencing her through his passion and obsession gave me an appreciation and love for her music as well. Janet was an amazing artist and next to her brother Michael, they were two of the most influential and iconic artists of that era.

Nikki was a girl with natural beauty, flawless caramel skin with a beauty mark above her lip. She had long, full, thick, black hair, just beautiful in every way. I began to experience feelings of intimidation, envy, and jealousy toward Nikki because of her looks. I had never been around a girl as pretty as she. I began to feel inferior, small and insignificant against her striking beauty. I felt obsolete, unworthy, and ugly. To add to these feelings, I was in a very vulnerable place, which allowed for feelings of loathing and insecurity to breed within me. I was experiencing the loss of my family, the confusion of it all and deep feelings of having to go through the confusion alone. I was a disfigured girl, with no family, and nothing to call my own, but a duffel bag full of hand-me-downs.

When I moved in, Nikki had to share her room with me. A panoramic view showed everything a young girl could ever want. She had a closet over flowing with clothes and shoes. I remember entering the room for the first time and having a flashback to my former life when I had everything. I instantly became jealous that I was living in the shadows of someone else's reality that was once mine. She had a window draped with frilly curtains, her bed looked expensive and was perfectly made. There was a large wooden book shelf of Barbie dolls in mint condition, all still in their original boxes with no evidence of having been played with. Nikki had Barbies that she played with, and the ones on the shelves that were off limits. There were several dolls that represented different ethnicities, and some that were special editions.

I remember she had a Holiday Barbie dressed in a big sparkly white dress, with white gloves that stopped at her elbows and she wore a crown. I wanted to play with her badly, but all of the dolls were off limits, and Nikki made sure to emphasize that point. I remember one day while Nikki was out, I snuck and played with the doll. I styled her pretty brown hair, and got lost in how beautiful she was. I was very careful in my deceit to place her back without any signs that she had been removed. Many of Nikki's dolls were vintage and untouched, therefore she never noticed when they were moved. I dressed Barbie in different outfits, and then back in her gown.

Nikki also had a Kenya doll, a popular doll representing the African culture of the '90s. Kenya came with the African garb and braids. The '90s was a time when blacks embraced and celebrated African culture, a statement of pride exhibited through music, art, clothing, hairstyles, and lifestyle. Just like Barbie, Kenya came with different themes and settings, but always remained consistent with the African culture. Unlike Barbie, Kenya was not heavily advertised through mainstream media, but the power of black influence helped to make Kenya popular; a special doll that made every little African American girl proud of her ethnicity. Young girls were also able to identify with Kenya; she came with hair accessories such as beads and barrettes, which allowed girls to replicate the same hairstyles they wore.

After spending much time with Nikki, I got to know her well. I got to know Nikki as a person, her nice ways, her generous ways, her kindness, but, also her prissiness, stubbornness, manipulative and cunning ways. She had lots of friends and cousins near in age. One cousin in particular was like her best friend. They were extremely close and did everything together. Either her cousin slept over or Nikki slept over her house.

When it was just Nikki and me, we talked, laughed and got along, which I grew hopeful that a bond was forming. However, when she and her cousin got together, her demeanor toward me changed, sometimes she did not include me, or treated me as if I was invisible.

Most of the times I hung with Nikki and her cousin, I felt like an outsider. I had absolutely nothing in common with the two, nor did I shared the same experiences. Both were very pretty girls and knew it. They took dance lessons, played instruments and modeled. I was just sharing the girl's space, wishing I could relate. Nikki's cousin was a very nice girl. She always spoke to me and was genuine. I sometimes felt Nikki did not want me to get close to her cousin, because when she saw us laughing or talking about something that she was not a part of, I believed Nikki did things out of spite. Many times Nikki interjected, and denied the things I said were true, or claimed I did not know what I was talking about, leaving me feeling furious with her.

Most of the time we got along well, but there were times when Nikki and I bickered like sisters. There were times when I believed she knew how privileged she was and threw it in my face, making me feel like an outsider and that I would never have the things she had. These tendencies caused me to sometimes resent and dislike Nikki.

I believed Nikki took advantage of the fact that there were two guilty culprits by default. When Nikki was angry with Shanika or me and wanted instant revenge, she found ways to place blame on either of us, I use to think, because we were easy targets.

However, Shanika was her preferred target. They constantly fought and argued, and half of the time I did not know what their issues were about. I could walk into the room and the two of them would be screaming back and forth at each other. I was just glad I had no part in the drama. Maybe getting us in trouble was Nikki's way of plotting revenge for having to unwillingly share her life with two strangers. Shanika often took things that belonged to Nikki or talked back with an attitude, or Nikki discovered upon returning home that Shanika was in her room when she was deliberately told to stay out.

Comparing myself to this privileged, beautiful girl only deepened the jealousy and anger that I could never be Nikki and have her seemingly perfect life. I internalized my feelings of resentment and jealousy that I felt toward Nikki. While putting on a superficial face in front of everyone, inside I was boiling over with rage. Sometimes in my thoughts I was cussing Nikki out, rolling my eyes, imagining I was in her face while telling her off. I had wished that when Nikki got in trouble with her parents, her punishments were severe; that when Ms. Jones scolded Nikki for something, she hurt Nikki's feelings the way she sometimes hurt mine. I wanted to be childish and knock down all of her dolls from off the shelves, destroying her prized possessions, because I knew how much they meant to her. I was infused with such anger because I felt as if Nikki thought that she was better than me.

I lived in Nikki's shadow. Many of the places she went, I tagged along, and many of the things she did I did them too. I think because we were so close in age, Mrs. Jones thought it would be a good way for us to bond, also to make my experience in their home fun and fulfilled. I remember feeling in the way, and a bother. I am sure Nikki did not like me always hanging around as much as I felt bad crowding her space. Whenever Nikki, her cousins, and their friends did things, I was usually the third wheel. It seemed every weekend there was something fun planned and we were always going out. Some of the fun things I would have loved to do, but my mother could not afford, such as going bowling, to the movies, and Chuck-E-Cheese.

As much as I anticipated the fun to be had, my fear of being exposed to other kids who I did not know trumped my excitement. I was fearful of having to defend myself. I was now on my own without my mother to advocate and protect me against the nasty comments and teasing.

As many times as I had seen my mother handle being in vulnerable situations, and even with her teaching me how to fight back, I did not know how to handle confrontation. I always wished for something to happen that would prevent us from attending, such as the event suddenly being canceled or the car on our way to the event broke down. I hoped for any excuse to turn around and go back to the house where I felt most comfortable, dodging the sharp darts of kids' ignorance and cruelty. I felt so afraid that I physically became sick, my hands shook, my head pounded, I felt disoriented and my stomach would ball up in knots, all because I was petrified of the inevitable comments and stares.

I also felt fearful of not fitting in, of what other kids thought of me, being made fun of, feeling ashamed and embarrassed of being exposed. I already felt out of place, but what made me feel even more out of place was that I could not do the things everyone else could do. I was ashamed to speak up and say that because of my injuries, I could not do this or that. I wanted to be accepted. I wanted so badly to make friends and for kids to like me. Instead, I brought more attention to myself that left me feeling even more vulnerable and humiliated.

There were two events in particular that ended up being nightmares for me. The first was a birthday party at a popular roller skating rink called WOW. I knew that it was impossible for me to skate considering the condition of my feet. I could barely keep my balance while walking a full block, let alone having the ability to balance myself walking on wheels. I allowed someone to convince me through their enthusiasm into trying. After a few paces I fell, got up, found something to hold on to, then fell again. Then an adult came and supported me up by holding my arms as she took me out into the middle of the slippery floor.

Eventually she had gone off to skate with others leaving me alone with no support. My legs began moving every which way. I tried holding on to the walls and railings, but could not stay up. Colorful lights flickered against the dark backdrop. I was hoping the darkness would hide my embarrassment, but it did not. I felt so embarrassed, clutching on to the railings, inching myself along to get off the floor. Kids were skating and having fun, while I struggled alone slipping, falling, and crying. It was a birthday party, but the facility was still opened to the public, so the place was packed with skaters.

Kids started to gather around me pointing and laughing. I could hear in the background, "Look at her face. Why she look like that? What's wrong with her?" No one cared that I was on the floor falling, nor did anyone cared to see that I was in need of help. Once the kids who laughed and teased had a pick at me, they skated off, glancing back, covering their chuckles. They skated off only to return with other kids to get a good look and join in on the taunting.

Another awkward and embarrassing event was at a sleepover I attended with Nikki and her cousin. It was a friend of theirs birthday. I was not excited about the night because I saw that I was surrounded around spoiled, snobbish girls who were conceited, and rightfully so. Immediately I felt intimidated and unworthy of being in the presence of so many pretty girls. As much as I did not want to be there, I quickly sensed the girls did not want me their either. I was not a part of the pretty girl clique.

My punishment for being the odd girl out, was that no one barely acknowledged me, more less talked to me for most of the night. They all talked amongst each other about what boys they liked, shopping and other stuff privileged girls talked about. I remember having a dry mouth from not talking, just sitting, listening, and observing, feeling sorry for myself that my physical loss put me at such a disadvantage. When night fell the girls began changing into their pajamas, I waited until everyone changed so that I could be the last, because it took me longer. I grew afraid when it was time for me to change into my night wear because I did not feel comfortable revealing any parts of my flawed body amongst girls who were seemingly perfect. I was about eight years old and was now wearing wigs. I had gone from being comfortable with not hiding my head, and being accepted in my truth, to covering it up and feeling ashamed.

The wig I had on was a dead giveaway, it was too much hair for my small framed face, and the style was not age appropriate. It was a style from out of the '50s, a bob with bangs and the ends curled upward. I felt uncomfortable wearing it, I felt insecure and desperately hoped no one called me on it.

I went into the bathroom with all of my things and cautiously locked the door out of fear that someone would walk in upon me removing my wig to change my shirt. When I went in, I could hear the girls laughing and whispering about me. When I came out of the bathroom, the girls were doing each other's hair. I prayed in my head, "Lord, please do not let anyone ask to play in mine." I remained quiet as though to blend in the background. I suddenly was brought to the forefront as a girl came over to me with a brush asking to do my hair. When I gestured that I did not want her to, she came out and asked if I was wearing a wig. Caught off guard and feeling the embarrassment trickling down through my body from my head, I immediately denied as I felt put on the spot, and nervously fished for a cover up. I quickly denied that I wore a wig, claiming it was all my hair. The girl who asked said, "No, it's not! Let me see!" Trembling, I held the prosthetic tightly to my head, fearful of her pulling it off.

She tried to inspect closer, at which point I stopped her by quickly exclaiming that my scalp was very sensitive and no one could touch my head. She backed off, by telling everyone that it was not my hair. I did not say anything, as embarrassment filled up inside of me, causing my eyes to overflow with tears as I began to cry. I wanted to run to hide my shame.

To my surprise, Nikki and her cousin came to my defense. They hovered around me, with sympathy; Nikki's cousin said to the girl, "That's a shame, leave her alone." The attention in the form of pity I received made me feel good. I felt included, heard, and noticed. The sympathy was a momentary gain of inclusion and recognition. Seeking pity through sympathy became a tool I would come to use to my advantage many times in my life. It became a way to cope with the constant rejection that was too painful to accept. I saw myself as a victim and looked to people to provide me with condolence. I thought, if I could not have genuine friendships, I would desperately take interactions with people by any means, even if they were superficial.

After pacifying me, the two girls found trivial things to talk and joke with me about in attempts to make me feel better. Once I had calmed down, next on the girl's agenda was doing each other's nails. Again I felt shame and embarrassment because I did not have any fingers or toe nails to paint. No one asked me to join, to avoid another awkward moment, I sat and thought, *I will just sit and watch*. In that moment, sitting and watching them do each other's makeup, paint their toes, I felt even worse about myself because I could not participate, I was so much different from them.

I felt hideous, I knew exposing any parts of my body would horrify the girls, so I slept in pajama pants, wore a long sleeved shirt and kept my socks on to hide my disfigurements. I had absolutely nothing in common with them and could not wait for it all to be over. The highlight was the next day when it was time to leave. I would never see those girls again and could not wait to escape the intimidation of their looks. I just wanted to crawl back into the security of myself, where I hid and felt safe.

I was not a permanent inclusion in the Jones's family, although they were nice to me and treated me like I was a part of the family; I felt I still had to be acquiescent and not bring any negative attention that would deem me ungrateful or subversive, for fear that they would get rid of me. I was quiet and understood my place as a child and also as an outsider, I understood that I was just passing through and eagerly anticipated returning back to my own family. I did what I was told and careful not to violate the privilege of having a good placement, although there was one incident when I almost lost that privilege.

Reuniting with my mother through scheduled visits was an ecstatic time for me, but also very disconcerting when it was time to leave her. My mother had the same unremitting attitude, spirit and radiant appearance that always assured me all was and would be well. However, it was extremely difficult to see my mother so helpless and unsettled in those circumstances. My mother was living in a shelter program called Project Rainbow. It was a transitional housing program established by the sisters of St. Francis, for single mothers, transitioning from homelessness to self-sufficiency.

Once after a visit, I was in such despair over my mother's situation that all I wanted was to help her. One day I was in the house with Anita, we had just returned from running errands. I was in Nikki's room, when I was called into Anita's room. I noticed her purse sitting on the dresser and saw that there was money sticking out from it. I waited for Anita to leave the room, with anticipation, fear, guilt and necessity, all coagulating inside my throat. When she left the room, I swallowed the huge mass as I swiftly snatched the wad and went back into the room I shared with her daughter.

I put the money in my jacket pocket so that I could give it to my mom the next time I saw her. I knew what I had done was wrong, but I was thinking that Mrs. Jones had lots of money and that my mom needed it more than she did. My mom needed it to get a house for us to be together. That is all we talked about during our visits—my mom working on getting a home for all of us to be together again. I did not get far with my scheme, immediately Anita returned to her room to discover the theft. There was no one in the house but she and I, so I was the only suspect. She called me into the room and demanded the money. The sound of anger resonated in Anita's voice. I suddenly wished I had not taken the money, realizing how I had disgraced Anita, and also how severely I had betrayed her trust. It was then, through her look of disappointment toward me, that I realized how much Anita cared and was deeply hurt by my actions.

Many years later, after I left and reunited with my mother and siblings, I revisited the Jones. Although everyone was happy to see me, including Anita, I still harbored guilt from stealing from her. So much time had passed, and Anita told me when the incident occurred that she was not mad, the guilt that I still felt made it difficult to look Anita in her face. I knew that I had lost her trust that day. A childish mistake, which I was certain tarnished and changed her perception of me. It is a mistake that I would have given anything to take back. Throughout the years since leaving the Jone's home, Nikki and I often ran into each other and reconnected. In high school, she dated a family member of a close friend, I then ran into her again while in college, and several times as adults. I have also spoken to her mom and brothers. Nikki and I remain in contact as adults, and are friends. We were very young and it was a difficult time for us both. I was just beginning to cope with the constant changes in my life, but through the Grace of God, yet again I made it through.

CHAPTER 6

Home Again

THE DAY FINALLY CAME when I left the Jones family to reunite with my own. I packed up everything I had accumulated while living with the family. I could not wait to see my brothers again, and to see my mother who was very pregnant with my little sister Erica. I was beyond excited to learn that there would finally be another girl joining the family. It was lonely being the only girl among so many boys. The days, hours, minutes and even seconds were painstakingly long, leading up to me stepping out of Ms. Pat's car and, into our very own home.

A new home and a new addition to the family, things were changing for the good, after many trials and tribulations. I could not wait to resume my life with my family. I could not wait to have my mommy back. Everyone looked the same, with the exception that my baby brothers were no longer babies. They were young boys, and Rasheen was a teenager. We all embraced each other with great appreciation to be in the other's presence, and held on tightly to make up for the hugs separation deprived us of. My mom expressed how much she loved and missed us, and how she promised me this day would come, as she swift me away in her arms. "Neesha, God is good, I told you baby girl He would work everything out.."

The year was 1990 and I was eight years old when my family opened the door to our new three story house on the fifty-nine hundred block of Warrington Avenue in the South West/Cobbs

Creek section of Philadelphia. My mother received housing through the Philadelphia Housing Authority's Section 8 program. PHA is a federal subsidized program established by the U.S. Department of Housing and Urban Development also known as (HUD) to make homeownership affordable for low income families. Some families are placed among other section 8 families living together in community developments. Others are placed in what are called scatter sites—individual housing throughout Philly that are among private owners and renters, but owned by PHA. We lived in a scatter site.

The row house set in the middle of the east side of the large two-way street. The bricked exterior had a small enclosed porch that encased a stoned bench with a small ironed latched gate. The gate opened to a small enclosed lawn with a large tree planted in the middle. The leaves of the tree shielded the front windows and made the porch more personal. The stretch of houses on the east side of the street were slightly oblique and the difference could be seen while standing on the opposite side of the street. Several feet from the curb, were a few steps that lead to the arched entry way that concealed the front door to the house.

The exterior of our house gave no indication to the enormity of its interior. It was a huge and spacious house. We were told that we had the biggest house on the block. The living room was the size of a ballroom. The dining room was slightly smaller, and there was an industrial size kitchen, it was the biggest attraction of the house.

Each room was sectioned off by large entry ways. The flooring throughout the living room and dining room was a dark, sandy wood; and white ceramic square slabs covered the entire kitchen floor. The walls in the kitchen were white and the walls throughout the entire house were a sky blue. Inside the kitchen were both top and bottom wooden drawers and cabinets, encasing a stainless steel sink with the stove. There were two large windows to the left of the kitchen and the back door which lead to an unsecured landing that we shared with the next door neighbors. In the middle of the landing was a dilapidated stair case that lead to the ground. A few months after we moved in, PHA renovated the porch with a modern wooden structure. The house was in good condition, with minor alterations needed. On the upper level, were four bed rooms. There was no need to argue over whose room was whose, because they all were favorable in size. The rooms throughout the house were so large that the bare walls amplified our voices. My mother claimed the front room, which was the biggest of course. The room had two oversized windows that allowed for the bright sun light to illuminate the walls of the large space. The windows revealed a great view of the entire block, from corner to corner. As large as the room was, there was a tiny closet right behind the entry door. Beside her room was the bathroom, which was moderate in size and the smallest room in the house. A couple of feet following a bare wall was Hakiem and Joshua's room, followed by the hall closet. Slightly around a small corner was the middle room, which was my room, smaller than the boy's room. About five feet was the back room, where Rasheen dwelled, the smallest of the bedrooms.

It would take some time before my mother was able to afford to furnish the house, but we did not care. At that moment, furniture seemed frivolous, because we were just happy to finally be together as a family again, and to have a beautiful home to call our own. It was the turn of a new decade, and my mother brought in the '90s with her seventh pregnancy and last child. My mother gave birth to a beautiful baby girl, months after moving in, on January 4, 1990.

I remember my aunt Evelyn, showing me how to hug my mom while she was pregnant, being careful not to hurt her giant belly. Having never seen a woman pregnant before, I was fearful of how big her stomach looked, and being scared for my mom, imagining that she was in so much pain. Her stomach reached far past her body. The day my mom gave birth, she was in active labor. I had mixed emotions, excited to meet my baby sister, but also fearful something terrible would happen to my mom. My thoughts were that she would not survive having something so huge in her body, not to mention the way my mom screamed and cried while in labor. To a child the loud screams were frightening to hear. My aunt, my mother's only living sister looked after us while my mother stayed in the hospital. The entire time I was fearful if she would come back home, until a couple of days later, when my mom returned, in hand with a tiny baby.

When my sister came, I had some reservations, I was not the youngest, but was the only girl and still given more attention than my brothers. I was in the middle of four boys and had grown accustomed to being mommy's little girl. Now there were two of us, and the attention that was directed toward me, would have to be shared with Erica.

I felt a little jealous, but not for the same reasons my mother feared having another girl. I felt a sense of jealousy because my mom's attention was now focused on a baby. My mom feared that I would become jealous over my sister's looks. She feared that I would look at my sister and have bitterness and hatred because she embodied the physical beauty that I did not have. I did not like her, but not because she was a pretty little girl, but because I did not like the fact that she just appeared and stole my thunder. For so long I was my mom's everything. When Erica came, she smiled, held and adored her the same as she did with me when I was younger. I was not getting the same attention any more, which I despised and for a while could not stand Erica for.

As my sister grew up, I believed my mother really felt guilty for having had another girl. Deep down, I believed she thought I secretly envied and felt inferior to my sister. My sister was a pretty little girl, the same dark brown completion as my mom, and had the same dark black, thick hair. Initially, to help me feel secure, my mom made sure to treat us both the same. I remember one Easter, she bought us both matching dresses. The dresses were a shiny silk, royal purple, with white lace embroidery outlining the dress. We both wore white stockings, with ruffled socks and white patent leather shoes, accented with white patent leather pocketbooks that held our Easter money of two dollars. A dollar had to be put into the offering plate at church and a dollar to spend at the store afterward.

After the word, we all attended Erica and Hakiem's grandmother' house for dinner. I remember my sister and I both looked cute and felt so pretty dressed in our puffy dresses, with ruffles and big shoulder pads (big shoulder pads were in style back then). No one could tell us we were not fly (slang of the '80s and '90s).

I had come to suspect the feelings of insecurity and jealousy over Erica's appearance were feelings my mother personally held toward my sister. I got the impression that my mom believed I inherited the same complex, because of my physical condition and would be in envy of my sister's beauty.

What parent would admit to feeling envious of their own child? As egregious as this may seem, knowing how deeply rooted my mother's insecurities stemmed, gave insight to why she held such bitterness toward Erica. I believe my physical trauma in conjunction with my mother's painful childhood experiences, truly traumatized her and shaped her ideology of beauty.

My mother shared with me stories about the cruelties done to her in her childhood. She experienced internalized racism by members of her family, mainly by her aunt and mother. My mom also came from a large family, consisting of three boys, and three girls. Among the girls, my mother was the youngest. Eileen, Evelyn and Eartha, named after the one and only legendary African American actress, Eartha Kit. Eartha Kit was known for her portrayal as the original Catwoman in the Batman series. My grandmother must have looked at my mom when she was born and saw something extraordinary in her to give her such a name.

Unfortunately, Eileen met an early demise from a tragic and untimely death. Eileen's death truly devastated my mother. By the description she gave of Eileen and how highly she spoke of her, Eileen may have been the only safe haven my mom had within her family. My mother emotionally shared how she was abused, mistreated and ostracized because of her dark skin and awkward looks as a child. My mom emotionally shared with me, that she was constantly teased because her eyes were crooked, for her shapeless frame and thick, brittle hair. According to my mom, most of the maltreatment was from her aunt. My mother shared how sinister her aunt was to her and how my mom was the least favorite; constantly compared to my aunt Evelyn, and harshly criticized for being darker, awkward, and unattractive.

My mom said she was emotionally and psychological impaired by being neglected, abused, traumatized, and told me that her needs as a child were unmet and ignored. She was treated poorly, and felt no care or concern went into her education. According to my mom, her aunt would beat her with whatever objects were most convenient or she was beaten with objects known to inflict extreme pain. My mom was told she was ugly, unwanted, disliked and would never amount to anything. My mom felt demoralized growing up, the trauma she experienced so young, aborted the development of a healthy and positive self-esteem. These painful experiences, in the form of internalized racism, would become the catalyst for the lifelong struggles and unfortunate circumstances my mom encountered, because of her internal conflict. I think in many ways, she was fearful of my sister and I reliving her painful experiences, not having a good relationship with each other, and that I might feel the pains of having to live in the shadows of my sister's beauty.

My mother always preached that looks did not mean anything in God's eye. "It's what's inside that matters most" she would say. Maybe this was subconsciously my mother's attempt to speak to herself as a child, validating the aspects of herself that no one else did. Maybe it was an epiphany that my mom had every time she made the statement, realizing that God had been with her all along. Maybe if she knew then that God's opinion of her was all that mattered, she could have had a fair chance to live in her truth.

My mom would sometimes add, "God don't like ugly and sure could care less about pretty." When she occasionally made the statement, it appeared to have been an entendre. The statement when directed toward me was gentle and sincere as if to comfort me, by affirming that although my looks had been altered, my beauty was evident by my personality and characteristics that made me a good person. The statement when directed toward my sister was outright an attack on her physical beauty and a malevolent conviction.

My mom told Erica often, although she had a pretty face, her attitude stunk. She constantly berated Erica, then compared her to me, in efforts to elevate my esteem and slay hers. A parent's positive influence is extremely critical during the impressionable early years of a child's life in shaping a healthy self-image, especially for a young girl. It is a travesty that my mother was unable to see the parallels, that she was doing to my sister, the very same that was done to her. My mom's criticisms detrimentally skewed the way Erica viewed herself, that only weakened an already immature and fragile self-esteem, the same my great aunt supposedly had done to my mom.

The way my mom spoke to my sister, was as if to suggest that Erica carried the thought that she was "all of that." Example, someone could tell Erica how pretty an outfit looked on her, or that her hair was long and pretty, my mom would say out of nowhere, "She is alright, don't hype her little head up, 'cause she gonna start thinking she cute." The things my mom said about Erica created such an unease and awkwardness that made me very uncomfortable and felt sorry for my sister.

According to my mother, the way she treated my sister was in efforts to humble her, which my mother believed she was doing with good intentions. I understood that my mom was trying to keep my feelings in mind, so I would never think that my sister was superior to me because of her looks. However, I never felt esteemed or good at the expense of my sister being humiliated and condemned. I felt Erica was being faulted for being born with her looks and without physical afflictions.

Contrary to my mother's belief that comments directed towards my sister would affect me, the comments or attention never did, and I thought my mother's approach was extreme. With my sister, I never felt any jealousy toward her. I cannot say that about every other female I came in contact with, but never with my sister. When Erica was younger, I agreed that she was pretty, and people were just stating the facts. I cannot think of a reason for being envious of my sister. Seeds of jealousy and envy over her beauty were never planted inside of me.

I have witnessed many battles my sister has fought while in combat with our mother. The more beautiful and successful Erica became, the more my mom attempted to ruin her self-esteem. Seeing how Erica struggled, persevered, and conquered, I could only see and celebrate her beauty. My mother was right, that beauty is in the heart and spirit of a person. My only wish was that my mother did not allow her internalized insecurities to inhibit her from seeing just how beautiful Erica really was.

I loved the idea of having a little sister, someone who looked up to me, therefore making me strive to be the best example for her to model after. I never looked at Erica and wished for a moment that she had not been born. She was in many ways a part of me, she was my sister. I felt that Erica was the gift after the loss of Nakisha. I was now the big sister, which I thought many times Nakisha's spirit watched over and blessed the covenant of our sisterly bond.

No relationship is perfect however, I had the same dislike for her as any older sister would with their younger sister. She was always in my stuff and in my space. With the exception of the expected bickering, irritation, probing of personal belongings and taking without asking, I absolutely loved my sister and have always felt special to have her in my life. Eventually my mom would come to realize there was no threat or sibling rivalry between Erica and me, but that our relationship was genuine.

The magic of our relationship was that there was a reciprocity. Having me as her sister was just as much a blessing for Erica. Through my adversity, my sister grew up to learn and understand the true meaning of beauty. She saw firsthand many of the obstacles I had to overcome and the accomplishments that resulted from never giving up. As life would later deal us similar hands, the purpose of our unique sisterhood would truly be defined as we both modeled strength and wisdom for each other.

In my role as the older sister, I enjoyed the responsibilities of having to help take care of Erica. So much so, that I eagerly convinced my mom that I was capable of doing things to assist her with Erica. What I did not know how to do, I had the willingness and desire to learn. One of the tasks I enjoyed helping my mom the most with was styling my sister's hair. I would sit and study my mom, as she combed, parted, greased, griped and created cute looks with Erica's bushel of thick hair. I sought opportunities when my sister's hair was undone and my mom had not set down to do it, to manipulate the barrettes.

It was difficult to figure out how to grip the hair, but I became very determined to learn how to style her hair as my mom had done. After carefully studying my mother's craft, each time I would lock myself in my room and sit for hours practicing on my dolls, what I had observed my mom do. I was able to take the hair by grasping it between the knuckles of my paw-like deformed hand, but struggled to figure a way to weave the hair with my good hand.

I became frustrated when a section of hair fell out of my weak grip when trying to rotate the locks into a braid. I could not figure out how to grasp the locks enough to make the braids tight so they would hold. The braids were loose and instantly unraveled; sometimes I sat with my doll between my legs all day, working on getting it right. I sat uninterrupted from sun up, until my mom turned out the lights in the house at night, determined on making at least one braid.

Hours turned into days, day turned into weeks before I eventually figured a way to tightly grasp the hair. When it came to crossing the hair over, the only way to keep the braid tight was to hold the sections of hair between crossing, in place using my chin. It served as an alternative for the lack of strength for gripping in between my two knuckles. Finally, I had made one braid that was secure and did not come undone. After much more practice, I finally taught myself how to grasp the hair with my amputated fingers, without using my chin. I had come to learn that I could only use very small locks of hair when braiding. The more I braided, the stronger the grip between my knuckles became, and eventually my grip strengthened to make bigger braids.

It was the first time I had ever felt such pride over what I had accomplished. The accomplishment of making just one braid, instilled an insatiable hunger to accomplish more. I had gained a new sense of confidence, and my identity would later be defined in part by my determination and unwillingness to give up, until I had accomplished what I set out to do.

In that moment, I was in a state of shock and bewilderment, it was surreal. I knew what I had worked hard to do, but could not believe the braid I was staring at, I had done. That one braid represented to me God's power. He had shown me that faith alone merely is not enough, but faith along with hard work can activate faith to its fullest capacity. Through a great loss, God was revealing an even greater gain, the belief in myself, that I was capable of doing whatever I put my mind to. This belief gave me hope that I would someday live the normal life predicted earlier in my convalescent state that I would never experience. From that moment, I understood anything worth having or accomplishing, required tenacity, which is the essence of hard work.

I had no idea at the time, that this significant personal enlightenment would become the fundamental to my life's meaning and purpose. I made a vow to never limit myself; to always at least try, and when something was proven to be too difficult, I found acceptance in knowing that I tried. In my mind there were no limitations. I learned that I had to find ways to modify tasks to accommodate my deformities. If I envisioned that I could, then I usually succeeded, and if I could not, then I accepted that the particular task at hand was not within my capability, after I had given it my all. At that point I was content with being able to let it go and move on. Haughty over my accomplishment to do something so complex as hair given the condition of my hands, I had pushed myself to go above and beyond to have many more. Suddenly I developed this steadfast attitude and unrelenting stubbornness to become successful.

My mom always had someone over in our kitchen doing their hair. She was a great stylist. Every time, I sat in the kitchen and watched avidly at what she was doing, then ran up to my room to practice on my dolls. I had not shown my mom what I could do, because I wanted to find the right time to show her, I wanted it to be a surprise.

One day after braiding my PJ Sparkles' entire head, I went into my mom's room to show her. I could not wait to show my mother this unprecedented accomplishment. This very accomplishment, solidified my mother's faith in believing that I was more than a hopeless tragedy. She raised her hands up, as uncontrollable tears flowed down each cheek. They were tears of joy and confirmation of what God had promised her, that I would not be bound or confined by my physical state. She looked with amazement and examined my doll's head a few times. "Oh my God, Neesha, you did this? Hallelujah, thank you, Jesus!" she cried out. "Wow, how... so this is what you have been spending all of your time alone in that room doing? God is so God! Nobody can't tell me my God ain't good. Neesha, you are a blessing."

Her excitement and praise only gave me more confidence. No one could tell me anything, I was unstoppable. I had styled my dolls' hair many more times and had become a pro at braiding. When I was about thirteen and my sister was about five, I tried my hands at styling Erica's hair. One day I got the stamp of approval from my mom after I had taken the initiative. My mom was so impressed, that I sometimes commandeered her headache of styling my little sister's hair.

I enjoyed with delight the task of sorting out colored barrettes to match the colors in the outfit put out for her to wear. I had so many interesting designs in my head that I had my sister sitting for long hours sometimes trying to perfect the style, making sure her edges were smooth and had a clean finish. I started one design, then halfway through, I would see something else forming and started all over. The colors of the barrettes, the parts all mattered to me. I took my time to make sure each part was perfectly straight. It was important to me that the lining of her scalp showed, because it meant the part was neat.

I wanted to give Erica a look of perfection, one that people would like and admire when they saw. I began to understand why my mom did not like doing Erica's hair. Having to comb and part my sister's thick bushel of hair was a tedious job. I was fixated on seeing commercials, advertising lots of child relaxer products that made little black girls' hair soft and flexible like Caucasians and Spanish girls. I spent so much time trying to make my sister's hair look straight and sleek like theirs. I wet the brush, and put lots of grease in Erica's hair, brushing until each frizz laid flat, her edges were straight and the lines in her scalp could be seen.

Erica was tender headed so she screamed, yelled and swarmed around as I yanked and pulled her hair. Erica would become extremely irritated with me. I took great pride in my creations, and wanted to replicate the styles in my head, just so she looked pretty.

As we got older, my sister always joked about the torture I put her through when doing her hair. She believed I intentionally wrapped the ballies tight as revenge for the times she took things without asking, or simply got on my nerves. She said that I had her walking around looking like an Asian doll, because her hair was so tight that it pulled the edges of her eyes back. Even when I finished, I chased her around the house with the brush to make sure a hair did not fall out of place.

My limited world had opened a lot wider as I courageously sought opportunities to take on incredible odds. Nothing was out of bounds. The more I began to discover about myself, the more eager I became to do more. I took on perfecting my illegible hand writing that resembled that of a kindergarten's. I learned to type, and even made beaded jewelry out of beads as tiny as specks of sand.

Since creating that one braid, I have had endless achievements, and with every accomplishment, my mom held the same reaction of wonder and pride. Anything I achieved, I anticipated the look of amazement in my mother's face. No one else's opinion mattered as much as hers, and as always, making my mom proud gave me validation. I still looked to make my mother happy, especially as I begun to notice that she appeared to look less and less happy. Something in her was different, unfamiliar, and unsettling. I did not want anything to change, after we had gone through so much to finally be in a good place. Unfortunately, I would learn throughout my life that good never lasted long.

CHAPTER 7

Calm Before the Storm

CALM BEFORE THE STORM is a great idiom to describe how things went from being good to becoming very bad. For much of the first year living in our new home, the only issues at that time were the financial hardships my mother faced, with the challenges of raising five children and maintaining a new home all on government assistance. However, our financial difficulties did not have a significant impact on us. It was nothing my mother appeared unable to handle, or anything that us as children realized as serious concerns. It was a time of making friends and just being kids. There may have been worries, but my mother did a great job of concealing them from us. It was a time of many great memories, and personal experiences that had an impact on me, as I continued to struggle with who I was, and trying to fit in amongst my peers.

We had many joyous moments in our new home. Many months later we were still trying to acclimate to our new life. For a period of time in the beginning, we resumed somewhat of the life we had before the changes. Despite my mother's limited income, she took care of us. Many times, we had what we needed and my mom went the extra mile to get us the things we wanted. Our refrigerator was full of food, the bills were paid, and we rarely wanted for anything. We made friends on the block, and played carefree until the street lights came on.

When we moved into the house, we were happy that for the first time in a very long time we all were together. We lived in an empty house, whose strident echoes could be heard throughout the bare, unadorned walls. We lived for about another year or so without furniture. With no beds, we slept on cots and mattresses, and used plastic orange milk crates for tables.

When my mother eventually did fill the house with furniture, it made the house look elegant and beautiful; it finally felt like a home. I remember the living room set being of suede material, a-postured in a dark gold color fabric, accented with embroidered leaves and oak wood detruding through the arm rests. The living room set came with the couch, love seat, a single chair, two small wooden in tables, and a wooden coffee table with glass as its center. My mom painted the walls a peach color with matching drapings for the windows. The dining room and kitchen had been put off so that my mom could focus on our bed rooms. My room was the first to be decorated.

I loved looking through the *Finger Hunt* magazines my mother subscribed, to pick out the perfect bedroom set. *Finger Hunt* was a catalogue as popular as Wal-Mart and Amazon are today. The magazine's concept made it convenient to afford good quality products. Everything from personal needs to electronics and furniture could be ordered and paid through monthly installments. I got lost in all the book had to offer, immediately skimming through to get to the girly stuff. I loved being a girl and seeing the girly colors—blues, pinks, yellows, and especially purples. I circled all of the things I wanted, and by the time I finished looking through the section, pretty much everything had my name printed beside it.

In one particular book, I saw a bedroom set that I fell in love with and had to have. The main attraction was a white canapé bed made out of the finest wood. It looked so perfect for me, I was sold! The set came with a twin bed with four wooden pillars; which held the dusty blue covering that draped across the bridge of the bed. There were two side small drawers, a tall chest, and a long dresser drawer with a large vanity mirror affixed. My mom accented the room with a beautiful golden touch lamp with glass in the folds of the gold shades. I had never seen anything so beautiful and magical.

Touching any areas of the gold metal miraculously turned the lamp on as well as dimmed the light gradually from high to very low.

One day after coming home from school, my mom took me to my room and when she opened the door I thought it was a dream. The entire bedroom set that I had seen in the picture was now in my room. It was the most beautiful sight. I felt like a princess. I absolutely loved the room, but I remember feeling afraid to sleep in it for a while alone. Prior to having my bedroom set, I slept in my mom's room on the mattress with her, or in the one bed with my brothers in their room. I had gotten used to always having someone around me at night, so it took some getting used to. I became more and more comfortable and eventually spent most of my time alone in my new palace.

My brothers' room was furnished and decorated afterward, with wooden bunk beds and décor of the animated cartoon *The Teenage Mutant Ninja Turtles*. My brothers lived for the pizza eating, nocturnal fighting, tortoise heroes that lived in the sewers, an animated craze popularized by the '90s.

I remember walking into their room and the feeling of being put under a trance, because of the radiant color schemes of green, purple, blue, red, orange, plastered on the backdrop of white on everything in their room. The entire bed collection included the shames, the curtains, lamp and adhesive icons of the shelled characters on the walls. For Christmas one year, they even got matching pajamas with the colored bandanas of their favorite character.

My fondest memory of those happy, earlier times was of our first Christmas at the house. That Christmas was beyond magical for many reasons. My mom told us her money was not as she had intended, because of having to put it into the house. My mom was not certain if she would be able to get us everything we wanted, but had promised to do her best. I do not think I fully grasped the concept because my mom did such a great job at providing for us.

I do not think it sunk in completely until Christmas Eve came and there was nothing under the tree. My younger brothers and sister went to bed feeling deeply disappointed. For children so young, no gifts under the tree was disheartening. My mom told us to pray before we went to bed and tell God the desires of our hearts. We darted up the stairs and got on our knees with tears in our eyes, praying with all our might. We went to bed confident that God would come through.

In the earliest of the morning, My mom crept into our rooms waking us all from our deep sleep with just a gentle whisper. "Tanisha, Joshua, Hakiem, Erica, wake up babies, it's Christmas!" Having been told not to expect much, we had no idea what to expect.

As we approached the top of the stairs and could see that the tree was in fact full of presents, our eyes widened, and the groggy feeling had instantly worn off. We all flew down the stairs. There were bikes for each of us and so many wrapped gifts that overflowed from underneath the tiny plastic tree. It truly was magical. For many years we believed in the magic of Christmas, only to discover as we got older, Santa was really our mother, who cleverly hid everything in the basement until we went to bed.

The second reason this particular Christmas was so special, was that it was the first distinct memory I have of my father re-entering my life. I remember telling him I wanted a three story beach Barbie house, a hot pink convertible, a changing colored fountain pool, and a beach Barbie and Ken doll. In addition to my long wish list, I had requested a PJ Sparkle doll.

I was so excited about PJ. She came in both the Caucasian and black version. Of course I wanted the black doll, she was the prettiest of the two, but more importantly, I identified with her. I saw my dad occasionally, and when I did, I was sure to remind him over and over each and every time what I wanted, to be sure that he did not forget.

When my dad re-entered my life, I did not hold animosity toward him being absent for so long, I was just happy I got whatever I asked him for no matter the cost. I remember him coming that Christmas with about four or five oversized Lionel Kiddie City bags. All I had to see was the brand's mascot, a happy kangaroo, and instantly went mad. As a kid, getting anything pertaining to Barbie, made me so excited. I was infatuated with Barbie and her plastic world. That Christmas every wish I had that was not granted by my mom was granted by my dad.

Another fondest memory in those early days was the friendships I made as soon as we moved on the block. During my aunt's stay to help care for us while my mom was in the hospital having my sister, she took the initiative to summon the kids from the block for a formal introduction. I shared with my aunt my trepidation about going outside, and fearful of making friends when we moved in. I was even more fearful of how the kids on the block would take to me.

My aunt Evelyn wasted no time, as she took me by the hand and marched me up and down the block. She collected any and every child she came across, regardless of age and brought them to my porch to meet me. Suddenly, there I was, surrounded by a crowd of at least ten kids, and all their eyes stared at me. I could not stand the pressure of one set of eyes staring, let alone ten sets.

My aunt stood in front of the kids who huddled on my porch, it was too small to accommodate so many. She wasted no time cutting to the chase, as is my aunt's personality, she explained to everyone what happened to me and why I looked as I did. She then highlighted all of my great qualities and why they should want to be my friend.

My aunt informed the group of kids that what happened to me could easily happen to anyone. She told them if she should hear that anyone was mistreating, or making fun of me, she would personally confront them and their mothers and it would not be pleasant. "This is my Neesha, anyone got anything to say about her, because of who she is and how she looks, got a serious problem with me. No one is gonna disrespect my baby because she did not deserve or could not control what happened to her."

My aunt concluded by asking everyone if they had any questions for me. Ten hands shot high in the sky. As I took over and began answering, I felt more and more comfortable and hopeful that this opportunity would help me make new friends. I quickly formed friendships with many of the kids after. The next day my door bell buzzed and my mom was asked by a tall slinky girl with many pony tails in her hair, if I could come outside to play.

Thereafter, a friendship quickly blossomed and became a very special one, that will forever remain close to my heart. Her name was

Malaysia, she lived down the street from me. Malaysia came from a large family consisting of both immediate and extended members, all living harmoniously together under one roof.

Malaysia's immediate family consisted of her mother, a younger sister and an older brother by a few years. Each of them was gorgeous. Their mother was young, and looked more like an older sister, but had always carried herself in a way that conveyed authority and commanded respect. She had a quiet, but firm presence; her children knew better than to disrespect her.

I had the biggest crush on Malaysia's brother, it was because of him, I developed an infatuation for light skinned guys. I could not wait to sit on my steps, just to watch Rodney walk up and down the streets, playing ball or just going. Every time he passed, he always smiled and waved at me. I became even more excited when Rodney came over our house to play Nintendo with Rasheen. While Malaysia and I played in my room, I easily became distracted or found reasons to be around Rodney. It was a smile worth a modeling contract; it brightened up any glum day.

Malaysia and I had much in common, we found ways to enjoy our mundane lives and neither of us expected more from the other. We both had similar personalities and came to accept one another as is, we instantly clicked. I was glad to have made such a special friend, who was pretty, very nice, considerate and compassionate, especially towards me; she protected and took up for me.

Kids who did not live on our block knew Malaysia and her brother. Both were well respected and other kids knew better than to step to either the wrong way. As nice as Malaysia was to me, the girl was far from a punk, and that fact was evident in the way she let people know she was not the one to mess with. There were a few times Malaysia had to hold her own, only because girls, mainly from other neighborhoods wanted to fight Malaysia, thinking she could not. Oh how they were misinformed.

Malaysia's mother taught both her daughters to be lady like and respectful, which they always were. Their mother also taught them an important street code, which was learned early—walk away from trouble, but if it finds you and puts you in a position of having to defend yourself, then that is what you do. Never let anyone put their hands on you! this was the most poignant clause.

Malaysia was a pretty girl, with coco smooth skin and thick, long, hair. She and her sister were the true definition of young ladies, because their mother only dressed them in skirts. I am sure the winter was the exception, but I do not remember ever seeing the sisters dressed in anything other than skirts. The skirts were loose cut, pleated and came in all colors. The sisters ran up and down the street, jumping rope and riding bikes, all in their skirts, and always maintained poise while doing so.

Our past time consisted of sitting outside on either's steps doing absolutely nothing, however those were the most fulfilled times. We talked and talked, about what happened in school and in our lives with our families. The conversations were more like two adult women, then two young girls. We found joy in the simplest things, such as watching the child play activity of the younger kids who lived on the block.

We then took breaks to walk to a small, well-known store within the community known as James's Market, but people in the neighborhood referred to as "Mr. James's". Mr. James ran his business for many years out of a shack on the corner of Sixtieth and Kingsessing street. Mr. James made the best hoagies in the neighborhood, most of his money was made from them I am sure. People packed the tiny place like sardines to place their orders. Hoagies where popular because they were a convenient and inexpensive way to feed a family lunch or dinner.

Mr. James was a generous and understanding man. Knowing the plight of many of his customers, he allowed them to use "store credit." Customers with whom he had established a rapport with, and who were unable to pay, were allowed to buy groceries they needed, with the agreement to pay when they could.

My mom was one of Mr. James trusted and loyal customers. She would send my brothers (I went a time or two) around the corner with a note to hand directly to him. The note always explained her current circumstance, including a small list of things she needed, ending with the promise of payment at the beginning of the month, when she received her stamps and money.

Mr. James took the note, no questions asked and gave my mother everything on her list. It was a great concrete support to have. Ten dollars of credit allowed for us to have breakfast or dinner. Were it not for his kindness, we would have experienced many times of being without. As promised, my mom sent one of us around the corner with the amount in stamps that was owed, but my mom always gave Mr. James a few dollars extra for his patience and understanding.

Malaysia and I walked to Mr. James to buy junk food, as much of our favorite snacks our two or three dollars put together could buy. We usually hung out on my porch, because it had the best view of everything that was happening on the block. We combined all of the popcorn, Cool Ranch Doritos, chips, pretzels, Dippsy Doodles we bought into a plastic bag, and then crushed the entire bag to make the snack last longer. Going to the store was more like an activity to help break up the monotony of an ordinary day with nothing much to do or going on. Therefore, most days consisted of asking for or finding money to go to the store.

At night, when the street lights came on, all the kids from the block, too many kids to name, gathered on my porch, which seemed to be the popular place to congregate despite the fact that I did not consider myself to be popular. It was another favorite time for me. The older kids played with the younger kids, and we ended up having nights full of playing games, such as red light-green light, tag, and hide-n-go-seek.

The day ended with parents yelling their kid's names from either ends of the street. It was the signal that it was time to go in for the night, which was usually no later than seven on the week days and nine on the weekends.

Jump rope was another popular game that filled the voids of most days. Jumping rope was a sport taken very seriously in black neighborhoods. Something so fun and upbeat often was the cause for many fights and the termination of friendships. I preferred to be an "ender," one of the two people who turned the ends of the rope. Playing "single" was easier for me, whereas double Dutch required holding two ends of a rope with both hands. With much practice, I ultimately learned to turn double Dutch. I wrapped the rope around my left hand a few times so that I could grasp it while turning. I loved jumping rope, the songs, the foot work others mastered and the whipping sound of the rope as it whisked and slapped the ground.

I was mostly a spectator, I did not feel comfortable jumping, either single or double Dutch, for fear of my wig falling off. There was a time when a few girls from another block came and asked to join in on a game. It's preferred to have more players than a few, so there were about five girls playing in front of my house. After everyone had a turn jumping, someone noticed I did not have a turn. I declined, telling them I never jumped and just liked turning. However, with much insistence, I decided to try my luck at jumping. I knew the grave risk, but had convinced myself that just once would not be too risky. I did not know how to jump in the rope while it turned. It took me a long time to jump in, but I felt good once I had gotten the hang of it. I had a few turns before my anticipated fear came true.

About three jumps in, the next time the rope went over my head, it did not make it fully over. It got caught in my wig and snatched it off. It was a surreal moment as I stared at my hair on the ground, it did not register that my hair was disconnected from my head. Instantly I felt the cool air on my scalp, realizing my greatest fear was really happening. I heard the girls who were not in my circle of friends, scream with laughter, covering their mouths as they pointed at me. In that moment the adrenaline had not filled my body to illicit a fight or flight response. I was frozen in a state of complete shock, standing there as people and cars passed by entertained by my embarrassment.

My mother, who had been by the window, saw everything and ran out of the house to my rescue with the look of sheer fright. "Oh my God!" she wailed as she rushed me into the house. My mom asked if I was okay, and that is when I broke down crying. I think I cried for several days straight. I was so embarrassed and humiliated that I was certain my life was over and no one would ever want to play with me again.

I was sure that I had lost my friends and that Malaysia would want nothing else to do with me now that she knew who I was. However, to my surprise, this was not in fact the case. She came to my house to comfort me. I was still feeling very much ashamed and embarrassed, so I tried smoothing over the situation by pretending that I had gotten over it. I did not know how to begin explaining who I was, but more frightening for me was losing my only good friend.

Malaysia, contradicted my thoughts by telling me it did not matter what happened to me, and she was not going to end our friendship because of my difference. She accepted me for who I was and nothing between us changed for the worse, instead it seemed to change for the better. After the situation, it appeared that Malaysia began to look out and take up for me more. If anyone had anything negative to say about me, she confronted them. She, her sister, and an aunt who was younger than Malaysia, but older than Malaysia's younger sister were a hard-knocks trio. I could not fight but was glad they could.

Many easily mistaken Malaysia's aunt for her cousin because of the closeness in age. Her aunt was very feisty and everyone thought she had a bad attitude. She appeared angry and unfriendly, but was very funny and entertaining to be around. Malaysia's aunt was always fighting someone, mostly because it did not take much to set her off. Her mouth was a fireball. She was tough, and did not take anything from anyone; she did not care who they were, a kid or an adult.

I never had problems with Malaysia's cousin, I was happy that I was among the limited few with whom she liked and got along with. Along with Malaysia, if anyone messed with me, Malaysia's aunt was in their face as well. The fact the girls had my back as they did, made me feel important and protected; it felt good to have popular friends who cared about me in such a way that they defended me.

I believed that humiliating moment allowed for Malaysia and me to become closer. I now felt I could share with her, personal and sensitive things that I was careful not to expose to others, such as my hair. I felt comfortable confiding in her about things that other kids never understood, and who made fun of me because of my condition.

After the incident, Malaysia was the only person outside of my immediate family I ever felt extremely comfortable with. I only walked freely around the house amongst my siblings, feeling most comfortable; Malaysia was now included. When someone knocked on the door, or if I heard a friend's voice in the house other than Malaysia's, who my brothers let in without knowing if I was dressed or not, I grew white with fright. I would try to stall them until I was presentable, fearful of being seen in my truth.

Malaysia never once made fun of me, or made me feel ashamed. I never got the impression that she felt awkward or uncomfortable. I even asked Malaysia once, and she said, "You're my friend, I accept you for you, you do not scare me, your nice fun and that is all I care about."

Malaysia and I had our ups and downs, trials that best friends experience within their friendships, but never anything too big that we did not get over. Many times she felt I had "traded" on her, by hanging around a girl who I began spending a lot of time with named Sara, with whom Malaysia occasionally did not like. My mother styled Sara's mother's hair for many years which was how we became friends.

Suddenly and without reason, as Malaysia and I entered our teenage years, distance eventually grew between us and we were no longer as close as we once were. I believed in part that we just grew apart. I also felt as we became teenagers, Malaysia grew closer to a group of girls, I did not fit in with. Malaysia was good friends with another girl on our block named Kia. Kia was an "it" girl very pretty, and popular. Malaysia began spending more time with Kia and her friends. Kia and a couple of teenage girls who also lived on the block were older than Malaysia and I by a couple of years.

They formed what my mom called the "pretty clique." The group of girls were the pretty, popular girls whose parents had money, which afforded them to stay current with the latest and popular trends and styles. The pretty clique was always the first to own the popular looks, and everyone else followed, soon after. Highly influenced by watching TV, music videos and popular movies, I was beginning to learn that one's appearance was very important. I discovered the more stuff I had, the more easier it became for me to make friends, because my physical appearance was proven to be difficult to accept. I had come to believe that I alone was not good enough, so it became my mission to be accepted by any means necessary.

My mom kept me in the latest fashions. The early '90s was as eclectic as the '80s. Stonewash was the must have and everything was exaggerated. Big hair, oversized and mixed match attire, lots of makeup, and bright colors were the fads.

I remember when LA Gear came out with sneakers that lit up with flickering lights on the heels, and were the must have brand. I badly wanted a pair, because everyone was wearing them. For my eleventh birthday, my mom came into my room and surprised me with a pair. They were white with the words "LA Gear" on the sides in a sparkly gray, laced up with three shoelaces made from different fabric: pink with silver glitter, gray, and the third was a white lace.

My mom also brought me a denim stonewash jean outfit, a skirt with a matching vest. The outfit had two large red stitched letters on the right upper chest of the vast and on the thigh of the skirt. I thought I was the "bomb" and could not wait to go to school to show off.

Having materialistic things—the latest toys, clothes, shoes— became a coping mechanism for me. I found that people noticed me, liked me and wanted to be my friend if I had and gave. Having stuff became arsenal for making friends. Giving and using the stuff that I had, compensated for the awkwardness and difficulties of trying to get people to accept me naturally. My appearance always solicited unwanted attention, and or caused people to dismiss me completely, whereas having stuff that people wanted made people notice and want to include me. I found that having stuff distracted people's attention from the way I looked. I was trying to perfect my image by having what others had, being like others, and following what others did, in hopes of earning genuine friendships. When my efforts failed, I settled for whatever kind of friends I ended up with, just as long as I was accepted and liked.

My mom made sure that I stayed current, by keeping me dressed in the latest fashions and hair styles. By this time in my life, I was no longer wearing out dated styled wigs that were a dead giveaway. My mom begun experimenting with styling wigs, using her skills as a stylist to perfect her own craft, and add versatility to her aesthetic. This was something exciting and new for the both of us, but more so for me because it gave me a new perspective on having to wear wigs. It also gave me a new sense of confidence as I could wear styles I wanted and felt comfortable in.

My world again had broadened and gave me hope in having a more normal appearance, one that I could begin to take pride in. Any style I wanted, my mom would sit me in the kitchen, where the magic happened, and used her gift to create. I distinctly remember the finger waves, the mushroom style with the side cut, and even braids. My mother styled my wigs to look inconspicuous, no one suspected. If anyone was suspicious, I lied saying my mom added extensions, and that most of it was mine. No one questioned it because most women wore hair extensions, it was a big trend; plus the styles were appropriate lengths, and volume. With each style, my mom became better and better in styling my hair to look natural.

I wanted to fit in, to be noticed and to be included in the circle of girls Malaysia hung with. I was very possessive of my friend and I wanted to be a part of whatever she did and whoever she was around. I did not understand why that could not be. I tried hard to be accepted. I even tried proving I could be as stylish as them. When the tennis attire became a trend, every girl for Easter wore polo collared shirts with the pleated long in the front and short in the back skirts.

I begged my mom to go out and get me the outfit as well as the white Ked sneakers, which were another popular brand. Then there was the year when everyone wore the mixed match Reebok high top sneakers, one color on one foot and another color on the other. Again when I saw the girls wearing the style, I asked my mom to get me two pairs of Reeboks, all so that I would be noticed.

The girls spoke to me in passing, sometimes engaged in conversations when Malaysia was around, but I was never invited to hang with them, whether at their houses or to sit on their steps to watch them play rope. I wanted to be a part of their circle because the girls were attractive and got all the attention from the boys in the neighborhood. I thought hanging around pretty girls would make me feel pretty too. I felt as we got older, Malaysia began spending most of her time with Kia, and hung around me less and less. I did not understand what was happening, I was losing my very first best friend and it hurt immensely.

What I appreciated about Malaysia was that she was not shallow or vain, even when constantly told how pretty she was. Malaysia had dimples in both cheeks when she smiled, and beautiful, white, straight teeth. As pretty as she was, Malaysia never acted on the complements. When we were around thirteen, Malaysia started getting her hair professionally done, and looked even more beautiful. Her new look made her more noticeable and I began to feel faded in the background of her spotlight. Malaysia was attractive and many boys from the block flirted and tried to pursue her.

A defining moment that formed my perception that beauty is conducive to success and acceptance, was from a comment made by a guy on the block, who I did not care much for named Steven. I could not put my finger specifically on why I did not like him. Other kids got along with Steven, and he got along with them. However, Steven hardily spoke to me, and when he did it was always with sarcasm. I was sure he did not like me, but did not know why. In passing I did not say anything to him, I knew the unlikeliness of Steven speaking to me, which made me resent him even more, because it was not a part of my character to be rude. Steven talked to other boys from the block about how "bad" (attractive) he thought other girls were. I would roll my eyes in disgust with his shallowness, while feeling angry and jealous that I was not among those in his consideration. Steven often talked about other's business, was very critical, and judged people on the block based on what they did and did not have.

As much as I did not like Steven growing up, I somehow formed an attraction to him as a teenager, although it was a brief one. During this brief time, I never told anyone I liked Steven, not even Malaysia. I was afraid of word getting back to Steven and that he would feel offended by my attraction to him. I had hoped, that if I took the initiative to start conversations, to smile more and show kindness toward him, then maybe it would change the way he treated me.

One day while sitting on my porch, Steven came over and I became nervous because of my attraction toward him. Malaysia and I were sitting and talking. Steven spoke to Malaysia but did not acknowledge me, which prompted me to say, "Hello to you too! How are you going to walk on my porch and only speak to one person?" I was being passive aggressive, telling him off but in a joking manner. My anger was masked with a smile.

He said, "What you mean? I did speak to you… Hello, Tanisha, if you didn't hear me the first time."

I rolled my eyes and continued with my conversation with Malaysia.

Malaysia had her hair cut in a bob. It was her first mature hairstyle. When I first saw the look, I could understand how many boys easily flocked to notice her, she was beautiful. Her beauty was pure and effortless. She was no longer the skinny girl, with the frizzled bangs in the front of her face, with the rest of her thick hair pulled back into a ponytail, she had transformed into a girl with permed stylish hair dos, arched, plucked eye brows, wearing the latest and walked with a new found confidence.

Steven intervened, breaking up the flow of whatever it was we were deeply conversing about. He told Malaysia she would have whatever she wanted in life. He added that she would never have to worry about getting a man, she was so pretty that men would always be available to her. Malaysia was the modest type, so she denied the comments and told him she did not want someone to want her just because of her looks. "That's not genuine, if that's all they are looking for," Malaysia concluded. In my spirit I was proud of her for dismissing his shallowness, and not agreeing to wear the label of vanity he attempted to place on her.

When Malaysia moved with her mom, brother and sister in their own apartment, that departure also signified the end of our friendship. It devastated me that our friendship was suddenly over. Nothing significant, no known reason or action taken that caused the fizzle of our friendship, it just ended. It was one of the most painful experiences. I believe we just grew apart, and I was so sadden by the lost, and grieved over it for years.

Throughout the years, we often saw each other, talked, and reminisced. It was during those times when I wanted to tell Malaysia how much I loved her and missed having her in my life, but never found the courage to do so. I did not think Malaysia felt the same since she had moved on with her life. I did not want to seem desperate or for Malaysia to think I was pathetic for being stuck in the past. I longed for our friendship, I did not think I would ever find another friend like her, and I would not. Malaysia meant more to me than she would ever know. She was the first friend who loved and accepted me as I was, showing me compassion during many vulnerable moments. I was grateful to have experienced her truth and simplicity, which validated those qualities in me. She was the first genuine female friend who gave me hope of experiencing another profound friendship again.

CHAPTER 8

Living with A Stranger

AS ANOTHER STORM ENDED with a beacon of hope after we all were reunited as a family, a massive one was slowly forming. The forecast for this storm would be poverty, violence, abuse and addiction, as drugs found their way back into my mother's life, turning our world upside down. Storms as they are known to do can form without prediction. The years proceeding would change the course of everything, shattering all that we knew as normal and just.

What I am most grateful for is having had the experiences with my mom when she was in a more stable state of mind. When her spirit was encouraged by her steadfast faith, when her smiles brightened up the atmosphere, and when she exuded with strength. Before the vices she used to cope began having adverse effects, and before giving up was inconceivable. When my mother knew God was with her, and knowing this one simple truth was all she needed to keep her going; and when affirmations were what helped her face adversity. More importantly, I am most grateful for having my mom by my side after my painful trauma, and for her never losing hope in my recovery.

These recollections gave me the ability to be there for my mom in her greatest times of need, by showing her the same loyalty, strength, unconditional love and compassion. Denoted by lifelong pain harbored deep within, masked with drugs, alcohol and men, nothing seemed strong enough to fill the void caused by her pain.

It was becoming too difficult for my mom to handle. Eventually a ticking bomb will detonate.

Behind clear skies on a day when the sun shines the brightest, is a storm accruing. Whatever happened to my mother, whatever she was going through at the time caused her to change. This was a devastating change, because it marked the death of who I had known my mother to be.

My mom still had her signature smile and striking appearance, but something about her spirit changed. It was as if she had let go of her faith and in doing so, the strength that held her together. She no longer had the same calmness, and gentleness that I was most familiar with before we were separated. I got my mother back, but she was different. Something happened that made her different and changed the dynamics of our family.

How I had known my mother would become a distant memory. Our happy ending quickly turned into a nightmare. Little did I know that my excitement and anticipation to resume the life I had known would turn to disappointment as everything quickly changed again, this time for the worse. As seasons change, so do people and situations.

A defining moment in my life was learning that nothing stays the same and those who you depend on to love and protect you, can also hurt and betray you. I had experienced how unfair life can be very early in my life. However, It was not until I experienced the subsequent difficult phases throughout my life, that I became cognizant of the fact that not only is life unjust, but it is unrelenting, unremorseful and rarely reconciles for the pain and suffering endured.

The '80s ended with the crisis of the crack epidemic, and the '90s began with an incredible amount of violence. With drugs came the greed for more and more money, creating the "by any means necessary" mentality to lucratively profit from it. Violent images constantly bombarded television through music videos, movies, and in the nightly news, giving accounts of the latest shootings, killings and other brutalities that occurred in Philly and across the country. The LA Riots in 1992, formed as a revolt from a community feed up with the racial attacks and injustice from law enforcement. After recordings surfaced of a black man being mercilessly assaulted by several Caucasian cops, racial tensions rose. This event seemed to antagonize people everywhere creating fury, in which violence became a cathartic outlet.

As a child indirectly exposed to violence by seeing and hearing violence on television, instilled another kind of fear inside of me. I became fearful of everything around me. Shows like America's Most Wanted, Cops and movies that portrayed people using drugs and being murdered, frightened me beyond my core. I found comfort in sleeping with the lights and radio on. I became hyper-vigilant, and paranoid, because most of the violence portrayed on TV took place in the same kind of environment I lived in, and looked like the people I saw every day. I lived with the fear of someone braking into our house and killing us. Even the faintest sounds of the floors creaking made me jumpy. With violence still at an all-time high, this is a fear that sometimes causes me the same unease and paranoia. I still cannot watch those types of shows and movies at night without feeling a sense of doom.

The violence I saw on television found its way into our home, breaking down the safe and stable foundation we had. Contrary to the fact that we were happy after reuniting and settling into our new home together again as a family, we were broken; and there were fragments that just could not be mended. I do not know what switch was turned on or off in my mother, but all of a sudden she developed into someone unbeknown to us. She was lesser of the warm, gentle and affectionate mother that I only knew her to be, and more of a hostile, aggressive, fearful and violent stranger.

Our home went from being innocuous, to being a nightmare of violence and abuse. The nascence of dysfunction, violence and abuse were perpetuated by my mother's addiction to drugs and alcohol and her habitual flings with men who shared the same self-destructing addiction. I remember one man she dated off and on; their relationship was volatile and eventually ran its course, and ended on a bloody note.

They screamed and fought constantly, and it was always a scary situation to be caught in the middle of. My siblings and I would be sound asleep and abruptly awaken in the middle of the night by loud sounds of objects being thrown, and the both of them yelling and cursing.

Many times we walked out of our rooms and into the hallway to find the both of them fighting each other. I was always fearful that my mom would get badly hurt or even killed. Most of the times I did not know what to do. As a child, there was nothing I could do, but watch and hope that my mother survived. Their fighting became a fearful norm and there were usually no warnings. Throughout the day things would be fine, they both would be in good spirits, but in the late hours of the night was when the drama took place. At night was when they fought.

One particular night, they were fighting and things went from bad to terrifying. I did not know it then, but my mother was in a drug induced rage. They both were high, and my mom lost it. They began fighting, but this situation was much scarier than any before. My mom was telling him to leave as she always threatened when they fought. This time, whatever infuriated her, she meant that she wanted him out. The fury in her eyes alarmed me. I was shaking uncontrollably, it was the first time I was absolutely terrified of my mother.

She was pacing around in the upstairs hallway, cursing and yelling at him. I stood at my bedroom door with one eye peaking. My mom had on a white t shirt that was ripped and stretched out, her hair was messy and her face fire with rage. I was fearful that she would notice and come after me, but I felt I had to see what was going on. I saw my mom run down the stairs as she continued to threaten him. A few seconds later, she returned back up the stairs swinging a steak knife.

My eyes grew wider with fright as my heart raced faster and faster. I did not know whether to scream out to caution my mother, or to stay out of sight. I went back into my room and hid under the covers. I then heard them fighting more with my mother sounding exhausted from exerting so much energy to fight. I then heard a long loud yelp from him, it sounded as if he was in pain by the way he screamed in agony. I found the courage to go back to the door to try convincing my mom to stop fighting him by yelling out, "Please, Mom!! Just stop!! leave him alone. Please, Mom!! you're going to go to jail, Mom!! What are we going to do if you go to jail, Mom?"

My plea went unheard as I saw my mom attack him biting his ear, nearly taking it off. There was red blood splattered on the egg shell hallway floor. I do not know if the blood came from him being stabbed or bitten. The cops were called, but my mom somehow evaded being sent to jail. I do not think he pressed charges, but I do know they were done with each other for certain afterward.

It would not however, be the last time I witnessed such violence with men my mom dated. There were times when things got violent and I waited for my mom to yell out to call the police. Times when they should have been called, but she forbid me to. When I was given the cue to call, I was always fearful the police would not make it in time to help her. However, as this kind of violent behavior became associated with every time my mother drank, we became used to the blue and red lights glaring outside our front door, hanging out our family's dirty laundry to the entire block.

Their intimidating pounding, demanding entrance to query about the ruckus, was stalled by my mother summoning us all to omit the truth when asked what happened. I did not know who to fear most, lie for my mom, or tell the cops the truth? I usually sided with my mom. I knew that moments later, the police would leave and I would be left with the consequences if did not. After the drama ended, the police turned off their sirens and sped off, and after everyone who had clustered around awaiting the weekly gossip returned inside their homes, my mother simply closed the door and acted as if nothing happened. By the time all was said and done, we were in our rooms, under the covers, still shaking, trying to forget the haunting images of the night to somehow return to a peaceful sleep.

Another event I will never forget, Joshua, Hakiem, and Erica were too young to remember when a fight broke out in our house where I saw a family member strike my mom in the head multiple times with a blunt object. I was nine, and remember my mom falling helplessly to the floor, as I was sure this time she was dead. I saw him beat her and heard the hard object hit against her head. I do not know what could have caused him to want to nearly kill my mother. She had to be treated for a concussion at the hospital, but I was relieved to see her return home with her head wrapped in bandages.

One day while outside playing at a block party, a brawl ensued with many people from the block physically involved, mostly women. I saw a metal rim from a bicycle, without the tire used to assault someone. I saw a woman bite another's breast, hair pulled out by the roots, and bloody, ripped clothes thrown every which way, all happening outside in the light of day in front of lots of children. It was the first time I saw a paddy wagon placing people in cuffs and hauling them off to jail.

Violence was all around me, and behind closed doors, it started affecting us by the hands of our mother. When my mom drank, it was the predictor of harsher things to come.

There were stages of her drinking that caused the onset of different mood swings and personalities. When she drank causally, her mood was relaxed, playful and her personality very carefree affectionate and confident. In this stage, she was the life of the party. After consuming way too much, usually hours of binge drinking, her mood became extremely erratic, and easily agitated. Her personality became aggressive, and she would purposely instigate fights with people so as to intentionally provoke them, therefore having a reason to become violent.

When fighting with her paramours, she hyped them up to hit her, "Hit me, I dare you." She got in their faces, hitting them, doing anything to antagonize them. Some fell into her trap and she would sustain minor injuries as a result, but most of the time she was the abuser.

We were never immune from her tyrants. The first account I remember of my mother abusing me was when she beat us all with a belt. She came home from an outing, got very intoxicated and came for us. She was angry about a chore that had not been done the way she anticipated and went ballistic. She yelled and cursed us out as she stormed up the stairs.

I remember she came into my brothers room where we all were, and started beating us. One by one she whipped us. My brothers yelled out while screaming from the top of their lungs. "Mommy I'm sorry! Mommy please! I won't do it again I'm sorry!" None of their pleas saved them. I did not think my mom would come for me, but she called me over from the corner of the room, where I had ran to out of fear and whipped my legs. My thin fragile layer of skin broke and bled. She told us to shut up or she would give us something to cry about.

Once I was hit with a broom stick across my elbow and could not bend my arm the next day. I went to my mom to tell her about my injury, in which she looked at me and said to get out of her face, "You shouldn't have made me hit you that hard." Later that day, while I was still in agony, she came up to my room offering no sympathy or remorse, but anger that I was making her feel guilty, for crying because I was still in pain.

Any time my mom had something to say, we learned to listen, and knew better then to show fear or have an attitude. Once, she got into my face, mad and yelling, I had slowly inched away from her, fearful of being struck again after she stuck me for no real reason. She told me to move back to where I was. When my mother treated me in such a way, I always looked my mother in her face, with fear and disgust. She demanded that we look her in the eyes, because if she sensed fear she would hit us again, but if we showed too much toughness she still hit us.

Any time after discovering our sustained injures, my mom unremorsefully showed no interest, and got upset if we brought them to her attention. There were times when it was apparently evident that we were really hurt. She then would be inclined to justify her need to put us in our place or rationalize that the abuse was because we had done something that caused her to act out of character. She then faulted us for bringing it on ourselves, then threatened that if we kept making her upset, she would put us away and we would never see her again.

My mom did not like for us to confront her, nor did she like to feel the guilt from her actions. When my mom felt guilty, we were beaten again for making her feel the discomfort, so we did everything we could to show we were in good spirits, that we were the ones in the wrong for making her upset and had to learn to show no reaction to being beaten.

Another time she attacked Rasheen with a broom, I heard the cracking sounds of the wood hitting against his bones, in which I think she fractured an arm, wrist or finger. Rasheen began running away from home because they both constantly fought. All the years of their conflict, Rasheen got to the point where he could not take it anymore and began to rebel against our mom.

He had gotten the video game system Nintendo for the second Christmas in the house. It was the only gift he wanted. The game became an escape from the daily uncertainties we faced with our mother's sporadic moods and behaviors. For Rasheen it was a way to defuse his anger and frustration. Rasheen barricaded himself in his room and obsessively played the system every day, whenever freedom presented itself. My mom became increasingly irritated with Rasheen playing it, because it distracted him from completing the tasks he was given. It had gotten to the point where Rasheen would hide the system after being forbidden to play it.

We all were addicted to playing the game. Rasheen had practically every popular Namco game, such as Pac Man, Burger Time, Diggiman, and Zelda. The game came with a cartridge featuring two games. Super Mario Brothers and Duck Hunt, Duck Hunt was my favorite game to play. It could only be played with the bright orange and gray virtual gun that also came with the system. The objective was to shoot the flying ducks that quickly flew across the screen. A hunting dog, covering his smile as he laughed, appeared from the bottom of the screen after each failed attempt. All of my suppressed aggression made me want to shoot the dog, rather than the ducks. I felt all the anger I had toward my mom rise in me and all I wanted to do was shoot some ducks to get it out.

One day, my mom stormed in cursing and fussing upon discovering that my brother had neglected his responsibilities of maintaining the house as he had been instructed to do. She snatched the system from the television and threw it out of the opened window. The rest of us, in the background, looked at each other in disbelief at what just happened. We did not have to see the damage done, the sound of the box crashing two stories down onto the cement ground was confirmation that it had been destroyed. Seeing the remains that laid in our backyard, upset my brother so much, he loved that system.

A few days had passed and we were still grieving the loss of our stimulus entertainment. Somehow Rasheen had snuck to retrieve it, aggregated all of the pieces that he believed were salvageable and miraculously put the system back together. It was without the top casing, exposing its hardware and wires, but it played as if it had never sustained such an impact. That system symbolized the resiliency my siblings and I possessed. We were not easily broken! Having the ability to bounce back became the essence of who we are, sustainable, even with the toughest of impacts.

The distinctive changes in my mom's temperament, behavior, and the dysfunction her unstableness caused in the household began to affect all of us negatively. Over time my brother became subversive, and tension rose between him and my mom that eventually escalated, resulting in Rasheen being permanently removed from the house and placed back into the system. His aberrant behavior, and emotional instability had been caused by long term abuse at the hand of our mother. When she felt traditional methods were not reformative, she resulted to outright forms of whipping us into shape.

One night, my brother came home from being out, and I believe he got in trouble because he either stayed out late or did not answer when my mom called him into the house. Back then, when it was time to come in the house from playing outside, my mom would yell out our names. An appropriate time to respond was no later than the second time our names were called. If we failed to return, it meant we were in a world wind of trouble, especially if we were found in someone's house without permission.

When my brother finally came in, my mother attacked him, whipping him with an extension cord. She beat Rasheen as he ran around the house seeking a place of protection while screaming from the top of his lungs in hopes that Rasheen could spare himself enough time to gain his composure. My mom caught him, holding the thick orange, extension cord whipping and striking him haphazardly with it. Every yelp and groan made her furiously beat Rasheen harder.

Afterward Rasheen was covered in blood and swollen, lacerations on his arms and legs.

Rasheen was about thirteen when he was put away. He was placed in a facility called St. Vincent Children's group home. He would not return to live with us for many years. This left me feeling sad to be separated again from my brother. I was also more fearful than ever because I was now the oldest, and afraid of what would become my fate. Minus one, the dysfunction and abuse continued with no end in sight.

For the rest of us left behind, we constantly lived on pins and needles. Anything appeared to set my mom off. Whenever any of us were in trouble, we more than likely were physically punished in some way as a result. We ran and hid in sheer fright, because we had come to learn that one person's impending terror was never solely about that person. It was a spillover effect that triggered a delayed reaction in my mom. After she finished beating one of us, she remembered something another had done days ago, that for whatever reason got passed her, and she would come after that child. We hid in closets and under beds, but my mom's intimidation convinced us to face the music.

Hakiem, however hid in clever places and sometimes would not come out for hours, waiting to come out after my mom left the house. Hakiem constantly told us his plans to run away, he could not take it anymore. Hakiem said he rather leave then stay and continue to be beaten and mistreated. I did not blame him for wanting to run, I wished I had somewhere to run to also.

My younger brothers were very close to each other growing up. Joshua was always the one who talked to Kiem to calm him down. That was Josh's nature, to be the peace maker. He was always reserved, quiet and diplomatic, which broke my heart every time to see him crying or beaten. Hakiem, would run out of the house and not come back for hours. Hakiem hoped that upon our mother's return her fury had dissipated, and that she had forgotten and forgave. It was wishful thinking, my mom would beat him terribly just because he ran.

The most frightening moment was the night I was convinced my mother was going to kill us. As seemed the norm, hell opened its gates late at night. I was eleven and can remember that night like it was last night. I just had surgery on my right leg a few days prior. It was fused in a hot pink cast from my knee to my toe. I could not walk and had to be confined to a wheelchair. I had the procedure done at Children's Hospital. It was not a procedure that permitted me to recuperate in the hospital, so I was sent home hours later.

When we returned home everything was fine, my mom helped me to my room and catered to me throughout the day. As always, whenever I had surgery, I received everyone's sympathy and was given full attention. My mom had given me a bird bath, because I could not get the cast wet. She then massaged my body with lotion, clothed me in new pajamas and helped me into bed. She kept the wheelchair the hospital provided me upstairs so that I could access the rooms and bathroom.

All appeared without concern, I felt somewhat secure that my physical state would ensure me immunity from my mom's wrath. I just assumed she had compassion for the fact that I was already in pain. On this particular night, I fell into a deep somber, with the aid of some prescribe medication to help relieve the post-op pain. Suddenly I awoke to the abrupt resonant sounds of banging, crashing, stumping and the sound of my mother yelling and screaming. As many times as I had awoke to her belligerent episodes, this time was peculiar.

She was shouting obscenities, screaming how much she hated everyone, how she could not take it anymore and that God was not helping her, no one was. Upon hearing that, I feared for the worse, and grew evermore fearful of the fact that I could not move out of her way. I then saw from the slit in my cracked door, the hallway light turned on, and nearly jumped from out of my skin when my mom suddenly busted it open. She had summoned all of us out into the hallway as she screamed for everyone to "get out of my house." She demanded that my brothers and sister move fast, threatening to break their legs if they did not.

We absolutely had no idea what was happening. All the while my mom was yelling and screaming that she was tired, that no one respected her and how fed up she was with everything. Josh managed to sneak into my room to try and help me down the stairs, but not before my mom rushed in behind him. The look in her eyes showed no mercy for me being incapacitated. She yelled and screamed at me to get out of the bed. I looked at her and said, "But, Mom, I can't walk." Joshua was waiting by the stairs to help me down, because he knew there was no way I could meet her demand. Hakiem saw it as an opportunity to hide.

My mom was still ordering me to find a way out of the bed before she was going to hurt me. "Tanisha, you better get out that bed before I hurt you girl, I'm not playing." She then got in my face yelling, as spit spattered across my face, about how tired she was. "I'm tired! Ain't nobody helping me, you better get out that bed and down those steps, y'all getting out my house, or I'm seriously going to hurt somebody."

I slowly dragged my casted leg out of the bed and the pain immediately shot right to my head, as gravity from the weight pulled my leg causing it to bang against the floor. I was in no condition to move. The whole time I was inching myself out of the bed and into the hallway, my mom was standing close by telling me to hurry up. I finally crawled my way to the head of the steps to where my brother stood against my moms' orders, waiting to help me. She got in Josh's face, smacking him around until he ran down the stairs crying.

My mom resumed her psychotic episode, now I was the only one left in the hallway. Again she threatened me that if I did not move, she would push me down. I was so scared, I tried with everything I had, but it was not good enough. Fighting through the pain, I managed to make it down one step, and that was when my mom kicked me down the stairs. I tumbled down the case, as Josh rushed behind to help me. I laid there too afraid to cry, restrained by my tremulous nerves; I thought my weakness would only make my mom lunge at me again. I just sat there huffing as I cried silently, praying for the strength to endure the night.

My mom went into her room and about ten minutes later came down the steps, I close my eyes and started praying. She knelt down beside me to say, "Get your butt back in that bed, and you better not tell no body. Keep your mouth shut." She told Josh to help me back to my room as she then wept. Seeing this, my anger and everything else I was feeling suddenly left me, and was replaced with sympathy for my mom, my heart wanted to forgive her. I gained my composure, but to no avail did I get over the fear, I was beyond timid. Angst was branded in me, from the constant fear I felt of my mother.

During these tumultuous times, I not only felt fearful, and unsafe, but also alone. I was baffled that with all of the commotion going on in our house, no one cared enough to want to help. Attention was often brought to our front door. With the fights, and police being called, I believed it was impossible for people not to be wary about the children inside. With all the yelling, thumping and banging that took place frequently in that house, I did not understand how no one found necessary to react.

No one got that involved in other people's domestic issues, other than to gossip; many had their own shameful iniquities and or fearful of the consequences brought on by another code of the streets known as "No snitching." Ironically, the height of the neighborhood watch program was becoming a popular movement. A project that was the biggest inner-city crusade, encouraging residents to participate as crime voyageurs in attempts to rid the urban community of violence that corroded its streets in the early '90s.

I desperately wished for someone to protect and rescue us. For someone to confront my mother, warning her of the potential of a greater loss, that of her kids – again. I wondered if any of her closest friends tried to convince her to get herself together to be a better mother. I am sure people on our block saw and knew what was going on, but maybe felt it was not their concern or place to intervene.

I looked for a hero, but we lived in a place and time where none existed. We were left alone to fend for ourselves and all we had were each other. The bond between my siblings and I grew ever so deep through the adversity we endured together. When there were no others to look to, we looked to each other. As time went on and things continued to be tumultuous, we found power and strength to preserver in each other.

CHAPTER 9

A means of Escape

THE STRESSFUL AND ABUSIVE environment I lived in caused me to find other means to escape the hell in my home. A few years past and the severity of the physical abuse subsided, but happened intermittently. The abuse went from physical to more verbal and emotional.

My mother's behaviors and moods became more and more unpredictable, causing me to feel very confused as to how to deal with her. The fear internalized and I became mute. At this time, I was really struggling with what I looked like, and making sense of what happened to me. Expressing my emotions, particularly regarding my appearance and the accident were not safe for me to talk about with my mom for a long time.

I found serenity in the plastic world of mettle. I was thirteen years old and very much still into playing with my Barbie dolls. I easily became subdued in imagination, as I had the freedom to create my own storyline. I was helpless as a child over my own circumstances. My imagination was the only outlet I had control over. I created a life for Barbie, Ken, and their family that I yearned for. Barbie and Ken were secure in a loving and caring relationship, where there was no yelling and fighting. They both had great jobs and enjoyed the finer things in Barbie's world. Whenever a new doll house or car hit the shelves, I asked for it. I wanted to give my dolls the life I could only dream of through them.

As a child I had a very mature and vivid imagination. I played behind closed doors because I did not want anyone seeing me imitate the preppy and proper voices I learned from my favorite shows.

Another temporary escape from the stresses I experienced at home was spending time over other people's houses. One friend's house I spent the most time over was Sara's. In efforts to save and make money, my mom bought clippers and cut my brothers hair instead of going to the shops. She had a regular cliental of women who requested to have their hair pressed and curled. Occasionally some requested intricate up dues such as buns and finger waves. My mom's most consistent client was Mrs. Rollins, my friend Sara's mom. Mrs. Rollins did not want to pay the expensive costs of a solon, when she found that my mom styled hair at a fraction of the costs, and did as good of a job.

The Rollins were always on the go and did lots of exciting things. The mother was a homemaker, and the husband had a high paying position with the city. He was a quiet, friendly man who worked a lot. Sara was the rightful heiress of her parent's hard work, and acted like a spoiled princess. She was the only child, and had everything a girl could want. Sara never seemed satisfied, she always wanted the latest things. When something new came out, she was among the first to have it, then a week later, lost interest, demanding something bigger and better, which her parents always met Sara's requests.

Sara and I became very good friends, playing at each other's house, borrowing and swapping each other's dolls and accessories. I loved being at Sara's house. Not only did she have dolls that I did not, but we did a lot of things that I would not have been privileged to do otherwise—we ate out, and went to fun places.

Sara's house was an escape from the discomforts of my home environment. Mrs. Camila knew about my circumstances and had such a big heart. I never had money of my own, but she always provided for me, without ever mentioning the fact. Whenever I spent time at Sara's house, Mrs. Camilla did for me the same as she did for her daughter. I felt embarrassed and out of place, even though Sara and her mom never made me feel out of place or ashamed. Despite her attitude and behaviors associated with being an only privileged child, I really liked Sara. Sara made me feel like I was an important friend to her. I did not have the money or finer things as she and her friends, but I felt included and a part of her circle.

Sara had a large, close knit extended family who maintained that closeness with many fun filled, and excited events. I often tagged along with Sara, becoming very well acquainted with many people in her family, after spending so much time around Sara's family, I felt included in hers.

I envied the closeness of Sara's family, because I did not have that with my extended relatives. I felt a sense of belonging that comforted me with her family. Her mother was nice and pleasant, which sadden me, because Mrs. Camila was easily walked over by her daughter. I often got upset with Sara by the way she treated her mother. I witness how sometimes Sara bellow, disrespect and call her mother names when Sara did not get her way. However, when Sara provoked her mother, Mrs. Camila lost her patience and fussed at Sara mostly out of frustration. At times I purposely distanced myself from Sara, feeling disgusted and irritated because of her behavior towards her mother. Sara knew her mother was soft hearted and that she would do every and anything for her.

Sara knew how to manipulate her mother and force her hand to get want she wanted. Watching Mrs. Camila put up with Sara's petty tantrums, made me feel sorry for Mrs. Camila's inability to command authority as a parent. There were a few awkward times I observed Mrs. Camila demand her respect, by striking her daughter letting Sara know she was very much still in control, and I silently cheer Mrs. Camila on for standing up to her daughter.

Mr. Rollins was quiet, and caring as well, but Sara knew that she could not get away with the same disrespect she showed her mother with her father. He did not play it. When her dad put Sara in her place, I felt a sense of justice for Mrs. Camila. I believed Mrs. Camila gave into Sara's demands, just so she would not have to put up with her tantrums. I resented Sara for being ungrateful to her mother. I envied Sara, not so much for the things that she had, but for the kind of parents she had. I would have given anything to have parents like hers. Whenever I spent time with the family, I always made sure to show Mrs. Camila the upmost respect, in compensation for the lack there of from her own daughter. I envisioned myself as her daughter and thought how my mother was not deserving of me as a daughter and how Sara was not deserving of Mrs. Camila as her mother.

Sara's sense of entitlement and obstinate ways made me want to distance myself from her as we got older. It was easy to do just that when the family moved to the suburbs in the far Southwest part of the city, and we just fell out of touch. I visited Sara's new house a few times, but things felt different. Aside from aspects of Sara I no longer wanted to tolerate, I also felt extremely jealous of their extravagant new home. I completely felt undeserving of being Sara's friend when I realized I could never live up to her expensive lifestyle. I realize I no longer fit in with Sara and her new friends, who all lived the same privileged and comfortable lifestyle. I tried my best to hold on to what we had, but we were teenagers now and so much had changed with Sara, that I could easily see I was no longer important to her as I once was. Her new circle of friends, intimidated me with their beauty, and all they had, that I did not. They were gorgeous girls. Again no one made me feel out of place, the times I did hang out with Sara, they all were really nice, fun girls, but I had convinced myself that I did not belong, feeling like the soar eye to look at against so many pretty faces. When distance created a divide between Sara and I, I was most grateful. Sara stopped calling and coming around for me, and my jealousy and intimation were relieved she no longer did.

Television was another great escape for me; I was an avid watcher. *Sweet Valley High* and *Saved by the Bell* were among my favorites. When I had surgery and was homebound, I watched *The Young and the Restless* with my mom. The shows I watched were mostly shows with white actors and actresses portraying picture perfect lives. Through the movies and television shows I watched, I received many biased messages about race, class and privilege. Many black shows and commercials depicted blacks in negative stereotypes. Storylines usually centered around a single parent struggling financially, also faced with secondary challenges such as drugs, gangs, murder, and life in the confines of the ghetto, whereas the white shows had storylines depicting nuclear families, that showed everything happy, fair, and glamorous.

I became infatuated with watching shows depicting a life better than the one that was mine. I became emotional, wishing that the television could open up like in the cult classic, Poltergeist, and I could step out of the ruts from my life and into the pleasantness of a perfect world. I wanted to live in a house with a white picket fence, manicured lawn, with parents who spoke in soft tones, and who were always loving and kind. Through play, I played out the life I wanted to someday have; I took what I observed from mostly white characters and recreated my life through pretend play.

I loved going to school and being in the presence of my teachers. In second grade I had two teachers, Mrs. Wright and Ms. White. Mrs. Wright was Caucasian and Mrs. White, was African American. I was very much going through a phase of wishing I were white, because whites had a seemingly better life. On TV and in person, they were nice, had money, drove nice cars and did fun stuff with their kids on the weekends.

They even embodied the idealism of beauty. The influences of beauty portrayed in the media, had many blacks denouncing their "blackness" for long, straight hair, thin waists and lighter skin. I learned at an early age, being black was a disadvantage, while being white afforded whites with the advantages and privileges to living a successful life. Growing up, I remember being teased and criticized for acting "white."

I did not see it as so. I wanted to be taken seriously, understood, and judged for my level of intelligence; none of which would happen speaking improperly, (using slang primary). These aspects were very much a part of me, because every black person I was surrounded around in my life as a child, spoke informally. Slang is embedded in the environment I lived in, it is very much a part of who I am, but I did not want it to be all of who I was. I knew that I would be judged more critically, because of my appearance, therefore, I understood that I had to be educated and intelligent, so I learned to speak the dialect of success. The streets are where I am from, and I am in love with the culture, because it reflects where I come from, but I have also come to believe that there is a time and place for everything. The hood chick from South West is very much a part of who I am, and can be seen when necessary, but it is important to maintain a balance. People playfully teased me, calling me a "white girl" because I talked proper and did not follow many common trends and behaviors of street culture. I always had a difficult time understanding why people associated properness with color, therefore insinuating a negative connotation to what being "black" represented. I never understood why people relish in the stigmatizations that have crippled and demoralized blacks in urban environments. Furthermore, having pride and defending a type of ignorance that has aided as a sustained hindrance, preventing so many from ascending beyond the cycles of dysfunction and plights that have mislead many blacks to see themselves only in the context of their environments.

Mrs. Wright sometimes brought to school her two children Andrew and Amanda. Amanda was in high school and had the most beautiful long hair I had ever seen. It was silky, blonde and stopped near the end of her back. She had pretty eyes and a spirit that suggested she lived without worry, fear and anxiety. I envied Amanda just because she was beautiful, her life was different than mine, I noticed she had many advantages over me simply because of her skin color. I cried internally wishing I was a part of their family, then maybe I could have had a fair chance at life. I hated when the school bell rung and it was time to go home. I felt the most anxiety at the end of the day when I knew I had to return to a place I dreaded and returned to a family nothing like the Wrights.

I would get on the school bus, sit in my seat next to the window and cry. My school was over an hour away from my house. I stared out of the window observing the conditions of the different sections of the city we passed through. First was the Olney section where my school was, then West Philly, where a few students were dropped off, and last was Southwest. Every area, neighborhood, and street slightly differed, but had the same look of hopelessness, and disregard. Maybe what I saw in the world around me was a reflection of how I was feeling at the time, I too felt hopeless and disregarded.

Turn by turn I dreaded driving closer to my house, having to return every day to a place I did not want to be.

I struggled with my feelings toward my mom and how to make sense of what became of our lives. I had mixed emotions of loving her, forgiving her, resenting her and at times hating her. Everything became confusing, it was as if she was multiple people in one body. Not all was bad, there were times when we still had fun together, and I had good heart to hearts with my mom. She still meant everything to me, because she was my mom. A child has no other choice but to adapt, to rely and depend on that parent when there is no one else. I loved my mom with everything in me and tried making sense as a child does, of the things that happen and why people acted as they did. I began to internalize everything, thinking, what was it I had done or we had done to make my mom so angry all of the time. Coming up with the conclusion that it would just be better to be good, be quiet and out of the way to keep her from becoming upset.

No matter what my mother personally went through, she continued to take care of us, even while using, my mom maintained her role as a functioning parent. She got up every morning, made sure we were dressed and off to school, and made sure we went to all of our appointments. My mother also mastered keeping up appearances, my mother's addiction was always inconspicuous. My mom deceived many people, especially many of those who knew her well. Nothing about my mother's appearance or disposition gave hint to her suffering from an addiction. To the outside world, my mother was pleasant, appeared confident and had it together. However, her persona was really insecure, vindictive, deeply depressed, addicted, and violent. Only a limited few experienced the true difficulties of her personas. As children we witnessed firsthand Jekyll turn into Hyde. We became terrified of our mother.

Around the age of thirteen, I began receiving burn treatment at Shriners Children's Hospital in Boston, Massachusetts. We traveled so far, because Shriners was the nearest hospital specializing in burn care, and that accepted my government insurance. My mother and I made the long commute to and from in a single day for appointments. We stayed in Boston during my recovery time after surgeries, and then commuted weekly or bi-weekly for post-op appointments. Through Shriners, no family had to bare the expenses of anything, including travel. Shriners paid for the cab service that picked us up from our house, returned us back, and flew us on commercial flights. Once we arrived at the airport, Shriners volunteers would meet us and take us to the hospital.

The long trips to Boston were many times the most awkward with my mother. The biggest challenge was dealing with my mother's personality. When engaging with people outside of our norm, my mom spoke as if she knew and understood everything. I thought to myself, how could this be when my mom's life never afforded her with the same experiences as those she conversed with. I witnessed how my mom struggled to fight back who she was, too afraid to let her truth show, knowing that people would look down upon her. When she switched up, appearing proper and trying to show she could relate, I just looked at her without saying anything about the way she acted. I did not want to put my mom on the spot or embarrass her, by letting her know that I knew what she was doing. My mom openly shared with us that she had not finished school; in those moments, I wished she had been able to. My heart felt the deepest sorrow and elicited the deepest compassion for my mom, she truly wanted to be more; so I stayed in my place as a child.

In order to keep the peace, I learned to keep quiet and agreed with everything she said to feed her need to always be right. There was not enough room for the three of us—me, my mom and her ego. Through compassion I saw that my mom wanted to be more than what her environment made her, and through her efforts, she tried proving she was. My mom wanted to show people that she could hold her own, that her circumstances were no indication of who she really was, despite the fact that in so many ways they had. My mom felt she needed to prove she was capable of engaging with even the best of them. Her ego needed to constantly be reminded that there was no difference between her and them, so what they had more and better. My mom found ways to minimize their shine, to protect herself from feeling less than one's success made her feel. Her pride remained stable in the fact that no matter the things others had, that deeply my mom longed for in herself, they did not have God the way she did. She was always able to find some holes in another's perfection, which comforted her ego and rebalanced the justice scale in her eyes. My mother's ego peeked through in the ways she defended her suffering and protected her pain. No one knew more than she; my mother's ego refused to allow success and intelligence to intimidate her. I began to learn this fact from our trips to and from the hospital, and many times throughout my life as my growth towards personal success began to separate me from my mom, therefore creating a distance as I worked hard to define my own identity, outside of what was to be expected from my environment.

As I got older and became smarter and more knowledgeable, it became difficult to continue to allow my mother's ego to run the show. Years past and we were still traveling to and from Boston. There were times when it was obvious my mother did not know or understand, and I disagreed, tried to explain or denied what my mom believed she knew, by seeking answers or understanding, which always caused conflict. My mom liked to believe that she had all of the answers, which frustrated me so much, when it was clear she did not know; she was so stubborn to admit not knowing or being wrong, especially being corrected. This infuriate my mom, and she would argue me down or become aggressive. I realized most of the time it was just better to allow her to be right, shut up and let her deal with the consequences that resulted.

However there were times when, I felt it was absolutely necessary to go against the grain by contradicting the fact that she knew everything, especially when I became fed up and frustrated with her. My efforts were never received as a means of constructive criticism. I remember once, we got lost in the airport, all because she thought she knew where the terminal was, causing us to almost miss our flight. Neither of us knew how to navigate the airport well, although we had taken the trip several times by that point. I had however learned to understand the boarding schedule, which I decided to refer to, rather than continue going back and forth with my mom, using the information to eventually direct us to the correct terminal. I took the lead by asking people along the way for assistance. We found the terminal, but my mom did not like to be wrong.

My mom rarely apologized for her mistakes. In correcting, or disagreeing with her, my mom sometimes cursed me out in front of people, and a few times, smacked me when no one was looking, expecting me to pretend all was fine. It became unbearable traveling with her. The more intelligent and articulate I became, the more conflict I noticed there was between my mom and I. I was able to hold full conversations with all kinds of people that my mom could not. She was both impressed and appeared to be intimidated at the same time.

When talking to different kinds of people, my mom expressed how proud she was that I could carry on and articulate conversations with a doctor or a business person seated beside us as we waited to board our plane. After we boarded the plane, or even after we returned home, she then scolded me or said hurtful things. "You think your better than me, don't you?" My mom sometimes brought it up later and told people that I thought I was better than everyone else. My mom would sarcastically speak proper, imitating the way I spoke. I always resented the comments, because they were far from the truth.

Being intelligent to me was not attributed to one race, but a way of being. I noticed the contrast between those from my own environment and those who were educated and successful. Whether they be characters on TV, or someone I came in contact with who conducted themselves proper, poised, and with more class than the kinds of people I was surrounded by, those were the ones I wanted to emulate. I wanted to better myself. Doctors, teachers, classmates' parents, I loved to observe people who had qualities I wanted to possess when I grew up. I was young, but began to see that the world was a much bigger place than what I was exposed to. This new insight was given to me by a very influential person who entered into my life with great purpose, my high school mentor Vita. She exposed me to the finer things in life; because of such exposure, I have a great appreciation for the arts, such as theater, and classical music. We traveled the city and discovered all of its hidden gems. She exposed me to any and everything, things that I had never heard of and did not appreciate before knowing her. More importantly Vita taught me about how to conduct myself as a lady, how to speak and present myself with poise, properness and grace. It is because of my experiences with Vita, I learned to read menus, understand the use of the many kinds of utensils used in classy restaurants, and how to behave in upscale social settings. It was because of Vita, I can say I have experienced seeing a Broadway show, the Opera and when I went to college understood art history from constant exposure to contemporary art. I knew that I wanted more for myself, and was learning the key to being better and having better was determined by the person I became. I wanted to be the best me, regardless of my circumstances not being the best. Education would become the most powerful tool to overcome the insurmountable adversity I dealt with at home and throughout my life.

After the first rocky few years, my mom realized she had serious problems that needed addressing. She understood her life was no longer manageable, that she was hurting and we were hurting. My mom realized it was time to clean up her act and get help for her addiction. Choosing to become clean and sober was one of the best decisions my mom ever made for herself. She owed herself that much to live life healthy and with a peace of mind.

When she became clean, we functioned like a normal, cohesive family. It was a sense of relief from the drama we had become accustomed to. My mom promised to make a new life free from the demons that haunted her by entering into rehab. When she started attending Narcotics Anonymous meetings, things began to turn around for the better. She began faithfully making meetings multiple times daily.

I remember my mom coming home with colorful key chains celebrating specific milestones in recovery. Starting with a white key chain entitled "Just for Today," then there was a chain for one month of sobriety, and different colors for every thirty days, then every three months, then a black chain for every year after the first. They were more than just key chains, they were tangible reminders of how far my mother had come in her recovery. They also were a constant reminder of all my mom had to lose if she went backward.

Every time my mom came home from a meeting she proudly showed us her new chain. I felt her sobriety was a gift to us, the gift of hope that our family had another chance to prosper. My mom showcased all of her prize possessions by hanging them on nails on the wall in her bedroom. My mom carried her NA book, along with her Bible everywhere she went. For several years my mom was consistent and serious about her recovery.

She faithfully attended meetings, had supportive friends also in recovery and a sponsor for continuous support. I remember attending my mom's one-year anniversary meeting, where she was the guest speaker, honored for being sober for one year. I sat there gleaming with pride to see my mother standing so proud and confident in her own accomplishments. It was inspiring to hear my mom speak in front of so many people who admired her strength and courage also. I remember feeling very emotional, because it was the first time in a very long time that I saw my mother truly happy and looking better than ever.

My mom was meeting many positive people in meetings and at NA functions. This was good for her, having relationships with people was something she valued deeply. She was always hoping to find that close girlfriend to fill the void of the sisterly bond she desperately wanted with my aunt. My mom and aunt would reconnect and for awhile be okay, but then distance grew between them and they became strangers again. There was something each held against the other that unfortunately created the distance which separated them. My mom sat and cried many days about not having a relationship with her sister. It really pained her that she could not have her sister in her life the way my sister and I had each other.

The friends my mom made, were mostly men. For my mom some habits were more difficult to break. Oftentimes people in recovery pick up new habits or addictions to fill voids left still empty. My mom was beginning to heal some old wounds, but others still left unattended continued to fester.

Her other drug of choice was men. She had some close girl-friends, however, there was only one woman at the time my mom trusted and considered to be her right hand, which was Ms. Pat who lived directly across the street from us. Ms. Pat for a long time was that sister my mother wanted and needed, and an additional aunt to us. Ms. Pat was the rock for my mother, because of her tough love. I sincerely loved Ms. Pat for her compassion, for loving my mother so deeply, and loving and caring for us the same as her children. As much as my mother desired to have meaningful and secure bonds with them, she appeared distrusting of women. I could never under-stand why, my mom was physically beautiful; she was a caring, nur-turing, smart and spiritual woman who many people admired. She had a special effect on people, especially men.

I saw the way men looked at and adored my mother, but my mom could never make sense of what others saw in her. I loved watch-ing my mom get dressed in her glamorous clothes as she prepared to go out. I always flattered her with as many compliments as I could think of to boost her confidence. I wanted her to see the beauty that I saw. I would say, "Mommy, you look so pretty, you are gorgeous." She replied by scrunching her face with a disgusted look, saying "You think so? No, I'm not." I truly thought my mom was being modest, but she really did not see her truth. It had been suppressed by years of the painful experiences that convinced her she was ugly. The mirrors lied to my mother, telling her she was not the fairest when in fact she was. The good thing was that it was there. Everyone could see it but her. Every time I looked at my mom, I prayed for God to show my mother her true reflection, of how beautiful she really was both inside and out. She was living as a reflection of her pain. I knew who she really was, I experienced her. I did not understand then, that my mom was also dealing with mental health issues. God was expanding the love in my heart to reach the deficits within her.

I wanted to think that all the love I had in my heart for my mom, would be enough to convince my mother of her worth. This was the naiveté of a child. I wanted to believe my love and the love from my siblings were all she needed to make her feel whole and complete. I wanted to believe I had the strength to be strong for my mom, and to take her pain away, but I could not. Her issues were deeply rooted in her brokenness. It pained me to see her force rigid and uneven fragments of that brokenness together in dire attempts to be made whole. In finding the pieces that made her life complete, some pieces fit perfectly, while others did not fit at all. Every man who came across her path, she hoped was that missing piece. With much effort and force, it was a huge disappointment to her when they just did not fit.

My mom continued to search for love, but the paths she took only lead her back to the same dead ends. Some of the men who passed through our lives, were good to my mom and good to us. A few had the potential of being great husbands for her. However, none stayed around for long periods of time—some a year or two, others for a couple of months. A few had recurring roles, but my mother never seemed to find stability with any of them, and for the promising ones, I never understood why my mother could not see their good qualities. The nicer and functional they were, the less interested my mom appeared, and the quicker it seemed she drove them away.

Whenever my mom entered into a new relationship, it became her purpose, although she never put a man before us, she just held them to higher standers then she did herself. She catered to them, and made it her obligation not to disappoint, even though they did not have the same regard or the same monogamous intentions. It was as if my mother craved and could not function without dysfunction and drama in her life, just as long as she was with someone.

It seemed as though my mom was more drawn to and comfortable around the volatile, unmotivated and emotionally unavailable men. Her skewed perception of a healthy relationship was mirrored by the dysfunctional and abusive relationships she experienced growing up. Having no real positive and or healthy relationships to model after, she was susceptible to attracting the same kind of men, despite her desires for wanting a man made from a higher quality of cloth.

My mom wanted better, but truly did not know how to accept better. Substandard became a more suitable and comfortable mate, because he was less threatening. It appeared my mom chose men with whom it was easy for her to control and manipulate. She was always the dominant one in her relationships. Control over others, especially men, gave her false validation. Constantly seeking to rescue and enable needy men, appeared to suffice the helplessness she felt within herself.

When one relationship ended another one began; there were times of brief intervals spent alone, before introducing us to yet another prospect. Jumping in and out of relationships became a normal occurrence. It got to the point where we did not share the same enthusiasm as my mom, when she told us about her latest beau. We expected nothing more than the typical kinds of men my mom was accustomed to, and never hopeful of them being the "one." We especially never expected anyone to play the role of any of our absentee fathers. We learned never to get real close, knowing that eventually they would either up and leave, unwilling to deal with her, or she would sabotage her own chance at finding what she was looking for.

My mother always went hard and gave every relationship her all. She was very nurturing, supportive and also encouraging, however everything she did was tactical. If she proved to be loyal and tended to their needs, then the men she dated would not have a reason to leave her. Unfortunately, they found reasons to; one way or another, they were gone and my mother was left feeling the deepest betrayal and heartache. She was baffled at how they could choose to run off with another woman, or how giving all of herself was not enough to make a man stay. She saw herself as the victim, and the man who left her as the adversary.

My mother always believed karma righted the wrong of any injustice done to her. She would confide in me about her problems and the cause of the brake up as if I were one of her girlfriends. Sometimes telling me things that were far beyond my immature comprehension, in which all I could do was sit and try to sympathize. I understood what it felt like to have my feelings hurt, and when someone treated me badly. I absolutely hated to see my mom cry, let alone hurting. I feared the state it would put her in. I feared her hurting herself, someone else or worse using to cope with the pain of being alone.

My siblings and I loved seeing our mother happy. When in relationships she became a different person, fun and easy to be around. When my mom felt hopeful of the relationship, it was as if she also had the motivation and stamina to do other things in her life. She enjoyed life, it was as if a good relationship was the windup in her back that propelled her. However, when the relationship was over, especially because of infidelity, she was not a pleasant person to deal with. She took her anger, frustration out on us; she became depressed, and very moody.

There was always a contradiction in the men she chose, the kind of man she wanted for herself was never the kind of man she dealt with. Despite that they were in recovery, there was still an element of deception to them. Many times, we were able to scope their motives or dispositions before my mom. Or it could have been that she very well knew what we suspected, and either chose to accept it or had the intentions of "fixing" them.

As I think back, I see the evidence that God was always with us, protecting my brothers, sister and me, when my mom lacked good judgment to ensure, particularly that Erica and I were safe around the men she brought home. There were a few men my mom dated who I felt uncomfortable around. Nothing serious, just an unsettling feeling about the way they looked at me, or were too touchy. Especially when both my mom and her paramour were inebriated. These things were constantly roaming my young mind, and in some ways I resented my mom for not being more conscious of such risks.

I did not understand then, the significant impact of being predisposed to my mother's behaviors and idealism related to relationships. I witnessed my mom rebound from one man to another, in search of the "one." It appeared that she compromised so much of herself just to prevent living a life alone. Her experiences were shaping my perception and giving me false messages about what it meant to be whole and fulfilled. I learned from my mother that I had to have a man in my life to be happy and complete.

What I saw was a woman who gave everything she had to those who were not worthy in any way of her love. I saw a woman enabling men to take advantage of her and hurt her, accepting others' brokenness, exhausting her efforts, convinced that she could change them into the type of man she wanted. I saw a woman who was constantly abandoned, hurt, rejected, desperately seeking acceptance, love and commitment to avoid loneliness. I saw a woman not knowing what real love looked like, misconstruing it to be pain, abuse and disrespect. In my mother I saw a woman who wanted nothing more than to be loved, and would not give up until she found him. More interesting was that in my mother I saw a glimpse of my own reflection and my own internal struggles, traveling down similar paths in pursuit of the same love with men in hope of feeling whole and complete.

CHAPTER 10

A Shameful Identity

I WAS OLD ENOUGH to realize just how devastating what happened to me was, and the negative impact it would have on my future experiences with people, and my place in the world. I was in school, and although the school I went to was for children with disabilities, it did not protect me from being made fun of by other children. The constant teasing and negative attention, was not only a heavy burden to bare, but one that I had to bear alone. I could not trust the one adult in my life to help me cope with any of the pain I was feeling, because my mom was the root cause of all of it. With no one to trust, I turned inward and began to shut down.

I wanted to spare my mother the guilt, mostly because I knew she could not handle it. This fact was proven every time I showed or verbalized my grief. Aware of just how painful it was to talk about the fire, I never treaded on what was considered for a long time forbidden territory. I avoided the topic for my mother's sake; despite the accumulated curiosity and feelings of entitlement to the truth.

Throughout my life, I learned more facts in attempts to put into place the missing pieces myself. The topic was never something I brought up. Situations presented opportunities where bits and pieces were disclosed by my mother. I remained cautious with whether it was okay to search further for elaboration. My mother, the primary capsulate of information was consumed immensely with guilt, shame and blame so I waited for times when she brought up memories through her reflection of the fire.

Opportunities presented themselves during some of our intimate times together, such as when I was younger and my mother maintain my real hair. She would sit me down in the kitchen by the stove, with a heated iron comb to straighten the patch of hair left on the right side of my head that the flames did not claim, the only remnants of the physical beauty before my accident.

My mom longed to have back that unaltered beauty I once had, so much so that it became necessary to keep up what little that remained of my former self. I believed the remnants symbolized hope, that someday I would return to a mere version of who I once was. My mom would tell me how doctors could use the hair that was left to regenerate a new full growth. Or she took the hair when it was straight and long and comb it around my head, optimistic that I had enough to cover my head completely. She then would have me look in the mirror to see what I thought about the style, I did not want to kill her enthusiasm, but I was thinking, *No, this will never work.*

I believed as is true with the process of grief, my mom was in the stage of denial. Even though so much time had passed, my mom somehow believed that I would one day grow out of my scars and disfigurement to be reborn, healed, and be even more beautiful, that was how strong her faith was. Once a month she washed, straightened and finally braided two neat, shiny plaits that gave indication of the soft, straight, luscious textured hair I naturally had. She would say, "There is nothing too hard for my God to solve. I'm telling you, Neesha, God gave me a vision of what you will someday look like, and its one where all of your scars are gone and there are no results of you having been burned. He told me and I believe Him!" How could I refute God, so I just sat and listened, but in my mind, I thought, *I wish I could see what she saw*, and that God could make that prediction true now, because I hated what I saw in the mirror. Many times I got angry when she talked about this vision because she strongly believed it would come true, while I honesty knew it was impossible.

For a long time, my mom's vision played out in reoccurring dreams. In these dreams, I transformed into a beautiful girl, with all of the features that I wished I had. I was well liked, admired and sought after by guys. In some I had a boyfriend who possessed the qualities I wanted in a partner. I hated experiencing a good dream, such as when the perfect guy gave me his number, then suddenly the dream was abruptly interrupted by the alarm clock, or the urgency to run to the bathroom in the middle of the night. I tried to remember the ten digit numbers, but never could. Maybe it was the fact that I was overly desperate to find someone, that I actually allowed myself to somehow believe the guys in my dreams could be real.

The process of my mom maintaining my hair was always awkward and emotional for the both of us. My mother reminisced over what used to be her pride and joy—my physical beauty. My mom grieved over who I was and who I could have been as I grew older. She repeatedly told me how beautiful I was as a baby, and how everyone admired my beauty. For my mother, I honestly think the task of doing my hair was a reminder of the past and the inability to clearly see the gruesome reality. Even as she stood looking at my scared, patched scalp, she somehow remained hopeful that all of my beautiful hair would grow back as she combed what remained.

Her prideful bragging of me as a baby sometimes ended in emotional tears of grief. I just sat in silence and tried to be strong for her, by not sharing in the emotion over the same loss I grieved as well. I was unsure of how to respond to my mom, because I did not want to exacerbate her grief by adding how I truly felt, for fear of further pain I would have caused her. I wanted so badly to interject and inquire more about her memories of my former self, but I knew how difficult and agonizing that would have been for her to do. I did not want to inflict more pain that I imagined she had already immersed herself in. I just listened, smiled and laughed along with her, to lighten up the atmosphere. At the same time, I waited and eagerly listened in hopes that she might mention anything about the event that took place in the winter of January 1983.

I often felt the most profound sympathy and compassion for my mother for what she went through and the huge detriment she was left with; therefore, I never wanted to put more on her psyche than she was capable of handling. Instead, I just listened, and learned to keep my emotions neutral.

When my mom finished, she made note of how much my hair had grown in length since the last sitting. She then pulled out a hand held mirror from the drawer to show me the results, which were two long braids that twisted down to touch my right shoulder. We both smiled at the results, and my mom always kissed my head before I got up. I then retreated to the bathroom to get a close up look at my beautiful long hair in the mirror.

I stood admiring the half side of my head, pretending that it was an actual full head of hair, tossing the two braids around, getting lost in the moment. Eventually looking in the mirror long enough, reality suddenly came in clear focus and I would suddenly catch myself looking at the real me and becoming emotional, because I was so angry and disgusted at the image that stared back.

I convinced myself that I was in a bad nightmare, wanting to break the mirror hoping to see my true reflection, one that everyone liked, felt comfortable around, and did not criticize. The reflection that constantly stared back at me was too painful to look at. I did not like her, was ashamed of her and felt sorry that something so horrific happened to her, and she was given no choice but to endure the discomfort it caused. A part of my spirit broke down as I realized that the image of a beautiful girl with long beautiful hair was a mirage of someone I would never become, and who could never be fixed. As I stared harder and longer at the hideous disfigured image, the emotion I restrained while in my mother's presence instantly flooded my eyes. Holding back tears until I got to my safe place, I calmly walked to my room, gently closed and locked my door, then quietly and hysterically let it all out.

I learned to internalize my pain because my mom was just too fragile, she could not handle her own pain, let alone mine. My mom could easily detect when something was wrong with me. She had very keen instincts. Wanting to confide in her, I would quickly pre-screen my mom's emotional state to determine if I felt safe talking to her, and if so, I had to choose wisely what and how much to disclose.

Everything depended on her moods and what was affecting that mood. If she was inebriated and going through something that placed her in a bad emotional place and she could sense I was down by being reclusive and quiet, she initially appeared concerned, asking me to tell her what was going on with me. I could see the discomfort in her humbleness, I could hear the guilt in her relaxed voice, as she immediately searched for comforting words to say. Deceived by her gentle candor, I divulged. While doing so, I quickly felt a sense of regret, for having shared my feelings.

I expressed my sadness over not having friends, constantly being rejected, feeling left out, or anger over why me. In her altered moods, everything became about my mom. No matter my attempts to reframe from saying anything that pointed the finger, my mom always interpreted what I said to mean, "I blame you for why this happened to me!" Instead of comforting me in my time of need, she retaliated by either blaming me for trying too hard to make friends and to be accepted; or blamed me for causing myself pain by dwelling on things too long, instead of having faith, and just let my feelings go. My mom would say, "If no one wants to be your friend, so what, all that matters is that you have your family who loves you and God. Don't focus on pleasing nobody, trying to make friends."

If my mom found me days or weeks later still feeling the same way after having our conversation, her demeanor became even less sympathetic. To my mother, continuing to allow myself to be affected by my emotions demonstrated the doings of the enemy, somehow attacking her with guilt. Again my mom found ways to make everything about her. She wanted me to trust in God and in the word, and if I just applied it to the way I was feeling, then I would be healed, with no question, no doubt; regardless if the pain was very much still present. Having faith meant that there was no such thing as being in pain.

Then there were times, when I sat and was able to have deep heartfelt conversations with my mom, and she responded appropriately, making me feel I could tell her more. These conversations went surprisingly well, not at all as what I expected, despite her feeling unease with the topic. My mom would tell me how God heard everything, that he truly loved me and was there for me. These moments trumped the difficulties I had communicating with my mom. It was during these special moments, that I developed the deepest admiration, compassion and respect for her.

Even in my mother's worse state, God still was using her with a sound mind to minister to me. My mom was not a bad person, and God showed me the depths of her heart, through her love for Him. I never doubted that my mom loved me, and realized that her issues were far more complex. I knew that my mom loved me and expressed that love the only way she knew how, which was by teaching me the word of God, giving me the same words that healed her when nothing else could. I believed my mother was so strong, because my mother's strength was the only source that kept her from letting go and dying in her pain. My mom's faith is what kept her grounded and going, because to stay stagnated in her suffering was like a slow suicide. I believed her intentions were good when she told me to let go and trust in God. However, it was a lot easier said than done. Throughout my life, I struggled spiritually with thinking that I had disappointed and failed God, by staying in my pain too long, which developed into spiritual guilt that affected me greatly.

My mom gave me great encouragement, by reiterating how much God loved me, reminding me how Jesus suffered on the cross, and that He understood my suffering. Through conversations, my mom talked to me about the importance of loving my enemies even though they did not understand and treated me badly. My mom told me to always hold my head up high and to be confident in knowing that I am God's child. "He will make your enemies your step stool. The devil is a liar and has no claim and victory over *you*!" She ended by giving me passages to read, and prayed with me.

Praying was the solution to every problem. I walked away feeling better, confident and powerful over my situation, because of the unique bond God and I had. When my mother told me the story of Jesus, and that He too was treated harshly; I was drawn closer to learn that He too suffered immensely. My comfort came in identifying myself in Jesus, reading in the Bible that "many were appalled at Him… His appearance was so disfigured beyond that of any human being and his form marred beyond human likeness" (Isaiah 52:14). I felt less alone knowing that Jesus understood my pain, if no one else did. Despite the negative feelings I had about myself, I continued to pray to God, knowing that He heard all. He was there, assuring me "My loving daughter my purpose for you is greater than your agony, your suffering will lead you to that purpose." I came to understand my cries over my loss were validated through the story of Job, which is the book I have found humbleness despite so much loss and suffering in my life.

It was especially difficult during that time in my life, not having anyone to talk to who understood what I was going through, and no one who I trusted enough to bare my soul. It was the beginning of my life long experience with loneliness. As a child having to cope with the traumas in my life, I should have been in counseling and I should not have been expected to minimize, get over or not have my feelings validated. I learned early on to ignore and devalue my feelings; the only one I could trust with them was God. Therefore, I retreated inside of myself, because the world and the people around me did not provide the safety to be myself.

I had so many unanswered questions and felt confused with who I was, while trying to make sense of what happened to me. I began to feel negatively about myself and those feelings isolated and convinced me that my existence meant nothing. I began to internalize the reasons for the hurtful ways people treated me, blaming myself because of my appearance. Most of my life, I automatically believed everything bad, hurtful and unfortunate that happened to me, resulted from my appearance, which caused me to think in a very general, black or white, all or nothing way. I felt like a victim for much of my life. My negative thoughts were manifested from my irrational beliefs, brought on by training my eyes to only see myself through the lens of my pain.

I struggled with accepting the ugly image that stared back at me. I hated myself, I had no one to guide me through my pain, so I found comfort in my loneliness. I found peace and acceptance in my solitude, just me and the powerful spirit of a being that was the only presence who understood.

I wished I could see Jesus, and that His hand could come out of the far distance, in my darkest hour, when I felt the greatest of pain, place it upon me, just once, as a discernible sign that everything would be okay. Instead I cried and cried until my well was dry. I listened to gospel music to uplift my spirit, It helped for the times I was at home safe from the hatred I experienced from the outside world every day. Once I had to leave the confines of that covenant, was when I felt the feelings of worthlessness, self-hatred, and self-blame, for making people feel uncomfortable by my appearance.

For a long time, I was appalled at what I looked like. I purposely avoided every mirror in the house, and when I was forced to look at myself in one, I angrily criticized the image that stared back at me. I said things like, "You are so ugly, no wonder people laugh at you and don't like you, you scare people." Constantly seeing beauty on TV, in magazines and everywhere around me, only heightened my shame-fulness and insecurities. I was angry to be the odd ball, the chosen one forced to wear such ugliness. I desperately was looking for the zipper to this costume, because I no longer wanted to be in the skin I was in. I felt so uncomfortable in it.

My mom would tell me, "You're more than a conqueror!" But I did not want to fight a battle that seemed impossible for me to win. "Why me, God?" I asked. I was much too young to understand any of it, and all I wanted was to be a normal kid. This was all too hard to deal with, and I was angry and resentful that I had to wear such heavy armor that was too difficult to walk in.

While out in public, when people stared, I felt they absolutely had the right to do so, and to feel frightened by me. My appearance was egregious, one that was similar to horror villains, monsters and zombies. I was even picked on every day in school, taunted by one boy in particular, Maurice, who called me Freddie Kruger. I did not blame him, because my appearance did resemble the character of the cult classic Nightmare on Elm Street movies. Freddie Krueger was a serial killer who was punished by being burned to his death by the community he wreaked havoc on. I too felt my scars were a result of being punished. I knew this thought did not logically make sense, but I felt punished. The movie was one of my favorite horror films, but I felt guilt over watching it, because of the resemblance. When watching with other people, I was fearful of them making reference to me looking as scary and ugly as he.

Almost every day, I feared walking down the halls; whenever Maurice was around, he yelled out, "There goes Freddie! I saw you in your movie last night." Everyone around him laughed at me. I was in the second grade when he began teasing me, and it lasted throughout the fourth grade. I would come home crying to my grandma, who was staying with us, and just cried in her lap. What made the situation hard to believe was that Maurice had a very noticeable physical disability, he was just as different as I was. It did not matter, words hurt regardless of who said them.

I found myself in a chronic state of feeling insecure about my deformities when interacting with people. I walked around with my head down so no one could get a good glimpse of my face. I also styled my hair to cover the left side of my face, it was the side that looked most awkward to me. While in public spaces, especially where there were large crowds, I always felt most uncomfortable. Although I had developed a tough skin so the stares and comments would not cut so deep, they still hurt. It is a condition of living in my skin that will always affect me; having dealt with this negative attention throughout my entire life, over time I have come to cope with and manage. I knew I would have to learn how to confront the fear of interacting with people and knowing when to quiet that negative voice inside that convinced me no one liked me.

I was fearful and full of anxiety while out in public. I was determined however to have normal experiences, and do things I loved, such as shopping and going out. I scanned out situations before approaching them, trying to determine how to attract the least amount of attention drawn to myself. When traveling on buses, I tried to sit closest to an exit, so that I could get off as quickly as possible. I would have something within my possession, as a distraction from the initial impact of all eyes being on me. When getting on the bus, in a crowed store or walking pass a group of guys, I pretended to be on my cell phone, or fixing my clothes, to appear distracted and unaware of their stares and comments. This was an avoidant tactic that helped lessen the blows of people's cruelty, also to mentally and emotionally prepare myself for the overload of discomfort.

A sense of paranoia took over me, as I began to think the entire world was looking at me at once. The feeling was unbearable. I felt it was expected of me to maintain control over my emotions at all times. To somehow endure people's rancid looks and maltreatment without being emotionally affected. Therefore, I pretended not to notice people staring at me, while observing their stares through my peripheral.

I felt I had no right to confront people about how their comments and stares made me feel. I felt like a statute on display in a museum, my hideous appearance attracted so much attention. I felt when anyone hurt my feelings, mistreated and disrespected me, I had to minimize and dismiss the maltreatment; I felt I had to try to understand and empathize with the person's behavior. Not confronting and holding people accountable for their actions, in fact allowed for the behaviors to continue.

Many people blatantly stared directly in my face and did not care. I gave them something interesting to look at. I would just turn my face to look in a different direction, hoping the message was conveyed that their staring made me feel uncomfortable. Some turned away, while others just continued to look. I fought back even one tear from falling; in my head I was praying for the moment to quickly pass. I somehow found the strength to hold it all in until I got home to cry. I said horrible things to myself for causing the attention. I wanted to blame and be mad at the ignorant person responsible, but instead I turned and took it out on myself.

It is amazing how not even children are immune to ignorance. At a young age, I learned making others feel discomfort and fearful came at the expense of living in my truth. My new image was not acceptable to a society that is fixated on flawlessness. Having the courage to embrace my scars was frowned upon, and I was punished for it. It did not matter that I had survived one of the worse disasters known to happen to man. I was deemed a threat and discomfort to society, and placed among the marginalized, the outcasts, and the invaluable. My existence was null and void.

I was the cautionary warning of the worst fear—to be physically damaged. I was the example given to make people feel better about their plight. I was the elephant in the room, whose appearance always commanded unwanted attention. I learned that there was a hefty price to pay in order to be accepted.

I felt, because of my physical difference, the world put me on trial to prove that I was deserving to exist, to be included, and respected. I felt that I have always had to fight for many privileges that are innately a part of most people's social experiences, that are easily overlooked and taken for granted. Privileges such as meeting people without having to always explain why I look as I do, having personal privacy, and not having to constantly be subjected to inexorable staring. I came to realize, that a socially acceptable appearance affords societal privileges, which is the entitlement to many of life's rights of passages.

Being included is a basic human need. There is not one person who could ever say they do not desire or are motivated to building connections with other human beings, whether it be a romantic relationship, or having someone to have lunch with at work. Most people take being included for granted because they are already among the privileged group of the accepted, therefore they are naturally unaware that there are others who do not have the same privileges.

It hurt not to be included. Most of my social experiences have been negative, resulting in some kind of rejection. All of my life I have felt a sense of social awkwardness, because of my lack of social experiences. I saw myself as one way, but could always see how people's perception of me did not match. I knew this to be true because in many situations, no matter how I acted or spoke, I often got the feeling that people had their reservations about me. They would smile in my face, tell me how great I was, but it was in those awkward moments that I knew they would not keep in touch, call or further want anything to do with me. Most people did not want or knew how to be put in the uncomfortable situation of having to deal with the ugliness, and sadness, that for a very long time was my life. A deep insecurity made me feel fearful and intimidated around people, constantly vigilant of myself, my facial expressions, how I spoke, unconscious of that intimidation seeping through into my confidence. I have dealt with this truth all of my life; in every school, with every job, I knew everyone and everyone knew and liked me, but I did not fit in, there were a few exceptions, but mostly everywhere I went, no matter the setting, the loneliness and awkwardness always followed. Seldom was I invited, remembered, considered or included. I could not describe the pain and resentment then, but it is an uncomfortable reality that I have finally come to terms with. Even those whose burns have not affected their faces, can still experience a sense of normalcy, are accepted, and included. This fact led me to conclude that much of the social exclusion I have experienced is because of the discomfort my appearance and disfigurements elicits in people. Feeling and being excluded over the course of my life created the strong need and desire to be accepted, therefore, I was always motivated to meet that need. One is not fulfilled in their humanness without meaningful and positive connections with others. I struggled immensely with inclusion. When no one sees you, you can see everything.

Without a flawless face, I became nonexistent even while my presence was obviously known. I was forced to hide and be ashamed of my imperfections, because having the audacity to show my scars of survival, was too much truth that contradicted the superficial world most rather live in. Ads of all kind send messages that the truth is not good enough, but manufactured truth affords the highest confidence, leading many to buy into. I was made to feel guilty for making people deal with the underlying issues of their deeply rooted insecurities.

Who I am creates fear of the truth, to embrace the imperfect is to admit that it exists, and to confront a universal pain that society has gone to great lengths to ignore. I was made to feel ashamed of what I looked like because my appearance threatened people's sense of security, which is then inflicted upon me as if the insecurity is my own.

At a young age, I began to understand that when people looked at me, they did not see a survivor, they saw a monster who threatened their comfort and tolerance for suffering. Losing my beauty represented the worse tragedy to happen to the physical condition. The way many people look at me, it is as if I am not a person. I offend people by demonstrating the nerve to show my face in public instead of hiding. I remember riding on Septa and a man walked up to me and said, "You know your mother should be ashamed of herself for letting you out the house looking like that, you make people feel very uncomfortable looking at you." His mouth turned downward and his eyes rolled as he walked to the back of the bus saying, "It's a sin to be that ugly. Go home, baby girl, you're scaring people." I huddled in the corner of the seat I was sitting in and cried. I covered my face so that no one could see me. His words really hurt, and had me believing I was at fault. I felt humiliated, and wished that day I had stayed home.

I was learning how to be my own worst enemy. My mother's favorite saying is "the devil is a liar." It's true, he is, but I believe he gets too much credit. I believe people have a part to play in the cause of their own plight. I always took responsibility when I could see that what I was going through was a result of my own doings. I reflected the ignorance, dislike, disapproval and hatred of others toward myself.

In hindsight, I see the way I treated myself then was a result of the cycle of victimization that I inherited from my family's history with injustice. By continuing the cycle, I became comfortable sitting in the injustice seat as the victim. By hurting myself as I had allowed others to do to me, I denied myself the power to create my own justice. The way I looked at myself and the things I told myself were cruel. I had adopted the same hatred the world had of me. I thought what others saw in me had to be true since I received the same reactions and treatment from mostly everyone I encountered. I became very vulnerable and susceptible to any kind of attention. I desperately wanted to have connections especially among my peers. I was deeply insecure and became hyper vigilant over everything a person said and did. Anytime I experienced rejection, or failed to do something right or expected from people, I in turn punished myself and felt unworthy. It was extremely important to me that everyone with whom I met liked me, and when that did not happen, I beat myself up.

How wrong was my mom when she said I should not care if no one wanted to be my friend, I was just a child, all kids need social interactions to build interpersonal skills. By pleasing people, I was seeking acceptance by sacrificing and compromising all that I was for the approval and validation of others. Pity became a tool of manipulation I used when I could not naturally get people to like or notice me. I used pity to manipulate attention by having people feel sorry for me. Using pity allowed me to be the victim of an unjust cause. For a long time in my life, I honestly felt and believed I was a helpless victim. Powerless over my circumstances to no fault of my own, therefore never thinking that I could be responsible in any way for the ways people victimized me. For me it was the external of my outward appearance solely responsible for the pain, suffering, and unhappiness I experienced.

My self-esteem was so impaired that I allowed people to walk all over me knowingly. I felt I was at their mercy, and I that I did not have a choice in anything that happened in my life. I felt my life was already predetermined by my adversity. Many people with disabilities are portrayed as living in the confines of their adversity, with no room or many opportunities to truly excel, to surpass the limits of the sky. Although I held a negative perception of myself, there was a part of me that aspired for better in my life and wanted to be more than what the world saw me as: a hopeless product of my circumstance.

I did not know how to ask for what I needed and wanted, because I believed I was undeserving. I worried so much about what people thought of me, that I feared asking for the simplest things, not wanting to come off as being demanding. I feared upsetting and disappointing people. Anything that went wrong, even if it logically did not make sense, I still felt guilty that I was to blame. I believed I was undeserving of a voice, to be heard, seen or acknowledged. I felt my appearance took away all of my rights and entitlement as a human, because my experiences of people mostly made me feel subhuman.

At home I was condemned and afraid to speak. In general, when I spoke no one listened, or seemed interested in the things I had to say. I took whatever treatment I received from people and found ways to cope with it. It was the price I felt I had to pay not to be alone; not knowing just how great of a cost I would pay later for continuing to sell myself short, experiencing pain at my own expense.

My fears of not being accepted became greater than my ability to assert myself. At home, my mom imposed fear through intimidation if we asserted ourselves against anything she did or said, so I learned to be timid, quiet and out of the way. Outside of home, I feared making my peers angry and they react by saying mean and hurtful things, or worse, wanting to fight me. It was obvious that in my physical condition, I could not defend myself. Even if in the wrong I admitted and apologized.

I adopted the belief that I had to do everything within my power to get people to like me. I put great pressure on myself to be that person everyone liked, admired and wanted to be around. I had to always smile, I only spoke when spoken to, I tried not to do anything that would bring additional negative attention to myself, and tried to always be careful to never give anyone a reason to become upset with me. I also had to avail myself when people were in need and gave, even if I had to find a way to.

I was most conscious never to offend anyone or hurt another's feelings, knowing firsthand what the feeling was like. Whether aware or unaware, I did not forgive myself. To that person, their experience of me was now a negative one. I was already physically imperfect, I thought I had to make up for such a loss, by being perfect in aspects of myself that I could control. I believed I needed to be grateful and show appreciation for all things even if it was not what I liked or wanted. Even if it caused me pain, I believed lessening myself to put others first was required of me. I felt I had to earn the right to exist. I had no boundaries, no filter and no point to which I held others responsible for how they treated me. I had high and unrealistic expectations to be what I believed others expected of me.

Out of these behaviors, thoughts and feelings emerged a false self. My true self did not feel safe or trusted anyone enough to expose the gut-wrenching pain that existed within my core. I easily misled people to believe all was well; over time I became a master of illusions just to hide that I was unhappy, unsatisfied with life and the many times I considered ending it. I became the great pretender, not one, not even those closest to me really knew me. Even as an adult, I continued to feel uncomfortable with people's cold and sinister looks, every stare and comment still affected me the same as it had as a child. The tolerance of people's negative reactions were misconstrued as confidence. I had no choice but to endure, while pretending I was strong. I learned to fake it just to make it for so long, that there was a point in which I felt maybe I did not know what being strong and courageous really was. On the surface, my strength showed that I was healed, but for a long time, my pain was hidden way down in the deepest pits of me, so deep that it was still sore and sensitive to the touch. Like an ulcer, it remained open and difficult to heal.

I was not aware then and for a long time after, just how badly I was hurting myself. Many times I wished I was dead and had not survived. Through my thoughts, feelings and behaviors, I was as good as dead, not physically, but spiritually. I had allowed my physical self to diminish my spirit through all of the self-hatred, self-blame, self-defeatism, and self-deprivation, to the point of nearly killing her off. However, when I wanted to give up my spirit would not let me die. God knew I would come into so many tough times, that He ensure my spirit was strong enough to hold me when I could not stand for myself. When the loneliness clogged my throat and drowned my voice, my spirit prayed for me. It comforted and encouraged me until my voice became loud and strong.

My loneliness and lack of interpersonal experiences, became unbearable to deal with, therefore, I began to compartmentalize, using my vivid imagination, escaping to utopic places that helped me cope with the daily pains of my reality. I often saw myself no longer with a disfigured face. A famous plastic surgeon came and rescued this ugly duckling, by creating a flawless face that everyone envied. The best part was that I got justice from everyone who ever teased or harmed me. I believed fantasizing about what could be, helped strengthen my faith for a better future. In dreaming, there was hope, and hope is a derivative of faith, and with faith I always found the strength to go on.

There is never a problem too challenging for God to solve or a soul too far gone that He cannot revive. My soul was on life support, and it would take even more time before there were any signs of life. Slowly God breathed life back into me as He had done when I was born, and again after I neared death in the fire. I have come to learn through my experiences that suffering is necessary in order to live. It gives life meaning, which meaning in turn provides reasons for living. God gave me reasons to live, which saved my soul from dying every time I was certain that I was defeated by this fight. Never truly clear, but I understood as time went on and as I matured, God's reasons do not always need to be clear and known to man, just followed by faith.

Coming into myself would be a painful, disheartening, shameful and regretful struggle, but one that I would need to go through in order to be revived, transformed and made new. I have come to know the reason my life had been spared time after time, is because it serves a purpose greater than the validation and acceptance of man, but for the Glory of God. I would come to learn that I am who God says I am: VICTORIOUS!

CHAPTER 11

There's Nothing Special About Me

I HAD NO IDEA the life God was preparing me for. I have always had the propensity to be determined, and the challenges, struggles and perils that I faced in my life would require this great strength. Soldiers in an army prepare for battle by undergoing vigorous training, being put through countless exercises to develop and sharpen themselves to effectively fight. So was I, at a young age, God was beginning to show me aspects of myself, that would become essential to living a functional life. He used my schooling as a platform to showcase the many skills, talents and capabilities, that defined the person I would become and essential to my independence and success. This phase of my life marked the beginning of everything that is my life. I often think of how differently my life could have turned out were it not for being determined to push against the barriers placed before me.

From the moment I started attending school, my mother enrolled me in schools to accommodate students with special needs. I vividly remember the days of riding on the wheel chair accessible yellow Bird "Cheese bus" that took me to and from the Widener Memorial school for children with physical and mental disabilities. Sitting in the seat nearest to the window in the third row, I astoundingly watched the various daily hustles and bustles of the world as we drove through parts of Philly, wanting to someday be a part of the fast pace confusion.

Somewhere around eight or nine years old, in the second or third grade, I remember feeling out of place and held back. I felt my place was to be out in the world and not hidden from it. The long rides consisted of picking up other disabled students along the way, those in wheelchairs, those who walked with crutches and walkers, some of whom who walked with limps and hops. There was a school bus attendant on board, who stepped off the bus to meet those needing aide just to walk the several feet from their door step to the bus. I felt as if I did not fit in with the convoy of those with special needs, because I did not feel I had any. I was well aware that I looked different, that I had to learn to do things differently, and even that it took longer for me to get things done, but I was still very much capable.

My mother enrolled me in Widener because she felt the need to protect me from the ferocious teasing, tormenting and insensitivities of children and even adults who knew no better. Although I was comfortable and accepted by my peers at Widener, my mom believed that would not be the case at a "regular school." She was afraid that it would be difficult for me to adjust and handle the scrutiny. My mother did what she believed was best for me at that very sensitive time, being so young. In a regular school setting, I would have been exposed to amplified attention, and she could not be there to defend me.

Before attending Widener, I attended John B. Kelly in the Wissahicken section of Philadelphia from kindergarten through second grade. This school accommodated, both children with special needs and those without. I do not know the reason for the switch, but I know that as I got older, my mom did not feel too comfortable with the idea of me going to a regular school.

I entered Widener in the early '90s at which time, I had to repeat the second grade. I was still having surgeries and lagged in many stages of my childhood development as well as academically. I was just learning how to do many things that children my age had mastered. I was held back to repeat the second grade because of many physical setbacks. These setbacks affected me academically, having difficulty holding pencils because I was unable to grip them, which delayed writing both handwritten words and cursive writing. With much help from teachers and persistence on my part, I eventually learned to write print and cursive.

Learning to write cursive was the most challenging because it required hand motions with streaming the letters cohesively without interruption that posed difficult, because of limitation with range of motion and dexterity in my right hand. I used my right hand for writing and mostly everything else. My mental capacity to learn and retain information put me at the head of my class, and deemed me a very bright and intelligent child.

I remember having to take a plethora of aptitude tests, showing skill and agility over a wide spectrum of things ranging from memory, comprehension, interpretation and many others. I remember sitting with instructors in trailers designated for administering these kinds of tests, where I was shown inkblot cards and asked to tell what I made of the shapeless images, build and arrange colored blocks, listen and respond to sounds heard through earphones, raising my hand upon every sound I heard, to putting beads on string, drawing, matching images and so on.

I enjoyed being tested, and did not feel the overwhelming anxiety of test taking. They were not much of a challenge for me, as I achieved and completed everything put in front of me. I remember feeling proud of myself for what I had accomplished. I believed there was nothing that I could not do. My teachers were amazed at my abilities and my eagerness to learn.

I loved school, I could not wait to get to school every day to see my friends and to be in the presence of my teachers. My second grade teachers, Mrs. Wright and Mrs. White, were the best teachers I had in elementary school. Not only was school another escape for me, but each day was filled with something new and exciting to learn.

Widener was special in that it provided many opportunities to its students and their families. Contributions and programs from organizations and sponsorships helped to grant wishes making memorable moments for children who had already gone through so much. The Variety Club sponsored such events like the Special Olympics and the make-a-wish foundation gave out lots of toys during the holidays and even made possible, trips to Disney World.

I remember one Christmas, making a wish list and receiving every toy on it. The school really went to great lengths to make the students feel special. More importantly, the school gave students the chance to thrive, break barriers and to discover their potential despite having a disability. Widener was special in that it brought out the best in its students. Widener taught me that I was not limited by my physical disabilities, only by the obstacles I chose to let limit me. Its approach was simple – to give students the tools and the encouragement needed to excel academically and to gain independence.

While at Widener I learned how talented and competitive I was. There were two art contests in particular that exposed my hidden talent as an artist. My art teacher was very impressed by my work and how creative I was, seeing my potential she took the initiative to enter me into two art contest. The first, I was not a winner, but my work was recognized among hundreds of talented students from across the country. I was excited that my painting was considered and well liked. I was fascinated with painting in bright, illuminating colors and drawn to painting mostly landscapes and flowers.

The painting submitted was of a dark background representing night, with florescent green trees whose leaves popped off the page. A turquoise, iridescent stream of water under a wooden bridge with bundles of bushes painted in hues of pinks, violets and blues, with dark opaque shadows of two people standing in the middle of the bridge. I loved being innovative and thinking outside of the box.

My art teacher bragged about my potential, and when I was in the seventh grade, she entered me into a regional art contest where contestants were asked to paint a portrait of someone who influenced them and the chosen's career. I chose to paint my mother, and her esthetic as a hair dresser. I painted her and in the background I painted all kinds of hair styling tools and accessories. I was proud to honor my mother in such a way, she was good at what she did.

Only a few students in the city were chosen as winners. The prize included a savings account and a fifty-dollar savings bond with Beneficial Savings Bank. Months passed when I was notified that I was a winner. In addition to the savings account and the savings bond, each of the winners had the honor of having their portraits displayed in the bank. I was so proud of my accomplishments. My growing accomplishments gave me confidence in myself, which compensated for the lack of confidence and esteem, because of my appearance.

From then on, I was bit by the competitive bug. I remember filling my room's wall with certificates and awards of all kinds, and bringing home numerous trophies. Josh and I would see who could bring home the most trophies. Eventually both of our accomplishments over our school years evenly took up all of the space in the living room. I loved showcasing my talent for all to see, but it was also a way to prove myself. It was an advantage to all of the disadvantages that made it very difficult for me to be noticed. I thought, if I was the best at something, then people would be forced to respect me for my intellect and skill. Focusing on my talents somehow took away the pain. No one saw my scars. They saw me for what I could do, in many cases better than those with no physical limitations. I learned to use my creative talents to channel my pain and express myself.

Writing became another important and creative outlet for me. In the seventh grade, I won a computer that was raffled by my school, as they were making room for new ones. Winning the computer was again like winning the lottery. Owning a computer was a luxury my mother could not afford. The day I brought it home, I remember never wanting to leave my room. It was an earlier edition of a Macintosh, Apple computer, that took floppy disks. As an added bonus, I also received an outdated printer. I had decided at that moment I was going to write all kinds of stories and, eventually become a renowned author.

My first short story was called the *Surrogate*, a story about a beautiful woman who had everything she every wanted, the house, money, clothes, and a gorgeous husband, but she was unable to bare him a child. She was angry and perplex that she was faced with this hardship, considering beauty had always gotten her any and everything she wanted. She believed only good things happened to beautiful people. She did not have the nicest personality, matter of fact it was her greatest and most ugliest defect. Her husband feared her, but overlooked her personality because she was so beautiful, and keeping up their image was most important to him. He wanted her to desperately have a girl, so she too would be flawlessly beautiful.

Then one day, the couple went to see a doctor who informed them that the wife would never be able to conceive, and that they should consider alternative options. When the doctor explained the concept of a surrogate, both the husband and wife agreed the idea was perfect. The surrogate would be inseminated and later reside with the family for the duration of the pregnancy, during which time she would be cared for at no expense to the surrogate. The woman was no match to the beauty of the wife. The wife purposely sought a less than fair woman, because she did not want anyone who looked half as good as she did or better.

After the surrogate moved in, the family bonded for a while, but the wife began to show her true colors. She began treating the surrogate the same as she did her husband, by being selfish, mean and un-empathetic. The wife thought everyone was memorized by her beauty and that she did not have to change. The husband and the surrogate began spending much time together because the wife worked; they bonded, having shared the same feelings of beratement and insignificance by the wife.

They eventually fell in love, and the husband was surprised by his feelings for the surrogate because he was not attracted to her physically. This confused him even more, because he equated love only with beauty. He could not however deny his feelings. Months later, the surrogate was in labor and had given birth to a baby girl. The wife cursed the surrogate, and blamed her because the child came out looking less beautiful than the wife, and she cried to her husband that she feared what life their daughter would have, being less than attractive. The husband told his wife that she should be ashamed of herself for being so shallow. "Looks are not everything." He then turned and kissed the surrogate. He divorced his wife and married the surrogate and they raised their daughter happily together.

I had always been told that I was mature far beyond my age. Going through and experiencing all that I had definitely gave me a different experience than that of my peers and most adults. Through my adversity and persecutions, as a result, I saw and experienced the world through a different lens. I was at the age where I was liking boys, seeing my peers talking about boys and having boyfriends. I dealt with the pain of not being noticed and having those normal experiences of being liked in my writing.

I saw the huge influence beauty had on being in relationships. I felt because of this, being in one would always be out of my reach. I sat in my room and wrote all kinds of short stories and poems about being in relationships, heartbreak and about the things that should count in a relationship. I had this knowledge and incredible insight about love and relationships, but had never been in one. I was writing from a place of observation of the good and bad from the world around me. I always had a strong sense of awareness about myself, which made me feel very much ahead of my time and the people around me.

I watched movies and saw other people, even my mom in relationships and wanted to experience the same magical bliss. That one comment made by Steven years ago, would haunt me for a very long time. Those words kept me cognizant that love may never come my way, because I did not possess the physical beauty deserving of it.

Throughout my time at Widener, I made lots of friends, people who I bonded with incredibly without ever focusing on their differences. I grew even closer to the circle of friends in my class because we all moved up grades as a cohort. Our class size was small. There were about ten of us: Brandon, Karl, Linh, Omar, Pedro, Danny, Nicole, Juan, then Ashley came along in the third grade and Nahara in the fifth grade.

As much as we were good friends, we also experienced the same drama as close friends do. Ashley was a girl with a coco colored complexion, who and had a wide smile that exposed all of her gaped white teeth. Ashley had Sickle Cell Anemia and had to permanently wear a breathing tube in her nose, attached to a portable oxygen tank, which she could not be without for long periods of time. The machine became a part of her, it traveled everywhere she went. Ashley had been told that she would not survive through her childhood because of the severity of the blood disease. Her courage and will to live was as strong as her personality. Ashley had to undergo routine blood transfusions throughout the course of her life; I believe it was her stubborn will to fight giving her life longevity that surpassed the short span doctors predicted.

Immediately, I did not like Ashley because she came in having the advantages of a newcomer, by stealing my thunder and taking attention away from me. I was popular among my circle of friends, but felt competition once she came. Ashley was pretty, and all the boys in my class liked her. Even the upper classmen boys who I had big crushes on, all talked about how they wanted to get with Ashley.

One of my classmates, who I had known before coming to Widener named Karl, had become one of my best friends in school. We were always together, so much so, that he became my first crush and first unofficial boyfriend in the third grade. Our relationship was innocent, we shared our snacks only with each other, held hands, and held seats for the other.

Karl's disability affected the muscles and joints in his feet and legs and the way he walked. However, I did not see a disability when I looked at Karl, I saw a caramel boy with dark eyes, bushy eyebrows, a chipped tooth, and a handsome face. I loved everything about Karl and could not wait to get to school to be around him. My heart sank at the sight of him and at the sound of his voice.

Our "relationship" was proven to be trivial and juvenile because as soon as Ashley unpacked her school supplies and stored them underneath the wooden toped desks we set in, he had claimed her as his girlfriend. I remember Valentine's Day we were getting ready for our class party, I was so excited to exchange my card with some Disney character on it that read "Happy Valentine's Day To: Karl, from: Tanisha."

Then in an instant, my world was rocked and capsized as I stood in sheer shock, watching Karl give Ashley a small, red heart-shaped box of assorted chocolate candies, and not me. I was hurt and felt as if my life was over and there was no pain greater than that of my first heartbreak. There was nothing cute about the anguish I felt from a supposed "puppy love," it was more like a pit-bull had took hold of my heart and ripped it to shreds. I remember crying my eyes out for days, every time I heard Baby Face and Pebble's "Love Make Things Happen," which was in heavy rotation on the radio. I recorded the song on a cassette tape and played it over and over, crying as if I had discovered upon the deceit for the first time every time the song played. I thought I would never get over him, but their relationship did not last, I got over it, and the three of us became very good friends.

The small class size allowed for us all to bond, and moving from grade to grade together, further strengthened and solidified our friendships with one another. Omar was the Casanova, he had a swagger style and voice that made all the girls from other classes adore him. Brandon was the joker of the bunch, but easy to make laugh, which we made jokes or told stories just to hear him laugh. He was very intelligent and had the softest heart. Brandon and I also knew each other before attending Widener. Pedro was the Latin athlete, who loved playing sports, he was on every team and was very laid back. Nahaira integrated into our circle quick, although she was a newcomer as well. She was Latin and had long beautiful thick black curly hair. Nahaira was smart, and wise beyond her years. Nahaira hated how most of the boys were so immature, so she was always putting someone in their place for approaching her wrong.

Linh was a cute Chinese girl who was the smartest person I knew that was so young. We were the closest out of the crew. We did everything together. I admired her intellect, especially in math, since that was the subject I struggled most in. I remember we used to play a math game called "24." It was played in groups of four or less and the goal was to use the numbers and symbols to equal 24. It was amazing how Linh was always the first to get 24. Linh was extremely good at math, she played in 24 competitions and came back a winner every time. For about six years, we all became more like brothers and sisters. Unfortunately, we would experience a great loss of one our sisters; Ashley had succumb to her disease, and died in her mid-teens. It was the first lost I had experienced, and she will always be missed.

Toward the middle of the school year, plans were underway for me to transfer to a "regular school" after completing my eighth grade year. I had been talking with the school counselor, Peggy Burger, who often met with me to discuss and plan for this major life changing event. My mom and I began exploring the idea more, and discussing in depth the pros and cons. Many of my teachers and staff, including Mrs. "Missy" Pitts my gym teacher, believed attending a "regular" school would be better for me. Mrs. Pitts was the most honest person I came across, and she was a no nonsense woman, but that was because she cared so much about her students. She wanted us to surpass our own expectations to discover our true purpose, undefined by a disability.

During my entire time at Widener, I was preparing for the moment when I would step into the real world and be able to handle it. All of my experiences had more so emotionally and mentally prepared me. I was given the weapons that I would eventually have to use to fight back against persecution. I gained the momentum to face the criticisms and discriminations that awaited me on the cruel outside, by learning who I was and what I was capable of. Widener taught me how to hold my own in the "real world," that I was just as qualified as anyone else, and I was capable of doing whatever I set my mind to. Widener allowed me the opportunities to find my talents, myself, and the powerful strength deep within my adversity.

Widener taught me to be proud and confident in my abilities. I learned to never take anything for granted, and that the word "disability" was an illusion. It represented a loss that inhibits functioning. What many do not realize is that when one loses functioning in one area, they gain more strength in other functioning areas. They may have to learn to do something differently, but with much determination, they learn to master a skill, sometimes better than someone who is fully able. My heart was trained to see and appreciate adversity. To accept and embrace its beautiful aspects and the splendors of its resiliency.

Widener taught me never to give up on myself, and how to persevere. Whenever the thought seeped into my mind, that I could not do something, it was in that very doubt that I told myself I could. I would think of all of the students I came across, who did extraordinary things, such as running in the school's annual Special Olympics races. I witnessed kids faced with challenges greater than mine, falling but getting back up to run, determined to finish the race. Even if they were the very last on the track, they eventually crossed it with the smile of a champion. At Widener, I saw the greatness and beauty of diverse people. The kinds of people that society separates itself from, deeming unfit, worthless and incapable. It is because of these experiences that I have the level of compassion, empathy, appreciation for people of all kinds; and why I have a high level of tolerance and deep understanding for human suffering. God turned me toward facing my adversity, instead of away from it, so that I could come into acceptance of not only myself, but others.

Academically I was excelling, but my counselor and many of my teachers thought I needed more of a challenge, which Widener could not offer me. I agreed that attending a regular school for high school would be best for me, after hearing similar stories of students who had also left to attend regular schools or who graduated. Many shared how they were academically unprepared for the high schools or even community colleges they attended. Hearing this strengthen my decision to leave.

I believed Ms. Peggy always had sight of my potential, and was waiting as I approached high school to encourage me to leave. Every time I went to her office, changing schools was mostly the topic of conversation. She talked to me about different schools that she thought would be a perfect fit, somewhere that was small and accessible for me to get around. Ms. Peggy was an easy going woman, short in stature and had a cleft lip, which slurred her speech when she spoke. I marveled at her imperfection as she was a model of the success I hope to become.

One day at one of our scheduled sessions, Mrs. Burger set me in her office and discussed with serious consideration, finally making the transition from Widener to a "regular" High school. I was ecstatic and after much brain storming, strategizing and scouting out possible schools that would accommodate my needs, the decision had been made. My long-awaited dream was becoming a reality.

My biggest concern was if I stayed at Widener, I would not have the opportunities of experiencing the world in its raw truth. I understood the reasons for my mom wanting to protect me, but I was thinking long term. I believed that I needed to have real social experiences, and high school would be the perfect time in my life to prepare me for the blunt realities of the world. Going to a good school that challenged me academically, would truly prepare me to succeed in college and beyond.

I could not hide from the world forever, because I knew there would come a point in life when I would have no choice but to face it. I was ready for whatever life threw at me. I felt strong enough to handle all of the things my mom feared would destroy me. I was becoming accepting of having to fight, still not comfortable with having to wear the heavy armor, but I had come to a place of acceptance that I had no choice but to prepare. If I had to fight, then I was going to prepare myself for victory. I claimed it, and God had already shown me through my accomplishments thus far that the battle was already won. I was a one-man army lead by the greatest general known to man. "Thou I walk through the valley of the shadow of death, I will fear no evil (Psalm 23:4)" I knew that God was with me in this journey that I could only fight alone and with that comfort, I was equipped and ready. High school, here I come!

CHAPTER 12

The Terrible Truth About High School

AFTER MUCH DEBATE AND canceling out, the school I chose was not any of the ones on the top of my list. Matter of fact it was not on my list at all. Bartram High School was my neighborhood school that was known for its violence and delinquency. I had known kids in my neighborhood who attended Bartram and was told by many, the school was known for having a notorious reputation. My mother was convinced Bartram would be best because of its location, I needed a school that had an easy commute.

During my last year at Widener, I had begun taking public transportation, again this was an idea that my mother was completely against. "Child, you have absolutely lost your mind?" No! I was thirteen and I could understand her concern, I was too vulnerable to travel the vicious streets alone. My reasoning was the same, I would have to eventually learn. Since my new school did not come with any special accommodations, such as school bus service, it was the perfect time to gain another level of independence. I admit that I was scared out of my mind, but I could never show my mom.

I convinced my mother that I was capable of handling my own after missing the school bus one day. She hated me missing school, so the opportunity presented itself at the perfect time. My mom set me down and taught me how to navigate the Septa trolley and subway system. She mapped out a precise route assuring that I would get there. My mother made me go straight to the school's office to call her, letting her know that I made it there safely. Once she heard my voice she was relieved, and proud that I had gotten myself from Southwest Philly to Olney all by myself. After that day, my mom allowed me to take the bus to school every Friday. I loved and took full advantage of my new found independence. I planned trips to the movies, to see my dad on the weekends, and shopped on Woodland Avenue as well as the popular Gallery in the city. By the time I started Bartram, I was very familiar and comfortable with taking the bus to school.

Bartram was such a large system, that it was divided into several annexes to accommodate its enormous student population. The main annex of Bartram had the largest enrollment, so that was definitely out of consideration. I knew I wanted to go to college, so I was looking for an annex that had some kind of college preparation focus. I was also interested in communications as a major. I was told by many that I had a great phone voice, and a bubbly personality. I was a talker and truly loved being artistic, therefore, I saw myself as a radio personality.

I was also looking for something small where I could get the individualized attention I knew I would need to catch up in subjects that I struggled in, particularly math. I wanted a school that valued academic growth, and also implemented creativity into their curriculum.

I visited many of the annexes; although they had the small class sizes, and appeared to have a lively personality, I was growing worried that non would be what I was looking for. I feared having to go to a school where I did not feel comfortable, that was too big and intimidating. Long and behold, the third annex I visited was the annex that would become my academic home for the next four years.

Bartram Motivation Center was located in the Penrose section, deep in southwest Philly. It was a small school nestled within the suburban cul-de-sacs near the Philadelphia airport. I had been given a tour of the three story building, which included the basement, were additional classrooms and the lunch room were located. Something within, instantly told me that I was in the right place. As I passed by classrooms in session, I noticed the small sizes, and envisioned myself in them. I loved that Motivation was accessible, there were only two sets of stairs at each end of the hallway. Not only was the building easy to navigate, it was also accessible regarding the daily commute to and from home. There were several shuttle busses that ran in the mornings and immediately after school. The shuttles either connected to the 36 trolley, or express shuttles that transported students directly to the main annex, Motivation and the last stop was the Communication annex less than a mile away.

My heart was definitely set on attending Motivation. The Communication annex was more technologically hands on, where I could get direct experience with surveying different aspects of the communications field, but Motivation had more of an intimate feel, the students seemed less angry and more motivated than the other annexes I visited. It had an excellent reputation, with students graduating and being accepted in high ranking colleges. Immediately after the tour, I told my mom that Motivation was my choice and just like that I was enrolled to attend in the fall.

I was so excited, unable to sleep the night before the first day of a new beginning. I laid thinking of all of the endless possibilities, making friends, going on prom and countless other events that were known to be a part of the high school experience. I was confident that I would make friends and be accepted once people saw that I was fun to be around; that once they took the time to get to know me, they would realize I was just like them.

In preparation to make the transition easier, my counselor and mother both thought of holding an assembly, an informal meet and greet with the students and teachers to tell my story in hopes of making everyone comfortable around me. I told my mother that although it was a great idea, it was unrealistic. I further explained that I would not be able to gather people around everywhere I went, college, a job, to explain myself, just to ease the discomfort my appearance caused. The real world was uncomfortable, hard and I had to begin to learn to be tolerant of it. I wanted people to want to know me genuinely, I did not want to be seen as being different or given special treatment. I especially did not want anyone to have pity and befriend me because it was the kind thing to do after hearing my story. I wanted people to gravitate toward me naturally.

The endless stream of thoughts kept me wide awake the night before school started. The morning of, I awoke eager to start the first day. I approached it fearlessly and with confidence that I was in control of my destiny, and there was no amount of nerves that could rattle me to renege my decision. I felt strong and courageous, I had no idea what to expect or how people would react to seeing me, but I was used to being criticized and judged so it was nothing that I was too phased by. I believed high school kids were more mature than younger kids, who had no filter, it was the least of my concerns, I was ready to take on whatever came my way.

It was September 1997 when I entered into high school, I just turned fifteen that summer, and was entering into the ninth grade. It was true that I watched too much TV, I was looking forward to the whole high school experience playing out just as they did on some of my favorite television shows such as *Saved by the Bell*, *Sweet Valley High*, and *90210*. Minus all of the soap opera drama, I was very excited about attending the prom and developing lifelong friend-ships that are often established while in high school.

I was beginning to understand more about myself and what was required of me to make people feel more at ease around me. I came to realize that my personality was critical in determining how people perceived me. Having a friendly demeanor eased the discom-fort and awkwardness people usually experience at the first sight of my appearance. I understood the difficulty, it is a part of the human condition to experience initial shock at something that is completely unfamiliar, and unexpected.

The reality is that my appearance is shocking, it is something that will forever be a grounding truth. I eventually came to learn how to predict people's reactions and level of comfort, within the first few seconds of initial eye contact. I came to realize just how much power I had in this minuscule amount of time to control one's immediate impression of me. I knew that I had to exude confidence, smile, have positive body language and great eye contact. Sometimes initiating conversation has been proven to help people feel more comfortable and is in many cases, the thin line between whether most accept or reject me.

This was a process that took time for me to truly understand and master. Again, I had to be tested and had to go through more self-exploration before getting to this level of comfort. I had to first feel comfortable with myself to then help others feel comfortable around me.

I understood it would take time for people to feel comfortable to approach me, but I also knew it required some effort on my part to facilitate that comfort. I knew once someone took the time to get to know me, they would be able to see past my scars and noticed that I was a great person to be around. I also knew my circumstances required extreme patience to allow such relationships to transpire. I understood and empathized with the delicacy of the process, that people first had to develop a level of sensitivity before they could see that I was not a threat.

Through coming to embrace and accept what I looked like, I began to understand I could not always take myself seriously, or expect other's to. I had to have enough confidence to facilitate comfort in others. Many people found it surprising when I joked lightly about myself and what happened to me, or openly talked about my insecurities and struggles as they related to my physical. I have learned the importance of pointing out the elephant in the room by initiating the conversation of what happened, when I could see someone struggling to inquire. Usually I find that once I speak candidly about myself in a way that speaks "I am okay with me," I see it lessens the stiffness and anxiety in the person, and they too then become "okay with me."

The kids at my school took to me well, although I had not made many friends, I knew it would take some time. By the end of my freshmen year, I became friends with a girl in my home room class named Clare, and we developed a short friendship. She was smart, but was condescending. She often belittled me and made me feel everything I said was stupid. My friendship with her ran its course fast, as I introduced her to a close friend and discovered that she was using me to get to him. Our friendship fizzled after she transferred to another school, which I was relieved about because she really was not a good friend to me.

Zeke, who was also friends with Clare, but someone with whom I found easy to befriend, as his heart was just as loving, caring, and open as mine. Zeke was tall and biracially beautiful. His eyes were pure and his smile exposed the deepest dimples; but was a smile that made me fall in love with him over and over, (I was not in love with him romantically, but spiritually). Zeke protected me with the concern and threat of a brother, but he was the gentlest guy I knew. Zeke especially had trouble understanding how people could be so cruel as he witnessed many times, while in public together just how ignorant people were to me. It always bothered him to the point where Zeke was ready to act in my defense. I think we gravitated towards each other because we understood the pain felt from being different, experiencing rejection and attacks from those who were unaccepting of our differences. Experiencing bullying by peers in our school, Zeke transferred to another school and again I lost another good friend.

Going into my sophomore year, I was optimistic that it would be a more eventful and promising year. The first semester was difficult. Clare and Zeke were gone and I was on my own. My homeroom class consisted of the same group of kids throughout the entire four years. Toward the end of my freshmen year, I had gotten to know everyone in the class, but none of whom I had formed any serious friendship with. I had known everyone by name, but I was still much like a fly on the wall. There were one or two who talked to me just to pass the half hour of time away until the bell rung. It was mostly small talk about common interest, such as TV shows, a shared favorite musical group, or other interest. By conversing, I thought that I was making connections, but after the bell rung and everyone disbursed into their cliques, I realized I was still without friends.

On most days, I sat watching the engagement in the room, as it appeared everyone had someone to talk to except me. I sat there, hoping someone noticed I was excluded and invite me in. When there were general conversations, I felt somewhat included, because it allowed for anyone to chime in. Putting forth effort, I gave my input here and there, and I felt good when someone agreed with, laughed at or elaborated on anything I had to say, but again after the conversations switched, I sat alone.

Lunch time was difficult for much of the year before Clare and I became friends, and the first part of my sophomore year. Everyone had friends or cliques, and lunch was the time to meet up to talk about the latest gossip. I spent much of my time sitting alone in a corner or somewhere where there were not many people. I purposely scouted out isolated places, just to sit and feel sorry for myself. Sitting alone time after time began to make me feel deep sadness, so much so, that I would sometimes go off into the bathroom and cry, or sit at the lunch room table in the corner staring down with my head covered so no one could see me cry. It was very difficult, I did not have the patience or understanding as I had in my freshmen year. So much time had passed and I was still without friends.

There were times when I walked passed boys, and could hear hurtful comments made. Once while in a chemistry class, we were using Bunsen burners for a project and I was joking around, placing my hand above the flame, telling someone that I was not afraid of fire, then a guy seated in front tells another guy out loud, "You would think that she learned her lesson playing with fire." The guy standing beside him began busting out laughing, and I sat feeling humiliated and embarrassed.

Socially, I was still finding it difficult to fit in, not just in school, but among my peers in general. I was still trying to cope with my unique identity, while constantly surrounded around pretty girls. Looking at so many images of beautiful, flawless women on TV, further created a deep insecurity complex. When I looked at myself in the mirror, I no longer viewed myself as a hideous monster, but I still was not comfortable with what I looked like. When I looked at myself in the mirror, I now focused on areas of myself that I hated and wished I could change. I became fixated on looking at pretty girls and wished I had aspects of them that I believed guys found attractive. I envied several girls in my class, because they were beautiful and boys were always in their faces. I looked at them, believing their lives were fulfilled, perfect, and effortless.

This faulty belief made sense in my head, because living life unattractive was lonely, and very difficult. Beauty has a striking appearance that brings about intimidation. Beautiful females understand that they have power, and standing in their light, I felt inadequate, inferior and void. I felt extremely uncomfortable in their presence and believed they could easily sense my insecurities. I believed pretty girls constantly overlooked me, because I was undeserving, and did not possess the likeness to qualify for the elite group.

Day after day, I felt more alone than the day before. Feeling helpless in attracting friends, I reverted to using pity to manipulate sympathy I believed would attract friends. If someone noticed me crying or noticed that something was wrong, they would come over to me and ask if everything was okay; initially I said "yes", but then after being asked if I was sure, I belted out my pain and said, "It is just hard that no one sees me, talks to me, or wants to be my friend." That would be all I needed to say for someone to then sit with me and comfort me. For a few days after, the same person may have sat with me if we had the same class, or made sure to talk to me in homeroom, or walked with me to the bus stop, but their time was always short, and after a while things returned to normal.

When one is lacking in something, especially if it is a deficit of a human basic need, and they have been deprived of that need for so long, then their only focus is to meet that need. I desperately wanted friends, to feel included and to be a part of, but felt I had to give more of myself to prove to people that I was worthy. I thought if I wanted it, I had to get it, or else it would not come.

It is human instinct to seek human contact, to seek a response, any response. Eventually, in the continued absence of responses, helplessness sets in and soon after comes despair. Left alone and rejected, I kept trying and trying to seek affection until natural efforts burned out. I then found myself in survival mode, taking anything that looked like acceptance.

In high school I started buying attention, I offered to buy kids lunch, go exceedingly out of my way to accommodate and flatter people, be extra friendly, and always made sure I had things to offer or give away, to appear as being the nicest person who was a good friend or best friend quality. I sought out the kids who looked down or sad, and always found right words to cheer them up.

If someone shared something personal, I looked to encourage, compliment, and even give them good advice that I should have been telling to comfort myself. If it was someone's birthday, or a special occasion, I went out of my way to buy them a card with a beautiful message in it, or a small gift. I put so much thought and work into the presentation of the gifts I gave, assuring myself that the gift would also buy their friendship. I knew every time I was taking a huge risk, but was sure every time would be different, but each time never was. My motives were deceitful, and my expectations were unrealistic. Pleasing people and compromising myself became a character defect that would take a long time to shed. Although the end result was the same every time I put myself out there attempting to please people, It did not stop me from thinking that the next person would be different.

By the second semester, of my freshmen year, my situation had changed tremendously. I now was included in a circle of girls, who I could call friends. Finally, I felt complete. It was not a formal inclusion or something that happened over night. Chanel was a girl who I not only went to school with, but we lived on the same block. We had always spoken to each other in passing, but never hung out until high school. Since we lived on the same block and went to the same school, it made sense that we traveled to and from school together. In the mornings, she walked down the street to my house and waited for me as I rushed to get myself together and out of the door on time to catch an uncrowded charter bus.

I was happy to have someone to travel with to school. Large crowds, especially teenagers, made me feel uncomfortable. Kids are cruel, but kids from the rough environment I grew up in were vicious. They said what they wanted, did what they wanted and dared anyone to have a problem with it. Being aggressive, insensitive, having a nonchalant and repugnant attitude were characteristics of living in areas perforated with crime, violence and intimidation. Having someone to travel with helped with the anxiety I constantly felt while traveling alone.

Chanel came from a large family too, she was the oldest of three brothers that included a set of twins and a sister who was the youngest. She lived with both her parents and directly across the street from her grandmother and aunts who were also twins. What I admired about her family was that they all were extremely close and shared the responsibilities of taking care of each other. Chanel's family was grounded in their Christian faith, they faithfully attended church, and had a keen knowledge and obedient spirit. Chanel was not an extremist, but knew when appropriate to right a wrong, or support an explanation with a quote from the Bible. Chanel was a smart girl, with a gentle heart. She was cautious with people with whom she did not know or got a good vibe from, which people who did not know her, misconstrued Chanel as being stuck up and unapproachable. Sometimes guys would ask me why my friend was so mean? My reply was, "Who, Chanel? That's because she don't know you." What I admired and liked most about Chanel was that she was humble, quiet and observant like me.

Chanel was Basic, she did not draw attention by flaunting herself or went to extremes to stand out. Unlike most girls, Chanel did not feel the urgency to keep up with fashion trends, she wore jeans, a shirt, sneakers and her hair either in a ponytail or straightened, and parted in the middle. Chanel had the type of look that she could tone down her appearance and still looked as if she applied effort to look so pretty.

Chanel and I hung out often, we went to the movies, the malls and South Street. I invited her out and she invited me on her travels. It meant a lot that Chanel considered me when she went places, because it meant that she was not ashamed to be seen with me, which made me feel important. I think because Chanel was a pretty girl, and I had my physical afflictions, I felt privileged she considered me equal to walk beside her.

Chanel and I spent hours sitting on each other's steps talking, well I was always the one who did most of the talking, she was a great listener and paid attention. I felt a special connection with Chanel, because we both came from a big family and had similar financial hardships that did not allow us to have the luxuries that a lot of our classmates and friends had. Much of our experiences seemed to happen at the same time, which made me feel someone understood many of the growing pains I experienced.

The small circle consisted of five girls. We all were in the same homeroom, but it was the separate connections we formed outside of homeroom that brought us close. Drita and Christine had known each other since they were younger. Three of the other girls and Chanel became good friends because they all shared most of their classes together. They also had the same lunch period before my schedule lined up with having the same lunch in the second semester. It was a bit awkward coming into the circle, seeing that everyone had already formed a bond with each other. However, they welcomed me in and I quickly felt included. Everyone developed a unique bond with one another in the group, but collectively, we were all really close. It was the first time I had felt a true connection with the girls.

The connection I had with Drita was stronger than with any of the other girls, because outside of school we both had been accepted into the same scholarship program called Philadelphia Futures. The program matched students with mentors; so we traveled together into the city, to attend workshops that prepared students for college. It was an amazing program; Furtures provided trips to various colleges, and provided vocational preparation that included our first work experience. At the completion of the program, we received a scholarship that assisted with the cost of college.

On our excursions as Drita called them, we made the most out of going into the city. We were two broke students, I was always more broke than Drita, but when we did have money, we went to music stores to buy the latest CD by our favorite artists. Drita and I shared the bond of music, we both especially loved pop music that not everyone shared a love for.

Drita came from a middle class family, that included her mother, younger brother and Sister. Although our worlds were slightly different, we shared the same burdens of being the oldest child and having to be responsible for assisting our mothers in caring for our siblings and running the house. Drita's mother was the definition of a hard working woman trying to obtain the American dream. She managed two jobs, therefore was barely home, and when she was, she ran a tight ship. Her mother was kind hearted and soft spirited, but she did not play, she kept her children in line by ruling with an iron fist. They feared their mother as children should. She governed her family by the traditions and principles of their native Caribbean country.

They were a traditional family but always stayed true to their culture. I loved hanging out at Drita's house and experiencing their culture, everything except eating fish eyes, and chicken feet with the claws still attached. I loved listening to the dialect, and Caribbean music. I became obsessed. Everywhere we traveled we were listening to the latest Reggae Gold album, in which Drita translated the words to a song, to help me learn the lyrics. I felt cocky when I could sing along to the fastness of the music, keeping up and singing with accuracy when most had no clue what was being said.

There were aspects about our friendship that I did not like, but never made mention of because I did not want to jeopardize a good thing. I did not expect Drita to be perfect, but over time, there were things that did not sit right with me. I felt Drita was dismissive of things I had to say even when I was being serious. I never said anything because I was more concerned with not making her upset, even though I knew she was the type of person who would understand. Drita had a sense of humor that I loved, she was extremely funny, all day everyday she had me in tears cracking up at the things she said; however there were times I knew she was subliminally speaking truth when she sarcastically said things about me. Nothing that hit below the belt, but small things that no one would catch on about, but I did. Looking back, I know my insecurities caused me to misinterpret and take many things the wrong way.

There were things I struggled with in high school, some beyond my control and others that were. By this time, my family had again hit a rough patch, our financial situation had hit an all-time low, most times we struggled immensely. Therefore, I did not have many outfits to choose from in my closet, nor did I have a selection of shoes to wear, only two pairs. I took care of what I had, because I knew it would be a long time before the old could be replaced with new.

What I could not control was not having many clothes to choose from, so I wore what I had, many were hand-me-downs, which some did not fit well, and I often wore the same things many times throughout the week. After wearing the same shoes for so long and the combination of having sweaty feet, my sneakers and boots began to smell. I tried masking the smell with powder, but over time the smell worsened.

I was also becoming depressed by my home situation, still struggling with the way I looked and the isolation I continued to feel in general. I was not aware then that I was depressed, I just knew that I was no longer motivated. I did not always have the energy to bathe, so I went to school with my arms smelling; I tried covering the stench with deodorant in the mornings before heading out, but it did nothing to elevate the smell. I did not care to check my nose when I should, going sometimes the entire day with it crusted and running, and expecting people not to notice. I started wearing foundation make up, that needed touching up every so often, but I stopped caring to maintain it, figuring that it did not stop people from staring, and no one noticed the difference when I wore it and when I did not. Drita made light of some of these issues in ways that she thought I did not catch on to, but I did and I secretly resented her for it.

The good times out weighted the bad with Drita, she made my years at Motivation eventful. We did everything together. We were both interested in communications and graphic design, and took a summer program together for film design at the Academy of the Arts. Drita was my voice when I did not have one, she boldly said the things I wanted to but was too afraid.

When out together in public, if Drita noticed someone making a cruel comment or staring at me too long, she intervened. Drita was always telling me how to respond to flinching comments or actions of people and how to adjust my attitude, so as to appear unaffected. I appreciated Drita's assertiveness and knew it was something I lacked. I felt being assertive meant being confrontational and of course I did not want people not to like me. We shared a lot of intimate things with each other regarding the pains of home. I confided in her about things that I wanted to with Chanel but felt more comfortable telling

Drita, because of how opened she was with me. I knew Drita cared about me, just as much as I cared about her.

I learned a lot from Drita, she found a job before me, and was the one who taught me how to balance a check book and write a check. I admit, I was jealous of her, because she had a means to money and I did not. When we went out, Drita was able to buy things that I could not, but Drita bought me food when everyone went to Wendy's for lunch or after school, and sometimes fronted me cash when we went out. I was grateful to call her a true friend.

The tenth grade academically was a difficult time because of one teacher in particular, Mrs. Wells who taught geometry. She was a smart woman, who knew and loved math, her favorite saying was "math is a beautiful science." I hated when she said it because it was not for me, matter of fact I had grown to hate school having to sit in her class everyday. Everyone knew Mrs. Wells was tough as nails, but many students liked her "I'm going to break you down" approach, because that was what she did. Mrs. Wells humiliated and put us on the spot when we got an answer wrong. She yelled and berated us for missing a concept or taking too long to figure a question out, and she did not allow anyone to offer help. There were two sisters in the class whose IQs together were larger than the class combined. Both sisters were beyond smart, they were geniuses. However, no one was immune to Mrs. Well's scrutiny, not even them. She was harsher on the sisters, than anyone else because she did not want the girls to toot their own horns, it was a way to humble them she would say.

At the start of each class, Mrs. Wells assigned everyone a question from homework, to write the answer on the board and then go over together as a class. I was happy when I got a question that I knew the answer to, and fearful when I had a question that I did not know the answer to. While in homeroom, many of us sat with someone we knew had the correct answers. We then shared the answers, and worked out the problems before class. One thing Mrs. Wells did not tolerate was anyone handing in homework that was incomplete, she did not care if the answers were wrong. It was a bad day for everyone when someone did not turn in their homework.

By the end of the school year, I had walked away feeling defeated and intimidated. It was evident that my struggles with math from my days at Widener followed me to high school. Mrs. Wells's approach and demeanor did not work with me; because of my experience of her, I developed great fear and anxiety in math. I felt intimidated and stupid, and resented her when she put me on the spot knowing that I struggled immensely; being in her class ruined any confidence I had in math. My fears and anxiety kept me from getting the help I needed and would later come back to haunt me in college. In subsequent math classes, I just gave up, I did not care to try because all I heard was that negative voice in my head reminding me how much of a failure I was. In the eleventh and twelfth grade, Mr. Phan, the trigonometry teacher, empathetically went out of his way to help me, because I was on the brink of failing. I did not care to put in the effort because I had given up on myself, I was too fearful and ashamed.

My sophomore year ended with me going on my Sop hop. It was my first dance and was one of the most exciting and memorable moments of my life, thanks to a great friend who was my date. He was even more special because he was the first guy I had ever gone out with. The best part was getting dressed up and having a date for the first time. I was excited for the whole experience, shopping for a dress, having friends and family gathered around the house to send me off, arriving in style and making a grand entrance.

The time leading up to the sop hop, my thoughts were consumed with fantasizing about how the night would play out and how people would react to seeing me. I had chosen a dusty purple satin spaghetti dress that stopped at the knee with a matching shawl. I also found shoes with a heal that was comfortable for me to walk in, and had them dyed to match the color of my dress. I was certain I would turn heads, not just with my dress, but with my date. No one expected I would be accompanied by such a handsome guy, which I was right, my class mate's mouths dropped when they saw him with me.

Anthony was a friend I met through another friend, and we hit it off in that very moment. The first time we hung out was playing basketball, in which Anthony claimed he let me win, but in fact I beat him about ten times in a row. It was one of our favorite stories Anthony loved to share. At first, I was extremely insecure around him, because guys either ignored or made fun of me. There were a few times when I allowed my insecurities try to push Anthony away, but he refused to be another guy, who did not recognize that I was a beautiful person. Anthony proved this by coming to my house, hanging out with my family and friends, introducing me to his friends and family and invited me to tag along during his track practices. To everyone he introduced me to, he proudly referred to me as one of his best friends.

Anthony reassured me time after time that he cared about me and that nothing would get in the way of us being friends. We both cared about each other so much, that we attempted to try at a relationship, but quickly decided that what we had was too special to ruin. In part, I was relieved it did not work, because I was fearful I was not good enough and that he would eventually discover all of my truth and run. I was not comfortable with myself being in a relationship with someone as attractive as Anthony, it was too much pressure.

It was Anthony's idea, to be my date after I shared with him my plans to go alone. Anthony knew about the tough times I was having with people, and he wanted to do something that would have me noticed for sure. Anthony was cocky, and bragged about himself and the girls who he believed found him irresistible. However, he was such a good hearted guy, that no one took offense to it, I just laughed and called him conceited.

I remember feeling proud and honored that Antony was my date, he was the perfect gentleman. However, I also felt awkward having never been around a guy long enough to experience intimacy in the sense of closeness and affection; therefore, I refused to dance with Anthony, I did not want to embarrass myself in front of him or in front of my classmates. Every song that played I promised to dance on the next, then promised to dance on the first slow song, hoping the DJ would continue the stream of fast-paced songs to get me off the hook. I allowed Anthony to dance with other girls, but being the guy that he was, Anthony refused, stating he was there for me. He went out on the dance floor to dance alone, in which his personality stole the show. I had never slow danced before, and I began to panic over showcasing my inexperience. When the inevitable happened, Anthony immediately came over to me, grabbed my hand, telling me to get up, and that a promise was a promise. I felt embarrassed that he would notice I could not dance, and when he did, Anthony kindly lead the way and told me to follow. Anthony held me close as he sang along to the theme song of the dance, "These Are the Times" by Dru Hill. It was the right song for a perfect evening.

The Sop Hop was by far better than both the eleventh and surely the twelfth grade proms. Anthony's friendship meant the world to me back then, it was a defining moment that taught me all guys were not the same. His compassion and sincerity made me hopeful of one day finding the same qualities in a mate.

My Junior year academically was my best year and most memorable because of one teacher. English was the only subject I felt academically strong in, was passionate about, and could express myself. My instructor, Mr. Weiss, was a tall, heavy man with white light hair. He had a gargantuan smile, and the largest hands I had ever seen. Mr. Weiss reminded me of the country singer Kenny Rogers and at times a lumber jack because of his statue and because he wore suspenders.

Mr. Weiss had a passion for literature and the arts. His enthusiasm and theatrics made me appreciate classic literature. Unlike any other teacher I had before, in high school, Mr. Weiss was my favorite. We mostly talked while waiting for students to get to class. We talked about whatever randomly came up and I appreciated the fact he sought interested in my story.

I talked to him about the ways I dealt with my hardships, such as surgeries, my home life and plans for college. During a summer when I had to be homeschooled because of a surgery, Mr. Weiss sent me get well cards. I saw that he felt deep compassion for me. Mr. Weiss always commend me for my courage, and for being an inspirational role model. I was also surprised to learn he often talked about me with his wife and daughter. I remember feeling moved that his daughter felt compelled to make crafts for me, and take the time to write heartfelt messages, sent via her father that brightened my day. It surprised me that a young girl with whom I had never met was inspired by my story.

Mr. Weiss taught both eleventh grade English and Drama, which was the class I had after English, therefore I spent a good length of time in his classroom. As a result, I was certain that Mr. Weiss was privy to the exclusion I experienced while in class, it was of no secret to any outside observer. The setup of the classroom facilitated a physical divide, with the desks on one side facing the desks on the other. Majority of the class set on the opposite side from where I was seated. I remember feeling like I was the only occupant on one side, while the popular kids set on the other, laughing and having fun among one another.

I felt my loneliness and the fact that I did not fit in was evident. It took everything in me to fight back tears, wanting to be a part of the laughter and conversations. I was embarrassed, thinking that my loneliness was so obvious. On most days, I felt awkward sitting for forty five minutes, hunched over, pretending to be reading a book or looking over homework, when I really was crying silently. I felt angry and hurt that I was invisible to my classmates. I resented them for not caring to notice me. To appear unaffected by the blatant rejection, I set in the seat closest to Mr. Weiss's desk, finding anything to talk about. I tried not to show I was affected, but I sensed Mr. Weiss knew that not being included saddened me.

I was however noticed for being a hard working student who easily comprehended the readings. Many of my class mates came to me for interpretation or help with homework and class projects. My thoughts were, *Oh I'm good enough to talk to when you need help, but not so socially.* I found myself feeling very bitter and angry with being ignored and rejected by most of my peers.

Twelfth grade came and went fast, and I was excited to end this chapter and move on to the next - college. I again became optimistic, having expectations that my social situation would for sure improve once in college. Hope is what keeps a soldier alive when it is surrounded around so much death, and destruction. What gives him energy and strength is knowing he has come too far to give up, even when giving up seems like the better choice.

I went out of high school with an unexpected bang! For much of the four years I was in school, I felt invisible, dismissed and unheard. For a long time, my voice was mute because I felt like no one cared about what I had to say, not knowing the opportunity would present itself that would change everything. I completed the Philadelphia Futures program and had not only been given the expected scholarship, but I unknowingly was nominated and chosen to receive the Lincoln Financial Award which came with ten thousand dollars toward the cost of college. I was on cloud nine. Going to college was not an option. With my condition I knew having a higher education would be the major factor in finding a career and being successful.

The surprises did not end there. Senior year was a good year. We all were looking forward to Move up Day. Move up Day was Motivation's graduation ceremony, an intimate commencement that celebrated the grade completion for grades ninth to twelfth. Each grade participated in taking the seats of the proceeding class, to symbolize moving up to the next grade. Each senior's name was called to the stage to receive a certificate, or remained standing while the principal announced scholarships and grants a student was awarded, for the colleges and universities each planned to attend. After each class exchanged seats, the senior class then left the building, symbolizing graduating and going off to college.

After so many years of participating in the tradition, to finally be seated in the Senior seats felt so good. I made it, when I was certain I would not, because of some academic struggles that almost prevented me from graduating. I made it! When my name was called and all of my scholarships were read, I was shocked to learn I was among the twins, to receive the highest amount of money to aide for collage. They got top dollar, because they were so smart.

The icing on the cake was my Principal had encouraged me to enter a contest that was open for Bartram high school, including all annexes. The contest was to write a powerful commencement speech. I did not think there was any way I could win, competing with so many students who wanted the unprecedented award. I was a great writer creatively, but doubted that I could actually win.

However, I began thinking about all that I had gone through in high school, feeling unseen and unheard, and now there was the chance of having the opportunity to finally be heard. I remember just writing what I defined success to be, and used my journey in the context of motivating my peers with the same hope and encouragement I used to see myself through the hard times. My speech won first place out of many who entered. The feeling was indescribable as I led the processional of flaggers holding the school banner and the American flag, with teachers, the valedictorian, and honor students all in tow as we walked toward the stage.

The entire Bartram High School graduated together, thousands of students with their loved ones packed the Temple University's Lacourse Center in the north section of Philadelphia. Its enormity was large enough to contain the graduates from Bartram High School, including each of the annexes, and all of their honored guests. I had never seen so many people before, nor did I ever imagine such an enormity would listen to a speech I wrote.

I stood firmly and spoke each word with passion and conviction. As my voice echoed throughout, it was the first time I had ever felt important, confident and bold. God gave me the last say. They may not have noticed me in school, but would remember what I had to say for a long time to come. This moment again changed the course of my life. I had come to realize that I had a voice, it was big, and loud, but more importantly its power touched people and made them listen.

CHAPTER 13

Hope Found in Makeup

HOPE CAN BE FOUND in the most dismal circumstances, the darkest places and even in the utmost of uncertainty. Hope was the one true thing that I held on to tightly. I was still struggling with who I was, finding my place, finding meaning in my suffering and God's reasoning to have me endure such pain. Every night I continued to pray for God's grace, for Him to give me the strength to continue, especially when I felt so warn out from being me. Walking around pretending I was okay, that I could handle my situation, and that it did not affect me, but it did. It affected me every minute of the day, and it was exhausting. My mom was great in giving me spiritual words of comfort and guidance, but I still felt despair.

I continued to pray to God for acceptance, confidence and self-love. I believed everything my mother told me about God. That He would never forsaking me, that my situation would work out for my good, and He had not brought me this far to leave me. My mom had me open the Bible and read whatever scripture my eyes landed on. Matthew chapter 5 became a pillow of comfort, where I rested my cares upon, "Blessed are those who mourn, for they will be comforted… blessed those who are persecuted because of their righteousness." I felt God speaking to me, reminding me my suffering would never be in vein. That I would be prosperous through my adversity because I had a good spirit. A good spirit that people easily dismissed because they were unable to get past what they saw.

They were unable to see the simplicity in what appeared to be a complex situation. All that mattered was that God saw me and what He saw was BEAUTIFUL. He just wanted me to see the beauty that I possessed for myself and understand the depths of it was far more alluring than the outer.

What I quickly learned about God's power was that He wastes no time in answering prayers. "Ask and you shall receive!" my mother would tell me. I had a burning desire to look in the mirror and truly love the reflection that stared back at me. God knew the desire of my heart was to stand firm and believe what my mother often declared, "You are who God says you are!" Slowly I would come to see and believe that I was beautiful. This declaration would eventually become the fundamentals of my strength and assurance.

Near the end of my freshmen year I had another surgery and finished my semester being home schooled. During one of my outpatient appointments at Children's Hospital, my mom and I were introduced to an esthetician who heard about my story, and wanted to meet me. She spoke to my mom about coming in for a consultation for a makeover. She went on about a camouflage foundation, that when applied to the face and body, concealed scarring. My mom was very excited, and I was excited because she was excited, but had no idea of what to expect. I had made some progress in that I was no longer ducking mirrors, but not standing too long in front of them either.

Regie was extremely beautiful physically and even more inside. She was vivacious and full of energy, her enthusiasm was contagious and I had instantly loosened up and became excited of what would become of this experience. The entire time while Regie applied the makeup, my mom was standing beside her, ooh-ing and ah-ing, her animation made me anxious to see my face. The process took about forty-five minutes of work, applying the foundation, drawing and filling in my lids, and tattooing my eye brows. I was unsure if I could follow through with carrying out the meticulous steps to recreate the same look. My mind became tangled with all kinds of thoughts about how this experience would change my life. I was hoping her aesthetic would create a face with no evidence of its flaws. My hopes were soaring. When it came time for the reveal, I was given a hand held mirror and closed my eyes. In that split second I said, "God, please let this be good."

I opened my eyes with mixed feelings, but knew the amount of hard work that went in to the production, and was aware of the response that was expected, so I attempted to put on the performance of a life time. As soon as I returned home, I went straight to my room, in hopes that I would feel indifferent with a thorough examination. I did not. As much as I appreciated the effort that went into giving me a new-found confidence, I struggled to accept my new look. Maybe it was because I had gotten so use to my normal face, that my first thought was I did not need to wear makeup, and would not use it again. Initially I did not like the makeup, because I thought the color was way off. I told my mom my concerns and she encouraged me to keep using it, that I would eventually become comfortable and would soon see the difference.

I thought about what people would think of me when I went to school. Would they like it, laugh or not say anything at all, but talk about how ridiculous I looked behind my back. I waited for a few days, dismissing the long list of instructions, and began playing with the makeup, until I found a way to use it to my liking. Looking in the mirror, I eventually noticed a difference in the reflection that was once too painful to look at. My face bared the same scars, the same deformation, but it suddenly had life. The fact that the makeup covered my scars, and gave me a smooth, even tone was amazing. The makeup was also used to cover scars on the entire body, but I was not concerned about showing the scars on my arms and legs, I comfortably wore dresses, skirts and short sleeves. I knew this experience would be beneficial to me, I just had to get to a point where I felt comfortable and mastered applying it to look inconspicuous.

After much dibbling and dabbling, I decided to wear it. I spent the entire night perfecting my look. I applied the makeup first, then followed the stencil of my eye brows that had been tattooed. The tattoo was not permanent and began to wear off after a few days. I then outlined my upper lip, using a black outliner pencil, then neatly colored within the black line with a brown liner, before blending the two colors together to make a natural toned upper lip. Applying a pink colored lip balm completed the look. I watched videos and closely tried to critique the trends in makeup, of the female artists and models. The trend then was a gradient effect with the lips outlined darker and then blended to a lighter color in the middle of both lips.

Through the art of makeup, I became a bit obsessed with female aesthetic and feminine features, especially the eyes and lips. If I noticed that a woman had beautiful features, I studied them and or their makeup, then tried to recreate the look on myself. Many times, I tried not to stare in a woman's face too hard, especially ones whose beauty stunned me, because I always feared they would catch me staring. I wanted to define a look for me that was natural and beautiful. The more I got into makeup, the more confident I grew in the possibilities and my evolution. I had found a way to aesthetically enhance the features I lost. It was amazing to look in the mirror and see the instant transformation of my face. Going from dark, discolored blemishes to a color tone, that matched my true skin color and concealed the pink area around my upper lip, where pigmentation was lost.

The first day of showing the world my new look I was very nervous. I wanted to come across natural and believable. None the less, I do not think people really noticed my difference as much. Some kids in school noticed there was something different, but they had never taken the time to notice me, to notice the significant change. I received many comments that the makeup looked nice and made me look different, but I figured people were just saying nice things because it was the good thing to do.

In my mind, just by covering up my scars and drawing facial features, I thought people would see and treat me as a regular person. I thought people would no longer look at me with fear and disgust as they had without makeup. Therefore, I became consumed and preoccupied with maintaining my new image. I constantly excused myself to go to the bathroom during class and in between classes to reapply my makeup. Whenever I applied my makeup, believing that I drew on my brows perfectly or my lips perfectly, I spent the entire day making sure I kept up with that look. What I came to realize was that if I thought I looked good and flawless, then I felt beautiful, and I also thought people saw me in the same light. On the contrary, if I did not feel my makeup was good that day, or if I had forgotten a small step when applying, or if I went too long without having checked my face, I became insecure and paranoid, thinking that people noticed.

With such a great gift came a curse. After becoming acclimated with wearing makeup, I became dependent on it, and wondered how had I survived, walking around before without it. The curse was that I had not yet found the right brand. Even with the expensive camouflage make up that I first started wearing, it transferred, it got all over my clothes and everything I came in contact with. I could barely pat my face without it getting everywhere. In the mornings, I applied it before putting my clothes on, but it smeared all over my clothes. So then I got dressed first, and then applied my make up, but there did not seem to be an easy way to avoid the makeup from smearing, it easily made messes.

When it was time to reorder, I do not remember if we had to pay or if it was covered by my insurance as a patient, but after becoming so frustrated with how messy it was, I decided to try other brands. I did not have the money to afford expensive brands, so I settled on affordable ones, that matched my skin color. This aspect was hard, because there were not many cheap choices for darker skinned women. Although I appeared very dark because of my burns, my true skin tone was determined by the unaffected skin of my neck and jaw bone, which is more like a mocha. Luckily one brand I began using had that one color as its only dark option. I saved my money to buy the liquid foundation and a press powder. The foundation alone made my skin look too oily, so I used the powder to give it balance. Using this brand appeared to be good in the beginning, I continued studying women and cosmetic trends and my aesthetic improved; my look was becoming more and more natural, however the makeup was also runny, and the powder was too light, making my face in the light look chalky and ghostly.

When applying my makeup, in dense lighting, it appeared to look fine, but looking in mirrors or seeing myself in pictures against the natural light of the sun, my face looked dusty, making me feel as if I looked like a circus clown. I felt embarrassed by this, but the brand was all I could afford. I pat moisturizer on my face after applying the powder to prevent it from looking dry.

I still did my best with what I had, and eventually developed a new confidence. Despite being hard on myself by noticing every detail, I was evolving. My appearance was forming into one that I was becoming comfortable with, and begun to admire. The vision God had given my mother was not one that would happen literally, but figuratively. I was beginning to understand that I would go through a physical evolution through makeup, altering my face in a way that did not make my scars look so obvious, which then in turn gave me a sense of normalcy.

With much effort and work throughout the years, God trained my hand to perfect my aesthetic skills, to create a face I would soon become very proud of. Make up was one of the best things that happened to me. From it, I developed a new sense of self, and the desire to reinvent a new me. I suddenly got this surge of esteem, confidence and conceitedness, that all I wanted to do was show off. For the first time ever I was feeling good about myself, and optimistic about the future. Not only was I learning to use makeup for enhancement purposes, but what is a beautiful face without a beautiful hair style.

My mother had been the greatest inspiration and teacher, and I was ready to apply all that I learned to create the cute looks I saw in music videos. I bought wigs, usually long ones, took them home and cut them up. I remember my first bob, it was crazy cute. As I had done when I was younger with my dolls, I sat and learned how to curl hair using my mother's stove curlers. The heaviness of the iron made it challenging to hold, but as I had always done, practiced, practiced, practiced. Eventually after many burns from the curlers falling and nicking me, I learned how to curl my wigs.

Back then most wigs were made of synthetic hair, which was all that I could afford. I burnt the hair many times and once, destroyed a brand new wig. Luckily I had an old one, that I washed and it magically came back to life. I eventually figured out how to curl the wigs without burning them, by making sure the curlers were not too hot, and by adding hair moisturizers. Not only did the hair curl, but the products made the hair look natural.

I especially loved the up dos, but I could not pin the hair up without the underlining of the wig showing. Playing in the mirror for a while, I manipulated the hair by raveling it up into a bun in the back, securing bobby pins into it and through my own hair to make it tight enough securing the wig. Next I folded the underlining of the wig, to make it discrete. I then left some hair out at the top, raveled the hair to make it appear curled with bobby pins, it was my version of an up do that worked for me. I then completed the look with a side long bang covering my left eye, because I was still uncomfortable showing it. There was one time, I had a good wig and was able to make a ponytail, no one could tell me I was not cute!

Even to this day, finding a good wig is like finding a diamond in the rough. I now have developed an eye for what I know will look good on me, without trying one on. Back then, it was pretty much a guessing game. If it was not the look I wanted, I worked with it until I created a look I liked. Usually after a few days of sleeping in them, brushing and styling them, the wigs appeared to look more natural. I hated wigs with too much hair or looked too synthetic, making it obvious. When shopping for a wig, I always opted out of trying them on because I did not want anyone seeing my head. I believed that not even the most seasoned hairstylist was prepared to handle the exposure. In most beauty hair stores where wigs are sold, there is only an area of space open for people to come and go while the person tries on wigs. I did not feel comfortable exposing myself, so I refused the service when offered.

For a long time, I felt a great sense of shame having to wear wigs, that I started wearing them all day every day as if it was my actual head of hair. Like when man felt shame when he realized he was naked, so did I. I had gone through a part of my life where I did not wear them, not even in public, to wearing, and not taking them off at night or when in the house. My shame had gotten to the point where I did not like to stare at myself without one on. I also began to feel shame around my family.

I liked my new image, and how I felt, the old was too much of a reminder of my truth. With makeup and fake hair I could cover that truth and develop a superficial truth that everyone believed, and that I would come to believe myself. I personified that I was in control, that I was confident, but had a long way before I could stand in that truth. I was confronted by the harsh realities of my truth many times before I could comfortably stand in it. God works in mysterious ways. What man meant for bad, God always uses to bless one in ways unimaginable. I had no idea what was happening to me, and how God was using and preparing me. This time in my life was more than the evolution of a new look, but an evolution of the person God spared my life to be. Through my deepest pain and insecurities, God was slowly molding me into a beautiful and strong wonder. In order to inhibit such qualities, I first had to understand their meaning.

Around the age of ten or eleven years old, I was introduced by my mother to a woman who became my source of inspiration, and the first role model I had who was successful, and who shared my experience of being physically disfigured in a fire. Her name was Rosemary; my mom told Rose she had a daughter who was also severely burned.

My mom came home one day, with tears streaming from her eyes in excitement to tell me about Rose. "Neesha, you are not alone, baby I met this amazing woman who was also burned, and I invited her over to meet you." A few weeks passed and we were introduced. My first impression was shock. There was a kid in my school, who had also been burned, so I had seen another person like me, but my shock was not because of the way she looked, but that I now knew a woman with whom I could physically relate to.

Rosemary shared with me that she had been severely burned in a car accident. I did not have the same sadness for her I felt for myself, because she was so inspiring. Seeing someone who looked like me, understood the depths of my pain, and the struggles that I experienced with the outside world, because she too had the exact struggles, made me emotional. All of the time I cried to God about feeling alone, God had given me Rosemary as a companion who understood the weight of the cross I had to bare, but for the first time in my life, I did not have to bare mine alone.

Rose was close in age to my mother, very stylish, drove a very expensive car, and lived in the most exquisite house I had ever been in. We gravitated toward each other instantly. I believed I was to her, everything she was to me. The fact that she was older and successful, gave me a new found hope I too would become successful. Rosemary broke the glass ceiling that kept me feeling confined because of my circumstances. I had this desire to excel and make something of myself, but seeing Rosemary made me want to put in the work to possess what she had, and to be the remarkable woman of such courage. She had the confidence of someone whose presence commanded respect and showed a woman of high esteem.

It was as if God had given me a vision of myself in the future. She drove a Mercedes Benz, which was all black, with black leather interior. I remember feeling like a celebrity every time we rode around the city listening to Baby Face's For the Cool In You album. We began spending a lot of time together, and I loved every minute spent with her. Rose took me out to eat, shopping, or just to ride around with her as she ran errands. I was convinced that I loved the life of luxury and I wanted it just as bad for myself.

With Rose I did not feel ashamed or uncomfortable when people stared as I did in public alone. While alone in public, people's malicious comments felt like sharp daggers cutting deep into my self-esteem. With Rose I wanted people to see me with her. It was as if to say, "Ha, look at us, driving in this bangin' car, despite what we look like, we living the life you wish you had." I saw how unaffected and secure Rose appeared when attention was focused on us. People often assumed we were mother and daughter, because of our disfigured faces. People asked "is she your mother?" my reply was "why because we both were burned in a fire?" I got so irritated with people's ignorance, but it was our social outings that presented teachable moments for me.

Rosemary was very graceful in the way she carried herself, which was the contrary for me, I was still very young, wild and loud.

Rose was carefully watching me and was the only person who began pointing out my flaws. "Tanisha why do you walk with your head down, you don't ever have to walk with your head down. I understand the stares, and that people can be hurtful, but you are God's child and have nothing to be ashamed of. He made you beautiful, even with your scars. Don't be afraid to ever show them." At first I was embarrassed that my insecurities were easily detected. Instead of detesting her observations, I was thankful for the criticism and eager to begin working on becoming a confident me. I never thought my insecurities were so evident, especially since I thought I was cleverly concealing them.

Her confrontation was never intended to embarrass me, but to bring to my attention the things that were affecting my esteem and therefore the ways people perceived me. I remember one time getting on the bus and it became crowded. A man got on and stood in front of me, holding on to the railing above. I hated being in situations where I felt stuck, because people would then have a close-up view of me and I could not escape. I became very uncomfortable, particularly because the person standing in front of me was a man. My insecurity rose and escaped through my mouth as I confronted him, sure that he was staring at my face and judging me. "I was burned in a fire, so could you please stop staring me down." The man softened his gaze and said "see that goes to show how insecure you are, I was actually admiring your eyes." I was taught a very valuable lesson that day, that I could not make assumptions of how people viewed me, based on my own faulty beliefs.

Rosemary was educating me on the importance of developing and maintaining a healthy and positive self-image. She emphasized the fact that because we looked different, it was even more critical to be mindful of how we presented ourselves while in public. She understood me better than I understood myself.

I remember her exact words "Make sure that you always take care of yourself Tanisha. Make sure you are always well groomed, that your hair is done, you smell good, your clothing is always well kept, that you are respectful, polite, forgiving and most importantly, educated. You have to strengthen the areas of who you are that will force people to see you beyond your scars. It is bad enough that people are going to judge and talk about you because of the obvious, let the obvious be the only aspect of yourself someone has to use against you. Not before long, the negative things people say about your appearance will not have much of an effect on you."

I found myself seeking solace from God in my isolation. I remember praying to Him and asking for success. I desperately wanted to be able to get to a point where I could see myself in the same way God saw me. I just wanted to be able to walk without feeling deep shame for who I was. Praying for success was not for material gain or professionalism, but to gain full acceptance, love, contentment and self-worth. I knew it was attainable because Rose typified such success for herself. I just wanted to be able to walk with my head held high and truly love myself inside and out.

I held on tightly to every word she spoke, they would eventually become the fundamentals of how I live my life. Rosemary became a huge influence in my life. Her guidance led me to begin exploring myself in true honesty. Facing the things about myself I struggled with was something I feared ever having to do, but knew that I had to if I wanted to become successful.

Before meeting Rose, I started attending a camp for children and adults with burn injuries. I attended Camp Susquahanna since its inception, until I had my first child. I remember the first year I attended. The kid I went to school with severe burned injuries was also in attendance, but besides him, I did not know any of the fifty or so kids and adults who had traveled to Lancaster PA, to the Franklin and Marshal College campus, where the camp had been held for many years. There are many misconceptions and stereotypes that people hold about people with disabilities.

The way the disabled are depicted, has conditioned people to unconsciously believe in these stereotypes. One is that people with disabilities or with physical afflictions are always nice, understanding and empathetic, to others with similar circumstances. This is far from the case. When I was at Widener, I had the same curiosity for people in wheelchairs, wondering how they performed the same tasks as people who could walk. I also automatically assumed that someone with a speech disability could not read or understand what was being said; or wanting to help someone pick up something whose disability affected their hands. However, spending enough time around these individuals, and witnessing their abilities made me realize they could do things better than I could, who did not have a problem with the particular task. Being conditioned to view people as helpless, just because they lack something or had a difference, caused me to instinctively make inaccurate assumptions.

I learned I was not immune to judging people based on the unconscious messages I was taught from the environment I lived in. I felt like a bad person for what I believed were shameful feelings, because I did not want to appear to be someone who lacked sympathy for someone, because of their differences. I learned through my reactions of many people at camp whose injuries were more severe than mine, that it had nothing to do with one's good intentions, but because of the human condition. A term known as implicit bias, which is an unawareness to ways of thinking and behaving that are rooted deep within the subconscious, and result from being conditioned. We all share the same feelings and reactions to things we see, and experiences that are egregious or unexpected. The appearance of someone who has been burn is both egregious and unexpected.

There were people's physicality that made me stare with bewilderment. Then I felt the discomfort of not wanting to get too close, fearful of being touched, not wanting to stare, but unable to keep my eyes off their uniqueness. Then I realized I too was just like them, but then to some degree I was not. There were aspects of my injuries that were less extreme than others, which made me feel grateful. There was a guy named Bobby, the first year of camp who was the definition of a cruel person. Bobby's story was similar in that he was burned by fire, but how he was burned was rumored to have been intentional. I did not feel bad for Bobby, because his spirit and attitude were not good. The first year he made my life and others extremely difficult. Bobby laughed and taunted us as if he did not share the same boat with everyone in the camp. I told him "Do you not realize that when you look in the mirror, your face looks just as burned as mine?"

Bobby bullied me every chance he could during the entire four days we were at camp. I could not wait to leave to get away from him. He made fun of the way I walked, what I wore and told me I looked like every grotesque monster in movies he could think of. It really hurt my feelings, and never did I think that I would come to a place of support and comfort to experience being ridiculed. Bobby was told he was not allowed to return to camp, I was relieved and happy.

A few years later there was a girl who came to the camp, she and her sister were burned severely, but had an incredible story. They were heroes in their hometown, because the fire affected their entire family. I thought their story was incredible and I had the deepest respect for them all. I however did not initially feel comfortable around Tracy. I was about twelve years old and had formed a little clique of my own, of about four girls younger than me, but their faces were not disfigured like mine and Tracy's. They were still pretty girls who looked up to and admired me. It was the first time I had my peers gravitate to me, and considered me the leader of the popular group, which everyone in the camp thought of us as. We were the hip black girls who introduced fashion, sass and urban culture.

When Tracy came and tried integrating herself in our crew, we all made it difficult for her to. Behind her back, some of the other girls said things about her, which I could never ever bring myself to do to anyone, not even to Bobby who I could not stand with a passion. My righteous conscious knew better, but more importantly knowing what it felt like to be teased. However, I treated Tracy badly by not including her, by subliminally rejecting her, although I talked to Tracy and smiled in her face. When we went off to do things as a clique, we purposely left Tracy behind, or did not save her a set on the bus to wherever we were going.

We were kids, but I knew what I was doing was wrong and hurtful. I was so insecure with myself that I rejected Tracy because I saw myself in her, and understood the fear and cruelty people treated me with. I inadvertently punished her, because that was what I felt from others. I did not want to be associated with Tracy, because she physically embodied the same disfigurements I had, and the discomfort I felt with her, I understood was the same others felt around me.

I was so concerned with the pretty girls liking me and having my ego affirmed by them following me around, that I hurt someone with a beautiful and accepting heart. In Tracy I saw myself and it was too painful.

Over the years at camp, and outside of it, I came to learn so much from Tracy. When I realized how smart, talented and deep Tracy was, I felt like a loser for the way I treated her as kids. Just listening to her speak and the way she described the world and the difficulties she experienced, I knew I needed to connect with her rather than pull away from her. Tracy strengthen and encouraged me many times when I wanted to give up, or talked to her about something I was struggling with. I felt stupid for complaining about whatever, after listening to Tracy's struggles that appeared more challenging than what I was crying about, but that she was handling with strong faith. Her optimism, humility, joy, and determination to rise above her suffering convicted me. Tracy ended our conversations with powerful words of encouragement that left me speechless.

Whenever I had an exceptionally difficult time with something, I became humbled and felt foolish knowing what Tracy was going through, was far greater. It was her deep faith and gratitude which taught me to complain less. Even though we lived hundreds of miles away, I felt her presence with me when I was in the greatest of distress. The beauty of her heart made me turn inward to see that I too possessed the same beauty, and courage.

I learned from Tracy that I had to replace the negativity I told myself with God's word. That was the great comfort she lent to me. I remember a conversation we once had. She was studying at a remote predominately Caucasian college and said to me, "Tanisha I refuse to be turned away from something that I am so passionate about. I do not expect for these kinds of people to ever understand what it is like for me. They treat me less than human, but I still walk with my head held high, because I am suppose to be here! I deserve to be here and will finish what I started."

One year I was approached by a reporter for a Lancaster newspaper who was doing a feature story about the camp, and wanted to interview one of the campers. I sat before the reporter answering all of his questions with truth and courage. When someone showed me the article the next day, I could not believe my picture was in the newspaper and people were interested in what I had to say.

In 1998, I was given the opportunity of a life time. A fellow camper was asked to be a guest on a popular day time talk show, but for legal issues surrounding how the person was burned, they could not tell their story. I do not know how my name was mentioned, but I got a phone call from a producer of the show, asking me if I wanted to be a guest. I literally hopped out of my skin with disbelief. I was going to be on national television, telling my story to the world, I was full of excitement. With the show finding me at the last minute, I was informed that a limo would arrive at my house to take me, my mom, and my mentor Vita to the show. It was truly a surreal moment. I thought about the popularity I would get at school, how those who did not notice me were finally going to, and how so many people would know my story.

When I met the host, he looked just as he did on TV. The show was transitioning from his iconic shows of people with rare and unprecedented medical and physical conditions, to more reality based. There were two other kids who were also going to share their courageous stories.

The night before the taping, I met with the producer of the show, who informed me they received a copy of an autobiography I wrote about myself in my freshmen year of high school. The director stated they wanted to focus on my life experience and the courage I showed to be an inspiration for others. Knowing how people with physical adversities are seen and depicted on TV and the repeated proverbial: "I'm just like everyone else." I wanted to reframe from being a cliché. I did not want to evoke pity, I wanted the world to see me as being strong and courageous. I wanted to say, "Yes, this happened to me, but I deal with it and I will not be completely defined by what has happened to me." I was convinced that everything was going to go as planned and the producers respected and valued my direction.

However, when I sat on stage the next day, the host opened my segment with "This is sixteen-year-old Tanisha, and she says she has no friends." The statement was followed by a sympathetic sigh from the audience at the cue from a technician directing the emotion of the crowd. In an instant I felt confused. When I eventually saw the tape, I noticed my facial expression went from encouraged to feeling defeated. I was just another guest whose plight elicited pity. I did not want to be seen in the ways people with disabilities were often stereotyped on television. It was propaganda and I did not want to sell it to boost better ratings. I wanted to tell my story, to talk about how cruel people can be, but focus primarily on how strong I was, having to live being constantly mistreated and marginalized.

The world did not see what I saw, which I was thankful for. Many came up to me as if I was a celebrity, telling me how much they admired me. I was on the show over twenty years ago, and I still get recognition for my appearance. Overall the feeling I got from being on TV was phenomenal. I appeared some months after my first appearance as the show's most asked about guest. I had been given two US postal service bags full of mail from thousands of people from across the country who wrote about how my story touched them.

After the show, my mom and I were flown out to LA by Dr. Drew Pinsky to shoot a pilot for a talk show. It was the experience I wanted with the other show. Dr. Drew asked questions in ways that conserved my dignity and was more informative and educational than exploitive. I was then contacted by another popular talk show of that time, who wanted me to be a guest, but when I told them what I would and would not talk about, they asked me if I knew of anyone else who had been severely burned and willing to be on the show instead. I could not believe it, but was not surprised that this talk show had shown the true intentions of media propaganda.

The experiences I had on television inspired me to narrow what I wanted to do with my life. I believed God's purpose for my life was beginning to come into focus. I loved speaking and realized that others were touched and changed by my testimony. Through speaking I again found my powerful voice. I had always felt a sense of insecurity in the way I spoke. Influenced by that faint voice that created a sense of fear, which caused me to think I was stupid and I did not know what I was talking about. The voice constantly whispered into my psyche, that no one cared to listen to what I had to say. This is an insecurity I have learned to turn into a strength through my speaking. My insecurity was a result of the time in my life when I was mute and wrote all of my feelings down.

As a motivational speaker, I feel God's presence with me, and all of the fears and insecurities takes a back seat to the power of my messages. I know through every word I speak, God is healing the brokenness and disparity in those I speak to, the same way He healed me during those difficult lonely times. All of my experiences I expose in raw truth, are meant to comfort that one individual who feels they are all alone in their suffering and think there can be no suffering greater. It has been through the words I have spoken while standing before the masses, that reminds me of how far I have come and the work still left to do. I am still very much in need of being spoken to and encouraged, so when I speak, I have realized the messages are more so meant to encourage myself.

The reason I have worked and pushed so hard to be successful is because my worth depended on it. It was very important that people see me as normal, able, intelligent and successful, because without all of these qualities, I would be seen as just another unfortunate individual overlooked and unimportant, therefore there would have been no point of me having survived the fire. If I was not seen, I was as good as dead, and speaking in part gave me the platform to be seen and heard. Success was my survival, the reasoning that made such a tragedy make sense and gave my existence purpose.

God said the road would be hard and long to success. I have learned that I will not have all of the essentials needed. However, it has been the small things I have pick up along the way that have preserved my energy, served as a compass to direct me when I have fallen off track, and things that have shown me the beauty of walking desolate and repelling paths. All I have gained throughout my life, has reminded me the arduous journey will be well worth it.

CHAPTER 14

Growing Up Too Fast

MY CURIOSITY OF BEING in a relationship began round age eleven. It was not the amorous affairs my mother had with men that caused this inquisitiveness, but what I mostly saw on television and later the relationships of my peers. Love, sex, and attraction were among the popular storylines of most shows, especially music videos. I was beyond obsessed with watching them. I loved to see the storylines of my favorite songs play out on screen. We intermittently had cable, and when we did, music videos were all I watched. I did not know the psychological impact videos were having on me and how they were shaping my perception about beauty and relationships.

At this age I was still playing with my Barbies, and played out the concepts of love and relationships that appeared to be correlated with physical attraction. Whether it was a movie, show or music video, physical beauty always seemed to be the highlighted focus, from the actors chosen to the storylines. Physical beauty then and now is the essence of music videos. I learned from watching them enough, that beautiful women are objectified simply for men's sexual desires. Especially in hip-hop and R&B videos, women have always been idolized for their voluptuous curves, big breasts, small waists, and even bigger backsides, along with a facial appearance ranking nothing less than a "10" on the good looks scale. In hip-hop and R&B culture, a woman judged as a "10" is referred to as a "dime." Music and its visuals can highly influence people's perceptions and expectations for what defines, in many cases love and attraction; beauty appeared to equate to both. From these messages, I began believing that infatuation and lust equated to love. Aware of these facts, I grew fearful and deeply concerned of what would become of my experiences with romantic relationships.

With Barbie, I sarcastically played out what I hated about the stereotypes of love and beauty seen on TV. In my skits, Barbie's main objective was to look as beautiful as she could; spending hours styling her hair, and trying on every article of clothing until she found the perfect outfit that was most revealing. Barbie's efforts went into satisfying and looking good at all times for her man, Barbie's equally beautiful partner Ken. She always had much competition, as every Barbie in the plastic world were tough acts to follow, since flawless beauty was the only important attribute. Barbie had to constantly keep up her perfect image if she wanted to keep her Ken.

With no effort required, Ken always found Barbie's flawless beauty irresistible, no matter what she wore, had or did. Subliminal messages are given to young girls who Barbie targets. In my opinion, Barbie was designed to epitomize the optimal physical beauty and the desired aspects of a woman that are believed to be ideal in attracting the perfect man. In the plastic world of Barbie, what man is more perfect than Ken? I sometimes forgot Barbie was not real, and grow envious of her, wishing to be her, look like her and live in her perfect world. I thought how easy it was for her to have everything, including true love with a heartthrob.

By the time I entered into junior high school, I developed a curvaceous shape, filling out more so in my hips and backside than in my chest, which I really wanted more than anything, as it appeared that girls with breast got more attention. When I was introduced to makeup, I was also given silicone inserts to place inside my bras for a full bust and to even out my lopsided chest. I was an 'A' cup and the inserts added about another size up. When the inserts became old from constant wear, I started inserting tissue. I wanted to feel feminine and having small scarred breast made me feel less feminine. I stuffed them until I got the desired look in my shirt. Eventually the charade was up.

One day I went to school and my shirt kept rising, unaware the tissue was showing, I noticed two classmates staring and pointing at me as they laughed. I looked down and was horrified that the tissue was bulging out of my shirt. I learned having a voluptuous backside was just as attractive as having a big bust. I was grateful to at least have something that made guys notice me. I was getting attention, although I did not like that the shape of my body was the only reason boys were interested.

I really wanted to have the same experiences as most girls, and having a boyfriend seemed to be most important for a girl's coming-of-age experience. At Widener, I rode the school bus with another student named Kesha who was much older than me. She and I became good friends from our long rides to and from school. Kesha was loud, wild and had much experience with boys. She sat beside me telling me about the latest guy in school who wanted to get with her. Allegedly, it was rumored that Kesha had been with many guys in school, a rumor that Kesha denied and despised.

Kesha dated several guys from school before settling down in a long term relationship with an older guy who did not attend Widener. One guy Kesha had a fling with rode the bus with us, we all sat in the back and my seat was across from theirs. Every day on the ride home, I laid down on the seat attempting to sleep during the long drive, but my attempts were many times interrupted by seeing the two of them kiss passionately during the entire ride. I covered my head with my jacket, not wanting them to see me watching, but curiosity kept me looking. I had never seen two people romantically kissed up front and personal. I stared on, wishing that someone kissed me that way.

Sex was something I was curious about, but way too young to think about doing. I believed the fear of my mother was the real reason I never considered doing it, even if I had the opportunity to. The topic of sex was the most uncomfortable talking to my mom about. All my mom said regarding sex was that I better not do it, and there was nothing I needed to know about it being so young. She just wrote it off by saying it was a sin before marriage and that God would not be pleased. I think the fact that my mom saw me as being innocent and "the good girl" who never gave her any problems, eliminated any suspicion that I might be interested in sex. When she eventually did attempt to have the talk with me, it was beyond uncomfortable and the way she went about it would forever traumatize me. It is a topic that even as an adult is never brought up for discussion.

In middle school I wanted boys to like me. I wondered what sex was about, seeing there was so much exposure of it on TV, and because it was all the older kids in school were either talking about or doing. In a way I was thankful for the lack of male attention, because it kept me from the pressures of finding out before I was ready. However, I was not so innocent, my curiosity only took me as far as fulfilling the wish to be kissed.

By the eighth grade, Maurice, who had teased and harassed me since the second grade, was no longer giving me as much of a difficult time, instead his comments became more flirtatious. Apparently others from his entourage were also becoming attracted to me. I felt a sense of pride in the fact that the popular guys were noticing me. That year I had swim class, and the boys would come pass the pool to see the girls. Maurice, Amir and Bam lurked around the pool flirting with me and Ashley, and commented on the way Ashley and I looked in our bathing suits. I remember feeling shy and uncomfortable with talking in such a mature way. Maurice was cute, but I was not attracted to him, I had a deep resentment for a long time because of the way he treated me in the past.

Every time I encountered the group of guys, they made references to the way my body looked in my clothes and continued to talk to me in ways that made me feel uncomfortable. I like the attention, but was unable to bring myself to tell them the content was out of my league. Choosing to feel uncomfortable, I just smiled and dismissed what they said, and tried to change the conversation. I was now well liked by those who use to humiliate me, and I did not want to compromise that. Any attention from boys was good attention. Although, I felt uncomfortable, the things they said and did appeared to be normal. It was no different than the ways guys treated and spoke to women in my neighborhood, in music videos and other forms of media, so I assumed maybe it was me, and something I had to learn to become comfortable with.

I wanted to be liked for who I was. I knew I was not pretty, but I wanted to think there was something favorable about me that was attractive, such as my personality, something other than just my body. Instead of telling the boys I felt offended by their sexual comments, I went along with it and played the part.

Their intentions became known as I realized their attraction to me was not genuine. They did not like me, they just wanted to get close to try their hands at groping me. This hurt my feelings greatly. I was more than hips and a protruding backside. I was nice, kind, and fun to be around, but these virtues were meaningless. I desperately wanted to stand up for myself and demand respect, but my low self-esteem craved the attention.

Bam was the raunchiest. For a guy to be so young, he had an incredible knowledge about sex. The things that came out of his mouth always left me dumbfounded. Despite his salacious dialogue, I sort of liked Bam, but not for those reasons. He was a big guy, with the cutest dimples when he smiled, and had a toughness that I was drawn to. I tried showing I was no baby, that I could handle the bedroom talk, simply by smiling and repeating: "Ya, okay, whatever," for lack of words. This was my response to everything he said. I heard the older kids and people talk explicitly all the time, so again, I just thought it was the way guys talked to girls when they liked them. I guess Bam had gotten tired of waiting for me to respond to his sexual innuendos, and figured, why waste time on me when there were other young girls who would find his immaturity flattering. I had become fed up with his denseness, and my interest had long since diverted toward his friend Amir.

During this same time, the "in crowd" had left the hallway were elementary and middle school classes were held, and graduated to high school. Widener taught grades K–12, the transition was a matter of relocating to one of the many separate sections of the huge single story building, which held grades ninth through twelve, known as the "High school Hallway."

I became attracted to Amir but never acted on it. I was too afraid to approach him, because I was so sure he did not feel the same about me. Amir was tall, slender, caramel complexion with slanted, dark eyes, and a gaping smile. He had a little mustache above his top lip indicating his evolving into manhood. Amir always had a fresh cut and dressed in named brand clothes, accented with matching baseball hats that made him even more attractive.

I never imagined Amir being interested in me, because I knew he had the biggest long-time crush on the only girl who was a part of their entourage named Tiffany. I felt I never stood a chance to her, as a result I became intimidated around Tiffany because she was pretty with long hair and every guy in school liked her. I felt I could not hold a candle to Tiffany, she was older and gorgeous. Tiffany had coco brown complexion with black, straight shoulder length hair. She had pristine white teeth that were perfectly aligned when she smiled through her plump pink lips. I believed in part, my feelings of intimidation came from the suspicious looks she gave to anyone who she thought was trying to come into her circle of friends, without her permission. I desperately wanted to be friends with Tiffany, but she always seemed unapproachable, so I stopped caring and kept it moving. (We eventually became friends after I left Widener).

Amir and I spoke while in passing, but for a while, never held full conversations, he would just say hi and nod his head at me with a smile. Amir was pretty much the quiet follower among his friends, he agreed with everyone and only put his two sense in when prompted. I guess he did not want his crew to know he liked me, let alone was talking to me more than just saying hi and bye in the hallways. As time went on, we exchanged numbers and talked a lot on the phone. After many conversations, Amir told me he liked me, but it had to be kept a secret, he did not want his friends to know. This bothered me because I did not know why we had to keep the fact that we had become good friends a secret. My general assumption was that Amir was ashamed of me, but never questioned him or made any demands, as I had become accustomed to doing, I just accepted it.

After talking on the phone so much, I had really grown fond of Amir. Amir began flirting with me, and although I did not like it when the others flirted, I liked it when Amir did; I even let down my guard by flirting back. I really wanted Amir to like me. A handsome boy was interested in me, and that was all I cared about. I was taken by Amir's looks and his looks alone.

I wanted to experience closeness with a guy, still wanting to know what it was like to be kissed, to have a guy put his arms around me and have that same connection I saw other teenage girls and boys share. Amir continued to talk to me, but it was always in secret when there was no one around. It became a routine, while in the presence of others, Amir never said anything leading on to the fact that he liked me. I began feeling upset about it, because I wanted to be his girlfriend and for everyone to know, I thought to myself, *Why not?* I became certain Amir was ashamed of me, which hurt my feelings deeply.

Talking on the phone so much about how he liked me and wanted to kiss me, tuned into Amir planning the perfect moment to implement his words into action. Never letting on to how nervous I was to have my first real romantic kiss, I grew more and more nervous as the day, then the moment approached. I knew I was in way over my head, but I was beyond curious at that point.

The plan was for me to meet Amir behind a large, oversized tree that set over by the back entrance of the library, far from where everyone gathered outside for the thirty-minute lunch break. The tree created a shade, where no one could see us. It took me some time though to actually meet up with Amir, because I was filled with shameful hesitation to experience my first kiss with someone who I believed felt embarrassed to be seen with me. I was also consumed with the fear of getting caught, at the same time excited to have my first kiss. I finally mustarded up the courage, against all risks and met with him.

All questions were answered and I was convinced I liked being kiss by Amir. We started to meet every chance we found, and kissed all through recess. My body felt numb and trembled the entire time, while fearing that someone would eventually catch on to us being missing, and discover our secret. Not only was I nervous about some-one calling us out, but after meeting up to kiss so many times, I begun to feel uncomfortable. Every time, I saw Amir, the only thing on his mind was kissing. I felt used, but again instead of speaking up and telling him how I felt, I kept up with the charade.

I knew the position I put myself in was wrong, and that I was only hurting myself, but I continued to meet with Amir, until the guilt and shame I felt, finally shook and grabbed a hold of me, making each time more and more uncomfortable. As I started to see the fact that Amir did not respect me and that he had no intentions of ever telling his friends about us, I began feeling really small, and knew it had to end. I really wanted Amir to prove me wrong, but he never did.

Finally, one day I did not show up. I never told Amir that I no longer wanted to see him, I assumed I was doing Amir a favor by pulling myself away, because it appeared he really did not want to be seen with me anyway. Amir persistently ask me to meet up, but I ignored him and did not show. I wanted to go back to preserving my innocence. Although I did not feel esteemed, I knew I wanted and deserved better. Even if I never experienced what I hoped to in a relationship with a guy, I still knew I deserved to be treated with respect.

Maybe it was the fact that we all were young and immature, but it still opened my eyes to the way guys were. I was trying to be too grown, too fast, coming to the realization that I had only set myself up to get hurt. I wanted to believe there was someone for me. Another one of my mother's sayings was "God will put the right man in your life, and he will accept you for who you are, just as you are. You will be able to show him every aspect of yourself and he will accept and love you." Again, I held on to hope that what she said was true. I thought that because I was a good person, a good guy would eventually love me for me.

One of the things my mom emphasized, was that we were in the world but not of the world, which meant that I had to know the difference between what was carnal and what was of God. If I focused on what was of God and lived my life according to what was right, then I would save myself from the troubles and pain of the world. By the time I had become a teenager, I had gotten tired of my mother's sanctified speeches. Above all that she said, I followed what she did.

Her example had always been that she needed to have a man around; therefore, I developed the perception that I needed one too.

Lust, attraction, and the need to be with someone were constantly glamorized in the media, and then normalized by so many in the environment I grew up in. These messages shaped the perception of love and relationships for an impressionable young me. The message read "You have to be desirable for a man to want you," and that anything less than a "10" was unacceptable. Physical attraction had such a high emphasis, that I could only hope personality and introverted aspects of myself could rein over what I lacked physically. I often heard clichés like "Beauty is in the eye of the beholder" or "It's what's inside that counts!" All I could do was hope that out of so many shallow guy/men in the world, there were a few who fundamentally believed in these truths.

Instead of focusing on things a teenager should have been focused on, I became determined to find someone. I did not like being the only one among my peers not having had similar experiences. I noticed how girls easily got attention, and how their confidence blossomed because of the constant admirations, affection and attention from guys. I also noticed how awkward I felt being able to count on one hand the number of times a guy showed me attention, let alone showed genuine interest in me. When around my friends, I kept the focus on them, about their experiences with their boyfriends, or guys trying to pursue them. In high school I felt extremely awkward and out of place anytime I was with an attractive girlfriend while in public. No matter who I was with, I noticed the attention that she easily received from guys and how easily I was ignored. I often wondered if the friend I was with noticed.

In high school, I started going on lots of outings with the girls I had become friends with. It was then that I began to feel optimistic about having a normal social life and meeting new people. My time was split between doing fun stuff with Drita or Chanel. I enjoyed doing things normal teenage girls did. When we went out, I dressed in my best, feeling cute. I felt my confidence came across to people in passing and they thought the same, but they often did not; although people still stared pointed and mocked, I did not care, I felt deserving of the feeling.

Whenever someone walked up and asked to talk to her, I walked away to the side giving them space. Sometimes there were two or three guys and not one even looked my way, let alone spoke to me. I felt shameful, embarrassed and hurt, but I never let on to the fact. I wondered if both Drita and Chanel caught on, but never said anything because they felt sorry for me.

I remember going to a Temple Party with Drita and a few of the other girls. We all laughed and talked, enjoying the surround sounds of the music and the atmosphere. One by one, the girls were pulled to talk or dance with a guy, and I was left standing alone. I felt embarrassed, it was obvious that no one wanted to dance with me, but I made no mention of it. When everyone came back to where I was standing, I quickly put the attention on them, digressing in hopes that no one pointed out the fact that I was not asked by a guy to dance.

I was ashamed that I did not have experiences to relate to girl talk. Therefore, I kept the interest on them and their stories so whoever I was talking with would not imply about me, because I never had anything to share. I was more ashamed to explain why guys were not interested in me, but I believed no one asked, because they already assumed the answer. I have always been told I give great relationship advice, this is because I have had so much time throughout my life to understand that looks were not as important as people weighed them.

There were several girlfriends with whom I believed only talked to me for this very reason. I was just happy to be highly considered for something. It pained me to sit and watch others have the experiences I wanted to have for myself, I thought it was unfair. I did not know what it felt like to be courted, for a guy to go out of his way to show how much he cared; I did not know what it felt like for someone to tell me they loved me first or put forth effort to show appreciation for me.

These things appeared to come easy for females whose appearance affords them these privileges. It appeared a female's attractiveness held greater value to a man than any other aspect. A woman's beauty is often considered to a male to be a prize won, an accomplishment that most cannot wait to show off to his male counterparts to be envied and commended for. A good looking woman symbolizes prestige, she represents high standards and success in finally getting it right. It appears all other essentials that should be considered in choosing a partner becomes caviler, and deemed trivial compared to a beautiful woman, a "10," a "dime."

Feeling discouraged in ever finding someone the traditional way, I took a different approach I thought would be easier for me to meet guys. I felt the only way someone was going to see me for who I was, and not quickly dismiss me because of my appearance was to meet people over the phone. I was sure this method would give me a great advantage.

The evolution of what we know today as social media, began with what was then referred to as "the party line." A network of hotlines where callers from all over the city, and country could call and be connected with other callers looking to converse, meet up and establish deeper connections. The expectations of forming a genuine connection were based on the accurate description on prerecorded messages involving erroneous and exaggerated superficial qualities. Callers were given many options of the kinds of people they wanted to connect with by choosing to enter designated "rooms" prompted by pushing the corresponding number on their landline phone.

Before MySpace, Facebook and now a slew of other dating sites, chat lines were the new age realm for meeting people, with the intentions of forming long term, meaningful relationships. I was among the many naïve and desperate seekers, who had resulted to the lows of hoping to meet Mr. Right. The truth was that the party line became a convenient and deceptive way to solicit one night stands and everything else. I first learned about the line from Hakiem, who he and his friends called to prank callers. Then there were those late night commercials advertising chat lines as the liveliest party happening in the city that anyone with a phone could easily join in on the fun, by dialing an eight hundred number.

I believed the guys on the party line would be more sensitive to my situation. I met people fast, solely on the sound of my voice, and then won them over once they fell in love with my personality. I have always been told I have an attractive voice, and I knew it could be potentially deceptive if I did not disclose. Therefore, I made it my first priority to be up front and honest about my appearance at the very beginning of every conversation I had with a new guy.

Most chat lines I called prompted callers to give descriptive massages; in this initial meet and greet, I was as forthcoming as I honestly could be. I was mindful of the stereotypes and misconceptions associated with impersonal and informal ways of meeting people. The most common is that a person seeking the option of anonymity to meet the opposite sex, must be extremely unattractive. Immediately when someone ask me what I looked like, I started out by describing aspects about myself that applied to any woman, such as my height, weight, hair length, eye color, stature, and complexion. Then depending on whether I decided to further the conversation, I eased into telling them the story of what happened.

I disclosed how much of my body was burned, trying to explain aspects of my disfigurement that no description could create an image for the caller to envision. I was careful with the words I chose to describe myself, such as never using the word disfigurement, because it sound so grotesque. I tried to be as distinctive and accurate as I could in describing myself to the fullest, hoping it would be enough to prepare them to imagine the worse. My thought was, if they were already expecting the worse, they might not feel I deceived them, or that they somehow would be prepared to handle my distinctive look.

In the back of my mind, I did not think the forum would be any different than meeting a guy in person. I understood there was a strong chance that once a guy saw me, he would not want anything to do with me, but the rationale that convinced me otherwise was feeling confident my personality would weigh far greater than my appearance.

I had one experience with meeting someone over the phone before ever dialing the party line. I was thirteen and for my birthday, my mom allowed me to have my own private phone, and got me the first AT&T cordless phone. Having a phone was the biggest thing for a teenage girl, it was a luxury, and an essential. A guy dialed my number, attempting to reach someone else. He was taken by my voice and we ended up talking on the phone for hours. Hours turned into days, then weeks, and then months. Will and I talked everyday all day, after school and sometimes all the way through the night and into the morning, with only an hour or two before we both had to get ready for school. We talked so much that my mom took my phone away, but that did not stop me because I either snuck into her room to retrieve it, or I used an old corded phone, that was clear exposing the wires and hardware. I loved the phone because I could turn the ringer off and knew when Will called by the colorful blinking lights.

Will and I became good friends through our conversations over the phone. We talked about everything there was that teenagers could talk about, to deeper conversations about our families and our future. In these conversations, I eventually told Will about my accident. What I learned to be true about talking to guys over the phone was that when I described, as best I could my physical details, they always assumed my injuries were not as extreme as I described them to be.

Guys could not imagine the severity, because the way they pictured me from my attractive voice, caused them to think I was overreacting. Sending pictures were not as convenient as they are today. Back then everything had to be sent through the mail. This gave me an advantage, because most did not request pictures. Fearful of meeting Will, I prolonged the times we scheduled to meet for the first time, and when that time came, I found an excuse to meet at another time. I purposely rescheduled, to allow more time to talk to Will, because I was just too fearful of him not liking me and losing a friend.

Will was the first of so many to say, "I don't care about what happened to you, I like the person I have come to know." With this assurance I was eager to meet him, but still hesitant at the same time. I knew Will was sincere, but also knew he did not know what to expect. I convinced myself that everything would be fine, because we had built something very strong.

The day came when I gave Will my address, I paced the entire time leading up to him ringing my door bell juggling the odds. It was too late, to back out, Will was on his way; then my doorbell rang. I told my dad Will was a friend I knew from another friend and he was coming over to hang out. My dad would have killed me if he knew the truth. At the moment when my hand was on the knob, I felt confident that I looked good and there was no way Will would not like me.

I opened the door and instantly caught the stunned look on Will's face, but he quickly switched to a face of false excitement to see me. I caught on to it immediately, and instantly knew it would be the last time I saw or spoke to him, it was all too much. I confronted Will with ease and understanding, but he denied that he was uncomfortable. As I would do with every guy I met this way, I tried to manipulate the situation by saying, "I know this is too much and I understand if you never want to see or talk to me again, I would not blame you." My hope was that they felt guilty for being shallow and felt compelled to stay around because in their own words, "You are an amazing person." I was sure my personality won the guys I met over, but then my inner self who had become so used to rejection, expected and facilitated rejection by pushing guys away before they had the opportunity to do so themselves.

Will visited me early in the day, and by the end of the night when he did not call, I was sure I was right. The next evening Will finally called, we had a long talk in which he confirmed my presumption, my appearance was too difficult for him to handle, but said he wanted to continue being friends. To my surprise, Will started to cry, we spent hours on the phone having an emotional conversation resulting from a mutual loss, of something special, that we both grieved. Will cried because he felt it was such an unfair situation and for being angry with himself for not being strong enough to deal with it. I was broken hearted, but still wanted Will to be in my life, so for a while we continued to talk, but not as we used to. I knew it would be a matter of time before the calls became fewer until we did not speak at all, and eventually the calls stopped.

To cope with the rejection, I used the party line over and over, trying to find that one who would eventually prove to be different. Despite the way I felt, I continued to do so and it became somewhat of an obsession, because in so many ways, it made me feel validated, important and attractive. From the sound of my voice, and the content of my conversation, I was desirable and the ideal of a "real" female that most guys claimed they were looking for. It was easy for me to be myself, while not having to worry about being judged by the way I looked, or instantly overlooked for the lack there of. What I was doing however, was putting myself through unnecessary disappointment. I knew I would run into the same kinds of guys no matter what age or type. I was learning that physical attraction was invaluable, and that I had no chance.

I got to the point where it was no longer about finding someone to be with, but just having a male companion to talk to. Anthony was my only male friend and since we both were away at college, I was lonely and just wanted to call a guy a friend. I also figured, being just friends with a guy with no intentions of anything else, would be less threatening. I did not think appearance determined a friendship, but it did, because they rejected me too.

Out of the many guys I spoke to, I only met a few, in non public places, knowing the situations in themselves were risky. Even with the one's I did meet, I was clearly not thinking at all about the potential danger and harm I was putting myself in, by meeting up with random guys. No one knew what I was doing, where I was going and who I was with. I did not know if the guys I was talking to were really who they claimed to be over the phone, and went as far as meeting up with a few at their houses alone.

God truly watched over me. Looking back at how vulnerable I was, being so young, and in my condition, a guy could have easily physically assaulted me, raped or even killed me for denying his advances. I was so naïve in believing they wanted to get to know me, when in fact, all they were interested in was sleeping with me. In moments of irrational thinking and many more moments of not thinking at all, I somehow had enough sense to know I did not want to lose my virginity to just anyone. I was going to great lengths to pursue someone, at that point anyone who would accept me, but had somehow managed to stick by my decision not to sleep with anyone until I was sure I found the right one.

By the middle of high school in the end of my Sophomore year, nothing changed. It was seldom that guys spoke to me, let alone approached me with sincere interest. There were those whose intentions were blatantly obvious. "Girl, I like what I see. Where your man at? Come here, let me get your number." I declined by lying that I had a boyfriend or that I did not have a phone number to give. Then there were the creepy guys, who made me feel extremely uncomfortable, who I gave incorrect numbers to, because I felt too afraid to say no when they asked. Then there were the guys, who appeared genuinely nice, attractive, and appeared to be decent with the intentions of getting to know me, but eventually after much wasted time, they revealed their true intentions.

I remember few comments made from guys, one who said, "You should be grateful that I even paid your ugly self some attention." I knew most guys would attempt to take advantage of me, if I allowed myself to fall for their ruse. I do not know where it came from, but despite my low self-esteem and strong desire to be with someone, was the courage to say no to the wrong attention.

Reality continued to kill my optimism as I finally realized that guys just were not into me. I was beginning to believe I was not entitled to attention or deserving of it. My frame of mind had gone from desperate to hopeless. I started convincing myself that I was going to live my life unhappy and alone. Therefore, having had exhausted all hope for the future, my disparity caused me to compromise all of my diligence to rise above the pressures to have sex, and made the crass decision to do so. I had just turned eighteen when I haphazardly met Keith, while heading to my dad's house on the bus, and with a "Yo girl, what's your name," we started to talk.

Keith was a guy who did not seem fazed about what happened to me, Keith was very smart, and had the potential to be someone with high credentials, such as a politician with his level of intellect. Instead he decided to be complacent living with his mother, who he constantly fought with because she wanted him to find a job and move out of her house. Keith was twenty-seven, and resembled a younger T.I. He spent most of his time in a marijuana fog, and when he was not smoking he was popping prescription pills and drinking until drunk. Keith had no goals, no ambition and suffered with depression, but he noticed me and that was good enough. There were no romantic preparations, Keith did not make me feel special, nor did he even care that it was my first time.

I do not remember much about my first time, maybe because it was quick and uneventful, nothing as I had anticipated it would be with the right guy. After, it immediately hit me what I had done to myself, an indefinite wrong that I could never correct. It was a mistake that caused me great shame, even when I eventually got to a place of self-acceptance, I found losing my virginity the way that I had hard to come to terms with.

Looking back, I can see that for a very long time I was truly lost, broken and confused. My spirit was in a devastating place, searching desperately for anything that resembled love and acceptance. From these experiences, I had not gotten the picture and I had not seen the light, because I would later fall back into these patterns to resume the search. I eventually learned that by standing for nothing, I truly fell for anything.

My misunderstanding then, and for a long time after, was that being with someone was the key to happiness and fulfillment. I was spiraling out of control. I continued to meet guys with whom I met over the phone and later the internet, expecting different results, in hopes that my personality would be more than enough. I would come to realize that every path I took in finding my worth in a guy, lead only to dead ends of feeling rejected, alone, broken hearted and extremely bitter. The condition of my heart and spirit were slowly deteriorating, and it would take a great amount of time to repair the insurmountable damage done to both.

CHAPTER 15

Carrying Mommy

UNFORTUNATELY, OLD DEMONS RESURFACED as my mother began to use again. After some successful years of sobriety and focus on building a new foundation, the bricks came tumbling down before the cement could completely dry. When she began using and drinking again it was such a disappointment. I feared for the worse as the drama and dysfunction were all too familiar. I was so angry with my mother for being selfish and irresponsible, yet again. I could not understand why she just could not get it together. As a child I did not understand the underlying causes and effects of addiction, all I knew was what I saw and experienced was traumatizing.

My mother's behaviors and affects where all too familiar when she drank and used. Therefore, I instinctively knew when she was using, despite her efforts to hide it from us. We were her children and had unfortunately become acquainted with her lifestyle.

It was very disheartening when she relapsed. My mom had been doing so well in her recovery. She had gone back to school to finally complete high school and received her diploma, she also worked a few jobs. All seemed promising. My siblings and I loved seeing her do well and looking good, it was the greatest part of our mother being clean. It was encouraging that my mother had a network of support; however, my mother appeared to not use discretion when choosing who was in her circle. Many of the men she met, were also in recovery. There was one man in particular whom she formed a relationship with who relapsed. Not long after meeting him, my mom soon followed. She was naïve to believe that she was strong and secure enough in her recovery to support him during his setback. We all knew he was trouble and strongly opposed her being with him, in no way did we like him, because he spurred my mother's addiction. She quickly fell back into old habits and slowly disengaged herself from her support network.

I instantly knew when my mother picked up and used again. When my mom got high, her mouth quivered and her speech became slurred, low and very calm. She did not say much because she did not want me to know that she was high, nor would she look at me, because she knew I would notice. When I detected her state, I went into my room, closed the door and become upset with her.

I suddenly had this physiological response, where my heart sunk deep within myself from the feeling of disappointment, then raced faster than its normal rhythm, as the rest of my body shook with anxiety. Anger kept me pacing back and forth, and fright clogged my throat causing me to be silent. Being so young, I became uncontrollably nervous when my mother was inebriated. One reason was because I never knew if whatever she was using would cause her heart to stop or cause her to go insane and she harmed herself. The second reason was that I thought each time would be her last time, I feared she was going to die.

There has always been a contrast to my mother, in the mist of her darker times, she managed to hold on to her spirituality. It was during these tougher times, that she found the strength not to completely let go. My mother's spiritual relationship with God meant everything to her. Even if she had a night full of cutting up, and flipping out, that very next morning she would be up before the sun illuminated the sky, on her knees praying, listening to praise and worship music, which started each day. We awoke to my mother praying along with her favorite host on WDAS Am, Mrs. Louise Williams, who took prayer requests from callers, and gave daily words of inspiration. Sometimes my mom could be heard through her closed bedroom door on the phone praying with and for others.

When my mother prayed, she prayed wholeheartedly and with conviction. Through her earnest faith, she sought out God to deliver her from the things that she was powerless over. No matter which way she strayed, the name of the Lord always flowed from her lips. She would always say to us, "I don't care what I do, don't judge me… God still has his hand on me."

My mother prayed like her life depended on it, because it did. She prayed with the expectancy that what she prayed for would come to fruition. My mother was what is known as a prayer warrior. The words she spoke were weapons in a vicious attempt to slay the enemy dead in its tracks for the havoc and calamity it caused in her life. Whether she was praying for whatever current issues she was fighting, or whether it was speaking over another person's situation, my mom was serious about "the word."

My mom shared her love for God with us, and taught us about the miraculous power of God and the importance of living a consecrated life. What I admired about my mother was how knowledgeable she was of the scriptures, but more importantly her devotion and passion for God. Regardless of her human faults, she prayed, she worshiped and honestly kept God first in her heart. No matter how many times, she fell, she got back up to praised God anyhow, her faith may have been weary, but she held on to it with a firm tight grip, because it was all she had to hold on to. Experiencing this aspect of my mother, made me pray for such spiritual strength.

My mother's spiritual truth could be seen any time when she arbitrarily was led by the spirit. In church she shouted, praised, and spoke in tongues, as the Spirit led her in the middle of the church ales with all eyes on her. When I was younger and did not understand, I was fearful that she might fall backward or attack someone with her wildness. I did not understand as a child the power of the Holy Spirit. With all that my mom was going through, she meant serious business when she went to God in prayer. She strongly depended on her faith for a break-through and through her praise and worship, she was spiritually fighting for it.

Most times after church we all gathered together in her room to listen to gospel music then took turns reading scriptures from the Bible, at which point my mom had us read whatever passage we randomly opened up to. My mom believed by doing so was God's way of leading us to a meaningful message. My mom explained to us what we read, and found how to apply its meaning to something about the person reading it. She then had us each interpret the meaning of what we read and ended by encouraging us to continue the things we were doing right and confronted us to change anything which was not Godly, or usually something that really irritated her. She used the word and God as virtuous tactics to make us feel spiritually guilty about things she could not get us to stop doing.

My mother's altered personality was of both righteous and malevolent. We witnessed the never-ending battles between both trying to reign supreme dominance over her. I wanted the righteous personality to knock the malevolent personality on its ugly backside, for trying to claim her spirit, and her joy. However, the nefarious strongholds that restrained my mother, seemed to overpower her spiritual will to be righteous. In these darker times, it was clear that the malevolent personality was running the show. Many times she crept in without warning or notice.

Nothing more difficult than my mom being inebriated, was dealing with the behaviors that followed. My mom usually designated the evenings for her recreational activity. Usually after we all had settled down for the night, and she was less likely to be disturbed. Her narcotic and drinking escapades became an everyday occurrence. When my mom drank her demeanor was violent, but when she got high, her demeanor was first calm, extremely nice, then not long after showing symptoms of psychosis.

When my mom used, it felt like hell for us. We were unable to get a good night sleep because of her hallucinatory and erratic behavior. She would have music blasting, walk around the house turn on every light, and check every door. She constantly paced around in a state of paranoia. Her rituals included spraying cans of air freshener to mask delusional smells that were only apparent to her. What she smelled were the fumes from the smoked crystallized substance.

Her erratic behavior also included bursting into our rooms in the middle of the night, waking us up to help chase away her hallucinations, insisting that someone was trying to break into the house. She would make us follow her around the house checking the front and back doors, and made sure every window, including the ones in the basement were locked. One time never was enough. She repeated the same things over and over until her high diminished, which wasn't until early in the mornings. In the mornings my mom appeared apologetic, cheerful, and sometimes moved to do things for us, such as give us money or buy us stuff in attempts to expiate any asperity or ill thoughts she may have thought we formulated about her. She probably hoped that our deep sleep would expunge the events of the night before.

My mom seldom got violent while high, so I looked to take advantage of the opportunity to get out my frustration and anger with her, by talking down to her, yelling, stumping around announcing how tired I was of her, and threatened to have her put in jail. I attempted to do whatever I could to make my mom feel guilt and remorse for what she was doing to us. My mom would later apologize, telling me how disappointed she was in herself and how it always was the last time. My love for my mom when she made these promises made me feel guilty for disrespecting her. When my mother's high wore off, she slept majority of the day, or acted as if nothing happened, only to do it all over again the next night.

My heart ached when my mom used, seeing her in such a dismal state destroyed me. I loved her so much that over time, I began disassociating by emotionally detaching myself. I began to think of the possibilities of my mom dying from drinking and using. In order to protect myself, I felt I had to create a tough exterior to prepare for the worse should anything happen to her, because I knew I would never be able to cope with the grief if anything had.

Seeing horrifying images of what drugs did to people on TV, I always thought, *What if my mother dies or someone hurts her while under the influence?* I remember being in the second grade and learning about drugs during the big "Just Say No" campaign with a dog named Ruff McGruff, a crime fighting, no nonsense mascot, who targeted young inner city children through hip hop. He relayed his messages through catchy raps and wore clothing that represented the urban culture. The mascot's ploy was to teach students how to stand up to pressures when presented with situations related to drugs. Ruff ended with the catchy slogan, "Just Say No." Police officers came to present to our class, the dangers of drugs. They had with them large display cases of sampled street drugs, ranging from pills, liquid, rocks and chalky, pallid powder substances. Underneath each drug, was a description of its rancid effects. I thought if just saying no was all a student had to do to stop drugs' powerful wrecking force, then why couldn't it be that simple for adults?

My mother's drug use was a closed kept secret, that we never revealed to anyone although many people in the neighborhood knew, because they were engaging in the same illicit behavior, and some got high with my mom. I could never wrap my mind around what was so bad in her life that made her want to destroy herself. I tried with everything to protect the innocuous image I had of her; I wanted to preserve my mother as I once knew her, at times to stop from hating her.

I never caught my mother in the act of using, nor did I ever see her in possession of it. This was because she showed a minimal consideration and respect by not using in front of us. I never wanted to accept the connotation, that my mom used drugs, because it was too painful to think of her using and knowing the consequences of it usage. I never cared about the details of my mother's addiction, quite frankly I wanted to pretend she was not using at all. I tried to be as far away from her as possible, to avoid the disgusting reality. Even when my mother divulged anything regarding her activity, I become nauseated.

I could not stomach to look my mom in the face when she was trashed, I refused to talk to her, and looked away from her, because I felt both sadness and embarrassment. My mother maintained her natural striking beauty, which made it even more easy for her to deny her addiction. I just could never come to accept that my mother was an addict. I did not want to think of my mother being a statistic, or a victim of the streets that failed to teach her how to "Just Say No." We all thought that if we made known the pain and disappointment she was causing us, it would be enough to make her stop, but it was not. She intermittently went to meetings, but her denial and manipulative behavior kept her active in her addiction.

Whenever she got high, we stumped and pranced around the house yelling and screaming, telling her how we wished she would just save us the agony and kill herself. It had gotten too much for us to deal with. I threatened to run away, and sometimes to harm myself, with the hope that the thought of me dying would scare her straight. Once, when I was in high school, I had gotten beyond fed up with her keeping us up all night, chasing away phantom intruders, predators and criminals. When we pleaded with her to let us sleep so as to wake up on time for school, she followed behind, opening doors turning on lights and telling us we had to stay up with her. I was so upset, that I grabbed a bottle of aspirin from the medicine cabinet, threatening to gulp them all down and kill myself, hoping to get her to stop indefinitely.

I had no real intentions of harming myself, just thought my dramatics would make her realize that she needed to stop. I held the bottle to my lips pretending to swallow it whole, but to no avail did it even phase her one bit. The drugs had her completely tranquil, she walked into my room, checked the window to see if anyone was trying to break in, told me to keep the windows locked and walked right back out of my room. I threw the bottle against the wall, and all of the pills bounced around like ping pong balls, before settling to the floor. I cried feeling helpless, tired and alone, feeling that we were the only ones living life with so much difficulty. I felt so sorry for myself, thinking, *Why can't I awake from this lifelong nightmare? How bad of a child have I been to endure everything that I have?* I did not talk about my home life, I was too ashamed to tell anyone the craziness I had to deal with, let alone that my mother was an addict.

Whether it was because of drugs or just her personality it became more and more difficult to deal with my mom. The physical abuse subsided in its severity and became more verbal and emotional. Although we were not experiencing the physical abuse, the harsh words she sometimes chose, and the impressions they left emotionally and mentally were just as traumatic. Now that we were of age and stature of maturity, my mother found other ways to keep us oppressed, although she truly believed she did it all in good faith and with loving intentions.

My mom gathered us all together for what were called "family meetings." The intentions of them were for us all to talk together about the issues we had as a family. However, the meetings quickly turned into interrogations and the opportunity for my mom to get off her chest things that we were doing that she did not like; things that irritated her, made her upset, and voiced whatever else she felt needed to be addressed. In these "family meetings," she used what she referred to as "healthy criticism" when pointing out sensitive things she felt we needed to know about ourselves. Her rationale was that "it is better to hear negative criticism from someone close to you who has good intentions, rather than hear it from someone with intentions to hurt you." I saw the meetings more as a vengeful agenda to talk down to us, curse us out, embarrass and berate us.

My mother was a devout Christian and used it as a double-edged sword. Her knowledge of God's word soothed the weary soul, but in these meetings, she used the word as a weapon of manipulation to evoke guilt, shame and condemnation. She would tell us that God gave her insight about our intentions, behavior and attitudes, and that He was not pleased. We all hated these meetings, I am sure my siblings shared the same dread and fear that I felt. The meetings usually allowed only our mother's thoughts, opinions and criticisms of us, but did not allow for us to share the same with her. If we were allowed to speak about issues we had with her, we treaded with caution, careful not to say anything that offended, upset, or made her feel guilt. What I had a problem with was that my mom used the word to convict, but she contradicted the word by her actions and lifestyle. My mom used religion as a means of control for her personal lack thereof.

If ever the meeting became contentious by someone disagreeing or challenging her, she felt moved to put us in place by smacking, shoving or threatening physical harm. My mother pick on us according to our ability to defend ourselves. I was always the one singled out; and victimized often because of the astringent sent of my vulnerability. When my brothers and sister became physically taller, in my mom's eyes, they were potential threats, with the ability to retaliate. My mom psychologically posed as a bigger threat through manipulation, and intimidation, using verbal aggression to humiliate them.

If my mom was upset, she many times tried to provoke my siblings, stepping in their faces, daring any one of them to retaliate so she would have probable cause to attack back. Therefore, we all responded to her scrutiny by remaining mute and unaffected. My brothers mastered tolerance and endurance, in which my mother tried her best to break them. She sometimes said the most atrocious things, getting close in their faces as she spoke with condescension, sometimes with formed clenched fists as if she was going to throw blows.

I however was not so stoic, my mouth got me in trouble, simply because I dared to correct her and stand up to the injustice we faced. Just the utterance of a word that refuted my mother's, angered her enough to get in my face and smack me around for thinking I knew more than she, or challenge her authority. I was nearing close to graduating high school and made it my mission to excel in my last two years to get accepted into college, knowing it was the only way out of that house.

With all of the dysfunction throughout the end of my childhood into my teenage years, my feelings toward my mom were more like an oxymoron, they interchangeably consisted of both love, strong dislike, but more so resentment. The drugs, men, emotional, physical, and mental abuse made me resent her, but my spiritual conviction made me feel guilty for feeling anything less than love, compassion, and sympathy.

I felt a deep sense of commitment and obligation to my mom, because she could have easily chosen to terminate my life, or chosen to give me away else's burden to deal with. Instead she kept me, loved me unconditionally, and had faith in me when no one else had. Now she was in dire need for me to do the same for her. As much as I wanted to hold my mom accountable, through empathy and compassion I learned to enable her. Holding on to hope that if I loved my mom passionately, unconditionally and helped lessen her suffering, then she would return as the mother I longed for her to be.

We had always struggled financially, but by this time, things had worsened. We did experience times when the heat was off, and had to boil water to make hot baths. There were times our cabinets and refrigerator were empty, and we became creative, using whatever we did have to make a meal. I remember my mom making pancakes out of flour and water, and spread jelly on them, to give the bland taste flavor. I used cheddar cheese spread to make cracker sandwiches. Most days I tried my best to get to school in time for breakfast; both breakfast and lunch were sometimes the only consistent meals I had. I figured if I ate two meals a day at school, I would be able to get through the night if we did not have much to eat for dinner.

When my mom relapsed, it took a financial toll on the household. The beginning of the month was the best time of the month, because my mom made sure to take care of the priorities first, before using the rest to get high. She shopped at convenient stores, stocking the fridge and cabinets with an assortment of cheap foods. We then had to be conscientious to make the food stretch for as long as we could, because usually within a week or two, we were without.

My mom wanted to stop, and well into her relapse, she tried demonstrating her efforts by having me hold on to money. As soon as she got paid, we both agreed on pay days, she would give me whatever money remained after the kids and priorities within the house were taken care of. I wanted to have something for emergencies, before my mom had a chance to irresponsibly spend it all. My mom knew that I was exceptionally good with saving money. When I was fourteen, I began working with a relative of a friend who owned her own daycare. I made twenty-five dollars a week, and by the end of the month, used my hundred dollars to help out around the house. The money I took from my mother, I then hid and we both agreed the money was to only be used for when a need arose in the house or with someone.

I sensed that my mom had the desire to get back into recovery, but I had a hard time believing her. Days or even sometimes later the same day she gave me the money, she demanded it back. I would remind her the purpose of me holding the money, and attempted to put my foot down, by refusing to give it to her.

My mom then cursed, stormed into my room throwing things around and even threatened me if I did not give her the money.

I was fearful of my mother, knowing it was a matter of time before her calm requests soon turned into aggressive and even violent demands. Even when she got into my face, I hoped to reach her with reasoning about why I refused to give her the money. Reminding my mom that something would come up that the money was needed for, such as an approaching birthday, or simply because it was all that was left for the month. My mom did not care, she would strike me or frighten me to the point where I just gave it to her.

This became a cycle, her giving me money to hold and later demanding it back to use. I had gotten to the point where, I realized I would have to step up in ways to provide a better means to an end, because the way we were living was unfair to the kids. I learned not to think of myself, my focus was on protecting and caring for my younger brothers and sister. I knew I had the strength to endure, but knew my siblings were not as stoic.

I started going out looking for after school jobs to help my mother out with taking care of the kids. A part of me was driven by the fear of my mother abandoning us again. My mom sometimes told us how hard it was becoming for her to care for us. Worse, was her threatening to leave to have her own life, and putting us away. This became a reoccurring threat, that I feared one day she would make good on her word. Being separated from my brothers once was too painful, and was something I was not going to allow happen again.

Since Rasheen's departure from the family, I had taken on the role as the oldest quite well, so well that at times I felt the roles switched, and I had become the parent caring for my mother. Whenever my mother did not feel like playing her role, or was unable to do so, I did. I cooked, cleaned, helped my siblings completed their homework, bathed and woke them up in the mornings for school. I loved my brothers and little sister so much, we were all each other had.

I assured them no matter what happened, I would do everything to see to it that we were always together and that I would take care of them. I talked to them about the importance of working together to get through those tough times, and promised everything would be okay. I comforted my siblings by telling them how much I loved them and how proud I was of who they were. I told them that we had to always pray for and love our mother regardless of what she did. I taught my siblings to never talk about her, explaining that she was sick and emphasized the importance that we all learn from her mistakes and aspire to do and be better. I added that no matter what we endured, we were strong; that God saw all and He would protect us and provide.

One of my greatest emphasis was on school, and how important it was to do well and graduate, because college was the only way out of the house and having a better life. Knowing we were able to confide in one another made the hell we went through bearable. I knew most importantly I had to exemplify the strength I was asking them to have.

Since I was young, I understood the importance of education, not just because it was the only advantage that I had to become successful, but because doing well would afford me the financial opportunity to get into a good college. The difficulties of our childhood, solidified the bond between me and my siblings. We all relied on each other for comfort and support. As the oldest, I not only became responsible for co-parenting, but I felt the responsibility to prepare my siblings for excellence.

I wrote out assignments in my lesson books, and used old workbooks and materials from school, that teachers no longer used, to play school with my siblings. Being as though Joshua and I were closer in age, I knew he would grasp the concepts better than the two younger ones. I looked at Joshua as my young protégé. He had a knack for learning, and I wanted to bring out the best in him. I sent my siblings to their rooms after play school with homework, that they had to return the next day, in which I graded. We had fun playing together, but I took the responsibility seriously, because I wanted them to be successful in life. I wanted us to be the change that would end the cycle of everything that represented failure in the generations of our family.

Joshua was a very bright, quiet, and shy child. The two of us were very much alike in the sense that we both were reserved and timid. Joshua was an exceptionally smart student, he always did well in school, his areas of expertise were science, math and vocabulary. I remember Joshua competed in a spelling bee every year at his middle school and brought home trophies for coming in either first or second place. Josh reminded me of myself in the sense that he loved to read books. His quietness and love for books bred an articulate and resourceful young scholar. I believed Josh channeled his anger and pain in books. Commotion could be taking place all around him, and Josh would be sitting in his room quietly reading.

We had no money, not even to buy books, so Josh borrowed books from his school's library. Most kids were interested in playing video games, but Joshua's idea of a good time when we were young, was nestling under a good book. Circulars came in the mail, and Josh and I went through to find anything containing ads for books. The great thing about buying books back then was that we could send away for the books we wanted, receive them a few weeks later, and then have to send a money order or check. Knowing that our mom had none of the methods of payments, we wrote a list of IOUs, and promised to pay them back when we were old enough to get a job.

My favorite series was the Baby Sitter's Club, and Josh's favorite was RL Stine's Goosebumps, which was based on the age appropriate horror, hit television show. Josh also loved the mystery books that allowed the reader to create their own ending, which I then stole from him to read. Both Joshua and I were the rational ones, level headed and most accepting of our mother, no matter how bad the error in her ways were, we always understood that we had to honor and obey her. Our hearts were tough enough to endure the pain, but at the same time, soft enough to compassionately love and show our mother grace. It would be this same love and compassion, that caused us to become the pillars that would later uphold the family.

While a sophomore in high school, I realized I needed to find a real job. I in the 9th grade, I started the job at my friend's relative's daycare making twenty-five dollars a week. When things bean getting financially difficult at home, I asked for a raise in my pay, the actuality was that one hundred dollars a month would not suffice an entire household. So I began looking for anything I could find. I went to the markets to bag people's groceries, which I was paid in tips, but they still were not enough. I then started looking every day after school for jobs. It was during these early searches for employment, I realized my physical limitations, limited the kinds of jobs I was capable of performing. Most jobs available to teenagers were in retail. I knew I could not physically manipulate money, especially scooping up coins out of the registers. I also could not sit and stand for long periods of time or lift heavy objects. Unfortunately for me, these limitations canceled out most jobs.

At sixteen, Philadelphia Futures connected us with our first legal jobs, which was a part of a summer job readiness program, but the job was only for a few months. I saved that money and continued my search. I eventually found a job working at a candy store, called the Candy Barrel located in the Liberty Place on Sixteenth and Chestnut Street. At the interview, I was upfront and honest about my physical situation, but shared my story, and need for a job. To my surprise, I received a call back and was offered the position stocking candy. The store was intimate and there were always two of us working along with the manager. He had helped to accommodate me, by limiting my duties to things I was able to do, such as stock and restock large barrels containing assortments of candies. It was my first job, where I made good money.

I was elated that I was finally making enough money to help out at home. I remember when I received my fist paycheck, it was close to two hundred dollars, but to me it felt like I had earned a million bucks. All I could think about was making my mom happy, and showing her she did not have to worry. The first thing I bought after cashing in my check was, a small bouquet of blue colored flowers for my mom, along with a card telling her how much I loved her with fifty dollars enclosed. When I got home she cried and thanked me. She told me she did not know what she would do without me.

By the winter of 1999, the job at the candy Barrel had come to an end, because the store was closing. I felt sad because I knew that I would not be able to find another job as accommodating and with a staff and manager who were so friendly and understanding. I continued to put in applications after school, but could not find anything. I became very discouraged, because the holiday season was slowly approaching and I knew my mom had no money for gifts. I did not care about receiving gifts, but I did care about my siblings having a Christmas. For at least the past two or three years, I was helping my mom buy Christmas gifts for my siblings, but this particular year was different; if I did not come through, they would not have received anything.

One day I went into Futures and spoke with my class coordinator, Mo, who was the definition of a beautiful soul. The best way to describe Mo was easy breezy and carefree. She had a calmness about her that instantly calmed the anxiety inside of me. Mo was a cute slender woman, with a stylish crew cut, very debonair and poised. She made looking ladylike very fashionable, with her cute handbags, that dangled on her wrist. What I loved most about Mo was that it did not matter where she was or what she was doing, she would stop to primp her lipstick, which was always a ruby red shade adding the final touch to her natural beauty.

Mo and I became exceptionally close, she was one of the few who I trusted to lay my burdens on. She was familiar with my plight at home and offered to allow me to come in to the office to do work in exchange for fifty-dollar cashier's checks that she gave me each week. I cashed the checks every week, and one by one brought the items on the kids Christmas List. I made close to four hundred dollars, in which I shopped every week for everything on my siblings Christmas list, including gifts for my mom. My brothers and sister knew our situation was bad, and did not expect to have gifts that Christmas, but I made it happen, they had enough disappointment, that they deserved to have a Christmas. I tagged the gifts mostly from my mom and a few from me, but they knew the truth.

My taking care of my siblings did not end when they were little. Joshua graduated in 2008 from Penn State University. I was so proud of my little brother, because there were now two college graduates in the family. I wanted to do something special for my brother's hard work. I saw how excited and eager Joshua was to enter the job market and I wanted him to make a grand entrance when he did. I had a little money saved in the bank, so I decided to use majority of one of my pay checks to invest into Josh's future by planting a small seed.

I felt it important to show Josh how to present himself with esteem and dignity when selling himself. Knowing even more how important image can be for a black man in search of not only a job, but a career. I needed to show my brother that I admired and appreciated his dedication of overcoming the odds. With all that we experienced as children, any young boy could have used his circumstances as excuses to do anything but succeed.

I always saw something special in Joshua, he was not an average black boy from the hood. He was destined for greatness, and every great man is seen in a mean suit; unfortunately my budget could only afford Ross. I took Josh shopping and began to school him on the important factors of success. I was not a man and did not have much experience professionally, but what I did know, I shared with my brother. One of the key factors is first impressions, which is highly influence by the way one presents himself. I knew Josh was shy and needed to gain more confidence. I was certain that looking the part for the career he wanted would give him a tremendous boost.

While shopping, Joshua questioned the things I picked out, but after I told him to trust my judgment, he ended up buying everything I styled for him. Josh walked out with five outfits and a pair of shoes. From that day on, Joshua has been sharp ever since. God showed this average boy just how extraordinary he was, and by this fact, Josh would go on to dedicate his life showing other young black boys who grew up like him, the greatness they too possess.

Joshua's first job was in the field of Human Resources with the Navy. From then on, he continued to climb the ladder of success to work for the Army, publish two books, started a tie line, founded a business and a non for profit, produced two musical albums, and is still climbing. Although my siblings have shown me their gratitude over and over for the things I have done for them, I could never take credit. I was just grateful that God positioned me to be there for my siblings when my mother could not be.

My brothers and sister attributes their childhood to me, but I did what I believe any older sibling would have done for their loved ones. I believed God used me in a powerful way to preserve and instill hope into our family. I am grateful He used me in such a way, that gave my siblings someone they could count on.

I was to them what I was looking for after Rasheen left. Someone there in the mist of the storm encouraging us to wait it out to see the beautiful rainbow at its end. I loved my siblings and there was no depth that I would not have gone to make them happy and to give them what they deserved to have–a childhood. It was being in this position as the "caregiver" that I learned the power of altruism. Through giving I received the greater blessing, to share the aspects of God's love to those in the greatest of need. Giving and caring for others became a part of my identity.

What I came to quickly learn, was that as big and loving as my heart was, I did not know that by helping, and supporting my mother, I was actually enabling her. I had tied a thick cord connecting us together, not realizing the weight of my mother would became more and more difficult for me to pull. Feeling dragged down and exhausted, I knew in order for me to move on, I had to cut the cord, and release myself from the overload that was weighing me down. However, I would find cutting through the thickness extremely difficult, but once the cord was cut, and I realized that I was finally free from her, I ran as fast and as far as I could. In the summer of 2001, when I left home to attend college, I left with the intention of never looking back.

CHAPTER 16

Valuable Lessons Learned

MY FEAR AND INTIMIDATION around people, particularly my peers pretty much spearheaded my choice in a college. I wanted to find an institution with programs in my interest of study, but I was more concerned with choosing an institution where I could feel safe in my insecurities. I did not want to go anywhere with a lot of students and where I could easily get lost in the crowd. I wanted to attend a college with an intimate class size, a comfortable environment that accommodated my needs, with students who appeared nice and easy to get along with. I was looking for the same qualities that determined my choice to attend Bartram Motivation. I was eager to meet mature and accepting people, who shared the same dreams, and who could relate to life's hardships and experiences. Most of all, I was hoping to be free from the superficial cliques, finding groups that I could be welcomed into and accepted because of common interest and intellect.

Unfortunately, majority of my negative experiences with insensitive people, have been from those of my own race in the culture I identified with. I believed if I went to a school that was not predominantly black, but diverse with Caucasians being the majority, then the possibility of being accepted and making friends would be greater. Up until I entered college, I held a bias, formed from the constant ignorance, disrespect, cruelty and intimidation experienced from the group of people I related to the most. Blacks in my environment did not hold back the disgust and fear they felt for me and had no discretion when it came to expressing how they felt. My experiences with other races were less crass. It was not that I did not receive the same negative responses and reactions, but they were more obscure and less appalling. I have found that outside of my race, people's ignorance was just that, not knowing. What I respected about Caucasians, Latinos, Asians, and others, was that they wanted to feed their curiosity with understanding. Even with their ignorance, they still showed empathy and compassion, and if the opportunity presented itself where I could explain what happened, it was the stone that broke the barrier of getting to know each other.

Looking over the course of my life and seeing how difficult it was for me to find acceptance, again I was hoping to manipulate what did not happen naturally. I figured I could do this with the careful selection of a college. Albright College in Reading Pennsylvania was my first choice because of its amazing communications program, and its small student population size. Eastern University was my second choice, not because of its' diversity, but because of its Christian base. Regardless of race, I was certain that people with strong conviction would certainly see pass my physical and recognize that beyond a mangled and maimed body was a pure and gentile soul. Another important reason that influenced my decision was its emphasis on providing academic supportive services.

I was not only worried about social, and spiritual experiences, but how I performed academically. I knew I was smart, but was still greatly affected from the academic trauma I experienced in high school with math and feeling I was in some ways, not smart enough for college. Although I had succeeded thus far, I knew college was going to be a challenge, and I did not feel quite confident in my academic performance.

What I did know was that my life greatly depended on doing well and completing. I was the very first in generations to attend college. If I had not succeeded in anything beyond that point in my life, I still had so much to be proud of in myself. I made no excuses, despite having many to choose from. Adversity is such a powerful force, in that it inspires one to exude strength, to become motivated and persevere, efforts that are not found in ordinary circumstances.

My physical trauma taught me that strengthening myself was imperative, and my childhood family trauma gave me the desire to want better and to be better.

The greater of my challenges was finding self-acceptance and developing a healthier self-esteem. As much as I had struggled throughout my life, I was at a point where I was consciously making efforts to improve in these areas. I really wanted to be better not only for my family, but for myself. I knew God loved me. I now wanted to get to a place where I could see the beauty that He saw, and acquire the same love and acceptance as He had for me. I understood enough to know that God would use me and what I had gone through for a greater purpose. Surviving the fire was of no coincidence, and I felt in my spirit God was preparing me for something epic, and entering college was going to be a critical time in my self-development.

I understood that after praying to God for success in true acceptance of myself, he wasted no time putting me through the rigors to earn that success. I had to work hard for what I wanted so badly. It was at this point that I understood, the saying "Faith without works is dead." I knew I had to have the courage and the tenacity to face my greatest adversary—myself. If I believed in my heart that God would truly make me successful, I had to also believe in myself to accomplish that success. I felt in my heart I was destined for greatness and that someday people would know me on a higher platform. I knew the power of my voice, and that I had something important to say that made people listen. Seeing how my experiences and others' who had gone through what I have, were products of an unjust and unconscious society, I felt I could make a difference in some way by using my experiences and the insight from them, to reach people in profound ways.

I had finalized a list of about ten colleges that I applied to, but then my guidance counselor told me about a Catholic college, Chestnut Hill College, late in the selection process. Initially, I was ready to dismiss it because the college was outside of my religion, although it was a perfect fit offering everything that I was looking for. What caught my attention was the fact that it was a single sex college for females. I immediately became aware of God's cleverness, and knew it was the college for me. I knew this was a test, and a critical one to my self-perception and esteem.

For so long I harbored a deep rooted inferiority complex, jealousy, envy and felt subordinate to attractive females. I knew I had to confront these fears in order to change my negative thinking and break free from the internal strongholds that imprisoned me because of my insecurities.

Initially I wanted to get as far away from what was my life, but realistically knew I could not. I still felt a sense of obligation to being there for my family. I liked Chestnut hill, because it was located North of Germantown Avenue. Within a few blocks, the distinction between poverty and wealth could be seen. At the top of the hill sat a huge castle, surrounded around acres of beautiful lush green hills and colorful landscapes. Chestnut Hill college was an oasis that made me feel far away from the harsh streets I grew up in, despite that the collage was a few miles from the impoverished sections, south of Germantown Avenue.

The college was not too far from home and the environment I had become accustomed to. As much as I wanted to get away from all that I knew to be reality, it also was very much a part of who I was, so I needed to be close to what I was most familiar with. I felt the same about my home situation, as far as I wanted to get away from everything, I felt I could not abandon my family completely. I had already felt guilty for leaving my siblings alone to fend for themselves, but knowing that getting a higher education was critical to helping my family break the chains of poverty that kept us contained in our family's generational plight.

I was in no way fearful of living on my own; with all of the responsibilities I had taking care of the house and my siblings, living on my own would not take much adjusting. For so long I saw myself as my own caregiver. In high school after telling my counselor about some of the things that were going on at home, she recommended that I strongly consider becoming emancipated.

I enjoyed talking to my guidance counselor. I felt that she genuinely cared about my future despite the many discreditable stories I heard about her loosing people's college applications. In one conversation, I ended up digressing from my plans for college to talking about wanting to leave home because living with my mother had at that point became intolerable. She spoke to me about becoming emancipated. She explained that although I was only seventeen, I could become my own legal guardian.

The more she explained to me what emancipation was, I realized that it was similar to my brother Rasheen's situation. After turning eighteen, and reaching the age limit to remain in group homes, Rasheen had been legally deemed his own guardian through an independent living program. He was given his own apartment and began making what could have been a successful life for himself.

When Rasheen returned home after living in the system for so many years, the relationship between him and my mom did not mend. Rasheen had too much resentment toward her for displacing him, and my mom disliked the fact that he was not obliged by her demands and subservient to her erratic behavior. Both egos often collided making it impossible for my brother to reside in the same house. Rasheen lacked the patience that Josh and I had to deal with our mother, nor did he have the level of empathy to excuse or forgive the things she did.

Rasheen was a very skilled and talented self-taught artist. He created his own logo that he designed on everything using his skill of calligraphy, and graffiti writing. He took plain sneakers and timberland boots creating his own unique, colorful designs, that made everyone want to wear what he created. Rasheen won several contests and received recognition for his abstract art and true to life self-portraits. Rasheen had such a promising future, but with the lack of support and no real outlet to process his pain, Rasheen's ambitions had no real opportunities to become achievements.

Now that Rasheen was older and no longer had to put up with our mother, he constantly tried showing her that she could not control him. However, my mother did not back down nor did she appear intimidated. She was a five-foot pistol who feared NO ONE. Her hard knock life, equipper her with an edge and mentality needed to sustain the mean streets. The only problem was that her response was the same in the house with her children, as it was with people who an aggressive persona was necessary to have.

My brother came home from juvenile rehabilitation, just to begin his many cycles of adult incarceration six months later. My brother challenged and confronted my mother. The underlying issue was there was so much pain between the two. Rasheen was hurting and resentful that our mother had not been there for him. The truth was that my mom was not understanding that he was a fractured boy in need of his mother, who failed him his entire life. He mostly resented her for putting him in the system. Rasheen had expressed his feelings of anger, the only way he knew how, which was by being explosive.

The reunion with Rasheen and our mom was brief. Weeks after being around, although he had been emancipated, and lived in his own apartment, my mom used her manipulative tactics to intimidate Rasheen. She randomly threatened to call the police or his probation officer and have him sent back to jail, whenever she got upset or did not get her way. Since coming home, Rasheen worked to do well and tried to make up for the time lost, but his efforts came with many challenges and temptations. Rasheen began hanging with the wrong people and doing the wrong things, which he believed was the only way to maintain his independent living. I do not know the specific details, but what I do remember was coming home from school to discovery Rasheen had been sent back to jail. He was placed in adult prison because he was of the legal age, and just like that I would not see Rasheen for about another five years.

Unfortunately, Rasheen would reenter prison many times throughout his life. Most of his adult years have been spent serving time behind bars. My heart has always ached for him. If only he had been given a chance, a chance to be a child without having to grow into shoes too big to fill. He was made to be a man without experiencing being a child. He did not have the chance to grieve the pain from the fire, which has always been the true cause for his anger. It saddens me what has become of my brother.

My brother was there for me in the beginning, when I was young, but much of my life, he spent in prison. During the times

Rasheen was around, he has always attempted to pick up where we left off as children, trying to protect and take care of me. My heart breaks to think of how big his heart is and how much love Rasheen has, to be there for and take care of others, but my mother did not know how to take care of him. She did not know how to tell Rasheen how much he mattered, or how to make him feel valuable. She did not tell Rasheen as a child, "Son, it was not your fault!" His lifelong persistence to still take care and protect me is evident that Rasheen continues to believe that me being burned was his fault. I often think where would my brother be today if only my mother had given him a real chance to be a child, and took the moment to hold him in her arms and say, "Baby, you were just a child and I left you to be a man, for that I am sorry."

I would have been required to present my situation before a judge explaining why I wanted to be emancipated while in the presence of my mother, which it would then be decided if the facts were enough. I feared the thought of having to explain why my mother was an unfit parent, right in front of her. I knew that once the Judge heard the overwhelming facts, there would be no way he would deny me the right. I practically was running a household by myself, while being a teenager in high school. Moreover, I felt apprehensive of airing all of our dirty laundry and risk the judge saying no.

I would be left with the consequence of trying to make my mother look bad. It all became too much, and I was afraid to face my mother, accusing her of being unfit, but more so what she would have done to me if I was returned back to her. I felt it was an act of betrayal and I was not prepared to slander her, even though everything I said would have been the truth.

I was really torn between being set free and leaving my brothers and sister. I felt that I could not live with myself for thinking only of myself, and making what appeared to me, as a selfish decision. My thoughts were, *what if my mom went home and took her anger out on them?* What if the judge heard my testimony and decided that it was not a safe environment for everyone, mandating that my brothers and sister go into foster care? I did not want them having to go through that. I decided that as good as an opportunity it was, I could not find the nerve to go through with it. My rationale was that I had one more year before I would have my independence, and that I could wait until I started college.

In the summer of 2001, weeks before students arrived on campus to officially start the Fall semester, I among a small selected number of students were given an early start to the fast pace and grueling demands of college. We all had been accepted into Chestnut Hill college's Act 101 summer preparatory program called Summer Success. Summer Success awarded qualified students with a grant toward the cost of tuition. It was a four-week program, which gave students a mock experience of what to expect academically, how to manage time and other strategies to make the college experience successful.

The summer program was intended for us to experience the intensity of a college semester, however it turned out to be more like an academic boot camp. Realistically, an actual semester's duration was about three months, for the program, an entire semester was compacted into four weeks.

The program was worth a four credit course toward the completion of our program of study and the final grade was added to our overall GPA. Therefore, we understood early on, the importance of doing well. It did not take long before we began to feel the pressures and anxieties known for making the grade in college, so with the fall semester officially starting, I was free from the freshmen anxiety.

My immediate feeling upon moving into the dorms was of optimism, that things would only get better. I had feelings of contentment and hope for making it thus far. Were it not for me listening to that inner voice on that school bus, telling me I was capable of so much more, I would not have had the chance to know my own potential and to excel to higher heights.

I was looking at attending college as a way to grow more spiritually, personally, socially, academically and professionally. I felt privileged for the opportunity and was looking forward to absorbing every lesson I needed to learn and situations I needed to experience, if it meant bringing out the best in me. I was looking forward to being challenged and inspired; determined to always face the biggest challenges, seeing the accomplishments in them as an added piece to the constructed puzzle of who I was destined to be. I never wanted to miss what God wanted to reveal to me about myself, knowing the opportunity may never present its self twice. I felt that refusing to face the challenges I feared, would stagnate my personal growth and move me further away from my purpose.

On the day of orientation, amongst a crowded room full of anticipating students and their teary eyed parents, I was greeted, by a girl who was full of energy and whose personality seemed to resembled a reflection of my own. She introduced herself in a high pitched voice, with what sound like a New Yorker's accent. "Hi, I'm Rhonda, what's your name?" The shadow of her tall statue hovered and swallowed my shortness, but her beautiful smile made me feel happy to be in her presence.

At first, I did not know why she approached me, she was absolutely beautiful. I felt intimidated and honored all at the same time to be in the presence of someone so stunning, and she was interested in getting to know me! Rhonda's tall, hour glass figure resembled that of the animated vixen Jessica Rabbit. Her striking physical beauty, highly resembled that of the singer Beyoncé, and her style was very similar to the then Destiny's Child lead singer. She wore platinum, blond, long extensions blackened at the roots, exaggerated, but well done make up and she was dressed in what appeared to be high end clothes. I had only saw her beauty on TV.

She walked over and began talking to me as though we were long lost friends who had not seen each other in a while. She just began talking to me with ease, and very interested in who I was and my background. Rhonda graduated from a well-known prominently Caucasian, higher-echelon high school located in the suburbs of the city. Rhonda spoke about her mother who was a retired school teacher, and how she sacrificed so much to put Rhonda, her brother and younger sister in the best educational programs, to create a successful path for her children.

In our first conversation, it was amazing to learn how much Rhonda and I had in common. From that day, we became inseparable, we shared the same dorm, set together, studied together and did everything else in between together. In such a short amount of time, Rhonda and I grew close and developed a great connection, because we shared so many interests, and had many similarities. It was unbelievable that someone so attractive was just like me in so many ways.

What I loved most about our friendship was that we talked. Rhonda was as much of a talker as I was, and just as loud; which was great, because I constantly had to be aware of my loudness that many times people found irritating. With Rhonda I felt such a relief because I was able to be myself, and knew that I could be around her. As we grew through Summer Success as friends, we grew even closer over the Freshmen Year.

We stayed up all night and talked about everything. I disclosed with her and she disclosed with me in ways that broadened my perspective, and clarified misconceptions I had formulated about physical beauty. It was listening to many of Rhonda's stories, as well as through careful observation of her, that truly redefined my outlook on beauty. I was surprised to learn over time, how much we related to one another.

Through Rhonda's stories I learned she dealt with many of the same personal conflicts, hardships and insecurities as me, which I found even more difficult to believe physically attractive females had insecurities. It just did not make sense to me, it was a great contradiction to the ways beauty was emulated and idealized. It was not until I entered into college that I got a closer view of the hidden ugly truths behind beauty. I saw how physical appearance in many ways, can be worn as a superficial mask that is highly deceptive.

Like any relationship, Rhonda and I experienced many ups and downs, which I believed was because we both were two strongly opinionated souls. We both loved hard and easily. In getting to know Rhonda, there were many things I loved and admired about her. She was affectionate, sensitive, and as generous as I was. She had a great sense of style, absolutely fun and dramatic. She was extremely creative and intelligent.

Then there were aspects that irritated me and pushed my buttons, like her messiness; but more so, her lack of awareness of how naïve she was to many things about herself that others close to her recognized, but that she could not, or refused to see. This issue appeared many times, as heated topics and confrontations became more frequent, eventually putting our friendship on a long hiatus.

Many thought Rhonda was trying too hard to be someone she was not. I felt her personality at the time grew too big and trampled me. I just remember after a while, feeling belittled, insulted and not considered by her. When I noticed character flaws, I attempted to say things to Rhonda out of love and concern. Being someone on the other end of the attraction spectrum, I could see things about Rhonda, that made her appear less attractive. Insecurities I easily detected in her, I had recognized in myself. I believed if brought to her attention, she would then be able to see in herself and change.

I quickly learned I too was a bit naive to believe that when I approached an attractive female with the intentions of helping her to recognize her truth beneath the exterior, it would not be received as such. Instead, many attractive females saw it as an insult, and mis-construed my sincerity as jealousy. To them it was the only concept that made sense. Many were so used to people confirming and vali-dating their physical beauty, instead of being the mirror that denoted they were not the fairest one of all.

This played out between Rhonda and I. One day I told her about herself and how at times she treated me, in which Ronda replied that she suspected I was jealous of her. To have heard Rhonda make such a claim hurt me immensely, because that was the furthest from the truth, and I was certain that she knew it. Getting to know Rhonda over time, I got to see the vulnerable side of her that no one else saw, and one of the reasons why I loved her; I saw beyond the physical beauty to see who she really was.

I saw something very interesting in our relationship, and this I learned was the work of God. I use this analogy: Rhonda looked as I was beginning to feel about myself, beautiful; and I looked the way she felt about herself at the time on the inside. The beauty that was adorned on the outside was not shown the same attention on the inside. Her personality had become unattractive and disfigured. Rhonda had a lot going on internally, and I thought as her friend she would respect the reflection of that truth coming from me, but she did not, causing a temporary end to our blooming friendship.

We have since come a long way in our relationship. I have always considered Rhonda to be a special friend, and it has been that bond and relatability that always kept us close. We would fall in and out of touch throughout the years, but when we needed each other, we picked up where we left off with no need to explain. There is an understanding and acceptance that we both have for each other. So many years later, Rhonda's beauty truly shines more than ever because the outer finally matches the inner. We were young and both had a lot of growing up to do. Our friendship is special in the sense that no matter how far apart life separates us, our love for each other always finds its way back.

During my years in college, I witnessed how trivial and insignificant physical beauty truly is in comparison to possessing great character. I learned that what lied underneath physical beauty is the true determination of one's worth. It is the building and maintaining of internal attributes that make up one's character, along with a good spirit that attracts and repels one from others. More importantly, they both are what sustains one through the trials and tribulations of life.

It always got to me when people emphasized beauty when rationalizing one being entitled to something. Take away the appearance and there exists a person. Under the beauty lies similar ugliness that determines the truth of one's circumstances. We as humans share universal responses to our environments, experiences and relationships. Beauty does not save someone from plunging to their death if they fell fifty stories down. Beauty does not prevent broken hearts or feeling worthless, despite constant attention and validation to the superficial self. These facts speak truth to the fact that physical beauty is worthless until character gives it value. Society teaches us that Beauty is the golden key to unlocking life's success. The media creates a smokescreen that blurs the truth, making it very difficult to see and accept when the smoke actually clears.

In asking God to help me become successful, it was during this time I came to realize that I already was. God showed me through observing other females that success is not determined by what one has or by their accomplishments, but is determined by the character demonstrated while dealing with life's' insurmountable circumstances.

I was successful because I had the characteristics that made me a conqueror over the adversity in my life. I believed God revealed to me early on that I would come into internal success, although I was very much still in pursuit of it. This revelation gave me the drive and perseverance to reach that personal success knowing someday I would have it.

Attractive females looked at me and instantly judged me, staring me up and down with pity, and never fathomed the thought of me being competition because of my disfigurement. I would then look right back with sympathy, observing and taking notice of their behaviors, personalities and situations, feeling grateful that I was nothing of their kind. There were females who believed they were God's gift to men. Females who never stopped to think they too were just collaterals in a guy's ploy to build upon his sexual reputation.

I felt sorry for girls with no real sense of confidence; confidence that can only result from the internal honors of honest self-work. Instead their confidence was superficially validated by men because of their looks. I felt more sorrow for those, who it was clear they relied solely on vanity, and had nothing but to fall back on. I felt sorry their good looks blinded them from the realities of the world that required increasingly more than attractiveness.

I recognized in so many females the same negative thoughts, feelings and low self-esteem that I had isolated to only my physical disfigurement. I was observing that many females also struggled with many of the same internal conflicts that I had, but engaged in self-destructive behaviors I could not personally relate to, such as drinking, using drugs, being promiscuous, physically hurting oneself as a means to escape, but more difficult to hear were the stories of failed attempts at suicide.

God was showing me through the different things I observed females go through, and from those who shared with me their pain in confidence, just how blessed I truly was. For so long, it did not make sense to me that many attractive girls did not feel good about themselves and even held the belief that they were unattractive, despite the obvious.

The common theme I began to notice among many attractive females was that they had their looks to use as a scapegoat to avoid having to deal with or expose their internal scars. However, when they found themselves in situations where physical beauty was irrelevant, they found the situations to be too difficult. I had come to observe many attractive females, were taught they only needed to rely on their looks. Unaware that there was more to them than just a pretty face, many females I came in contact with while in college and within this time of new insight, felt defeated, and gave up. Seeing that this fact was true with so many females, I began to not only see the beauty in my tragedy, but the insurmountable strength.

I realized that having to wear my scars on the outside, forced me to see the beauty of my spirit, and the good qualities I possessed. I had no idea that all of the challenges in my life and all of the pain I had experienced was building great character. The many attributes I gained through these experiences would become the reservoir of everything needed to face anything that came my way. I was beginning to see there was so much about myself to be proud of and have esteem in.

Being surrounded by so many females, caused me to pay closer attention and study them in contrast to my experiences, in the ways I viewed myself. I came to understand what my mother meant when she spoke of people being intimidated and envious of me; not because of how I looked, but for the character I possessed that many wish they had. Despite the way I looked, I knew I was truly blessed with having the intelligence that allowed me to think decisively, to be articulate, and having a profound spirituality that exuded strength and courage to live in my truth, despite having a physical truth that contradicted most female's perception of beauty.

For so long I had a jealous and envious spirit, not realizing that many of the same feelings I experienced were universal to women in general. What I found disheartening was that attractive females also had it difficult in the sense of being falsely judged by their appearance. Guys took advantage of them just the same—for their looks. I realized the same ways I viewed attractive females was a part of a social stigma: all attractive females have life easy, they do not go through hardships or have trouble with being accepted. After talking to many girls, I learned how people only saw value in them because of their looks, and how attractive females struggled to be seen for who they were or taken seriously. I heard stories of girls being exploited and sexually assaulted, and even using their beauty and body to get ahead, because they were convinced there was nothing else worthy about themselves.

One female shared with me that guys only saw her for her pretty face, and how she feared she would never find someone who would love her with the darkness and pain inside. She said when she looked in the mirror, she did not see the same beauty others saw. She saw an ugly, unworthy person who blamed herself for the pains of her childhood.

My perspective changed, I now had a greater appreciation for all females. These stories and lessons truly touched my heart, and gave me deep empathy for women as a whole. Hearing so many stories did not make me feel better about myself. It hurt me to see and hear the loneliness many attractive females also experienced, because their issues had not been validated. Hearing many share with me, the pressures of having to live up to what other's expected of them, and feeling they were viewed as just a pretty face, saddened me.

The same female went on to say, "Don't believe that the grass is greener on the other side. I have a lot of friends, but most of them are only around for what they can get from me. I have always felt alone, so much so that many days I wish I were nonexistent. No one sees who I really am. I would trade my looks to have your confidence any day. You Tanisha have real confidence, because your beauty shines so bright from within you, that I don't see your scars. I wish people saw mine in my heart, they are ugly and painful."

From these experiences I learned to see the beauty females possess both inside and out, and that all beauty bare scars. Considering the difficulties we all faced, I realized I was no different from those who judged me for the way I looked, because I too passed judgment based on looks. I decided to work hard on my insecurities and not allow them to cloud my judgment. I vowed to always uplift and bring to the attention of any woman the beauty I recognized in her, because there is a chance no one has ever validated her truth. I believe it is all of our responsibility as females to love each other, because we are a reflection of each other's beauty.

When I looked at the young woman I was growing into, I felt I was becoming more secure with who I was. My new experiences were teaching me to see the world outside of my bias, which began to give me freedom from my own self-criticism and negative thinking. I was beginning to see how favored I was.

I was given a uniqueness that set me apart from so many distractions and ill intent people who meant me no good, shielding me from getting involved with the wrong people. Good people could easily see and were attracted to the good in me. Although extremely painful and difficult to deal with, the solitude and loneliness I experienced, provided opportunities for deep reflection, self-analysis and to hear God's voice. It was while in this space where I replenished my strength in finding acceptance, and that first year in college, I had reached a pivotal milestone in moving closer toward it.

My plan was to go to school, find a good stable job, where I could save money and be able to find a place when I finished school. A place where my brothers and sister could come to if my mother decided to never clean up her act. I felt everything was weighing heavily on my shoulders, which helped me to focus and concentrate on doing well in school.

My intentions were to commute back and forth home regularly to help and to remain as a support for both my mom and siblings. Once I got settled into forming my own life and seeing how peaceful it was, I will admit my trips back home became infrequent. I dreaded going home so much that I requested and was among a handful of feign exchange students allowed to continue to reside on campus during college breaks.

When most students went home on weekends, I stayed in my dorm. I did not want to deal with the horrors I was hearing about from my siblings. Hearing from my siblings not much had changed, that my mom was using still, made me not want to return home. I will admit I was happy I had the option of not having to deal with the stress and anxiety, but felt guilty and shameful for choosing to avoid the drama, knowing that my siblings had to endure it. Still I chose not to deal with it, and realized I did not have to.

I was enjoying my independence, coming and going as I pleased, doing what I wanted without feeling as if I had to put others first, but still I did. I had a work study job on campus, throughout college. It was a great financial support, but I continued to do what I had always done, set aside all of my money to assisting my mother with the household. In my freshmen year, I often brought my siblings to the campus to meet my friends, they all knew about my home situation. I knew Marquita from Philadelphia Futures, but grew closer to her while in the Summer Success program, Rhanda, Marquita, Sharee, and I all became friends through the program, but grew closer through our freshmen year.

Marquita stressed the fact that I was being too kind hearted and emphasized the importance of me breaking away from enabling my mother and doing so much for my siblings. She told me that it was not selfish to take care and live for myself. I knew Marquita was telling the truth, because she had dealt with similar circumstance, and was also the one everyone in her family turned to. She had gotten to the point where she saw that she had to put her foot down and do for herself, so I knew she was only looking out for me.

One day Marquita came into my dorm room, I had just gone Christmas shopping and stuffed bags in my closet full of things for my siblings. Over time I had accumulated mounds of bags all for my family. Marquita said, "Tanisha, your siblings are spoiled, you spoil them. They need to learn to do without you." I thought she was being too harsh and did not understand my reasons for providing for them, especially for Christmas. She said, "I do, I get it, but anytime your sister or brother [Erica and Hakiem] want something, you go out of your way to get it for them." It was true, I rationalized it because they mostly did not have or got the things they wanted, and a part of me felt good to put a smile on their faces and make them happy, in attempts to take away the pain and sadness they lived with.

In the summer before my Sophomore year, I traveled to Boston for a skin grafting procedure to my chest. This particular trip to Boston, I had gone without my mother, and with my then boyfriend Kareem. While there, I spoke with the hospital's social worker, who knew my mom and I well from working with us over the years. She too was aware and had even witnessed many of my embarrassing moments with my mom during my recovery at the hospital.

It was this time around, that she asked how things were, and I shared with her about college and the financial hardships I was facing personally, while at the same time trying to help my mom and house-hold. She was well aware of my mom and stated that it was time I stopped allowing her to take advantage of me. I had no idea what she meant by what I believed was an insensitive comment. I at the time did not see it that way.

The social worker asked me about my Social Security benefits, in which I had no idea of what she was talking about. I listened as she told me I may have been entitled to receiving supplemental money as a result of my disability; that my mother would have been the primary beneficiary or "payee" until I reached the age of eighteen. When I stumbled upon this information, I was consumed with so many feelings, but mostly anger that my mother never disclosed such information to me. I also was elated to be entitled to money that would lessen my financial burden while in school.

The counselor set with me one day and had me call social security to confirm if I was receiving money, how much, and what I could do to become my own payee. She then explained to me how I was being an enabler to my mother, that by justifying the things she did, I was only allowing my mother to continue to have her way. I was confused as to what I should do, but motivated at the same time to do what I needed to for myself.

At that time, all I thought about was what that money could allow me to do. My first thought, was of taking care of my brothers and sister, and not care what my mother chose to do with her life. During this time, her addiction had gotten worse, although no one told me what was going on at home, because they did not want me to worry, my conscious told me otherwise. My suspicions were confirmed when I called and heard about the things my brothers and sister were going through.

I called Social Security to in fact learn that I was receiving a little over five hundred dollars a month. As a college student, this was a significant amount of money. I confronted my mother about the money in which she confirmed she had been receiving checks for me since I was very young. Mrs. Pat, the family social worker also assisted my mom in applying for benefits for me.

When I asked my mom why had she not told me about the money, she said she intended to when I turned eighteen, I was almost twenty one. A payee is determined based on the ability to responsibly manage their money. Based on this fact, I should have been my own payee a lot sooner. I was not extremely mad because I saw how my mom put money to good use to take care of us throughout the years before things worsened, but I was upset to know that it was my money she was using to support her addiction. If I had known about the money, I would have snatched the rug right from beneath her.

I really did not know what to do, and every time the counselor met with me during my stay, she would ask me what I was thinking. I kept putting the matter off because I was terrified of going against my mother. I did not want to cause a rift between us, even though I was entitled to my money. I did not want her to see it as me selfishly taking away from her, but gaining to support and better myself.

When I returned to school, I made the call and became my own payee. When I told my mother, she blew a gasket, attempting to manipulate me by saying if I made the changes, she would lose her housing. All the while, I learned this was not in fact true, because her housing was based on her income, therefore she would not have to pay rent. She then threatened to never speak to me again. Although these ploys affected me, I knew I had to do what was best for me.

While in school, I was without support, I saw how other students had support from their parents financially and in between, how they were able to settle into the comforts of just focusing on their studies and enjoy college. I, on the other hand, could not go to either my mother or father for much support, especially financially. I was responsible for finding ways to pay for my books and anything else that tuition did not cover. I had help from my mentor Vita and Philadelphia Futures, but the checks I received from my SSI, helped significantly.

By my Junior year of college, I found myself back in a familiar place of feeling alone. Academically I was getting by, and trying to make up for the hit to my GPA, the year before. In my sophomore year, I struggled a lot with math and many of the English classes I had since English was my minor. My fears from high school followed me to college and during one of those semesters, I failed math. The "F" had not only lowered my GPA, but also my confidence in my academic performance, I felt like a "Failure." English that year was also tough for me because I had a very challenging professor.

My lack of confidence and substandard performance affected my grades. Although I worked hard, I still seemed to struggle. My insecurities because of my performance led me again to believe that my professors did not like me. Therefore, I became ashamed and did not seek help. I was a very hard worker, and did well, but in some classes, I really struggled.

I was also becoming severely depressed, and I knew that my mood played into why I struggled. In my sophomore year much had changed, most of the students I had formed great relationships with in Summer Success left for various reasons, including Rhonda and Marquita. I was not close to Sharee when Rhonda and Marquita were around, but after, she and I along with another girl named Mya, formed a friendship. We did not share any classes together and had different schedules, but bonded over having lunch and mostly dinner together. Sharee was a commuter, while Mya lived on the opposite ends of the large Rotunda and went home on most weekends. When all three of us were available, it was a good time for me. I really enjoyed their presence because they both were easy, calm and simple. I missed them when they were not around and felt out of place having to sit alone to eat in a large cafeteria where tables were filled with cliques.

I sometimes joined cliques when invited to, but knew I was invited because they noticed I was sitting alone. I became embarrassed by always sitting alone, that I sometimes skipped meals, and regularly began boxing my food to eat in my dorm where I was comfortable with my loneliness. Again people noticed when I walked around quiet and when something was wrong. I resulted to that place of pity, hoping that my sad story of not being noticed would facilitate friendships. It got people to listen and I am sure feel sorry for me, but that was it.

My routine was going to class and then returning to my room. I joined groups and put myself out there, but I still found myself solo. I began feeling very depressed, so much so that there were days when I would not leave my room at all. I began skipping classes, exaggerating the swelling of my legs and feet as an excuse. Some classes met twice a week, so I sometimes missed an entire week of class. My absences were the real reason I struggled so much in my classes, because I was missing out on lectures. I began to feel unmotivated, while at the same time very much aware that I could not fail college. It was my only option to a better life. So I tried my best to fight against the strongholds of my depression, just to at least pass. Some days I was focused and determined, but most days I was stuck in darkness.

I became so depressed by my loneliness that I began thinking if I were to kill myself in my room, no one would know, that was how invisible I felt. I was truly thankful for Mya and Sharee, they were the occasional reminders that I was not completely alone. They both were good to me and sensitive to what I was going through. As good as they were, I longed for Drita.

Drita went to a well-known university in the city, and since graduating, we did not see each other much, however we managed to talk to each other often. I missed my friend, considering how alone I felt at school. I visited Drita at school and she visited me. When Drita came to visit, she did not know it, but I dreaded her having to leave. Drita's presence took me back to a time when we had so much fun together.

Just as many people find destructive ways to cope and mask their pain, I resulted to shopping. I began spending lots of money on clothing, shoes, purses, jewelry and CDs. Music helped to tune out the silence. I rationalized my shopping as harmless, considering the more destructive vises people resulted to. I got such a thrill from having stuff, lots of stuff to compensate for the lack of people in my life.

I figured if I looked good, wore things that made people notice me or want what I had, I would get attention. Not only wanting girls to like and befriend me, but I also wanting to be noticed by guys. I was dressing good and feeling good about the way I looked and for the first time started to feel confident in attracting the opposite sex. I went shopping alone, to the movies alone, did everything alone, but as long as I was spending, I felt good. A temporary frivolous gain would later have a lifelong effect. At the time, I felt the more I had, I had to have even more.

The game changed when I found out that I was approved for credit cards. "CREDIT!" I had what is known as a "Poverty Mentality," finally able to afford the things that I never had. My thinking was only in the present, focused on consuming expensive things that were thought to make me feel valuable, be envied and accepted. I knew the importance of saving, but was not worried about it at that time. I was not thinking about my financial future, and understanding just how crucial having good credit was. My emotions caused me to only live in the immediate moment. I convinced myself that I would not go in over my head, but before I knew it, I maxed the three cards I had in less than five months.

My senior year brought me full circle with what I had been trying to avoid all throughout college—math! During my freshmen year, I had to take a math proficiency test, which I failed. Nothing was required of me after, and I thought I had dodged a bullet. I was methodical in trying to avoid math at all costs, so I was happy to find the communications track did not require math. Every semester since having to take the prerequisite math course, I made it a point to avoid taking any math courses. However, in my senior year, the score from that test came back to haunt me. About a month before graduation, I was told I had to retake the test and pass or I would not graduate. I had gotten so far, and truly felt defeated. I heard a familiar voice in my head, laughing and reminding me how incompetent I was, it was the voice of my tenth grade teacher Mrs. Wells.

I thought it would take a miracle for me to pass. God would have to come down Himself and take the test on my behalf. I cried for days, until I realized there was too much at stake to give up. My siblings were depending on me and the hope I had for a better life hung in the balance. I knew God had not brought me this far not to graduate. I faced my fear and attended tutoring. The tutor availed herself to me whenever I needed her, and even tracked me down when she did not hear from me. I realized I had to push myself beyond my fear to get the help I needed. It was the persistent, dedication and encouragement from the director of the math department who took me by the hand and pursued me when I wanted to give up. She showed me that I knew more than I thought.

In about two weeks, I had learned years worth of math in a way that was easy for me to comprehend. The tutor would always say "Math is a Beautiful science!" it was as if my past came to literally haunt me. I resented the statement in tenth grade, and then in college but by the end of our sessions, I had come to agree. I realized that once I had a better understanding, math was no longer intimidating. I took the test and passed with an impressive score.

Walking at graduation was even more special because I felt after all of my struggles, I truly earned my degree in Communications and Technology, with a minor in English. However, walking across that stage was bitter sweet, I looked happy, but was wearing a smile to cover up the distress I was in from the unbelievable events that led up to arriving at graduation.

What took place on and before that day precipitated a series of unfortunate events that would create a huge rippling effect throughout my life. I had reached a pinnacle in my life, only to find myself days later deep in despair. As everyone congratulated me on such a success, I feared what would become of me now that school was over and I was released into the world to find my way toward reaching the limits of the sky, that I had been told I could do throughout my school years.

I was eager to make it and I convinced myself that I would. I quickly learned however, that in order to reach the sky, one must have in position and available to them opportunities, resources and supports that made the journey up possible. I learned that the statement was biased. Not everyone had the same opportunities to excel so high. Many were bound to the ground by plights and injustices that made the journey to success nearly impossible. Despite being held down, I never lost sight of that reach, I was determined to break the barriers placed before me to climb as far as I could, giving it my all to one-day touch the sky!

CHAPTER 17

The Beginning of Everything

THE WEEK BEFORE GRADUATION, every student on campus had to have their stuff out of the dorms. I dreaded the moment, more so because I had been unsuccessful in finding a place of my own. Realistically, with my income finding one did not happen as fast as I had hoped. I was now in debt and had been working on reestablishing the credit that I tarnished as a result of being comforted by impulse. I had three credit cards, one of them was a major card. I had also broken contracts with two major cell phone companies. In the search of finding a place, I felt the brunt of splurging without care, as I learned that credit was a factor in securing a place.

I began paying off what I could afford to eliminate as much debt as possible, but the amounts grew larger from interest. My problem was not so much being in debt, but the fact that I did not have the lump sum for a security deposit, or the financial means to maintain rent. My payments from Social Security was not enough for market rent. So I began researching and learned about subsidized housing programs that tenants were eligible for because of their Social Security Income (SSI). I thought that I would not have a problem finding housing through the HUD program, because I met the income requirements.

The downfall was I had to come to the realization that I would have to temporarily move back home. During college, the times I did go home to visit, my stay was usually brief, maybe for a few hours.

My mother's behavior usually determined the length of time I stayed around. As soon as I got there I was eager to leave.

During my Junior year of college, I began attending campus counseling. I was matched with a wonderful therapist in training and we did great work together. It was the first time I had ever been in counseling, and I loved having someone to talk to, who could help me work through the tough things I was dealing with. My main reasons for seeking therapy were to learn how to create boundaries with my mother and how to separate myself from her without feeling guilty for choosing to live my own life.

I found the months of talking and reflecting very cathartic. I walked away with an understanding that my parents are who they are, and that I had to find acceptance in the fact that they may never meet my expectations. I learned a lot about addiction. It was through this eye opening experience that my compassion for my mother deepened. Most importantly, I learned I no longer had to tolerate her manipulation and unacceptable behavior. The therapist pointed out something very interesting that really got me thinking about my childhood experiences. She defined all of the dysfunction I experienced throughout my childhood as trauma.

When she explained what trauma was, and the physiological reactions I experienced in response to the trauma, it made me look at what I had gone through a little deeper and pay closer attention to how certain things affected me. Although she was not in the position to diagnose me, she concluded from many of the symptoms I shared, that I was possibly suffering from Post Traumatic Stress Disorder (PTSD).

The more I began to look at myself, the things I did, and some of my ways, I saw how this could be true. I had developed a fear of being intoxicated so I abstain from drinking alcohol of any kind; the fear is being outside of myself in an altered state where I have no control. I feared most experiencing the behaviors of being inebriated. I also have a big thing about wasting food. I really feel extremely guilty having to throw food away. These two are not symptoms of PTSD, but they are greatly affected by my childhood experiences.

I talked with the therapist mostly about my anxiety, which was a symptom of PTSD, and how it manifested inside of me. My anxiety was mostly fear from things my mother did, that when done or seen by others, made me feel nervous or extremely uneasy, and took me back to times when I felt unsafe; things that happen, that still affect me as an adult. Such things are the slamming of doors, the sound of stumping, yelling that includes profanity, and seeing children be hit and cursed at, makes me extremely anxious and overly emotional. My fear manifested in my personality, and could be seen through my sometimes timid, quiet and reservation amongst people who appear loud, aggressive and or intimidating.

I also shared with my therapist, reoccurring dreams that I continued to have for many years after. In the dreams, I was always screaming at my mother loud and ferociously, until I lost my voice. I would stop momentarily to catch my breath and then continue. All the while, I am assaulting my mother with such force and such rage until my limbs gave out. Deeply disturbed by these dreams, I forced myself to wake up, feeling horrible.

The therapist asked for my interpretation of the dreams. Consciously I never thought of ever hurting my mother, but I interpreted the dreams to mean subconsciously I wanted to stand up for myself. To position myself in a way that made me dominant and powerful over the fear and intimidation I felt towards my mother for much of my life. The loud and ferociousness symbolized asserting myself in a way that I was heard and that demanded respect. I will not deny that the undertones were definitely anger and resentment, and having the feelings of wanting my mother to feel the pain that she had inflicted on me, by being physical with her. As difficult as it would prove to be, I began standing up to my mother, in hopes of one day being free from the fear I had of her.

Once I realized that I had to suck it up and move back home with my mom, it was the most difficult reality to come to terms with. I had come so far in gaining my independence and had just come to terms with being able to deal with my anxiety and the trauma that I faced while living at home, just to have to turn around and walk back into the fire. I was scared, I honestly feared for my safety and mental state, because nothing had changed and my mothers' addiction was still a current issue.

I had no other options, places to go or people to stay with. For summer breaks while in college, I stayed with my father. However, by the time I graduated, the owner of the house decided to sell it, so my dad moved into a one-bedroom apartment, with no space to accommodate an additional person. Knowing my level of discomfort was high living with my mother, it took much prayer for me to get through every passing minute.

The first day or two went by rather fast, I was hoping that subsequent days would pass with rapid speed until I found a job, and could move out. My mother appeared excited to have me home, but within a day or two, I was not immune from her fiery. I noticed her drinking, but what was different was that she did not go to any great measures to hid it from me as she had always done.

Things seemed to be tense around the house. My brothers and sister were ecstatic to see me back home, but my mom did not show much affection toward me. She mentioned how proud she was of me for finishing school, but the feeling I got from her did not match her words. I knew better than to have expectations that my mother would be doing flips and cartwheels over my accomplishments, although I knew she had the pride of a parent. It appeared my mom became jealous when attention went to someone other than herself, for doing things that she wished she had done. Therefore, I learned not to gloat too much in my accomplishments. I always down played my excitement as though it was not that big of a deal in front of her, just so my mom would not have any hard feelings. I realized that my successes were painful reminders of all that my mom had not accomplished in her life.

I came home and quickly blended into the everyday mundane and uneventfulness in the house. I was graduating in two days, but day by day, it seemed the excitement had died, my mom did not speak of it in anticipation, so I contained my excitement. I had so much to be excited about, I was the first in my family to receive a degree from college.

So much seemed to change since I was gone, my siblings were all taller and older, their personalities were different, but what saddened me the most, was seeing how they appeared acclimated to all the confusion taken place. They were less timid, anxious, but more prepared and alert. Most nights, my mother drank and acted accordingly, but I chose to pay her no mind. I kept my focus on my big day. I had gone shopping for a nice outfit that I was excited to wear, and had styled my hair in layered curls, a style I had never worn before, but thought it was perfect for the outfit and the occasion. I just sat in my room asking God to be with me and give me the same tolerance that He had given my siblings to be unaffected by the ciaos. I was determined to handle situations differently with my mom. I knew I had grown and changed, and wanted to show my mother I would no longer be victimized or tolerate anything less than respect.

Through my silence I had gained a voice. I learned to speak against my mother, showing her that she no longer had the power or the authority to break me down. Even after a few times of having to stand up to her, the walls crumbled around me, yet I was not moved.

The day before my graduation would be the catalyst that would cause true struggle and hardships over the course of my life. The day started out as any other, my mother was sobering from the night before, and every one kind of stayed separate and quiet. My mother awoke in a cranky and hostile mood, which was considered normal the mornings after she sobered.

She was yelling around the house at Hakiem and Erica for no apparent reason. We walked around on eggshells, just trying to avoid her, which irritated and fueled my mother's anger even more. For days she kept finding things to complain about with regards to the bags of clothing I brought with me. Knowing that I was returning to my moms and I no longer had my own space, I made an effort to take with me as least I could. I mostly gave a lot of things that would take up space away, to anyone in the dorms willing to take them. I never liked to hold on to a lot of stuff that created clutter, so important things such as books and all of my art projects, paintings and drawings from my art course, I kept in my dad's storage. I only had three trash bags full of clothing and essentials. Needing to find something to complain about, at least once a day, my mom would tell me how my things were cluttering up the room that I was sharing with Erica.

The whole morning my mom appeared motivated to antagonize us, because she was just in a bad mood. I knew my mother well, and it seemed the closer graduation came for me, the more she stirred the pot, until it boiled and spilled over. Joshua walked in the house and suddenly out of nowhere, my mother started ranting on him about not taking the trash out the night before. I was standing nearby, and already annoyed by the way she was acting all day, but the extent to which she was screaming and berating him, rubbed me the wrong way. I had had enough and confronted her, asking why she was yelling at Josh instead of just reminding him that he had not taken the trash out. I felt the tension brewing all day, and it was finally unleashed! My mom lunged at me, cursed and grabbed me, asking who I thought I was, calling me all kinds of names, while swinging clenched fists at me.

I was extremely surprised when Joshua intervened to my defense. I had seen the evidence of years of pent up anger and frustration in Josh as he defended and helped to get me out of the way of our mother. I had never seen my little brother, ever utter a word toward my mom, let alone stand up to her in the way he had. What I was most impressed with, was that even in the mist of such anger, my brother confronted her in a way that was respectful, but powerful. He did not say anything out of turn, but he boldly stepped outside of his timidness that day. Josh always stayed quite in the background, and I think years of silence caused him to react. He stood in front of her, the sound of his bold voice was enough intimidation to restrain my mother from me. Joshua stood firm looking her square in the eye as he told her she better not think about touching me. My mother then switched from trying to attack me and lunged at my brother, picking up a broom and started hitting him with it. Rasheen raced into the house after hearing the commotion outside, ran in and started pulling my mom off of Josh.

Suddenly the kitchen filled with people and everyone was yelling and screaming. When Rasheen finally got a hold of Josh, to see if he was okay, my mom began cursing everyone out as if we were no kin to her. Josh then told her she was just jealous that I was graduating from college and she had not. He added that I was more than she would ever be, in hopes she felt shame and repentance for what she had done. It hurt me more to see my mother attack Josh, to see him cry hysterically, and had been taken outside of his character. I was more affected by my brother being hurt physically and emotionally than what I was feeling.

The uproar in the house was enough to antagonize Rasheen, who always seemed to look for the right opportunity to give our mother a pieces of his mind. It also seemed that his rage had been fueled by so many years of pent up anger. His fanning of the flames made the fire worse. He and my mom started to fight, which lead someone to call the police. While in the midst of all the commotion, I had been feeling pressure on my face and went upstairs to look into the mirror to discover that my eye was slightly swollen, realizing that my mom had struck me in the eye.

The police were called, and when they came, everyone migrated in front of the house, continuing to yell and scream. someone talking to an officer, pointed toward me, and reported that I had been hit. My mom then came outside commanding the scene as she always did, to claim that she was in fact the damsel in distress. However, I had the burden of proof that I was the victim with my eye swollen. I was very fearful, trying to get the police to see that I was in jeopardy and needed for them to not leave me feeling unsafe.

My mother was yelling and screaming obscenities at me, telling the officers I was trespassing and my name was no longer on the lease, asking them to remove me from the premises. I began yelling and screaming back at her that I did have the right. In attempt to break up the commotion, the officer yelled at me and said, "Ma'am, do I have to handcuff you?" I was appalled and even more angered that the officer clearly did not see I was the victim. I quickly followed his orders and set on the steps to calm down. He then asked if I had anywhere else to go, I told him no. In the background I saw the other officer put my mother into the squad car to separate us, he returned and they both began to examine my eye and asked if I wanted to press charges.

To stall from answering the dreaded question, I asked the officer if I could make some calls to see who I could stay with. The only two possibilities were my dad and my aunt. I knew my dad's situation, but thought that under the circumstances, he would make room for me. Surprised by his refusal, I felt hurt that he would not at least try to find space for me. I hung up while he was in mid-sentence, and tried calling my aunt who had a house on the next block from where my father previously lived.

Through my hysteria, I tried to compose myself in order to tell her what was going on, and that I was in desperate need of a place to stay. she immediately heard all of the noise in the background and said, "Oh no, you can't stay here!" choosing the wrong time to be noisy, my aunt began asking me every other question about what was going on rather than aid me. I begged and pleaded saying "this is me, your niece, the one you said you would do anything for." Now was the time when I really was in need, but instead she said she did not want any drama.

I felt abandoned by both, and set there crying with nowhere to go and seemingly no other prospects of whom I could turn to. Then the police officer returned, asked me the question again, if I wanted to press charges on my mother. I hated being put in such a position, a part of me felt it was the ultimate act of betrayal, despite what she had done to me. On the other hand, I knew if I allowed my mother to get away, yet again with her behavior, she would never learn. She needed to feel the repercussions of her actions.

Finally, I decided that I would press charges, with the motive of getting my mother the help she needed. I told the officer I would with the conditions that she be placed into a treatment facility. He informed me I would be given a court date for a hearing, at which time I could address my recommendations with the court. At the same time, I could hear my mother pleading with me as she sat in the back of the car. She seemed to calm down, crying and pleading with me not to do so. Of course her manipulation tugged at my heart strings, but I felt secure in my decision. It was hard to see her in that position, and as much as I wanted to tell them that I had changed my mind, I remembered that I would only be enabling her if I had. I knew it was time to show my mother some tough love, and I was sure sitting in jail for a day or two would scare her straight. If she had to get help by force, then I felt it was necessary, so she could finally come to terms with the things she was battling.

Late that evening, a police officer arrived to escort me to the precinct to take my statement. By the time I walked out of the precinct and was taken back home, the sun was rising. It was the day of my graduation. Feeling conflicted, I went home and got dressed. Initially my attitude was that nothing was going to stop me from walking down that aisle!

Considering all I had just experienced, made me more determined to enjoy my day, because I had earned it. I thought to myself, not even the absence of my mother would make me miss my day. I attempted to put the drama of the day and night before, behind me to focus on graduating. However once there, and around other students happily enjoying the moment with their parents, many sharing gifts such as large amounts of money and cars, I really was saddened my mother was not there to see me walk. Nothing could ever change the fact that she was my mother, and my love for her was deeper than the pain she caused. I cried because I felt so alone. Although I had my dad, my brothers, sister and others there I had invited at the last minute, just to use the tickets I had, I felt the day was incomplete without my mother being there.

Once at school, I put on my cap and gown, and blended in with the happy crowd of students, giving off no indications of the hell I had been through that morning and the night before. I walked down the prestigious aisle, and received my degree when my name was called. I had no idea how the day would end or where I was going to reside for shelter, but in that moment nothing else mattered, because I owed it to myself to relish in it. I tried distracting my roaming mind with positive thoughts, although I was extremely fearful. I felt comforted in the belief that whatever my immediate future held, God was working it all out for my good, so I let go and put my trust in Him.

Since my mother was not in the house, I stayed the night, unsuccessful in finding anywhere else to go. I had no idea when my mother would be released, and prayed that I had found somewhere to go before she was. The next day, I began making phone calls to find out what kind of services were out there for emergency shelter situations. To my surprise, my mother walked through the door later that afternoon. I could not think straight when I heard the sound of her voice. I began gathering things to appear as though I had been there to gather my stuff, but I still had not found anywhere to go. I was talking on the phone with the director from Camp Susquehanna, asking her for suggestions of what I should do for immediate residency. She offered me to stay at her house for a few days so that I could figure out a plan.

While I was gathering my stuff, my mom asked me a few times if I was planning to go through with pressing charges. I told her I did not know what I was going to do, while rushing to pack my things, hoping my friend Chris, who I had called to take me to our friend's house, was waiting outside. I lied to my mom, telling her I had to wait to receive letters in the mail with the court date, before I could make a decision. Clearly I had my mind made up, but knew better than to tell her. She followed me around as I was packing, whispering underneath her breath that I better not go through with it, if I knew what was good for me. I kept my mouth closed, avoiding her, to prevent another altercation. I had gathered enough things to hold me over for a few days, and told my siblings I would be in touch to get the rest of my stuff when my mother was not around. I did not know what I was going to do, or where I was going to go. I was homeless, but did not lose hope that God would never allow things to get too bad.

When I got to my friend's house, we set and talked, I told her a little of what happened, enough to explain my situation. I stayed at her beautiful three story house in the City Line Avenue section of the city for about five days. During the day, I hung out with my longtime friend Chris, who also had been burned and attended burn camp, trying to find options for work and housing. My main focus was finding a place to lay my head next.

Chris took me to the Philadelphia Housing Authority, where we both put our names on their waiting list for subsidized housing. I was hoping there were immediate vacancies, especially after answering questions about having a disability, until I was told the average wait time for housing was about seven to ten years. It was 2005, and the clerk stated they were servicing applicants from 1998 to 2000. I could not believe what I was hearing, I was upset that I had set for hours filling out an application and waiting to speak with someone, just to find out that kind of information.

Upon learning the only option for expediting housing was to go into a shelter, I really became discouraged. I lead the way out of the office, not counting on the program being of any use to me. Picking up where I had left off in my search, I reached out to two sisters, who I knew were now working in the field of social work. I had become good friends with the sisters who were Seniors at Chestnut Hill when I was a Sophomore. Their mother worked in City Hall and had given me the contact of a woman who worked with Councilwoman Jannie Blackwell. The women dealt with subsidized housing, and was willing to help me.

Just when I was about to lose hope, and began feeling desperate, I received a call from Joshua's ex-girlfriend, who had become a good friend. When I heard the bubbly, squeaky sound of her voice on the other end say, "Hey, Neesha! I was thinking of you." I attempted to match her enthusiasm, but I was mentally in a different space. I hesitated at first to tell her what was going on. I honestly felt ashamed to tell her I had nowhere to stay, but I trusted Jessica, because she was no stranger to hardships and adversity.

Jessica was in the very same kind of independent living program through DHS, that Rasheen had been in. Jessica's life was a plot for a Lifetime movie. She had been through so much, but had this amazing personality that inspired me, even though she said the same about me and my story. To say the least, when my brother introduced me to Jessica while they were dating, I fell in love with her resilient spirit the moment we met. From then on, we clicked and became like sisters.

After a few days at the director of the burn camp's house, I felt I had stayed long enough, and feared out staying my welcome, although she offered me to stay longer. In my conversation with Jessica, when I disclosed what happened with my mom, and that I had nowhere to stay, she insisted I stay with her. Feeling a sense of relief, I was grateful for Jessica's generosity. Jessica was madly in love with my brother, although they parted ways, but from that love grew a deep love and loyalty to me. That same night, Chris drove me to Jessica's house.

Once I arrived, we sat up all night talking. She comforted me, and for the first time I felt safe and comfortable to let out all of the emotions I had been holding in. I cried big and loud in her arms. Knowing one of the similarities we shared was having a nurturing spirit, I felt good to let everything out. I explained to her that I expected my stay to be short, because I was hopeful the contact at City Hall, would help me find a place quick, once she heard my story.

I sought out finding housing with the same determination as finding a job. I knew I would not be able to afford market rent with my SSI, so my search entailed anything that was under five hundred dollars a month. I knew rent within this range would consist of efficiencies, shared spaces, and room rentals, which I was uncomfortable with all, but I was desperate. I also looked for jobs, now having a degree, I figured I would have better luck than when I was younger.

Jessica was a bubbly, energetic, and talkative, petite girl with a head full of long, luscious, brown curls. She did not distinguish herself as belonging to any particular race and or ethnicity. She told people who asked, that she was a cross breed of everything. To make things more simple, she referred to herself as being "rainbow." This illustrated just how quirky and carefree Jessica was. Jessica had the most beautiful smile, and chestnut eyes; she was a cute girl, but was modest and humble when it came to beauty. I believed who Jessica was inside and out epitomize true beauty.

Jessica's wounds were still fresh from the breakup with Josh, so I was surprised she was willing to let me stay with her such a difficult. I feared I would be a constant, painful reminder of Josh, but she insisted I stay. Jessica said having me there would be great company for her. It proved to be a trying time for the both of us, which was great to have each other to lean on for support.

I was ever so grateful to Jessica, because she was risking her living situation by having me stay with her. She and the occupant of the upper apartment were in the custody of DHS, and their apartment came with strict rules, one of which prohibited anyone staying over. Jessica informed me that the agency did "pop up" visits, which were unannounced. Jessica assured me that she was within good standing with her social worker, and did not worry about them popping up on her, but Jessica wanted to be prepared if anyone should.

So Jessica devised a plan, just to be safe. She created a space in the back of her tiny closet for me to hide behind her dresses, which hung long enough to cover me entirely. Jessica was convinced it was a spot anyone was less likely to check. Again we never had to put the scenario into action. God shed his grace over us, because during the two long months I stayed with her, no one visited.

Living with Jessica was a dream. We never fought or disagreed. I felt her space was mine, but all the while, I felt bad she was taking such a risk having me there. Every day I made calls to the contact I had, and finally she retuned my call telling me to meet with her. I sat explaining my situation, and emphasized the desperation I was in. After my tearful plea for help, she informed me of subsidized housing programs she knew I would be eligible for because of my SSI.

She handed me a hefty list and told me to call each listing for vacancies. I immediately noticed there were more vacancies available for mothers with children. My time was running very thin, I only had till the end of the summer to find housing. Jessica had been accepted to a Pennsylvania University, and was giving up her lease to move on campus. From the time I moved in, I had two months to find, and move into a place of my own, so I began to feel the pressure. As dire as everything appeared, deep within, I believed God would continue to provide for me as He had always done. It just meant I had to work hard and be persistent with exhausting every option, and took advantage of every resource I came into.

After I contacted all the programs on the list, I then began going to City Hall nearly every day for about a month. When I was not there, I was calling the coordinator back to back. I was not going to allow her to forget me. When I went, I sat sometimes for hours, waiting to meet with her. I felt disappointed when she told me she had no updates from her viable contacts. I had no other options and Jessica was leaving for college in two weeks. I began to grow weary, because I did not have a backup plan. I refused, however, to give up, and continued to press hard.

Finally, a few days later, the woman from City Hall called to informed me of a potential program with a vacancy near Broad Street in Philadelphia. I did not waste any time to call to schedule a meeting with the property Manager. There was no doubt in my mind that I had found a place, and knew their only opening was meant for me. I had been saving as much of my monthly checks as I could. It was being in a situation as such that I wished I had managed my money better, when I had the chance.

When I went to the interview for the apartment, I was nervous but confident. I just knew I would get the apartment... I had to. I met with an African American full figured woman whose statue made her appear very intimidating; she had a no nonsense mannerism but was pleasant. I had with me all of the documents I was told to bring and eager to begin the interview. The property manager proceeded to give me a brief history about the historic building, and informed me about the requirements, expectations and residents. She explained the program was a living facility for people who were disabled and the elderly who were able to care for themselves. She then took me on a tour around the building, before showing me the vacant unit.

The unit was a small efficiency, its entirety was about the size of my mother's kitchen. It was newly renovated and although small, It felt comfortable. As soon as I entered, I envisioned what the space would look like once I added my décor. It was just myself, and I had only planned to stay until I was able to secure a career and made enough money to afford my ideal place.

When we returned to the office, the manager introduced me to the rest of the staff, before proceeding with the interview. My excitement could be seen though my smiling, and making small talk, as though I was friends with everyone in the room. The manager did not seem fazed as she continued to work behind her desk. She looked at me with a stern face and asked me about my situation. I told her everything that lead up to that moment. She appeared impressed with my recent accolades, and became interested in knowing more about me. For a moment I was sure I had the interview in the bag. I had everything needed to move in immediately, even the security deposit.

I then cringed when I heard her say the last thing she required was a credit check. It was at that moment that I wished I could have gone back in time and declined the offer to those credit cards. In fact, they came up, and when she asked about them, I assured her that I was in the process of paying them off. My excitement turned immediately into fear. I was sure she was going to turn me away based on that infraction. I sat holding my breath while she stroked her computer keys with momentary glances at me in between.

She then told me that as soon as I could have a deposit for first and last month's rent, which was calculated based on thirty percent of my supplemental income, I could move in. I told her I was prepared to pay the deposit right then and there. I went to the nearest check cashing place, and retuned shortly after with a money order for the amount. I filled out the necessary paperwork, and when the interview was over, I walked out with a copy of my new lease, and was told to return the next day to receive the keys to my unit. I walked out crying, thanking God the entire way back to Jessica's house. I was extremely proud of myself for persevering through extreme uncertainty. From the people and the opportunities God put into place as stepping stones to get from bad to good, my faith in Him could not have been stronger. What I would soon learn was that things were far from good, the fact of the matter was that my trials were far from over. All that was about to happen would truly test the unshakeable faith I had built up to that point. This next phase of my life would require me to use everything in my arsenal, from waving that red flag of defeat.

CHAPTER 18

Finding Myself on My Own

I MOVED IN THE next day with only the few bags I had with me at Jessica's place. It was late August, and I just remember feeling a sign of relief and favor. As I was moving into my place, Jessica was packing up to leave that week for college. I kept thanking Jessica, I could not thank her enough. I never could repay her generosity. During my time living with Jessica, we truly bonded.

It took me time to accumulate things my apartment needed. I had enough to buy a full-sized mattress and its essentials. Someone who was moving out of their apartment around the time I was moving in gave me their TV, after introducing themselves and seeing that I was without one. In that moment, I was just happy to be on my feet again and with a place to call my own.

By the time I moved into the apartment complex South of Broad street, closest to Penns Landing, I had mended things with my mother, enough that we were on speaking terms again. I was a forgiving person, although I never forgot. I believed God expected me to always show grace and compassion to my mother, because she needed it. She needed me and she needed my love. I however was no longer enabling her. We talked, laughed and appeared close, but emotionally I was distant. I struggled spiritually with the resistance I had with her, and felt extreme guilt. Years after overlooking so much and learning to forgive by default, as time went on I realized the emotional resistance was because deep within my spirit I had not forgiven her.

While living with Jessica, I went to court for the incident before my graduation. I was nervous to stand in a court room for the first time in front of a judge. My intentions remained the same, that I wanted my mother to get help. I practiced everyday what I wanted to say, in hopes of gaining the judge's sympathy for my mother, rather than look at her with disgust. I wanted them to see I was pleading for her life. I was fearful, however of the possibility that pressing charges would send my mother to jail. In my pitch, I stated I did not want the latter to happen several times. The day came and seeing that my mother and I were within a few feet from one another as we waited for the hearing, my fear heightened. I feared my mother would try to intimidate me minutes before testifying against her, so I did not speak or look at her. I was appointed a court representative in which I told her my plan. When the case was called into the courtroom I prayed for the best, that God showed my mom mercy and she would finally get help – she did. The judge stated to my mother that she ought to be grateful for having a daughter who did what I had done for her. She cried in relief, and I cried with hope. Outside I hugged my mother and told her I only wanted the best for her, even if it meant having to put her in an uncomfortable situation.

I absolutely loved my new place. weeks in, I was in the best mental and emotional space I had been in a long time. Every day I found something to do and somewhere to go. I would put on my best and take the Market Frankford line, which was the main connection near my apartment to everywhere in the city. For a while I did everything on Septa, but realized doing things such as going grocery shopping on the bus became extremely difficult. I was only able to travel with two, maybe three light bags at a time. I knew I had to find a car, and a job.

In the meantime, Jessica often came home and when she did, we got together and hung out. One of the fun things we did together was frequent the circuits of clubs that were scattered around the neighborhood I lived in. The area was a fascinating mixture of diversity. Behind my apartment building was a housing project, which the only oversized window in my unit, revealed a secluded portion of the cul-de-sac, and gave me an unwanted view both day and night, of people using drugs and even engaging in sexual acts. My apartment was on the second floor; I figured if I was close enough to see the details of what was going on, then others could easily see me. Therefore, I kept the large single pull shade that was already installed when I moved in, down at all times. Up and down the major street, were all kinds of businesses and upscale apartments. I was a few miles from the city's river front which surrounded expensive hotels and attractions, and a few miles further was South street.

In my area alone there were seven or eight nightclubs. Every night the surroundings of the apartment became a hot spot, where party goes gathered in large crowds to frequent the clubs up, down and around where I lived. Seeing pandemonium, I wanted to be a part of it. I was older, and felt more secure in my skin. In college, I came to figure, if I wanted guys to see me for who I was, I had to come across more confident and comfortable with myself if I wanted them to be comfortable with me. I even had been in two relationships, one at the end of high school and the other while in college. I finally experienced what I longed to for so long, only to be hurt and left feeling that my appearance played a significance in their endings.

I still received attention from guys with obvious intentions, but I felt a new sense of optimism of finding someone, because I felt better about myself. I now was twenty-three and thinking about the future in hopes it would one day include children. I figured if I was going to meet anyone, I would have to step my game up, so I learned to challenge my insecurities. Instead of looking away, I looked guys square in the eye. If approached, I made sure to show off my personality, and conscious not to let my intimidation show, even when inside I was filled with anxiety.

Many times I took a bolder step by initiating a guy. If I saw someone who I thought was attractive, I pushed myself to walk up and tell him. I wanted to confront my fears to see if the worse I believed could happen really would. They did not, I was surprised to see that some guys found my level of confidence attractive and was often the reason one further perused me by asking for my number or gave me theirs. I had come further in my craft of makeup and hair, and looked completely different. I felt beautiful and was randomly told by guys that I was. As it does with women who are use to it and or even expecting of it, the attention gave me a huge boost in confidence.

I still was cautious with the guys who I met, I knew what their game was, but believed if I could get them to see me, then they would respect and see the good in me. Eventually many guys gave up, eliminating many of the "guy friends" in my contact list, who I had met at different times and places. There were many times when I felt the loneliness of not having anyone, that I reconsidered compromising myself just to have someone to be with. Everyone else did it, causal dating and the "no strings attached" preference seemed to be expected and highly encouraged.

I thought many times, *I'm grown*, and tried convincing myself I would be okay with a "no feelings involved" situation. Shortly after the thought, I came to my senses realizing doing so was out of my character, and I was unwilling to do that to myself. I had to be in a meaningful relationship to give myself whole heartedly, that was the case with the two relationships, and would be the same with the next. I believed my patience would pay off when the time was right.

In the meantime, I was focused on the next phase of my plan, which was to find and secure a good paying job. My degree was fresh and I was eager to see what was out there. Although I had a degree in communications, by the time I graduated, I had come to realize my interest changed from pursuing a career in media and graphic design to the human services field.

In my junior year of college, I was given the opportunity of a lifetime. Gerry Straub, a well-known Hollywood producer turned award-winning filmmaker who left the glitz and glamour to expose the dark and devastating plight of poverty here in the U.S., as well as internationally, presented a phenomenal presentation at Chestnut Hill on leprosy in an impoverished third-world country. The film reignited to the core of my pain. Worlds apart, I identified with the disfigured women portrayed in the film and the feelings associated with being marginalized and deemed an outcast because of the disease. The film evoked emotion from me in a way that I became visually inconsolable.

At the conclusion of the film, Mr. Straub and I were introduced and I shared how I identified with the suffering shown in his film. Moved and inspired by me, I was contacted by Mr. Straub personally and offered to travel and work with him. Mr. Straub and his family were willing to open their home to me for a year until I was able to support myself. Mr. Straub believed I could add to the power of his productions and I was honored. It was an incredible opportunity that after much thought, I respectfully declined. I had nothing holding me back, except the offer meant I would not be able to finish my last year of college. I was truly torn, but felt in my spirit I had worked so hard and was so close to graduating. My thought was, what if Hollywood did not work out, I then would be left with nothing, including an education. I felt it was too great of a risk that I could not afford to take.

Around the same time, my friend Chris proposed the idea of starting a non for profit organization for burn survivors called the United States Burn support Organization. The idea was to offer supportive services to those suffering from fire-related incidents and injuries, and to also provide awareness, education, and prevention. We were two inexperienced people spending all of our time starting the organization from the ground. I designed our logo, slogan and wrote the proposal. Chris did all of the foot work with financing and promoting it. Creating and running the organization solidify my purpose, which was service. We began speaking at many organizations, programs, groups and events. Several events where I spoke, the former Fire Commissioner Lloyd Ayres was present and I got the opportunity to impress him, which was great.

We were working on growing the organization, in between my search for employment. I continued to use the organization as a platform to speak, which I realized I loved doing each time I did so. I was really enjoying what I was doing and decided I wanted to work more directly with people in need. I also realized how infectious speaking was, and the fact that I really had the propensity to encourage people. I began looking for more venues where I could speak. I met a police officer at an event, who was impressed by one of my speeches, and invited me to be the guest speaker at an annual community event she held. That was a success, which allowed me to begin networking and getting my name out as an inspirational and motivational speaker.

After much effort searching for jobs, I found it difficult to find anything in the field of human services with a communication degree, and no experience. I had come to find there were not many jobs in the communications field outside of IT or programming, neither of which were my area of expertise. I then was given information about a temporary staffing agency from Rose Mary in King of Prussia. I was grateful for the connection, and after I went in for the interview, I think it was a combination of the woman I interviewed with knowing Rose, and the fact that she was impressed with my credentials and skills.

My first temp job was with the Muscular Dystrophy Association in Broomall PA. There, I was a Disability Awareness coordinator, where I recruited schools to sign up for the program's special fundraisers and events. The coordinator was impressed with my ability to meet my quotas, which I had also been successful at my former summer job working as a debt collector. The entire three months employed for the collections agency, I maintained either the first, second or rarely third position as the top collector for that site. At the MDA, I also was given a quota, in which I exceeded within the three months employed. The money was not great but, I felt dignified. I was grateful for the benefits I received from SSI, but I never wanted to be complacent with them. I saw it as a support until I could stand securely on my own.

Months acclimated in my apartment, I met many of the elderly tenants. I believed besides me, there was another young family residing there. They were a common law husband and wife with a boy and girl. The fact that most of the residents were elderly, was great because it made it easier to keep to myself. I was conscious that I was a single, young female living alone, so I wanted to be safe.

The facility had around the clock security, a guard who secured the parameters of the building and ensured the residences were okay. Just because there were mostly elderly residents, did not mean the complex was free from drama. Something was always going on whether big or small. In my comings and goings, I spoke to the security guard who seemed to blend in more as a resident than asserting authority. I would always see him outside talking to residents or seated in the office with residents coming and going as they conversed with him. It was not long before he introduced himself to me as Raymond. Raymond was a tall slender brown skinned guy with a shiny bald head that was fitting for his appearance, and a striking smile that revealed a chip tooth, but did not take away from his handsomeness.

I saw how everyone gravitated to Raymond and had nothing but wonderful things to say about him. He was described by many of the tenants as being sensitive, extremely helpful, polite, thoughtful and generous. I was also informed by the young lady with the husband and two children, that he was quite the ladies' man. She told me how Raymond was always flirting with every good looking woman who passed through the complex doors. She warned me to be careful because he was slick. I did not think anything of it, initially I was not attracted to Raymond and could not see why women gave him the time of day.

Through my passing, I noticed Raymond seemed eager to talk to me, or offered his assistance if I needed it. Always stating that I was fine, Raymond then began trying to strike up conversations with me either before leaving or upon returning. I eventually caught on to what he was doing and made a mental note to keep watch, and stay clear, however I could not deny that Raymond was funny and always had interesting things to talk about. With not having hardly anyone in the building who I could relate or talk to, I found Raymond's company pleasant. It was good to just sit and talk to someone who I could relate to. Raymond then began inviting me to sit in the office at night. It apparently became an after hour hangout spot where many residents congregated to talk to Raymond and play the Xbox video game system he carried around with him.

I questioned his ability to do his job while playing video games. Raymond told me it was no distraction, just a way to kill time in his five PM to six AM shift. He had to make rounds in and around the building once an hour, which did not take him long to do. Raymond told me that he and the manager were good friends, that she had given him the job when he was in need of one. I had nothing to do but sit in my apartment bored watching TV most nights, so I began going down to play Xbox.

After talking and playing for hours, Raymond revealed that he was forty years old. I could not believe it, even if Raymond showed me his birth certificate, because he looked so young. Raymond was well preserved, and looked no more than maybe thirty, and even younger when he wore his baseball caps. I was attracted to older guys, but no more than five years older. I was turned off at how much older Raymond was; I was only twenty-three, and forty seemed so old.

Initially I did not mind the flirting, but after learning Raymond's age, I felt somewhat uncomfortable. However the more time I spent talking to Raymond, I began enjoying our time together; his age no longer was an issue as I found myself becoming attracted to him. When Raymond made advances at me, I did not mind. I was concerned about getting involved with a man who worked where I lived. I did not remember hearing anything about not fraternizing with staff, but it was one of those unspoken rules I knew existed. Raymond's age meant that he was a well experienced man, and knew exactly what he was doing to manipulate a young naïve woman like myself. I would come to learn that Raymond preferred younger women. I should have paid attention when my suspicious radar began to beam after Raymond told me he was friends with a woman my age, whom he no longer dated, but claimed her two children as his own.

I would sit in the office with Raymond while he and the "friend" had what appeared to be platonic conversations. After much convincing, Raymond assured me they had not been together in a long time; being gullible, I took him at his word. The way Raymond showed he was into me, made me dismiss the thought that the two of them were still involved. Like I said I was young and naïve and fixated on the attention.

After much persistence, I eventually let my guard down and started seeing Raymond. We were now a couple, but in secret. Raymond was fearful of losing his job if management found out, so we found ways to be discrete. Raymond would sneak to my apartment as soon as he began his shift and after they were over. After a while, Raymond brazenly slept over, but always left early enough to make his last rounds before heading home. I was falling for Raymond and I really thought we had something special. This feeling did not last long however, because my suspicions about the woman he was supposedly just friends with came to light and revealed they were in fact still involved.

Things quickly went from being blissful to being nothing I ever imagined I would find myself dealing with. When I discovered Raymond was in a relationship with the both of us, I immediately demanded that he break things off with her. Raymond repeatedly told me he was not involved with her, but then attempted to cover his lies by saying he mislead her to believe they were together. The woman had an addiction and Raymond used being genuinely concerned for her stability and the welfare of the girls, as his plausible reason for continuing the relationship. I did not buy it and began resulting to my own measures to find the truth.

I began checking his phone to see if they were talking, what messages they were sending each other both verbal and through text. I eventually became obsessed and crazed with becoming a vigilante. I snuck around, looked through Raymond's stuff and while he slept I went through his phone to see who he had been talking to. I took her phone number and called from his phone, then stayed quite as she answered, before hanging up. The true test was to see if Raymond answered the phone when she called back after I hung up. I confronted Raymond over and over until she was all we talked about day and night. I then decided to call her and made myself known. I figured she would back down knowing he was with me. To my surprised she had known about me, and that we were together, but did not care. She said she and Raymond had been together for about five years and he always went back to her, despite who he was with.

After talking with her, I became paranoid, thinking about what Raymond was doing when he was not with me, feeling anxious that he was with her. Raymond always assured me he was not dealing with her. Raymond constantly professed his love for me, then reverted to using manipulative tactics such as threatened to leave me if I continued to accuse him of cheating. Raymond tried to convince me that it was impossible for him to be with her when he spent most or all of his time with me. I bought it, even though in my mind I knew he was lying. I allowed my emotions to convince my womanly intuition otherwise. I had gotten to a point that after putting up such a fight and seeing the anger, frustration and tears, did not faze him, I did not care anymore. I had fallen for Raymond in such a way that being with him was better than being without him, even if it meant I had to share him. I was feeling vulnerable and desperate to make the relationship work. I settled and knew I was, for someone who appeared to have it all together, but as time went on, I would come to know the real Raymond.

It had been discovered that Raymond and I were together, after the rumors made their way to management. I was so far gone in trying to catch Raymond in his lies, that I had lost sight of trying to conceal our affair. I'm sure many of the older women with nothing to do, but sit around while time past them, noticed what was going on with us. Some of our heated discussions probably could be heard bouncing around hollow walls, and I'm sure people took noticed to the fact that Raymond and I were inseparable. However, when Raymond told me, "Linda knows about us," I was fearful of what that meant for us both. Would they kick me out, and would Raymond lose his job? Well, one of the two happened, Raymond was fired.

Raymond was told he was fired because other residents reported that he was not doing what he should have been while on the clock, which was because Raymond was most likely in my apartment. It was a messy situation on every level. I believe the actual cause was that something happened either with a resident or in the building and Raymond was nowhere around to respond.

However, Raymond being fired did not prevent him from coming around. Raymond was still allowed to come whenever he wanted, and it did not seem to affect the relationship he had with management. It felt good to no longer have to sneak around. Raymond spent much of his time with me, that he practically moved in. Most of Raymond's things were at my place, and he stayed with me most nights, however nothing changed, we were still arguing all of the time about the same things. It had gotten to the point where I became depressed and cried all of the time. I did not want to keep dealing with the disrespect, but I tolerated it because I did not want to be alone.

In addition to Raymond cheating with the other woman, I discovered he was smoking weed and drinking. I felt uncomfortable knowing he engaged in those things, after vowing to never deal with someone who used drugs, but I chose to be uncomfortable. I justified his behavior by telling myself it was okay as long as it was not an addiction, which the weed was the only frequent substance I saw him engage in; I figured it was harmless since so many guys did it.

Raymond did not have a job, so I assumed the responsibility of caring for him. I bought him clothes, sneakers, boots and gave him money whenever he asked. Supporting Raymond became a tool of manipulation to get him to do the things I wanted him to do. I figured the more I had, the more of a reason Raymond had to stay with me. I knew he was going between me and the other woman, but I thought if I loved him more, it would be enough for Raymond to eventually choose me. I was hoping she got tired and saw I was not going anywhere, but I'm sure she was thinking the same thing. All the while, we were only stroking Raymond's ego by fighting over him.

I constantly poured my heart out to him, hoping that my cries showed Raymond how badly he was hurting me, but they did not. Raymond would see me upset and say things like, "What is wrong with you, why are you always crying and looking depressed." Or if I was still hurt from a previous situation, he would say, "You're still upset about what happened yesterday?" I was more afraid of him leaving me, so I just continued to deal with the disrespect, and emotional attacks.

I even went as far as befriending and getting close to his family in hopes of building an alliance. I figured if I fit in well and formed close bonds with his family, then they would convince Raymond I was the one. Raymond had 2 sisters, one of whom I did form a close relationship with, but the other and his mother could not stand me and I never knew why. I remember the sister I was closest to told me once, "Girl, you mean to tell me you never had a man cheat on you? Ain't no man gonna be faithful to you. I don't care how good to them you are."

I was in love with a man who never was faithful his whole life. Raymond was very much a native of the hard streets, as I learned he served hard time in the '80s. After Raymond's long stent, he wanted better, but women were always his major downfall.

Just when I had decided enough was enough and that I had had enough, seeing that Raymond was not going to change, toward the end of October 2006, I noticed I did not have a cycle. I instantly knew I was pregnant. This news changed the way I felt about the situation, and I instantly had hope that a baby would change things. Raymond had a grown son in his twenties, with whom he did not have much of a relationship with, because Raymond had not been around for much of his son's life. Again I was missing the clear bells, lights and whistles that were going off all of the time about Raymond. It had gotten to the point where my intuition stopped alarming me. What was the point, I was clearly far gone in this dysfunctional relationship, but it was one I felt if I hung on to, things would eventually get better.

I was excited to tell Raymond the news and knew he would be as well. Raymond was always telling me if he had another child, he wanted a little girl. It was my hope that the baby I was carrying was a girl, just to make him happy. What I did not know was that Raymond would have a baby girl in the upcoming months, but not by me. I found out shortly after I announced I was pregnant, the other woman was also pregnant, and was already three months along. My entire world fell apart. I could not believe what was happening. I felt beyond betrayed. To make matters worse, during my entire pregnancy, Raymond was not there for me as he was for the other woman. He made every appointment with her, and only a few out of my entire nine months. I remember feeling frightened and alone, this was my first child and I had no idea what to expect. All I could think about were the horror stories of how painful child birth was. I was terrified.

However, I was determined to enjoy my pregnancy. For so long, I thought I would be unable to carry a baby because of the extensive scarring around my abdomen, so when I became pregnant and carried full term, the baby was a blessing. Raymond attended two appointments early in the beginning, but the rest I attended alone, including the ultrasound to discover the sex of the baby; although I reached out to Raymond, eventually I stopped trying. I tried overcoming my emotions over Raymond expecting another baby, knowing the stress could potentially have negative effects on my baby, but all I did was cry, every day and every night. I was so depressed that I had to force myself to eat. At one point I was concerned the stress and depression would cause complications, so I fought to pull it together. I decided that if Raymond did not want to be a part of my pregnancy, then I was not going to force him.

After the temp job ended with the MDA, I was offered another position in December of 2005. I worked for a health care agency that provided insured employees with various companies, the options of additional support. I performed wellbeing surveys that created a multifaceted snapshot of a client's overall health history, to determine if they would benefit from the company's services. I then asked if clients were interested in having a registered nurse contact them monthly about concerns found in the questionnaire.

CorSolutions was located in Norristown PA. The job was by far the best place to be every day, with an assortment of people and personalities; it was the first time I felt I was in a place where I fit in. What I hated was the daily commute. I had to travel two hours, taking a train and two buses. The bus that dropped me in front of the building only came hourly. I got up at five in the morning every day, left at six, and returned close to eleven in the evening. By the time I started to physically show, I was determined to continue to work my entire pregnancy. I needed the money, but more importantly, I loved the job. There was the possibility of the position going from temporary to permanent. Several temps who started along with me, had already been offered permanent positions, and I believed I would be next. As the weather tuned to winter, I struggled physically in the brutal cold. I was trying to save up for a car, and fought everyday to push through. I sometimes missed the hourly bus, and had to stand in the cold, pregnant with a large belly, that made walking and standing even more difficult for an additional hour. When the second bus, which dropped me off in front of my apartment, also took too long, I began walking the two miles from the bus stop to my apartment. Scared and alone, vulnerable to the dangers of the night, I prayed the whole way home every night. As soon as I got home, I could feel the pressure of both my legs and feet as they swelled the moment I sat down. In pain I soaked them, got in the bed, and repeated the same routine every day until months later when I was finally able to afford a car.

Around the time when I was five or six months, I was told of the possibility that my baby could be born with down syndrome. Because of Raymond's age, the probability of my child being born with the genetic disorder was high. I was educated about a test known as an Amniocentesis. It came with a fifty percent chance of miscarriage, but would be able to identify if the baby would be born with the disorder. I was told to consider the option, but felt I was more so being intimidated and coerced into taking the test. None the less, I was confident that my child would be fine, and born healthy. It meant everything to me to have a child, because I knew that in them, I would finally have the chance to see the beauty I would have possessed if I had not been burned. I felt by looking at my physical features as a reflection in my child, I could truly be content with my own appearance.

I was excited for my ultrasound appointment, I again made attempts to reach out to Raymond to attend, and when Raymond did not, it dawned on me I was really about to parent my first child alone. He still was of no support to me. With the hormones from the pregnancy and the emotional state I was in over feeling abandoned and betrayed, I became even more stressed and severely depressed. I did not get much sleep and could not stop thinking of Raymond being there for the other woman and not at all there for me.

When the ultrasound revealed that I was having a boy, I was disappointed for a couple of reasons. I had always wanted a girl, because I was sure she would look just like me and mirror my exact image as a baby. I also thought having a girl would make Raymond happy and remain in our lives. Then when I saw the images and inspected the several pictures I was given to take with me, I became overwhelmed with joy and excitement about having a baby boy.

I eventually found support, not from Raymond, but from a Dula. I had decided to attend camp Susquahanna that year in June. I was seven months pregnant, and needed to get away from all of the stress, and be in the presence of people who I knew cared about me. It was there that I was approached by a long time camp counselor, who I had become close to throughout the years of attending camp. Karen offered to come to my house to support and coach me throughout the remainder of my pregnancy and helped deliver my baby.

Having Karen beside me was God sending his angle, knowing I could not get through the rest of my pregnancy alone. I had the most beautiful experience with Karen, she prepared and educated me about everything there was to know about labor and delivery, to the point that when I gave birth, I was able to deliver calmly and without complications. My labor proved to be a challenging one, I experienced the agony of labor for two days and ten hours. I was miserable, but Karen was there every step of the way, giving me techniques to help ease the unexplainable pain from the contractions. I felt loved and supported by Karen, which made giving birth comfortable and less fearful.

My world forever changed from the first sound of my baby's cries. When I saw his head full of hair, I knew that all was well with my baby boy. I named him Keyan Anthony (after my father) Carter. Once we locked eyes on each other, I felt a love I had never experienced. Nothing else in the world mattered to me, but him. While in the hospital, I had to fill out paperwork, one of which was the birth certificate. As the clerk explained to me that the father's name would not be listed because of his absence during birth, somewhere in the middle of the disclaimer, I began to cry. I was overcome with the feeling of shame and embarrassment. I felt I had failed my child hours after he had come into the world. I was even more annoyed with the clerk, for minimizing my reaction by saying to me, "Don't cry, you are not the only one to go through this." Her words reinforced my feelings of shame to know that I was among the many single women raising a child alone. My pain was casually dismissed because I now was a statistic.

A few days later, my baby and I left Hahnemann Hospital to begin our new life together. I was beyond scared. I was grateful to have had my family's support, but I feared most what would happen when I was left to care for this tiny, helpless being alone. Not only was I a single mother, but I also had physical limitations and would have to figure out ways to care for my son efficiently. My greatest fear was not being able to physically take care of him, and it be noticed, resulting in him being taken away from me by social services. This possibility forced me to work harder at being independent in ways and I had never considered before. Keyan depended on me and I promised to never let him down. No one could love him or appreciate Keyan's existence as much as I did, so I knew I had to push hard for my son.

My family was by my side helping and supporting me. My dad provided many of the essentials I would have otherwise been unable to afford, such as a crib and stroller with a car seat. I believed he was more excited about his first grandson, that it gave him great pleasure to spoil and provide for him. My mom was also a much needed support, but with the stress and high emotional state I was in, it was not long before we clashed and things became even more stressful for me.

From the time Keyan was put into my arms, my mother appeared to be overbearing and controlling. As with any of my accomplishments, I felt my mother was looking to sabotage my happiest moment. She condescendingly spoke to me, as if I knew absolutely nothing and talked down to me about everything I did wrong. She constantly said how she raised seven children and knew more than me; and manipulated me by saying how she listened to her mother when she had her first child, when she did not. I knew this was a manipulative tactic, because my grandmother and my mother always had a tumultuous relationship when she was alive.

Once I returned home with Keyan, my mother agreed to stay to help me get acclimated with caring for Keyan until I felt confident enough to manage on my own. It ended up being the longest and most difficult two weeks. I immediately realized upon coming home that my emotional state met the symptoms for Postpartum Depression. I read a lot about pregnancy, delivery and post-delivery; I had been educated by the doctor, for signs of onset of the mood disorder.

The first night home was by far hell. I could not get Keyan to sleep, and to stop crying. In addition, I had my mother in my ear yelling and belittling me. I cried, feeling extremely helpless. By the next day, I had become sick of my mother and a big screaming match erupted over her not allowing me to learn on my own what I needed to do for the baby. I called my father crying, in which he told me to try my best to deal with her and make peace, because I needed her help. I was miserable, and already felt I was failing as a mother. Instead of taking my father's advice, I asked my mother to leave, which infuriated her. She got into my face, screaming and curing at me, before telling me not to call her no matter what, as she stormed out and slammed the door behind her.

The minute she left, I felt completely alone, but unwilling to allow my mother to make me feel incompetent regardless of how much I needed her help. I figured I had gotten through so many difficult situations in which I had to figure how to manage without help, so I saw this situation as no different. My strategy was to think ahead and take my time with every step and everything I did. My biggest concern and fear was traveling with Keyan and how to get him from the apartment, then in and out of the car. Foreseeing the action steps in my mind and what they would require, helped me to prepare. It was great the building had an elevator, because all I had to do was strap Keyan in his seat, attach the seat to the stroller, and take the elevator down to the car. When leaving the hospital, I had my father teach me how to install the car seat's base and then practiced over and over several times reconnecting the seat to ensure I physically could do so when having to secure it alone.

My greatest fear was to be out in public alone with Keyan. I feared that someone would see me as a vulnerable target because of my limitations and appearance to potentially take my baby. Therefore, I limited my exposure to potential risks, by leaving the house only when necessary, which was mainly to go food shopping, to the clinic and to the Woman, Infant, Children program (WIC) appointments.

Once I knew I was pregnant, I knew I would need to rely on governmental assistance to supplement my income, because I did not make enough to support myself, let alone a child. The day I had to walk into a welfare office for the first time to apply for food stamps and Medicaid was very difficult for me, although I was grateful the services were available until I could do better for myself. I thanked God for everything, even what would be considered degrading and had a lot of stigma attached. I knew who I was and that I was not looking to take advantage of the system, without it, I do not know how I would have made it through.

The day after I gave birth, I traveled in the sweltering July heat, with Keyan to the local county assistance office. The summer's heat was brutal. I was drenched from sweating profusely, and in agonizing pain because of the engorging of my breast from the pile up of unused milk, after choosing not to breast feed. I had attempted to breast-feed, knowing that it was the healthiest option for the baby; however with the physical pain I experienced, on even the first attempt, with him latching on, I knew I would have to bottle feed. I sat in the unventilated office, lactating with cabbage leaves on my chest for five hours waiting to be seen. After demanding that I be seen because my physicality made it very difficult to "just come back," as it had been suggested I do, I was finally seen and apologized to for the inconvenience.

Weeks after establishing a routine and figuring how to do things that worked well for me, I became less uncomfortable, I felt more in control and capable of taking care of my son. However, the Postpartum Depression worsened. As sleepless nights turned into five months of dealing with a colic baby, I felt I had reached my wits end. I tried every possible thing I could think of to get Keyan to sleep, my father even came in the middle of the night to drive Keyan around to get him to sleep. I began feeling frustrated and detached from Keyan in the first few months. I felt extremely guilty that I did not feel emotionally connected to my baby for almost the first year. It was hard, and even when I sought help, I omitted how depressed I was and my feelings of detachment, for fear that my honesty would have my child taken. Instead, I prayed and when Keyan was about seven months, his sleeping became normal and eventually the depression subsided.

Raymond came around off and on, after Keyan was born. As much as I wanted to punish him for neglecting me while pregnant, and not being present for the delivery, I realized I had to deal with my anger and not allow it to interfere with Raymond having a relationship with his son. When Keyan was first born, I took the baby to see Raymond's mother, in hopes that she would inform Raymond that I had given birth to a beautiful baby. I also hoped he felt guilty for not being present to see Keyan come into the world. I was hurt by his actions, but I wanted my child to know and have his father in his life, and I did not want anything on my part to the reason why he did not. I believed God knew all and saw all, and Raymond would have to deal with the consequences of having to one day explain to Keyan, why he was absent from his life.

In truth, a part of me really held on to hope that Keyan would bring Raymond and I together, and to make Raymond want to do right by the both of us. Raymond eventually came around, and of course fell in love with Keyan. He suddenly was around every day after meeting his son. I lowered my guard, accepted Raymond's apology for not being there for me, and that easily, I allowed Raymond to re-enter and pick up where he left off with the disrespect. For a while into the relationship, I suspected he was still with the mother of his baby girl, but learned it was not just her, Raymond was in several relationships.

When Keyan turned two, we moved into a new efficiency, and was also when things with Raymond and I really became out of control. I became sick of the women, but more so sick with myself for putting up with what I had allowed Raymond to do to me. I made noise, and spoke to the women trying to keep tabs on him, but they were effortless attempts to hold on to Raymond and make him do right by me.

Raymond began running off with my car, leaving me stuck in the house many times for days with a baby and no way to get to the places I needed to go. I always feared my car being taken by the police, because Raymond was driving around without a license. My car was all I had and I had no way of replacing it. That is, however until one day my fears came true, when the police saw Raymond getting into my car. They approached him, and then contacted me asking if I had given him permission to drive my vehicle, I told them I had not, so they proceeded to arrest Raymond. The officer pulled me to the side and asked if I wanted to press charges for theft. The officer spoke to me about not having mercy for Raymond, and if he cared about me, he would not have taken advantage of me. When I said no, the officer said, "Okay, I don't want to see you in a situation where I have to come out again, because you allowed this guy to do what he wants." It was not before long that I realized I should had listened to the officer and cut my ties with Raymond.

Months later, Raymond drove me to work, because we agreed he would take Keyan to his doctor's appointment. I was upset Raymond was late picking me up, after class, I had been waiting nearly an hour. He was not answering his phone and I became very concerned. When Raymond finally arrived, I got into the driver side to drive and immediately noticed the gas gage was a notch before being empty. I asked why he did not filled the tank, since he had been driving it all day. He then began to ignore me, after claiming to have put gas in earlier. I told Raymond I did not have any money and that he should had made sure there was gas before making the long drive.

Class let out at nine in the evening, so I preferred to take I-76, because there usually was no traffic during that time. I was enrolled in my first semester of taking graduate classes, I had been inspired by my mom's struggles with addiction, and I always was fascinated with understanding human behaviors. I believed with having knowledge in mental health, in conjunction with my own personal experiences, I could help so many people.

After driving for about two miles we caught up with the congestion of stalled cars, and were forced to merge into traffic because there were no exits in sight. Raymond became extremely agitated with me for choosing to take the route, as if I knew one lane for about six miles was available due to construction. Raymond began cursing and calling me stupid, when he realized the gas light chimed as we inched along through traffic.

I told Raymond I did not appreciate him yelling and disrespecting me in front of our son, who was about fourteen months and asleep in the back. I told Raymond it was his fault, and he should have put gas in the car. All I could do was pray we made it to the nearest exit. Raymond then received a phone call that changed the course of everything. He answered the phone, and I immediately realized it was a woman. The tone of his voice suggested Raymond knew the woman very well. What I found most unsettling was that he spoke to her as if I was not sitting beside him. I heard Raymond tell the woman he would see her as soon after he was finished. The impression I got from the snippet of their brief conversation, was that Raymond was very much involved with her.

When he got off the phone, I asked Raymond who was he talking to and outright asked him if he had been staying with another woman during the days he was not with me. Raymond did not provide an answer, just told me I needed to be concerned with driving. I started to cry and asked Raymond why did he like hurting me, and why he just could not have been honest. I reminded Raymond of all the times I had been there for him and had gone out of my way to show I loved him. Raymond told me to mind my business and how tired he was of hearing my mouth.

Raymond's behavior and attitude suddenly changed drastically, he was no longer the guy I met and fell for. By this time, we were off again, on again, and I was still holding onto hope. He was staying with who I thought was his sister most days, but I learned he in fact had been staying with the woman on the phone. Raymond had become angry, aggressive and easily agitated. I did not know the person in the car with me that night.

I cried because Raymond was being insensitive by not showing any concern for my feelings. He told me he could care less about me crying, calling me a drama queen, adding, "All you do is cry and cause me a headache." Raymond went on to blame me for why things never worked out.

Raymond then proceeded to go through my bag, taking the money he had given me earlier to pay for my course books. Raymond told me he had changed his mind, wanted his money back and did not care about me. I begged him not to take the money, because I was already weeks into the semester without books. Raymond refused, I started crying, while telling him how cruel he was; Raymond kept telling me to shut up, calling me all sorts of names and threatening me. I then yelled at Raymond, "Stop disrespecting me!" Suddenly, out of nowhere, he yelled, "SHUT UP!!!"

The next thing I knew, I was seeing stars against blackness, and felt a massive blow to my right eye, Raymond had punched me in my face, while I was driving. I slightly lost control of the wheel as traffic began to pick up when the lanes finally opened. I tried to open my eye to see the dark road, but everything was so blurry. I had to reduce my speed to about fifteen miles per hour, to prevent from crashing. The brightness of lights from the construction area allowed me to see enough to see the exit for City Line Avenue. I screamed, "You hit me in my eye! I can't see!" Raymond kept yelling at me to drive the car, threatening that I better not get us into an accident. I told Raymond I could not see where I was, he replied by calling me a liar and told me how much he hated me for lying.

As soon as we got off the intersection, and into a gas station, Raymond jumped out of the car. I kept crying telling him I could not see out of my right eye, it was sealed shut, and I could not open it. I was relying on my left eye, which I could not see that good out of to begin with. I begged Raymond not to leave me and the baby with no means to get home, I had no money and no gas. Raymond then walked back toward the car and said he would get the gas, but afterward he never wanted to see me again. Sitting in the car waiting for him to pump the gas, I opened up the panel above my head to look at my eye to see how bad it was. When the small light shone in my eye, it was as if I was staring directly into ultra ray light. My eye was hideous. I was able to open it enough to see that my eyeball was bloodshot red. It was extremely painful to open, but I was more fearful because it was my good eye, and that I might lose my sight in it.

When Raymond made his way back to the car, he continued to accuse me of lying, claiming there was nothing wrong with my eye, while muffling obscenities and smart comments under his breath making me feel more nervous. I told him to look at my eye, but he refused, I knew Raymond felt guilty. Raymond pumped the gas, hung up the pump and walked off. When he saw that I was still sitting in my car at the pump, he came back asking me why was I still there, accusing me of wanting to draw attention. I begged Raymond to drive us home and then go on his way, because I could not see. He got into the car and began driving. I could not do anything but quietly cry in pain. Raymond got even angrier seeing me cry, saying it was my fault, and that I had pushed him too far.

When we were a block away from my apartment, I asked Raymond if he could drive me to the hospital because I could not open my eye, and by that time it had swelled more. Raymond again denied there was anything wrong with me, stopping the car while the light turned red and got out. Someone walking by asked if I was okay, and I replied that I was not, telling the woman I had just been assaulted. Somehow I had become convinced by Raymond there was nothing wrong with me, that I asked the stranger to confirm the trauma to my eye, which she did. Raymond saw me talking to her, rushed back over, and began telling the woman not to listen to anything I told her, that I was exaggerating, and threatened me to go home.

I managed to drive the few blocks to my apartment, and managed to take Keyan out of the car and walked into the entrance of my place, where I had no intentions of hiding my face. One of the women who worked the day shift was seated at the front desk and asked me if I was all right. Just as I was about to tell her the events of the evening, Raymond stormed in trying to overpower me to deny everything I was saying. She told him to leave and when he did, I went up to my apartment, called a cab, and both Keyan and I went to the hospital.

I sat waiting to be seen feeling ashamed, embarrassed, and alone. The relationship with Raymond passed through my head, and thoughts of how I had allowed myself to be in such a situation caused me to break down. I could not believe what Raymond had done to me, but more so that he had no remorse. I spent hours waiting to be seen and each time I had been asked to recall what happened, I felt more ashamed and embarrassed, having to relive it, and having to expose myself in the openness for others to see. I felt the nurses and the doctor did not truly care about what happened, it was protocol and I was seen as another battered woman, with a story they probably heard many times before.

I thought to myself, I should not be here, how did this happen to me, why did it? When I finally was seen, the doctor did not offer much sympathy. She spoke to me as if I was another case, asking me a list of questions, as if she already knew the answers to. Her tone was more uncomfortable and colder than her touch. I was asked if I had a safe place to go, and if I wanted to press charges. As soon as I said I did not need the police to get involved, her demeanor grew colder and unyielding.

She checked me out, and seemed agitated when I was in too much pain to do what she asked of me. The doctor kept instructing me to open my eye, which was too painful to do. It felt as if I had something lodged in my eye, and I was afraid of the pain from the intensity of the florescent light. The doctor became impatient when I kept flinching at the sensation of her coming toward me with a pin light. The luminosity of the pen sized flashlight sent a sharp shooting pain through my eye that sent a shock through every part of my body. I had never felt such pain before. I am sure the scream I let out, echoed throughout the entire ward, but the doctor became stern, forcing my eye open so that she could administer some eye drops. I'm sure at that point, she was just ready to be done with me and move on to the next patient on her ever growing list in the ER.

The only prescription given was to keep my eye closed to rest it, apply ice for the swelling and to avoid light for several days. She then left without offering words of comfort, other than to take care of myself in a tone that suggested she did not care whether I did or did not. I had expectations of being consoled and told everything would be okay, and treated with concern and empathy, instead I left feeling even worse. I felt like I was just another victim, left to come to terms with what happened to me alone. I felt judged and as if what happened to me was my fault.

It was five in the morning when Keyan and I hopped into the cab, the sky had changed to a lighter blue, the air was cool and calming, as it flowed through the cracked window. The Muslim driver was listening to music in Arabic, in which the foreign sound drew me in, anything to distract my mind from what I was going though was sweet music to my ears. My mind cleared, and I began to drift off to sleep, feeling for a split second that the ride would carry my cares away. I awoke to the driver opening the passenger door and helped me step out of the cab. He helped me to open Keyan's stroller and strapped him in.

It was very early, so no one was around when I entered the building except for the woman who worked the overnight shift. She came out of the office to ask if everything was okay. When she saw my eye, she helped me with the baby up to my apartment and was extremely upset with Raymond. I told her that I did not plan on dealing with him any longer and I was serious. Later that day, I spoke to the social worker, who got word of what happened to me. When she saw my eye, she was also very concerned, leaving to return with phone numbers for domestic abuse organizations. I thought it was all a bit much, I did not want to think of myself as being a victim of domestic violence. It was hard and painful for me to come to terms with.

More difficult was the phone call I had to make to my mother, because I was in no condition to care for myself or Keyan. Surprisingly, she came to my aid in a calm and rational manner, I told her what happened and she remained speechless, no "I told you so" or nothing that made me feel worse than I already felt. A part of me wanted to forgive Raymond and take him back, but a bigger part of me knew being physically abused was something I could not compromise with.

My mom helped me gather all of his things in my apartment, we drove Raymond's stuff to where he was in North Philly, and just like that I was done and over him. One thing about me was I loved hard, but when I fell out of love, that was it. Abuse was not love. The day Raymond put his hands on me was when I fell out of love with him, and I never looked back. It was something I could never rationalize or tolerate. Although we were not good for each other, Raymond loved and had a great bond with Keyan, and had never done anything to hurt him. Raymond was and is a good person, but just had many unresolved issues. I eventually dealt with that trauma, although it is a truth Raymond continued to find difficult to acknowledge happened. Despite it all, I found it in my heart to forgive him and we eventually set aside our differences to be cordial for the sake of our son.

Being in this relationship began to open my eyes to what I have gone through in relationships before Raymond, how men perceived me and how I perceived myself in relationships. I would go through much more heartache before I came to realize the problem was with me, with my fears and insecurities. I realized that until I truly faced and dealt with both, I would continue to experience unhealthy relationships. Relationships that were formed with men out of desperation and fear of being alone. I had to go deeper within myself to understand the root of the strongholds with men. What I discovered about myself would eventually lead me to a place of true self love and acceptance of what is. I would go through much more agony and humiliation, before I finally realized just how much pain I was allowing myself to go through just to find love.

CHAPTER 19

The Misconception of Love

BEING IN A RELATIONSHIP was something I desperately wanted, so much so that I became the antagonist in much of my own suffering. All I wanted, was to experience the bliss I saw so many people in relationships have. I prayed to God for someone and when a guy came, in whatever form, I believed he was the answer to my prayers. I knew what I wanted, but when I did not see it in the guys who approached me, I usually accepted them anyway. I believed I was not in the position to be choosy or have too many expectations, and felt I was not beautiful enough to have preferences. I knew I wanted to be with someone attractive, and even though my expectations were not high, I still had them. I had a type, and understood men had them too. For most, that type is heavily weighed on appearance. I was hopeful a man could and was willing to look past my scars to see that I was beautiful.

However, a part of me was not completely undignified, I valued myself enough to be selective in who I gave myself to. I vowed that no matter how desperate I believed I was, I would not have allowed myself to be completely destroyed and taken advantage of by sleeping around with any and everyone. I valued what a relationship represented, which was love, and I decided after just giving my virginity away indiscriminately, I would choose with much discretion. I convinced myself I had to be in a meaningful relationship where the feelings were mutual.

TANISHA CARTER

It did not matter if he was uneducated, had no job, had nothing going for himself, I just wanted to be with someone. In fact, I minimized the lack of attributes, ambitions, and success by believing I had to accept him as he was if I was expecting him to do the same with me. His lack thereof actually became an advantage to me, the more in need he was, the better the advantage I felt I had over him. I knew when guys were interested in me because I had something they wanted or needed, but I chose to ignore the signs. I put their needs before my own. I gave of myself wholeheartedly, there was no me, everything was about them.

I denied my wants needs and desires. If something bothered or upset me, I ignored how I felt, too fearful of pushing them away, by putting the attention on me. I believed I could not make mistakes or give him a reason to leave, already knowing how great the possibility was, because of the way I looked. In some situations, I felt the pressure to say yes, even when I did not like, agree with or felt comfortable. I thought I needed to be grateful they wanted to be with me, when he could have chosen anyone else.

Seldom did I hear men say physical attraction was not important to them. A few said, "It's what's inside that matters most," but that quickly changed either after meeting me or after exposure to my scars and deformities. Many of my experiences showed me the men who claimed looks did not matter had the intentions of being "a good person" and a part of being a good person, meant not to appear shallow and superficial. However, most men did not come across a woman who looked like me, and their inability to handle everything that is me, defied good intentions. Being someone who could handle the difficulty and the discomfort of my truth, relied on being predisposed to adversity that has sensitized them.

I have come to realize that it would take someone with a sound mind and spirit who truly understands the fundamentals of love, and who is secure within themselves enough, to know that being with an attractive woman will not boost his esteem and or validate himself as a man. I have found this to be true by observing and being with guys who could not handle being with me for fear of what others might think of them, because there was a deficit within themselves.

Many of the men in the environment I grew up in came from broken and dysfunctional backgrounds, where they lacked affection from a mother or true guidance from a man; where the concept of love was introduced and defined through lust and attraction. As young as a toddler, many boys are encouraged to "get the pretty girls." Boys then grow up with a bias of beauty. Many learn to see beauty as being only physical, and rarely learn to appreciate and understand beauty comes in all forms, even those that differ from the norms. Then the media and culture reinforce what has been taught, therefore many guys develop an intolerance and ignorance for anything contrary to what is considered acceptable. My beauty is considered by many to be unacceptable.

Constantly experiencing rejection, I felt I had to be grateful for whoever came my way. Being rejected so many times, I could not take much more of it. Since I have been rejected by most men, I allowed it to control and dictate any possibilities of future relationships. I lost hope in ever meeting a man who could truly accept and love me for all that I am.

Rejection from men left me feeling unworthy, insecure and ashamed. So much so that I felt anxiety in the presences of men, fearful of looking in their eyes to avoid their looks of disgust and disapproval. I could get attention from a guy who has yet to see my face, but may have been drawn to me because of my figure. Many times while driving guys will pull up beside me in cars, only seeing my profile, he then will call out to me, misled by what he sees, and unprepared for when I show my face. When I do turn for him to see my face, their face revels the look of shock and many times disgust.

Some quickly search for something to say, "Sorry, I thought you were someone else." Others outright say what is on their mind their minds and not hide their reactions. Once, a guy noticed me walking and rushed to catch up with me. Knowing what his reaction would be, I tried walking faster, but he finally sped up. All the while I kept responding, "I'm sorry, I'm not interested," but once he caught up with me and saw my face, he yelled out, "Oh my God, she is a monster." He laughed as he turned and ran back towards his friends.

He then described my face, and they all ran toward me to get a look, then turned back, laughed and made fun of me.

I remember going out to clubs, and guys pulling for me in the darkness, only seeing my silhouette. I enjoyed the attention, taking advantage of the moment, knowing I would not have it if the lights were on. Sometimes I was asked by a guy to dance, in which I would always turn my back toward them so they could not get an up close view of my face. I quickly walked away after the song, ignoring their further advances.

Once, I was dancing with a guy during a couple of songs, and afterward, we struck up a conversation. I noticed he had a few drinks, but he appeared alert and I really enjoyed talking and dancing with him. Before leaving, he asked me for my phone number, which I gave to him, and he gave me his. I took the initiative to call him a few days later, he vaguely remembered me, but asked if I could send him a photo to jar his memory. I did not think anything of it, and sent a photo to his phone. I was sure he would remember me considering we talked for a while in the club. When he received it, he said, "Oh, wow, I must have drunk too much, what happened to you." I explained, he did not reply, but hung up the phone.

I knew it took a special kind of man with the strength and the confidence to handle being with me, but I believed he did not exist. My mother would always say there was someone out there for me, I just had to trust and wait on God, but deep within my core, I did not believe. I had strong faith in many things, but when it came to situations where I saw attraction played a significant role, I felt I was the exception to God's power. I was looking at all of my experiences and began to believe if I wanted someone, then I had to take matters into my own hands. When I did, that was when I often confused my desperation and naiveté as a blessing.

For a long time, I strayed away from God, clearly knowing in my spirit that leaning to my own understanding would have dire consequences. I felt angry that it appeared God was blessing everyone with relationships, and many of whom appeared undeserving and unappreciative of them, but I had to wait. My thought was, *What exactly am I waiting for?* I feared I would have no experiences if I waited, so I did what I wanted, and was ready to experience what came my way. I learned from my experiences something very important; because I did not adhere to God's many warnings, I set myself up for much unnecessary pain and suffering.

I did not believe a man could fall in love with me, because I lacked what I believed was the essential factor that made men fall in love with a woman - beauty. I believed I had to convince them I was worthy of being in love with, by earning their love and affection. I knew a man would have to love me unconditionally, but my perception of men caused me to believe he did not exist.

Still I wanted to prove myself wrong, that there was someone special for me, and looked for the hope of him being in the men I found myself with. In these relationships, what I experienced were variations of good, bad and ugly. I would come to see how the pathology I brought to the relationship along with the dysfunction he brought, made for situations that caused me more pain than the blissful feelings I had hoped to experience.

In the summer of the end of my Junior year of high school, I met who I considered to be, my first boyfriend named Kareem. We had been introduced by a mutual friend; in theory, Shay was supposed to be more like a stepmother, because she was dating my father at the time, she was close in age to me and was more like a friend. Shay and Kareem were long time acquaintances from growing up in the same housing development. I had accompanied Shay to the housing units in the Holmesburg section of Philadelphia.

Immediately upon being introduced to Kareem, Shay said to me, "Here is someone you could take on your prom." I shared with Shay my thoughts of attending my senior prom alone. After going to both my sop hop and junior prom with someone, having a date for the senior prom was not that big of a deal. Matter of fact, everyone in my group of friends decided to attend the prom together without dates.

My first impression of Kareem was not much. Considering the suspicious surroundings we were in, and the dilapidated condition of the projects, I was certain that he was just another hood dude. Kareem was about six feet, dark brown skin, with cornrows snaking toward the back of his head. Kareem followed the oversized style that was trending at the time, baggy pants, and shirt. His whole attire seemed to devour his physique. I was not interested in considering him in anyway.

Kareem seemed to be someone of great importance and popularity as everyone who passed by shouted out, "Yo, what's up, Reem!" I noticed how cocky he grew as more and more people acknowledged his presence. It was a warm summer's day and people filled the enclosed cul-de-sac, barbequing, and enjoying the beautiful weather, in their private alcoves. Children ran around spraying the rough atmosphere with their cherub laughter as they played. It seemed like one big block party. Kareem seemed very interested in getting to know me, based on the very little information provided by our mutual friend. As soon as he learned I was in school and was preparing to go to college, Kareem became even more intrigued with me.

While Shay became distracted with talking to others she had not seen in a while, Kareem came over and started talking to me as if we were long time acquaintances. Kareem asked me questions and we started a conversation. Not before long, he had invited me to a less noisy area to further our conversation. The more I shared about myself from his probing, the more Kareem seemed impressed by me. Kareem asked if I had a boyfriend and I told him no, in which he said he was shocked at the fact that someone as focused, ambitious and cute, was not involved with anyone. I thought his flattery calling me cute, was nothing more than sarcasm, because I just could not accept that he honestly found me attractive. I simply saw Kareem as being overly nice. I am sure my insecurity and discomfort gleamed through me, but he did not let on.

Kareem did however ask what happened to me, while grabbing my arm to exam my scars. My anxiety rose, I felt completely outside of my comfort zone, and fearful that with further examination he would be appalled, so I gently pulled away. Kareem then turned to me and said, "Your scars are beautiful!" The way he positioned himself in front of me forced me look at him. Every second that passed in what had to be about thirty seconds was too painful to stand, as Kareem gazed into my eyes with seriousness.

I wanted to get up and run, while at the same time enjoyed being looked at with such intensity. I tried looking for familiar signs to get a feel for his intentions, but I just could not read him. I wanted to believe Kareem, but my experiences with guys made me disbelieve his sincerity. My way of dealing with discomfort was to avoid it. I laughed and moved around a lot so as to avoid the awkwardness and still moments of exchanged glances, sitting and standing close to each other. We ended up talking for what seemed like hours, but in fact was about a half of an hour. I wanted and tried to loosen up to come out of my shyness, but I could not. At the end of our conversation, Kareem asked for my phone number, I was excited that he wanted to talk further, but did not let him know. I waited for Kareem to ask a few more times before I gave it to him. I refused to take his, because I wanted to know if he was really interested in me by calling first. Kareem promised he would call and my response was it was okay if he did not, saying it was nice meeting him and thanked Kareem for the conversation. Inside I was excited and hoped he would.

A couple of days later, I received a phone call from Kareem, I answered the phone unfazed to hear from him, but was excited that he called. In our conversation Kareem wasted no time asking if he could take me out. I struggled for a response, I did not know what to say, no one had asked me out before. His question was rhetorical, because he quickly said, "It does not matter if you say "yes" or no I'm still taking you out."

A few nights later, Kareem pulled up to my house to pick me up. I felt on top of the world! Kareem was a few years older than me, who drove, had a job, but most of all, was interested in who I was and not ashamed to be seen with me. As with many of my first moments, I cherished my outing with Kareem as if I would never have one like it again. I came to understand that because of my differences, my life would be limited of the experiences many people frequently have and become reoccurrences in their lives. I expected many interpersonal and social experiences for me would be few and far between, so I made it a point to take advantage of experiences I feared might be my last.

Kareem took me out to dinner and a movie, but the highlight of the night was driving around, visiting seemingly every member of his family to introduce me. The look on his face, as he talked highly of me and my accomplishments was of pride and excitement. It was as if Kareem had found a high priced gem in the gutters of the hood, sitting in plain sight, but easily overlooked, because no one expected to find such a treasure in the slums of the streets.

Kareem seemed excited to show others his invaluable gain in hopes they would be in awe and proud of his random luck. Kareem saw something valuable in me, worthy of showing off. The only thing was I struggled to see what he saw in me, so much so that I found it hard to believe his feelings for me were real. My guard was still up, and despite what appeared to be good about Kareem, and the relationship we started to build, I did not fully trust the authenticity of his intentions.

Everyone Kareem introduced me to had the same reaction of shock that he brought someone like me to meet the family. His family was extremely close, so if Kareem brought a girl to meet his sisters, brothers, mother and father, he must have been serious about them. Apparently Kareen finding interest in me showed unexpected signs of maturity, considering the types of girls he typically was into were the complete opposite of who I was.

Initially, Kareem appeared to have a good head on his shoulder and he appeared to have many things I was looking for, well mannered, ambitious and hard working. As time passed and I spent more time with Kareem, there were things about him that caught my attention, but I chose to overlook. In the beginning, I did not find Kareem physically attractive, and there were other aspects about him I had reservations about. Kareem was four years older than me and had an infant son, from a long term relationship, which I quickly caught on to the fact that he was obviously very much still hurt and bitter over. He lived at home with his parents in conditions that I struggled feeling comfortable in. Kareem dropped out of middle school, which his reasons were that he did not do well and felt he did not fit in, so he chose to leave and hung around those with whom he did. At the time Kareem smoked marijuana, and had this "I don't care, or see the seriousness in the error of my ways" mentality. For lack of better words, Kareem was immature. I rationalized his flaws with the fact that Kareem was caring, but more importantly was accepting of me, which made me quickly dismissed my feelings towards him. I did not want to be a hypocrite, judge or dismiss someone because of their imperfections, seeing that it was the reason people instantly dismissed and rejected me.

I wanted to be in a relationship, and when it looked like one was forming, I became apprehensive. However, contrary to my strong desire to be in a relationship, because of my insecurities, I was looking for ways to sabotage the chance of having someone in my life. I had convinced myself I was undeserving. There was a part of me that did not know if I could handle being proven I was.

I was beginning to like Kareem, but was afraid to let my guard down and allow myself to be vulnerable, only to be let down and hurt, which I was sure would eventually happen. I was so fearful of rejection that I scrupulously looked for what I believed were signs of it; therefore, counteracting the outcome. I did not want to be rejected, but my fear antagonize it. Lead by fear, I decided it would be best that we no longer talk.

I avoided Kareem's phone calls for about two weeks, but he kept calling, leaving messages, wondering what happened. When we finally spoke and I told him the truth, Kareem assured me that I had nothing to worry about. As much as I wanted to believe him, I was flooded with the constant thoughts of my appearance being too much for Kareem to deal with. I foresaw what he could not— thoughts about being seen in public, fearing how uncomfortable stares would make him feel, and the ridicule he would be subjected to for being with me.

My greatest fear was of deep intimacy, what would happen if we grew closer and I would have to reveal all of my scars, deformities and imperfections. The scars and disproportion of my chest, the scars on my legs and the deformity of my feet—aspects of a woman that are most attractive and desirable to a man. I envied beauty, its appeal, its allure, its easiness, its effect, and its power. A women's movements are truly the essence of attraction, such as the effortless flow of her body, especially in the way she walks. These elements create the seductiveness that easily attracts males, and facilitates a level of confidence in a woman's sexuality. Having these aspects of myself physically altered, made it difficult to embrace such confidence.

I did not feel like a woman, and I was sure Kareem would be repulsed when he truly saw me. Although I had been intimate with someone, I did so without revealing much of my body. Affection was not a factor, so I dodged a bullet without having to take barely anything off. As things began to progress with Kareem, I wanted my time with him to be different, which lead me to think, was being in a relationship really worth the humility and exposure? The biggest of these was if he wanted to touch and stoke my hair, and while feeling it, became curious if it was real or not. What if his fingers got caught causing it to move or slip? I just thought it best that I end things before anything started.

As fearful as I was of being exposed, I challenged myself to think, what if things did work out and I was depriving myself the chance at love. I soon came to realize how much Kareem cared, because he did not back down, as many times as I tried pushing him away. Kareem told me he understood how cruel people were to me, but he was not one of them; and Kareem's feelings for me were strong. After spending a lot of time together, I began to see his actions matched what he said, so I gave him a chance.

I began spending all of my time with Kareem, telling my mother that I was hanging out or staying over at Drita's, when I was really staying over Kareem's house. I got to know his family extremely well, but I never invited him around mine because I was sure my mother would not have approved of me having a boyfriend. When she did finally meet Kareem for the first time, my mom interrogated me every day after, asking if he was my boyfriend, and if I was sexually active with him. I knew that it was a double ended question, which required a quick "no" response if I wanted to avoid the repercussions of answering "yes". Talking about sex was extremely uncomfortable with my mother, because of the fear and shame she made me feel. She then accused me of being a liar, before threatening to harm me if she ever found out I was active.

I was still consumed with extreme guilt and shame for having lost my virginity the way I had, and wanted to right that wrong with a real meaningful experience. After knowing Kareem, I was saddened that I had not waited for him. I never told him about the guy I lost my virginity to, because I was desperately trying to forget. I was hoping by forgetting it ever happened, would give me back my virginity. I wanted nothing more than for Kareem to be my first, so I told him he was.

Making the decision to take the relationship to the next level, was nothing like what I feared. Kareem pulled my face in his hands looking me straight in my eyes and told me how much he loved me, whether we did anything or not. Kareem then told me he had no intentions of leaving or hurting me, that I had been through so much and needed to be loved. As tears rolled down my face, saturating his hands, it was then that I was not afraid for him to see me in my truth. It was the first time and the only experience I have had with a man where I actually felt loved and respected.

Kareem accepted and appreciated the imperfections of my body that were still difficult for me to embrace. Being with him was comfortable and for the first time I was in love. As time went on and more was revealed about myself beyond my control, I realized Kareem accepted me for me.

One day while playing with his son who was an infant at the time, the baby grabbed at my hair and Kareem noticed the way it moved, blatantly asking if I was wearing a wig. Mortified, I contested and he said, "Yes, it is. Let me see." When he saw that I became uncomfortable, he moved toward me saying, "I don't care, it doesn't change anything," and it did not. Kareem did become more and more curious with what was hidden underneath, and even after many times of asking, I denied, vowing to never show anyone, because I never saw myself being comfortable. I needed to hold on to my femininity; my hair, whether real or not, made me feel feminine and I was not willing or able to compromise.

Kareem also eventually discovered that my face was made up. I found awkward ways to sleep to prevent my makeup from smearing and coming off, but when it did, feeling self-conscious, I would wake up extremely early, apply my makeup and sneak back into bed. However, Kareem caught me one morning and stood in the door way fascinated at how my face changed in less than five minutes. After seeing how obsessed I became over time, Kareem got upset with me saying "Why do you wear that stuff? You don't need it! Look I don't care about your made up face or your hair. I care about you. I care about the person you are, inside you are beautiful."

It was not only the fact he accepted me as I was, but Kareem also put himself in positions to try to empathize with me. A special time Kareem and I shared, that I will never forget was when he accompanied me to Boston for one of my surgeries. My mother could not go, so Kareem convinced her to allow him to take her place. It was the most random and unexpected thing, but the most sensitive and compassionate acts a guy had every done for me. While there, he played and interacted with other children with severe burn injuries who were also being treated. Never once did he stare, seem uncomfortable, or ask questions. Kareem teared up saying how the patients gave him a deeper understanding of strength.

Certain that Kareem would cringe at the sight of blood or anything more extreme than a cut, I kept everything hidden. When it came time to have my bandages changed, I asked him to leave the room because I did not feel comfortable with my boyfriend seeing me in the condition I was in. It was too much for the regular eye, and depending on the extent of my wounds, the sights were too much for me. During one session, Kareem insisted on staying, so I gave in and allowed him to, and to my surprise he did well. Kareem hugged and told me he had never met anyone so strong.

While out in public, Kareem would confront people who stared or who made smug comments. Kareem had no filter, and there was no holding him back when someone pushed his buttons. Kareem's favorite saying was "take a picture, it lasts longer." I attempted to calm him down, but he would look at me and say, "Babe, I don't care, they have no right to disrespect you, and they won't while you're with me." I understood his reasons for wanting to stand up for me, and greatly appreciated them, but I did not like the added drama. People's reactions toward me were a part of my life, something I had learned to adjust to and tolerate. The way I coped was by ignoring, and was what I wanted for people around me to do. Kareem gave me the nickname "book smarts." He constantly told me how proud he was that I was different from other girls he had ever been involved with. It felt good he thought so highly of me. Kareem wanted to be with someone who had their priorities straight so they could help him grow to be better. There were times when Kareem felt he was taking up too much of my time, and it should be used to study, especially whenever I told him of a bad grade or a missed assignment. He would not call me and refused to see me until I did better or caught up. Kareem dropped out of high school at I believe the ninth grade, he said how it was too difficult and he did not have the support to help him in school.

I really grew to care deeply for Kareem; for all that he had done for me and the ways he showed he cared, I did so in return. In overlooking his flaws, I was choosing to ignore someone with many struggles, setbacks and no concept of who he was, who looked to women to fulfill his emotional emptiness. Kareem appeared to be a man, but inside was an underdeveloped child, who threw tantrums when things did not go his way. The ways I showed my love would become a pattern in all of my relationships, which was attempting to change Kareem. I wanted to mend his broken pieces to create a masterpiece.

I also saw the opportunity in the men I dated to be a "fixer," the more vulnerable a guy was, the more of an opportunity there was for me to attempt to make them into the man I wanted. In reality, I was too fearful and insecure to pursue the kind of man I wanted, believing I was undeserving of the kind. Why would a good looking and successful man want to work hard to be with someone like me when they could easily find a woman who they were attracted to, and who it was easy to be with. I believed it was unfair to expect someone to handle what was still difficult for me to handle. I did not want for him to resent me for being me and making the relationship hard for him. I believed physical beauty could only attract the same.

There was also a part of me who assumed the role as the "fixer" because I genuinely felt a sense of compassion for people. Whether it be a man or anybody, I understood what being judged felt like, and felt I had no right to judge others, but to see them in their need and try to make a difference. I believed the term "a diamond in the rough" and loved picking someone up to help them to stand.

However, the other part of me, the deceptive part, learned the art of manipulation. While easily overlooking a man's faults and dispositions, and looking at his intent and potentials, I saw these issues as leverage. The more destitute and down-on-his-luck a man was, the more confident I felt in locking him in. I had an advantage over them, whether it be having money, my own place, resources, intellect, anything that would give them a reason for needing me and therefore staying because of that need.

Behind the helping, devoted "fixer" mentality, was really a selfish ploy to play the role of the loyal and God sent woman, whom they would be crazy to leave. I had no filter, worse I had no self-respect. I was very cognizant that what I was doing was self-degrading, but I did not care. What would have been worse at the time for me was being alone.

I pacified, rationalized, scapegoated, accepted, and denied, creating an image that "all is well" and "all is good." I convinced myself the bad was not the worse, just to keep up the charade to ensure my ulterior motives were met, which was to hold on to the guy and keep the relationship going. In my delusion, all was fine, and manageable. As long as there was a relationship, then there was a chance things would improve and he could change. As long as he remained in the state I found him in, then my purpose was validated. I began to like "fixing" their brokenness. It gave me a sense of pride, bragging rights that I had taken a scruffy man in need of revitalization, and created a fresh, new image that even took him by surprise. My role in their lives made me feel indispensable. My thoughts were what would they do without me? I hoped the more I did for them, the more they would love me in return.

Although Kareem accepted me as I was, I struggled to do the same with him. I was mostly bothered by his hoodlum mentality. I felt ashamed of him because of the way he chose to live his life also because he was unmotivated and complacent with not making anything of himself. Opposites do attract, but after a while they lose friction, and repel. Kareem was into the streets and I was poised and proper. I was naïve to the games played by guys, and although I did believe his love for me was genuine, I was not enough. Kareem had a huge ego, inflated by validation from others, especially women. Kareem was very insecure, and needed to be in the position of dominating women. I realized that things changed between us because Kareem felt intimidated by me and my success. What caused us to break up was when I discovered, while away at college, Kareem had been involved with a woman who he moved into his house and fathered a son and twins with. I was devastated.

Years pasted and in 2010 we reunited. We both were older and I thought more mature. I listened to Kareem tell me how he made the biggest mistake of his life doing what he had done to me. I again found myself in a vulnerable and lonely place, which allowed me to easily forgive and allowed him another chance. I again ignored my feelings of discomfort. My feelings for him were not as they once were, but he was familiar and comfortable. I had changed, but Kareem appeared the same as he did almost ten years prior. Kareem was in a bad place, he had formed an addiction to marijuana and drank all of the time. He worked, but it was nothing legitimate.

I was studying mental health and saw alarming signs of multiple issues, and I quickly assumed my role to fix him. However, I noticed a darkness in Kareem that made me realize he was unwilling to change. Still I stayed and settled for the craziness. In between the time we were together, Kareem told the story of how his life had spiraled out of control because of jail, fathering another child, doing and selling drugs. It all should have been enough for me to walk away shaking my head "No", but I stayed.

It was the worse decision I made, we argued over women I suspected he was involved with, his drinking, smoking and his behavior. Nothing was as it once was, and for about nine months, I settled. As history often does, it repeated itself, Kareem was still Kareem, and I was still naïve. I found out he had been sleeping around, and had been arrested for possession of marijuana. Being the loyal girlfriend I was, I paid the money for his bail. Kareem then was ordered to attend a treatment program, where he met a woman, quickly formed a relationship with her, and again I was the last to know. What was worse was that I did not even get a "thank you" for introducing them. I realized the second time around was shame on me.

In between the hiatus with Kareem, I met Brice, whose attractiveness caused me to constantly compare and judge myself, feeling inferior, because I lacked the same external attractiveness. I constantly looked at pretty females and aspects that made her beautiful, attractive and desirable, and wished I too possessed those same aspects. I began analyzing her and became critical of myself. If only I had fingers and could get my nails done, if only my feet had not been so badly burned, and I could wear high heels, or, if only my body was burned and not my face. I grieved mostly over my face having been disfigured. I noticed that even people who have been burned on places other than their faces, are able to still experience the same privilege of being accepted, than those with severe facial scaring and deformities, which only proved the face truly holds significant power. I stared at attractive females thinking, if only I had their beauty, then maybe Brice would have felt more confident and proud to be with me. Maybe he would have shown me off, loved me and shown me affection. Many times I observed couples and particularly watched how the man interacted with his attractive lady, noticing how affectionate, tender, interested and attentive he was with her, then feeling unfortunate that Brice had not looked or interacted with me in the same ways.

While out in public with Brice, I watched closely to see if he tried to discreetly look at other women. I became paranoid, feeling insecure that Brice was feeling the same being seen with me. I believed I created more anxiety for Brice, then what he was willing to admit to. Brice was extremely good looking, and knew it. We met over the phone and talked for a long time, so when we finally met, Brice told me he was emotionally invested and wanted to try at a relationship. I noticed how Brice struggled to be with me, but I was impressed with his willingness and effort to cope and accept. Brice was very stuck on his looks; as much as I loved being with a handsome man, it made me that more insecure. It bothered me to notice that while out together, Brice snuck to look at women. Brice made joking comments, that made me cynical of him, because there were aspects of Brice that were superficial, I knew his comments held truth. Brice constantly criticized things about my body and made fun of me in subtle ways. He said things like, "Have you ever thought about getting breast implants?" or "Babe, have you ever talked to a doctor about correcting this or that?" Once he said, "You're okay looking, but if this did not happen, I am sure you would have been beautiful." I was beginning to build my esteem, and his shots knocked down the blocks that built it one by one, until there were none.

Then there was Rick from South Carolina whom I also met online, and finally met after many months of talking, when he came to visit family. When we met, it was obvious Rick was uncomfortable, but he did not let on and neither did I. We spent time together and I thought maybe I was overreacting, because we had connected so well. It was not long before I realized I was being taken advantage of, because Rick was always without, and I was always doing and supplying. When it was time for him to return to South Carolina, he had no way of getting back. I ended up buying his plane ticket, and when he landed, I did not hear from him again. I called, texted, emailed, and when he finally responded, it was the cliché "It's not you, it's me." I then learned through social media weeks later, he was back in a relationship with his children's mother.

After many failed relationships, I formed a deep rooted resentment toward men. It appeared I did not matter. This was a skewed perception, because the truth was that many of the issues were with me. I was choosing superficial men, who I knew did not have the level of understanding to accept me. I gave and gave, knowing that many of them were not able or willing to. I accepted little, but expected more from men who were incapable of giving because they did not have much to give.

In relationships, I grew resentful for having gone out of my way to please and do for men, while they did not consider or acknowledged me; I felt cheated, because the relationships were only one sided. I was angry the guys I was with were not privy to my needs, wants and desires, but even more frustrated with myself for not verbalizing and standing up for myself.

I was susceptible to picking the wrong men because of the deficit within myself. I chose men who were broken, in attempts to fix the brokenness that I could not or did not know how to fix within myself. I learned being loved was conditional and how much I was deserving of it from a man, was contingent on how much I was willing to compromise myself to meet his expectations. I was taught how to devalue myself by giving a man more than what I had to give to myself. Deep down dysfunction made me feel secure and I realized that I thrived from it, and a part of me did not know how to function without it.

I convinced myself I was in love with them, because I was in love with the idea of being in love. I got lost in the fantasy of what I envisioned I wanted a relationship to be, despite the painful and miserable reality of what they really were.

There is a saying that goes, "A person has to be sick and tired of being sick and tired," and I had not reached that point yet. I still needed to be in control, because I felt my appearance already dictated my fate, but I felt I could change it. No matter how many times I got hurt, I was hopeful that the next would be the one. I wanted to be in a relationship at the expense of losing myself, and it would take just that, before I finally became tired of being sick.

CHAPTER 20

The System Doesn't Like Me

WHEN KEYAN TURNED ONE-YEAR-OLD, I decided to resume my search for employment. There was no guarantee of returning to the health care agency, and when they did not have a position, I then applied to an ad for a position I felt confident I would be hired for. I was confident, because I had the experiences they were looking for, which was in debt collection. What I thought was going to be a successful interview turned out to be a defining moment in my life.

I had experienced discrimination my entire life, but nothing as blatant as what I had that day. I went dressed in my best, with multiple copies of my resume, my prepared interview questions for the interviewer, and a thank you letter sealed to be dropped in the mail after the interview concluded. My optimism assured me I would get the job. I went in with the smile that always created ease from the initial shock of my appearance. I went in sat down and within a few minutes of talking, felt uncomfortable by the direction of the conversation.

I learned to use discretion when sharing what happened to me, and vowed only to do so when I felt it was relevant and effective. I was secure with myself and knew people had to be responsible for dealing with their own issues as they related to being in my presence. The only thing I disclosed about my personal injuries was that a friend and I started a non profit for people affected by burn injuries and fire, because there were no programs and or resources that offered support. I shared this information because it was a part of my credentials and experience. The interviewer then spent majority of the interview talking about a family member, trying to relate to my story. I felt it was a very inappropriate use of my time.

Throughout the interview, I noticed the subtle looks from the interviewer toward me that made me feel extremely uncomfortable. The interviewer then asked questions about my abilities to perform the task in a way that made me feel I was being judged. I had never experienced such a conversation before during an interview and my feelings of discomfort exacerbated.

The one question that stood out the most was "Well, are you able to type?" The condescending tone jolted me inside, and my reply was "Not to perfection, but I can type at a speed to get the job done." I felt disrespected and thought to myself, *If you look at my credentials you can see what I'm capable of doing.* At that point I wanted it all to be over, and when it was, I thanked them for their time, and silently cried as I walked out of the door, knowing I did not get the job, and I did not.

I never wanted to play the "discrimination card," but I felt it was necessary. The feeling was too strong in my spirit that I experienced a blatant injustice. I did some research and found a program that assisted people with disabilities with legal matters, such as employment discrimination, and was certain justice would be served. However, it was not, I felt in part the program did not properly inform, educate or prepare me, and felt I had experienced another injustice as a result of the lack of support and care to the sensitive matter.

About a month later, I went into arbitration, only to leave feeling worse about the situation. I felt I had no choice but to settle for an insignificant amount, and left with significant damage to my confidence and psyche, that seemed irreparable. This experience left a lasting impression on me and changed the way I viewed myself. It caused me to doubt my own capabilities, which I always held great pride in. I wanted to give up, thinking no company would hire me because of my appearance and felt I would never be taken seriously as a professional. A fear of applying to high position jobs developed as I began telling myself I was not good enough to work the kinds of jobs I knew I worked hard for; again, from this experience it appeared success was based on appearance. I suddenly became fearful of applying for jobs, so I stopped searching.

Not long after, I was contacted by a faculty member at a small liberal arts college near Philadelphia to work with her on a project that was near and dear to her heart. It assisted student teachers obtaining their Masters, to become certified as Special Education teachers. The students had to take a number of specific courses designed to educate teachers, not only how to teach children with special needs, but how to speak their language, to embrace and learn about their culture. The faculty member sought interest in me because we shared the experiences of overcoming odds related to our individual adversities.

The faculty member remembered me from a summer program I attended as an undergrad, and thought I would be a great point of contact for the students, seeing as how I was an example of someone who has overcome many forms of adversities. When the opportunities presented themselves, we found time to talk, nothing in depth, but the exchanges were enough to leave an everlasting impression on her, to remember me years later for the project. I had just turned twenty-five in June, and began my position in October of 2007. I was offered the position because of my adversity. She wanted every aspect of the project to reflect the strength of adversity, therefore I felt honored she saw something special in me to make an impression on the project and the students.

I was excited to finally have a "real job" that was long term and consistent. I did not get paid much, but it was a fortune compared to the five hundred and change I was receiving from Social Security a month. I was relieved to break free from the shackles of the system, and hopeful of a successful future that would afford me financial security.

I loved working with the students, I felt I had a sense of purpose and I was doing something meaningful. My boss was extremely supportive of me. As time passed we merged a friendship. She was gentile, and beyond kind hearted. She shared with me the challenges she struggled with as a child, and through her additional sharing, I learned we had even more in common. She understood the difficulties, the stigmas and biases of having a disability, which made me draw even closer to her.

She gained insight of the plights I was dealing with and went out of her way to help me. When I struggled with the smallest things, whether it be having money for gas to put in my car; and when I found myself again without one, she began offering me rides since my apartment was not far from where she lived. She supported my vision for creating my own graphic design business, by referring me to my first client, her hair dresser, whose salon I designed brochures for. A part of my duties was designing publications, advertising to schools, other affiliates, as well as for events related to the program. I was good at my craft and my boss helped me get exposure. She became a great confident. My boss really fought and advocated for me. I was grateful to have worked alongside someone who had found success through adversity.

I worked on the project for about five years, and during these years, many things were happening. For many of those years, I found myself falling deeper and deeper into the pitch black dark crevices of depression. My life was not forming as I had hoped it would, it became harder to believe I would be successful. I was living slightly below the poverty line, black, a woman and disfigured, strikes against me that made crawling out of the systematic box I was involuntarily placed in, nearly impossible. I often felt like a ping pong in the system being tossed around every so often, but never hit with enough force to pop outside of the box. It became harder and harder because of these aspects. I had to fight exhaustingly, and had to prove my worth, over and over again.

Two years into my work at the college, I became discouraged because I was still struggling financially, and every aspect of my life felt the impact of not having enough to sustain. I began looking for other jobs, but after being discriminated, fear began to overpower my determination. I felt no matter how smart or experienced I was, people only saw my scars. I felt even more pressure assuring Keyan the safety and security I did not have as a child.

More so, I had always envisioned myself as being this extraordinary person, but was living in ways that did not reflect how great of a person I was. I refused to be defined by my limitations or content with an allocated amount of money to live off of, determined for a type of people, deemed adequate to survive. I did not want to be content with what was barely manageable, and resented I was expected to settle.

The more obstacles I pushed out of my way, there were even more that proved to be too enormous with my strength alone. During this time, I never felt more alone. Dealing with the system became a lifelong battle and it did not care what I had gone through, what I had accomplished or that I was extraordinary. In the eye of the system, I was just another hand reaching out in need. I became infused with so much anger and resentment. I was an individual with a purpose and a right to success, I just needed help to help myself. I sought assistance with an agency that assisted the disabled to find employment, surely they would see my accomplishments and be able to match me with a job that reflected my level of education. Instead I was told that since I had experience with working, despite my hardships with actually securing a career, let alone a job, there was nothing they could do to assist me.

While working, I was on what is called a "ticket to work" through Social Security, which allows a person receiving benefits to continue to receive their benefits while working for a "trial period" of nine months. In this time, if a person is deemed unable to work, they can then stop and resume receiving their benefits. If after the trial period, the person continues to not only work, but make what is determined to be a substantial amount of money, that exceeds the eligible amount, then the person is no longer deemed to be disabled, but capable to work. In certain circumstances one could continue to receive their benefits after this time, if they can prove that special accommodations and or supports are needed in order to maintain employment.

It always baffled me, because my impairment was permanent, and I was struggling to make a life for myself because of it. Regardless of how long, how many hours, or based on a meager gross income limit that a panel of people calculated to be sufficient, I still needed help.

Having to prove I have a disability after a period of working just to have my benefits with Social Security reinstated is by far the most frustrating. I have worked so hard to be seen as an individual apart from my disability, but it does not matter to agencies within the system. I am seen only as what I am labeled as. In the case of Social Security, there have been times that I have felt very undignified, having to walk into offices without my make up, and having to run down all of my limitations to a stranger, just to prove that I am still as disabled as I was the last time I received benefits.

What I did not understand was that I was working hard to be independent from supplemental programs, but was not supported in those efforts. I still had to rely on Welfare for medical assistance and food stamps. While working, I would have to pay to add Keyan to my insurance, and even after paying thirty percent of my income for subsidized rent and utilities, I still could not afford the luxury of healthy foods for the month. I was blessed to learn humbleness so early in my life and learned to appreciate frugality during these tough times, because I had no problem stretching what little I had. Sometimes when the food stamps ran out and did not last throughout the month, my main concern was making sure my son was well fed, while many nights and days I went without.

Then there was the maintenance of a car, which I would find myself going through maybe ten vehicles to date. Buying whatever I could afford, which always came with more problems than I could afford to fix. I did not understand why a car was not considered a necessary means to maintain employment, because for me it was my crutch, without it my disability was evident and exacerbated.

Living in poverty and having to rely on assistance is contrary to what many perceive an easy hand out. At least for me it was hard work, stressful, and traumatic. I constantly lived in fight or flight mode from the anxiety of the constant uncertainty and insecurity. I became fearful of opening mail just to be informed that I was cut off from one of these life lines, many times resulting from clerical errors, which included not being promptly informed of required information, redetermination deadlines, or simply because of other errors on their part.

Systematic programs oftentimes lack sensitivity, understanding or compassion for the population it serves that requires such. There are many who do take advantage of the system, but there are those who really have the willingness and desires to improve their quality of life, but are assumed to have the same intentions. This has created a general stigma and perception of those who have to rely on the system. Many times, I was put in the position of having to show that I was educated and confront many who attempted to pass judgment or showed anything less than the respect I deserved.

It always hurt that I was not seen for who I am. Dealing with the system is difficult because it rarely looks at the person for who they are and the uniqueness of their situation. I had come to learn that my life's urgency related to a vital service, was only a numerical order in a long line of other people's urgencies. My issues were not considered important, but as another day's work for the agency handling cases. In dealing with this, I learned the art of being aggressive, in order for the agency handling my case to see my urgency.

One strong trait I inherited from my father was learning how to talk persuasively and when necessary, use my trump card to play the role of the victim. I have come to see that when I am aggressive in the manner of taking charge to get the answers or results I need, I found my situation was given attention and handled. I learned early that no one would fight for my life, I had to learn how to fight to better it for myself. Through my crisis, I learned to research in efforts to educate myself about the services, and laws regarding my situations, to then effectively articulate and debate my issue, and communicate my needs and rights. If I did not know, I would definitely find out. Educating myself with information many times put me in the position of being more knowledgeable than the professionals who were supposed to be experts in the related subject. Having this skill has helped me greatly to help myself and to get the best results.

I begun to feel I had no control over my life, and there was no end in the foreseeable future of matters improving. The pieces of my life hung on the thin string of manageable, and when that sting unraveled, all of the pieces came crashing down. I eventually became use to mending the string, searching for each of the missing pieces to reattach, while thanking God each day they stayed in place. I struggled just to maintain the basic necessities that every human being in life should be entitled to have, such as shelter and food; everything else for me was considered a luxury. I become grateful for every which way my money stretched. I learned to thank God for everything that went right, just for the current moment of contentment, and for every day I was able to maintain. This allowed me to keep my humbleness in perspective. Unfortunately though, with so much effort I became very tired. Living became more and more exhausting. It was not enjoyable, I was existing.

I developed an anger that no one understood my pain, and suffering. I began to see just how most of my suffering correlated with my physical appearance, lack of resources and lack of support. There is a truth to the fears, insecurities, feelings and struggles that I have experienced, which most people do not possess the ability to understand. This fact often made me feel even more isolated, convinced there was something wrong with me, and that I was to blame for my constant suffering.

Suffering is a result of the way the world turns, when it is off its axes, creating an unbalance, felt most by those on the opposite side of its gravitational pull. Constantly falling, trying to keep up, but unable to because of their positioning.

Suffering has always been the status quo no one really likes to address, instead the expectation is to suck it up, accept it, deal with it and move on. No one wants to deal with the long-term effects of suffering, it then becomes the sufferer's fault for continuing to be affected by the pains true suffering causes. Many times I was made to feel unentitled to my feelings, therefore I felt I had to deal with the agony of suffering alone. The nature of my suffering was already determined when my body reconfigured in the fire. Once I lost the privilege that afforded me this world's ideals of happiness and fortune, I came into perennial suffering.

The fire that left me disfigured and scared also affected my reality. It was now different, complicated and painful to accept. Living in a world where people are reluctant to see the part they play in the plight of others, in many ways has worsened my suffering. When society ignores the stigmatization, discrimination, and rejection of people with unpleasant adversities, so many in those groups suffer because of the lack of responsibility from society to take ownership in the major role it plays. Eyes become closed and backs are quickly turned, while the finger shamefully points to the sufferer as reason to blame. What I hate the most is being denied the right to feel the emotional effects of my suffering, having my experiences minimized, dismissed and ignored. To blame is society's inabilities to consciously see that it is insensitive, insecure, and in many ways, intolerable to adversity.

I have always understood the suffering I have endured is a primary result of what has physically happened to me, followed by the unfortunate circumstances of not having a stable family to support me, followed by a system that works to aid those working towards self sufficiency. I once felt the desires of my heart may only be experienced in my dreams, because I constantly lived in the realities of a nightmare that seemed impossible to awake from. My thinking was: What is a life without living, what is living without a sense of belonging, having success and happiness; my appearance kept me from experiencing all in my life. I felt I had nothing and was unable to feel. I then became mentally and emotionally entangled in the loss of myself, of purpose, of hope. I felt undeserving, which then caused the onset of depression, which then continued my suffering.

The difficult part was dealing with the pains alone. After much rejection from people and the fear of being judged and condemned, I chose to suffered in silence. I felt ashamed to tell people what I was going through, because I believed people had the expectation of me to always be strong, which I felt incapable of meeting all of the time. The expectation of having to remain strong put tremendous pressure on me, which lead to the belief, that I could never show anything less; to do so would have only facilitated pity.

With all I had been dealing with, I really needed a friend, so I reached out to Drita. I had not seen Drita since she visited me in college. Time passed as we both lived our lives, and we easily fell out of touch. I looked Drita up on social media and saw that she had children and had gotten married.

I connected with Drita and when she called, we both expressed excitement to hear each other's voice. As soon as she said, "Scc-oo-tt-aa—" it took me back, and I was hoping to pick up where we left off in our friendship, I was in need of a Drita and Tanisha moment. We updated each other about what was happening in each other's lives and planned to meet up. When we did, it felt so good to be in the presence of someone safe and familiar.

I had taken the trip to the second house Drita grew up in, not far from where I grew up. When I walked in, I noticed little had changed, it was still a beautiful house. Her mother was hard working, which her efforts showed in the family's lifestyle and in the ways she cared for her children. It was no surprise her children would also become successful. Drita's younger sister was away at college and her younger brother was in high school doing very well also. At some point, Drita's mother saw that I was there and approached me with excitement and surprise to see me.

She asked how I was and I told her what was safe to say that made me sound just as accomplished as what I was hearing about her children, such as working and starting a nonprofit. Drita and her mom continued to talk about what was going on with other members of the family and we joked and laughed about the past. Things quickly shifted when I told Drita's mother that I also had a son. She raised her brows as she asked how old he was and how I felt about being a mother. Drita's mother then asked about his father, and when I told her we were no longer together, I felt the air grow cold. I could see the look of judgment and disapproval in her eyes, which made me become defensive and shameful. She asked a barrage of questions, one of which was, was he helping to raise him. I told her they had a great relationship, and just like that, there was nothing more I wanted to do than to flee from the interrogation. When Drita and I left the house to run some errands, I was so relieved to have escaped being in the "hot seat."

Drita and I rode around the area laughing and joking, a part of me was happy to have my friend back. However, I had realized by observing Drita and taking into account all that happened at her house, we were now very different. Drita's demeanor changed, she had this great success, a beautiful family of her own, and a career. The way she talked and what she talked about suggested she had no room in her life for anything that was not as high on the peddle stool she appeared to sit on.

I was truly happy for her success, while feeling ashamed and embarrassed that I was not successful. I then became saddened as I realized our friendship would only be a memory, and that it would not continue. Our differences had created a huge separation. Drita had always been empathetic and accepting of me, knowing all I had gone through in high school, but this time was different, there was something about Drita that caused me to feel I could not welcome her into my dark and complicated life. Our time together was bitter sweet for me, because I knew it would be the last time; and it was.

Although I was working hard to improve my circumstances, I felt my efforts were not good enough, because I was still suffering. I began to feel ashamed for not having the success I saw so many of my peers from high school and College had, such as getting married, having great jobs, traveling and just appearing happy. I was envious of the security I saw other people have, while I lived in fear, loneliness uncertainty daily. I envied anyone who could afford the luxury of a nice reliable car, a beautiful home, had financial security, and climbed the ladders of success. For so long I felt like a spectator watching life happen for others, while forcefully showing excitement for their happiness, success and major accomplishments, when inside I felt sad, jealous and angry that there was a less than slim chance I too would experience the same. More so, these feelings came into play when in my mind life appeared easy, just and successful for everyone, but me.

I became resentful of others who appeared to come into success easily, thinking to myself, *It makes sense that they have these things, because they look the part.* Beauty has always been played up, especially through the media. Attached to it has always been superiority, and carries with it even higher expectations. For example, in many cases, it appears to be shocking when bad things happen to attractive people; because one is attractive, they must be great, successful, deserving, and have the best.

A woman's attractiveness gives her the privilege to do anything and go anywhere. I was always very self-conscious about a lot of the places I went and felt limited by the things I could do, such as getting pedicures, manicures, and going to spas, anything that emphasized the beauty of a woman or places intended to attack beautiful people caused me to feel intimidated, and out of place. An attractive woman can in many ways control how long she is alone; therefore, when she decides she no longer wants to be, she does not have to. I on the other hand, do not have such an advantage, I could not just walk up to a guy I was interested in and feel confident that I could have him if I wanted. I would be confined to my loneliness until someone saw interest and comfort in being with me.

Many times I felt my appearance put me at a huge disadvantage, thinking, *If only I was pretty.* Quickly I decreased, diminishing inside of my feelings of shame and ugliness as the image of beauty overpowered me. I saw how a woman's beauty made her a winner just because of it. I then looked at myself and became infuriated that I have worked, struggled and fought hard, but still was not looked at as a winner. No matter how hard I tried, I felt my disfigured appearance made a loser by default.

It is as if beauty encompasses all that is good in the world, and unattractiveness or anything less is associated with everything bad and unwanted. It appeared to me that appearance was a key factor and a determination of success and living comfortably, and my experience with discrimination only supported my perspective.

Growing up, I was taught the sound doctrine of the Bible. When counseled, many believers were strict to the word, leaving little room for compassion and empathy. This created the guilt and shame I held for not just getting over whatever I was going through, or not being strong enough to endure, or by not having enough faith to just let things go and not be bothered by them. Not just church folks, but sometimes family and friends would say, "You can't do this, you have to do this because the Bible says so." As many times as I tried to pray the pain away and walk away from it sanctified and unaffected, I could not, and I punished myself by believing I was no longer in favor of God's blessings and love.

I grew up in the church so I looked at church as being the refuge that I could go to be completely vulnerable and real about what I was dealing with. I believed those who attended church were authentic in their spirituality and who instantly saw God when they looked at me and not my scars; those who unconditionally would accept me, and help to relieve the overload that I carried. Instead my experiences pushed me away from the church and I became guarded, feeling negatively judged. I saw that many religious people were just as limited by human conditioning as everyone else, which was when I began to see that people are people first, before their titles. Even the righteous can be misled by flawed perceptions taught by a carnal world. Not everyone can see what God sees, because if they did, then many would see me. God speaks only of love, understanding and empathy, so why does the world cover their ears when my lips speak?

When I went to church, in between the "hallelujahs," "Praise the Lord" and "Thank you, Jesus" were quick and subtle glances at me. I noticed through my peripheral view, people's heads turning, trying to get a good look, watching, and studying my every move, as if shocked to see that I acted the same as any human. I felt the attention from those in church to be more difficult to handle than from someone off the street. I just expected those who considered themselves righteous and claimed to live as so to know better and understand deeper.

A defining moment was during the eye of the storm at that time in my life. I was going through a lot at work, my boss was a great person and had gone out of her way time after time to accommodate and empathize with me. However, I also felt constant belittlement, condensation, and felt I was always doing something wrong by the ways my boss unknowingly came across. My biggest issue was frustration over miss communication, and her jumping to conclusions based on her own assumptions. This became a constant theme. Her intentions were good, I knew she had my best interest at heart. I was in debt to her, because she defended me and put up with much of my personal issues that constantly affected my work. I constantly called out, from what I told her were physical setbacks, but unbeknownst to anyone, majority of my frequent absences over the course of time, were related to my depression. Knowing how she accommodated my needs and excused my unprofessionalism, made me feel I had no right to my feelings.

Initially I believed that because we both were victors over our personal adversities, and similar experiences, my boss understood me. However there were several comments she made which made me realize we were really two worlds apart. In one situation, I had pitched to her my goals as a motivational speaker. I do not remember specifically what we were discussing, but I remember my boss saying verbatim, "It sounds good, but it's very hard to be a successful speaker and make a lot of money." This small comment had a profound effect on me, coming from someone who I respected so highly for how she overcame so much. The comment made me feel my boss did not believe I could reach my goals. I thought, "What was it about me that she saw or did not see, that lead her to doubt I could obtain such success?" I think it bothered me coming from someone who I was expecting to tell me "You can do anything you put your mind to and work hard for." Considering the odds she overcame, I am sure many people questioned and or doubted her abilities to reach for the success she set her mind to achieve. I heard the comment as: *Its possible, but unlikely to happen for you.* Knowing the kind of woman my boss was and the nature of her spirit, I am certain she did not mean the statement as it came across. I knew she believed in me and saw my potential, but the comment made me feel my dream was impossible.

However, if there was ever a time when I felt my boss truly did not understand me, was when she once said, "Your problem is that you are too strong." Years later, I would come to understand what she meant by the statement, but at that time, I was going through so much and it was heavy. What infuriated me was that she had no idea having a stoic demeanor was how I survived. I had to be tough in order to weather many raging storms. Being tough caused me to turn off my emotions while constantly being in fight or flight mode. Being fearful became integrated into who I was. Bursts of adrenaline kept me ready to react. My only goal was to get through to make it to the other side. I felt I had to contain my emotions because I did not want anyone to know just how much pain I was in. She was dead on, I was proud and too suborned to ask for help.

I had gotten use to doing everything on my own, after so many people failed me. When things were difficult, I had no one to turn to for help, and people seemed to turn away the more in need I was in. As a result, I became guarded and distrustful of people's sincerity and intentions. My only concern was trying to keep up to prevent from falling down. Control became my tool for feeling out of control. In my pain I smiled to keep from crying, it was confirmation that I was still here. Being strong was the only thing that protected me. Both comments revealed to me, that not everyone sees me as I see myself, despite how determined and capable I present myself as, people see and react to me according to the ways in which they perceive me.

I began hating going to work, I was not excited about it anymore. I did not have friendships or much communication with peer colleagues from other departments. The administrators and faculty in the department where I worked, were wonderful people, but I did not have much in common with many of them; I was the youngest employee and did not share the same interest, knowledge and professional experiences as everyone in the department. People greeted me with smiles and said "hi" and bye in passing, and sometimes engage in small talk, but for the first few years, I spent all of my days alone.

One of the biggest issues was being without a working vehicle. My car broke down, and I had no money for repairs. I had to rely again on public transportation to get Keyan to daycare and myself to work. Taking the bus was my greatest concern, having to travel with a toddler. Luckily Keyan's daycare was a block away, and the bus stopped in front of the apartment building. My issues did not stop there, just like with any governmental subsidized program, there are a barrage of rules and requirements; many of which are contingent on a recipient's income, determined by a family's size that cannot exceed a predetermined gross amount. While living at the apartment, it was always my intention to reside there until I was able to get on my feet. I informed management as soon as I began working; from the conversation, it was to my understanding that they were going to support my efforts to save money to move. However out of nowhere, I was called to the office, during an audit, and was interrogated about my earnings and employment, as if I had never informed management of my financial change. I was told, that with both my new job and my benefits, because I was still within my trial period, made me ineligible for subsidized rent. The change in my income meant I had to either pay market rent, or remain on SSI for my rent to stay the same.

Given this ultimatum also meant I would have had to quit my job, but more devastating, I would have had to resign from graduate school, which I had recently started. It did not take long for me to decide. In no way was I going to compromise my dignity. I had worked so hard to get to where I was, and I refused to be held back or denied by my adversities. I knew the purpose of my life would propel me to surpass the limits placed on me by society. I chose to leave, without knowing where my child and I were going to go, I was weary, but again knew God would make a way.

With all that I was dealing with in just two years, I spiraled into a deep rooted depression, that possessed me. I had dealt with depression since high school, but it had gotten worse. Triggered by voluntary isolation and further exacerbated by self-pity, self-defeating thoughts and feelings of helplessness and despair. Extreme bouts of depression for me lasted anywhere from two weeks to a month. While in this state, I let myself go, lost consciousness of the world around me, grew increasingly angry, resentful, lost interest, and motivation to do anything. I did not clean, and was written up many times for cleanliness.

Worse was that Keyan suffered. I constantly yelled out of frustration and anger that had nothing to do with him, but he was a target because he was there. I was insensitive, somehow expected a two-year-old to comply with my demands, by making it easy for me to sulk in my misery. I then became even more depressed, because there was nothing more important to me than protecting my child's spirit.

In all of these things I was hiding behind a smile and the aphorism that "everything was fine" when asked how I was doing. I always resented the question, seeing how telling the truth appeared to be too much for many to handle or be bothered with. The perception I formed about myself was that in order to be strong, I could not show weakness. I convinced myself I had to always have it together, because people took one look at my appearance and assumed I must be weak and helpless.

I became enslaved to my pathology and paranoid by my faulty thinking.

As open as I became, I was also very guarded, fearful of exposing who I was and my ways of being, how I learned to adapt to my reality; I knew most people did not have the ability to comprehend and or accept my truth. As comfortable as I am with silence, many are not. The humble ways I have learned to adapt to my plight, others judge. Therefore, I decided it was safest to hide what living was really like for me, not only from people in general, but from many in my family. I never had to hear them, the criticism was in people's actions, the lack of compassion, empathy and understanding was evident in their distance, absence and minimum participation.

I felt a sense of shame and always the need to explain my plight, for fear of being looked down upon. I learned most people do not want to be associated with pain, failure, and those who force them to feel uncomfortable, because of another's hardships. I never understood why people shunned away from those who experience times and seasons where they are anything but their best. Struggling with depression, emotional and mental pain, suicidality, loneliness, poverty and brokenness. Being genuinely present for someone in their deepest time of need shows the sincerity of the human spirit and its understanding that love is unconditional. Most people in my life, failed to be there for me during my times of internal conflict, where I simultaneously struggled with all of these issues. The lack of genuine support throughout my life, caused me to refuse to let people in. I have noticed with many people, when life is good and they are on top, it is beneath them to associate with anyone not on their level. Since I could not get it together in the time or fashion people expected, I isolated myself. I felt I had nothing to contribute, after hearing about another's normal and exciting experiences; I felt that it was inappropriate for me to talk about how sad, hard and uneventful my life was. What is there to say when suffering is unfortunately all you have to talk about.

No romantic experiences, being subject to the confines of my home because I lived in poverty that did not afford me the privilege to have fun, go out or have the latest. I was ashamed to show people how I learned to adapt to living poorly. Here I was this person so many admired and in awe with, but none interested in befriending me, dating me or engaging with me on deeper levels. It takes a strong person to live their days with little, and to have minimal to no interactions with people. I eventually became use to spending day after day with no calls, no knocks on my door to check to see if I was ok, no invites from so called friends to have girl's night out. No male companions to just talk with. It takes a strong person, to accept the fate of living each day feeling uncared for, and unthought-of. It takes tremendous strength to live in loneliness and with rejection. To trust that God has built me tough enough to endure it all, is to go through knowing that God will always provide comfort and replenish my strength to continue to endure and accept the aspects of my life that I truly believed I had little to no control over.

I was in such dire need of help, but too fearful and lacked the courage to seek it, until everything became too much and I knew that I needed refuge. I began attending a church my family frequented and instantly fell in love with the atmosphere. The word was always unique and powerful from the man of God who delivered it. I met a lot of people and everyone was great. I knew I needed to be back in church, because I felt such a relief when there. My spirit was in great need of respite. I was fighting as I was accustomed to doing, but felt like I no longer had the energy.

I remember one particular time I was sitting during praise and worship, with my eyes closed, silently crying and praying, asking God to prepare me for the uncertainty my son and I was about to face with not having a place to live. Out of nowhere an official discovered me seated, walked over and laid their hand on me to pray. Immediately, I felt something was not right, but I believed in the power of hands being laid, so I trusted they were going to speak to the core of my pain. Instead the prayer consisted of them asking God to give me strength to accept the way I physically looked, and everything else about the prayer was in reference to my physical appearance. The person was way off, I had done a lot of hard work in the area of accepting my appearance, I had come a long way, and it was not among my heavy burdens carried; I was facing homelessness!

A few other times I experienced the same, which made me begin to caution who I allowed to lay hands on me. I began to observe a pattern—many who are religious believe and seek to have authority, to be in the position to judge, using the Bible and one's hard earned title to validate that authority. Many looked at me as being completely helpless and saw an opportunity to heal me. "Oh I see what has happened to you, sister, and God wants to heal you," but then misinterpret their personal perceptions to be that of discernment.

What hurt the most was when another official who I had been talking to, much like a mentor, told me, "You must not believe in God if you are dwelling on this issue. If you say you love God and believe, then you would not be allowing these issues to affect you. This is why you are suffering because you are weary and show no faith." I felt worse than when I came in, consumed with even more guilt and shame. My soul felt unworthy of God's love and even more distrusting of people. I was supposed to go to church and leave better than when I entered, instead I left feeling there was no place that would truly accept me as I was.

The criticism and spiritual expectations from many people inside and outside of the church made me feel I had to work harder to show that I was faithful and not as many believed, complaining. I set aside my love for R&B, for the uplifting sounds of gospel music. I tried to make sure I was not tardy for church and that my attendance was not poked with absences, from being unable to afford gas to make it every Sunday, which appeared to disqualify me from participating in many of the church's ministries that proved to be more healing than any other means. I practiced none stop speaking in tongues, the distinct language of God. As well as becoming more consciously aware of the negative thoughts I was told welcomed the devil into my heart to wreak havoc. When all of these efforts failed to produce righteousness, I found myself pulling further away from God, believing that since I failed to prove to the church my faithfulness, then God must be just as disappointed in me.

I remember the pastor saying to me once, "You are stronger than you think." Now those words woke my spirit right up! It was not until then, that I noticed I did have faith, and it was stronger than many Christians who can recite the Bible without looking, and who follows every commandment to the "T." I had come to realize that in my imperfectness, God fit perfectly inside of me. I was dealing with issues that were meant to flinch my faith, but instead God used them to strength it. I hung on to the fact that God says, all I needed was "faith the size of a mustard seed," and for a long time, that was all I had. I would come into people whose faith were as superficial as the lifestyle they sought after. They looked good, had comfort, but that was where their efforts stopped. For many God is as good as one's circumstances, but as soon as their circumstances become crucial, and it reveals the ugliness, pain and injustice of life, they easily question and lose sight of God. Their faith sways like nimble branches against the powerful winds of a raging storm. Many only having a bias perspective of God based on one's limited experiences, finding that they truly do not know who He is, and the spectrum of His love when they are faced with adversity that contradicts their perspective.

I realized I was not rejected by many church folks, because to them I showed no faith, but they were purposely dismissed by God from my life, because they had not experienced God as I had. I have learned that I cannot reveal pain to just anyone, because not everyone has the experience to sit with me in such despair.

I never felt more alone and therefore my reasons for isolating myself became rationale during these bouts of major depression. Extreme isolation became my most used, unhealthy coping skill.

My depression caused me to push those closest, and with whom I had great relationships with away, by completely isolating myself. When I became depressed, its onset easily crept in by way of constant loneliness and when faced with difficulties that made me feel afraid, helpless and wronged, which was most of the time. When things were good, I was able to function, but when they were bad, so was my mental state. Depression not only plagued my mind, but also my body. At times it was so debilitating that it acted like a tranquilizer, paralyzing every part of my body. I tried prying myself from its firm grips, my mind would tell me "It time to clean," or "Time to get up," or "Time to take care of your child," but my body remained unable to move.

With a server episode, I became saddened, cried uncontrollably and my mind flooded with negative and self-deprecating thoughts, each made me sink deeper and deeper into hopelessness. I knew I had to put on face that I was okay, I had to go to work, take care of my child and manage everything in between, but depression only slowed me down to where I could barely manage.

My comfort was found in sleeping. Most days I slept the day away, sometimes it seemed to be the only thing that elevated the pain in my mind. Many days I crawled into the dark corner of myself and refused to see or talk to anyone for days, week, and months. I literally sat in darkness, I came to love the ambiance of the dark, never allowing the light to shine through; I always kept the shades and curtains closed. When my mom came over, she would open the shades and curtains, asking, "Why is it so dark in here? Maybe if you let some light in, you will feel better." Like a vampire, I thrived best in darkness and felt the need to flee the bright outside light that represented life and happiness. Many days I wanted to disappear into darkness.

I had come to be very suspicious of people, distrusting of being vulnerable around anyone, and when I was at my worst, I closed myself off. I did not want to be alone, but I had become comfortable and safest without the judgment of others. I saw family calling, wanting to reach for the phone, but always felt a pull preventing me from answering.

I occasionally came across good people, some of whom were willing to be there for me, but I felt the risk too great to trust letting them in. I remember befriending a beautiful spirited woman at the church I attended who was an artist, and for months we grew close, she introduced me to her family, and felt drawn to me because her sister also had a disability. I knew that she was genuine, but as my problems worsened, I cut her off, I stopped calling and refused her calls. I left her a message, which her reply was "From the sound of your message, it sounds like your saying goodbye. I am here for you, but if you do not want me to be, I will not." It hurt me that I knew I had hurt her, but my heart had hardened and I could not trust.

There have been many good people I have pushed out of my life, either because I was ashamed to let them see the pain I was in, the struggle I constantly lived with, or because I did not feel good enough to be in their lives. There was one person in particular who to this day I terribly regret pushing away. Sharee and I grew closer after college. As we grew closer as friends, we realized we had the same souls. She was sensitive, generous, deeply caring and compassionate. Sharee was the essences of authentic beauty, she had the most beautiful captivating big eyes, and the brightest smile I had ever seen on a person. She kept true to her African pride by naturally maintaining her cotton, thick, long hair.

There was nothing either of us would not have done for the other. She was the definition of a true friend, and Sharee was that to me for many years after college. We had became close and considered ourselves as sisters. When she got married, I designed her invitations and made her and her Bride's maids faces for the wedding.

We both were dealing with a lot, and it was very comforting that Sharee understood the pain I was going through on many levels because she too felt the same. We went to each other when we did not feel comfortable confiding in those closest to us. Her husband was the definition of a beautiful soul, a good noble man who was brilliant. The way he spoke and the level of knowledge he had impressed me every time we sat around listening to his point of view. Together, they were the epitome of a strong, loyal and committed couple. I never seen a couple as strong as they were, and it made me so proud to be in their close knit circle.

Sharee wanted to spend as much time together as we could and do everything together. I loved that she wanted me around so much, and I wanted to be there for her as a best friend should. For a while, I really tried to call Sharee at least every other day if even to check in, because I knew how much talking to each other meant to her. I was very aware of my tendency to be a run-away-friend, sister, daughter, and I knew I needed to stop running when things got hard and let people in, but I was sure they would eventually get tired of me and my baggage.

In the height of one of my crisis, I grew extremely depressed and overwhelmed with my obligations as being Sharee's best friend. I was dealing with so much, while trying to be there for her as her right hand. She and her husband would have their other close friends gather at their beautiful new home on the weekends, which I attended when I could. I tried to be there for Sharee, knowing she too was dealing with a lot. However, after a while I felt Sharee expected me to be there for her more than I was able to. She expressed her feelings of being hurt when I did not call frequently. I knew my tendency to go missing for days and weeks, and the effort I put into being consistent with Sharee actually helped me to become better at reaching out to others.

I hated when I disappointed my friend, because I loved her so much, and I knew she unconditionally loved and accepted me. However, we began to clash more and more, as I sunk deeper into my depression and stressed over things in my life, I felt were just becoming too much for me to deal with. I had the pressures of trying to provide shelter for my child and I, I wanted Sharee to understand how consuming and emotionally draining it was for me. I was however, at fault for never fully disclosing these issues, because I tried to juggle my issues and being the friend she need.

I began to avoid Sharee until she started writing me, telling me how she felt, that I was not there for her. I replied telling her, I believed it was unfair that the validation of our friendship was contingent on a series of expectations, and my inability to constantly meet them, causing her to question my loyalty as her friend. I wanted to hang out, but there were times I could not, because I had a child and still living in a shelter. I could not always afford to hang out, or I was just too stressed or depressed to talk. I knew I could have at least kept better contact, but my head was always in survival mode, that I often did not think of anything else.

I began feeling more depressed for hurting my friend, which was never my intention. Sharee had always been there for me and good to me, which was why I thought it be best that I remove myself from her life completely, since I continued to cause her pain and disappointment. I was not happy or in a good emotional space, and knew I could not avail myself at the time to her, which was what Sharee was in need of during that time. I wrote Sharee a letter, to apologize for not being the friend she wanted or expected. I concluded that I loved her enough to remove myself, instead of continuing to hurt her, by failing to be there as she needed. Once I hit send, I painfully forced myself to close the door on our friendship.

Once closed and sealed, I immediately resented what I had done. I loved her and her family so much and every day since, I have thought of my friend. I have thought of how strong our friendship could have been today. The pain in my heart over such a great loss has always been felt. Her and Josh remained good friends for some time after. Josh would say many times, "You have friends Neesh, you have Sharee." I thought to myself, *Only if you knew*. It made me question if it was true, but I could not imagine how badly I hurt her and because of that fear, I never attempted to reach out to her.

However, I never stopped praying for Sharee and her family, which last I checked her social page, included the son she and her husband always wanted. I have lived with the guilt and regret of ending our friendship. Many times I have wanted to reach out to Sharee, knowing that I am in a much better emotional place, but feared facing the pain I had caused Sharee and her family. In my mind and in my heart Sharee will always be my sister.

I hated loneliness, while at the same time it became my greatest comfort, a twisted paradox. For over ten years, since graduating College I was engaged in this dysfunctional relationship with loneliness:

Depression had devoured me into an empty, dark abyss of sorrow where I found the comfort in loneliness. After becoming familiar with it, I eventually felt controlled by it. I wanted to escape it, but no matter the efforts to release myself from it, nothing seemed to work, it had me and tightened its grips the more I brazenly attempted to release myself. Loneliness welcomed itself into my life, it took over my mind and corrupted it, and lead me to believe I had no purpose.

Just as the lurking, sneaky serpent, had slithered its way into Eve's ear and easily persuaded her to go against God's orders, so did my loneliness. It convinced me that it was the best thing for me, causing me to bring further pain to myself. It was the only thing that accepted me as I was, so I believed I needed it.

Loneliness left me confused, and believing I could not stand outside of it—too fearful to leave, but so desperate to escape. I began taking matters into my own hands, choosing to go against the grain and take charge of my fate. I believed, if I wanted to have a chance at happiness and love, I would have to push myself to make those relationships happen.

Here and there, I experienced momentary relief from it, but loneliness intermittently reappeared, a reminder that it would never truly be gone. It was jealous and possessive and was not content to see me happy with anyone. It demanded its presence and I had no choice but to let it back in. It had a hold on me, creeping in without notice, penetrating my head, heart, and spirit, trying to convince me that death would be the only way of escaping. This unwanted matrimony with loneliness had me feeling trapped and contrite. I desperately wanted out of this unhealthy arrangement. I went to great lengths to seek and find temporary companionships, but they never lasted long, because of my own efforts to sabotage anything with the potential of refuting my fears, that I was worthy and enough.

Like with any dysfunctional relationship, loneliness became a false sense of comfort, that I learned to solely depend on, for the fear of better. As much as I hated it, tried to reject it, cheat it, deny it, I could not, so I felt I had no other choice but to embrace it, accommodate it, and to be consumed by it. I allowed people in, but never close, because I was too afraid of exposing my loneliness.

Loneliness became a significant part of me. My spirit attempted to rise up in my defense, filling my heart and mind briefly with encouragement, affirming me and lending strength in attempts to leave yet again. However, loneliness understood the depths of my emotions and played on them to trick me into staying. Its roots were firmly planted in my pain, that whenever I experienced it and felt rejected, it grew stronger and more difficult to break free from.

Loneliness had always been aware of my many attempts to bravely overcome it, but also knew that my efforts were as weak as my ability to confidently stand against it. Everywhere I went in my life, loneliness was never too far behind. Its spirit overshadowed mine, until my authentic self could not be seen. Loneliness was derived from my fear, but I was also in a comfortable relationship with fear, and could not make a decision, they both allow me to be avoidant.

Loneliness was an altar, that superficially protected me from the immense pain my psyche held. My fear split into fragmented parts that made up my false self, acting as a functioning version of myself that got by and helped to evade even more pain. People were threatened by what they saw when they looked at me, without taking the time to find meaning and understanding. People disliked me, rejected me, abandoned me and deem me unworthy, but loneliness was the only thing constant and always accepting. A matter of fact, it preferred that I experience these pains, so it could be sure to have significant authority over me. I felt stuck with my loneliness, and believed it was the world's fault I could not leave, not seeing that I was partially responsible for choosing to stay. Loneliness became my state of mind, it had complete power over my existence. No one saw the abuse from this relationship. I was always careful to conceal my scars from it, until I periodically broke down, because no one caught on to the fact that I needed to be rescued.

I hated to admit that my loneliness was right, no one saw or cared for me. The only escape was complete isolation, turning further inward and going deeper inside my depression where loneliness awaited to comfort me. I needed to leave for good, but how would I do so? I believed no one wanted me, the world seemed better without me. I deserve loneliness for being different, I did not fit in, I felt forgotten and unwanted. Fear reminded me I would only hurt myself more without them. I was not strong enough to deal with reality. There were times when my spirit peeked through to inform me that I was worthy, but loneliness again convinced me that was far from the truth. I then distortedly looked at myself and did not see the truth that my spirit saw. Loneliness had broken me down for so long, that I believed it knew me better. It selfishly hid me from having long term relationships, and diminished any hope I had; it compromised my faith. I got lost in the trance of this powerful spirit unaware that I in fact possessed more control.

CHAPTER 21

The Problem with Family

KEYAN AND I MOVED in with my father, it was a situation that neither my father or I was excited about, but staying with him was my only option, considering that I had to move so abruptly. I explained the situation and told him it would be a temporary stay, hearing the reservation of having us unexpectedly invade his space. My father purchased a house a few blocks from the house he rented that was sold, so he now had the space to accommodate us. I knew my dad would not allow his grandson to be without a place to stay. While there, I offered to pay a bill or contribute to the household. Knowing that I did not make enough, I was relieved when he told me to just do what I needed to get on my feet.

For the most part, my father and I had a good relationship, and created many great memories as a child. One of my fondest memories was driving down to Virginia where we visited my aunt and cousin. It was a very long drive, which consisted of my dad, me my uncle and a few other family members. I was a very talkative child and loved to converse. My dad and Uncle rotated driving, while I remained in the passenger seat. My dad did not seem fazed by my talking so I picked up where I left off, when my uncle switched with my dad to drive. At some point, my uncle Vess pulled over, and quietly, without warning, walked around to my door, opened it, picked me up, and quietly put me in the back of the travel van. He then said,

"Talk those in the back to death," and that is what I did. It is a story my dad loves to tell.

There were many things I admired and loved about my dad. One was the fact he had become a fire fighter after I was burned, that made me feel it was his way of honoring me for what happened. I looked up to my dad with high regard and pride. He was good looking, had a great job that I loved to tell people about, and for the time he reentered my life, the preferred parent during the times I was going through so much at home with my mom.

My dad provided for me when in need and of course for birthdays and holidays, and was always in my cheering section when there was cause to celebrate any of my accomplishments. My father had always been the type who showed his emotions by doing and giving. I knew he loved me with everything, I saw how proud he was of me, as I was just as proud that he was my dad. My father did not actively raise me, but was very involved in my life growing up, which quickly made up for the time missed in my early childhood.

According to my mother's version, my father's absence caused her to have deep resentment toward him for a long time. There was a portion of my life when my father had not been present before reentering around the age of ten. It had not affected me, I loved my dad and got excited to see him every time he came around. My mother on the other hand, resented the fact that I did not harbor the same resentment she felt for how he just up and left us after the fire. I was a child and just wanted my daddy. Growing up, I felt my mother believed I was choosing my father over her. They both had their faults, but they were my parents and all I knew how to do was love them.

Although my father did so much for me and financially provided in ways that my mother could not, I always felt somewhat of a disconnect with him. He was nothing like my mother, my dad never yelled, cursed or ever raised a hand toward me, but there was something about him that evoked a sense of fear. My dad had many good qualities, but struggled to give emotionally. Even as I think of him now, there has always been this mysteriousness about him. Throughout the years, my dad would confide in me, telling me bits and pieces of his difficult life. It had shed some light on the way he was, and also gave me a deeper sense of compassion and empathy for him. As a result of his adversity, he decided to go into the military and then, after the fire, was inspired to become a firefighter. My dad was very reserved and closed off, so I loved when he shared stories of his life.

When I was younger, my mother told me how my father left us and abandoned her, because he was ashamed of the way I looked. Hearing this, did not match how my dad treated me when I was little, but made me wonder if there was any truth to it. When I was in high school, my dad and I talked about the fire and he assured me that he loved me, and felt blessed to have me as his daughter. This made me proud to hear, and cleared any further doubts and or suspicions. My father gave me the nickname "scoot-a-boot." As a baby, I could not crawl because of the injuries to my hands, so I got around by scooting on my butt. It is a special and unique name that symbolizes our bond. My dad is the only one who calls me by the name. Drita and Rasheen were the exceptions to whom I allowed to refer to me by my nickname.

What I did not see much in my father was emotion. Even when he shared his version and perspective with regards to the fire, there was not much emotion. I knew every human being had them, but it always has been a mystery to me why it was so difficult for my dad to express any. What he did show however was a tough and intolerable, authoritative persona. There was a part of my father the outside world did not see, and would have been in disbelief if they had, because of the lively, caring, giving and warm person he is perceived as being; these qualities were genuine, but not mostly how my younger brother Mark and I experienced our father. Mark is my only brother with whom I share with my father, and who is a split image of him. My father never raised a hand towards me and barley raised his voice, but his use of intimidation always hit harder and spoke louder. He would give what we joke about as the "Carter stare," fixating his eyes on one of us when upset or needing to make himself understood. The few seconds his eyes focused on us felt like burning rays piecing through us creating fear. Not able to emotionally connect, I felt unease which caused me to become distant.

When I was younger and spent time with my dad at his house, I would make sure not to be in his way, so as not to irritate him, or make him uncomfortable, which I most often sensed. I am my father's child and know that part of my desire to isolate myself stems from my father's propensity to be to himself and prefer it. Just give him a recliner, a cup of ice filled will his favorite ice tea, and a remote, he is at peace and content. I am the very same way. I would come over and spend all of my time upstairs while he was down stairs, not wanting to make him uncomfortable by being in his presence.

Feeling bothered by his inability to emotionally connect, I looked for opportunities to soften him up and help him to be more affectionate, by hugging on him, sitting next to him, putting my head on his shoulder, and telling my dad I loved him. Usually at the end of a conversation, I have made it a habit to say "I love you," because my dad may not always say it unless prompted. Even when he does, I can sense how it is an effort for him to say the simple three words.

My father is an amazing person who has always gone out of his way for others. I have come to learn that he expresses himself emotionally through service, and the reputation he has with so many through his acts of service are unspeakable. I just wish that we could have broken down many of the emotional barriers that to this day prevent us from being even closer.

A few of those barriers have always been related to empathy, and understanding each other through effective communication. There have been a few times where my father and I did not get along and had fall outs over mainly communication. I exploded when I felt I was not being heard, and when my dad used manipulation or verbal aggression to make his point. In my dad's point of view, he was always right and knew more than what others knew. I was always left feeling as if I knew nothing, even though I had experience and knowledge that proved I did.

Especially when it came to the ways I chose to parent Keyan. My method was far different than his. I preferred to talk and explain to Keyan in ways that a child would understand instead of punish Keyan constantly for every mistake he made. Keyan was my first and I knew I had a lot to learn, but one thing I did know, I was not going to break my child down just to assert my authority as a parent. If I spoke to Keyan in a way that my dad did not agree with, he would confront me in a cautionary tone that suggested I was too lenient. When I attempted to explain my approach, it became a yelling match, me trying to get a word in, while my dad continued to talk, and bully anything I tried to say. In efforts to just avoid any eruptions, I learned not to say anything and allowed him to have his way, however that usually that did not happen.

What frustrated me the most was while living with my father, I knew eventually time would bring with it tension, and that tension would cause a problem. We stayed at my father's for nine months, and every day I was going to work, taking Keyan to school, buying our own food and trying to stay out of my father's way as much as possible. I felt guilty for inconveniencing him, furthermore, I did not ever want to give him reasons to become easily irritated or complain, which were habits of his.

My dad made good money as a firefighter, but was very conscientious and frugal. The complaining was in my opinion, a passive way to avoid saying what was really on his mind. I knew when I called my dad saying, "We need a place to stay," that he did not want us there. While there, my dad began getting on me about the water bill being fifty dollars more than usual, or something as insignificant as normal wear and tear. It had reached the point to where I got the hint and needed to figure my next plan of action, but again was stuck, because I did not have the money to afford market rent. I was just hoping to suck it up, continue grad school, look for another job, and stay as long as possible.

One day it was clear that something was bothering my dad, because he was in a bad mood and finding any and everything to fuss about. My dad suddenly got on me saying he was tired of me being there, and not contribute to the bills. My dad claimed his bills were mounting and the situation was becoming too much. I reminded him that in our initial conversation regarding what was expected of me while living there, he stated all I needed to do was save my money. The end result was both of us yelling and screaming at one another. I was trying to clearly understand why my dad was upset and why had he not spoken up sooner. I knew the reasons were not the real reasons my dad was upset; he just was tired of having us there.

I often felt attacked because of my dad's inability to be sensitive to whatever issues I was going through. Therefore, I had chosen to be cautious of the things I told my father, because emotionally I knew he would not be sensitive to my truth. I also did not want him to see me as a failure. My dad would constantly tell me "You need to try harder," "Everyone has issues, I did but I dealt with them," I found his words to be insensitive and made me feel the hardships I experienced because of my adversity were meager excuses. Although I was grateful for all of the things my father had done for me in times of need, I resented having to ask or be in a position where I needed his help.

My dad had this "you owe me" mentality, anything he did that cost him good money, he expected me to pay him back for. After I had Keyan, my dad ended up giving me his 2000 Chevy Impala soon after he purchased it, because I could no longer afford to make payments on my latest car. After a couple of years of driving it, it needed maintenance, which ended up costing him over two grand. When I found myself in a shelter after living with him, the first thing my dad asked was when I was going to pay him back. My dad constantly threw what he did in my face. Therefore, I began only relying on him when there was absolutely no one else to call. In a conversation once I told my mother that whenever I came into a lot of money, the first thing I planned to do was pay my dad back every cent he had given to me when in need. I no longer wanted to be in debt to him or have a reason for my dad to hold anything against me. My mother's reply was "Tanisha, you do not owe your father anything. He should want to go out of his way to do, and be there for you considering all you have gone through."

My father made me feel I had to figure everything out on my own. If it happened to me then it was my problem and my problem alone, and would not have been if I somehow did better in preventing the need to occur. It truly hurt that my dad did not understand the reasons for so many of the hardships I endure in my life. What hurt even more was seemingly, his unwillingness to accept that what has happened to me made life difficult and created majority of the challenges that I faced. My father's insensitivity was another contributing factor to the reasons I blamed myself, and developed the belief I was responsible for my suffering, that I was at fault for not working hard enough, this belief primarily was my reasoning for feeling ashamed to ask for help.

This however changed when I had no other choice but to. Immediately after the blow up with my dad, I told him he no longer had to worry, because we were leaving. I had always held in my frustration with my dad, which up until that point, I had no real understanding where the frustration stemmed from. It was probably the second time I had ever expressed such rage toward my father. After I finally calmed down, I realized I was leaving, but again had nowhere to go.

The next day, I told my boss what was going on and she immediately consulted another professor, who had given her information about a shelter program in Philadelphia called Interfaith Hospitality Network of the Northeast. I called and spoke to a soft spoken woman by the name of Rachael Falkove whose composure was the perfect remedy for my fear and anxiety. I explained my situation, which by then, I had become accustomed to doing. I felt my life had become one big interview and housing was usually what I was vying for.

Rachael could hear the pain in my voice and believed my feelings were justified. I could hear both sincerity and regret as she proceeded to inform me that there were no available spaces in the program's shelter at that time. Moved by my unique situation, Rachael was eager to find me services.

In my own search, I called every shelter and housing program I believed could be prospects. Some shelters I inquired had specific requirements intended for clients with issues that did not pertain to me, or the cause of my plight. One program mandated clients to attend basic education courses, behavioral health counseling and basic job readiness courses; because I would not have benefited from any of the programs, I was denied shelter. Another shelter for women and children had a mandatory curfew, but the program was unwilling to accommodate my work and school schedule.

A few days later, Rachael called me stating she had contacted another extension of the program located in Ambler, Pennsylvania, that would accept me. Rachael stated, "They owe me a favor." Apparently, the program in Ambled needed the same favor of the Northwest location. Just like that God made a way again! Throughout the frequent moves, our possessions became fewer, being condensed to a number of large black trash bags holding mostly clothing and any of Keyan's toys that were easy to transfer.

I remember feeling a huge relief from no longer having to walk on egg shells around my father, and the feeling of being unwelcomed. What saddened me was Keyan witnessed the arguing between my father and I, and although he was two years old, he verbalized his concerns and feelings over seeing us talk to each in the ways we had. Keyan's age was no indication of his intelligence. He was smart enough to understand that there was something wrong. He used what I had taught him about love, respect and the importance of family to point out the error in the part I played, that convicted me to eventually make amends with my dad. "Mommy, that is your dad, you both should love each other and not fight, you need to say sorry."

I also remember feeling a deep sense of sadness that my life had gotten to the point where I was about to enter a shelter. The night before, I set in my old room at my mom's house crying on Joshua's shoulder, expressing how fearful I was, because I had no idea what to expect, other than the perception I had from what I've seen and heard about shelters on television. Josh held me, while telling me that God would be with me and would give me the strength to get through it. Josh commended me for my bravery and for doing what I needed for my son and myself.

During the program's orientation, the process and what to expect had been explained. Families accepted into the program resided at churches within in the network, that participated by serving as "host" sites, where families lived for an extended period of time. At the end of stay, families would move to another church. Each church made necessary accommodations for the number of families, by converting spaces into living quarters where each family had their own private space. Members of the churches volunteered their time to "host" dinners for a particular night, usually a different host for each of the nights stayed. In efforts to make the difficult experience more comfortable, both the program and churches accommodated and showed consideration for the families by providing familiar and preferred foods. Dinner was always provided, but additional foods were provided for meals that were not.

The program as a system ran the same, although both locations differed in the length of time spent at each church, the number of churches housing families and the number of families accepted. Keyan and I were among two other families at the Ambler location. What made the program in Ambler different from the Interfaith program in Philadelphia, was that it offered transitional housing. There were a total of about eight functional multiroom apartments, that were also hosted by specific churches. Participating churches were within close proximity to the program's headquarters, so when it was time to move, it was always a short distance between churches.

The fact that I had a vehicle, an income, and motivated to better my circumstances, by being enrolled in grad school, bettered my chances of being one of the few families accepted. The program's director, Cindy and social worker, Mattie, were extremely impressed with my ambition and determination, despite having gone through so much. I developed a great relationship with the director and Mattie, however Mattie and I formed a special bond. She was a beautiful middle age woman, who looked more like my peer. Mattie resembled Jennifer Aniston and had what I joked "perfect white girl hair." Mattie was incredibly intelligent, with a background in theology. Her level of knowledge made me crave for her wisdom and insight. Mattie was an angelic spirit that constantly uplifted mine, and assured me that while I was at the shelter, I would be in good hands, and I was.

The Ambler Interfaith Hospitality program transitioned between three churches before accepting families into one of their transitional apartments or assisted finding housing outside of the program. Keyan and I stayed in the shelter portion of the program for three months, each month at different churches. Our experiences were not what I had imagined. Ambler was a small and quaint town, surrounded around beautiful landscapes and history. We were away from the city and had a peaceful and supportive experience.

Everyone we came in contact with was pleasant, caring and deeply compassionate about what we were going through. At the end of the three months, we were accepted into the program's transitional apartments. Keyan and I were housed in apartment six, which had been sponsored by a Jewish synagogue. Keyan and I became good friends with the woman who was the appointed person in charge of assisting our family for the duration of being housed in the apartment. Carol was a short woman in statue, but a spitfire who never took no for an answer when there was something she really wanted. After learning about my story, and then meeting Keyan and I, Carol and her husband became enamored with us. Just as Project Rainbow made Christmas special for my family as a child, Carol made sure Keyan and I had the same experiences. The synagogue provided us with everything one would have at Christmas, including gifts. Keyan received everything he wanted. Keyan and I became close with Carol, her husband and a volunteer. Carol was highly impressed with me and moved by my determination to persevere, work, and deal with the demands of graduate school, all while being homeless. One semester she purchased all of my course books, and paid for a course my work credit did not cover, that I could not afford to pay. We all would get together at Carol's beautiful, upscale home, enjoying each other's company, which eventually lead to forming a friendship.

Our time in the program did not feel as though we were experiencing a crisis. I continued to take care of Keyan and provided for him, so he never knew that we were homeless; he was only four and did not understand the concept, which I was grateful for. Our apartment had two mid-size bedrooms, which was the first time Keyan and I had our own separate spaces. I knew our situation was temporary, but it was the first time I felt I had something that was mine.

While living in the HUD apartment, my father's and then the churches, Keyan and I slept together. At the churches, we were given a queen size air mattress, which was convenient and easy to transport along with our several bags of clothes. Our bond only grew stronger during that time. My main priority was to keep Keyan's spirits up, by never letting on that I was ever scared or uncertain about what was going to happen next. We had each other and I believed having Keyan motivated me to push harder to make life better for us both.

After about a year and a few months living in transitional housing, I was told my time for termination was approaching. Panic filled as I tried to find a place that was affordable to live. The same time I had been accepted into the program, ironically PHA attempted to contact me. Apparently after so much time had passed since Chris and I applied, my name came up on the list, but PHA claimed I was ineligible because I had no address for them to notify me. Both Mattie and I attempted to explain my constant moving and need for stable housing. PHA's response was simply that I had to reapply, after so many years of waiting, and in critical need, I had to simply go to the back of the line and just wait.

For weeks I searched but could not find anything decent and within my budget. Rachael knew of a realtor and gave me information to a local property agent that leased many properties in the less appealing sections of the Germantown area. I did not know of the company and their practices until I began dealing with them. When I viewed the property, I was excited because it was on the cusps of Chestnut Hill and the harsher parts of Germantown Avenue. The small apartment building was on the street that literally separated the well off from the underserved. I looked at a two-bedroom apartment on the ground floor, it was newly renovated and accommodated many of my needs. When I chose to move in, Carol paid for my security deposit. Carol was extremely supportive but, I also felt a sense of pressure to maintain the high expectations Carol had for me. She thought so highly of me and I did not want to disappoint her.

For so long it had just been Keyan and I. I was very cautious of who I brought around my son, and careful who I exposed the difficulties of my life to. When Kareem and I reconnected, he wondered why I never invited him over my place. I told Kareem I had an apartment, but did not tell him it was a part of a shelter program. I did not want men to view me as being vulnerable or to feel sorry for me. I needed to appear strong and together.

After things ended with him, I began talking to men online specifically to meet new friends, which I was still desperately without. I again figured that since it was difficult finding someone to be in a relationship with, that I could create profiles, indicating that I was only interested in friendships and not dating. With social media, putting up pictures of myself, I believed it would make finding friends easier, because they could see what I looked like and could use their discretion.

I noticed there was a growing trend of women who used their appearance to show off personal aspects of themselves to attract persons of interest. I however wanted to be taken seriously and did not want to exploit myself in such a way that would give men the wrong impression of me, defeating the purpose of finding a genuine friendship. I only put pictures up of my face, and maybe a pose or two, but nothing with sexual innuendoes. I knew I was taking a risk by putting myself out there with hopes of meeting someone genuine and truthful, when everything about social media was deceitful and superficial. I displayed my art, poetry, pictures with captions that showed my esteem and daily quotes of personal inspiration. I was hoping that if people saw me in my truth, then maybe it would inspire them to look a little closer at what beauty really was. I was certain my truth would separate the good from the bad, and those who sought interest in me did so with understanding and acceptance.

As I had done in the past, I met a few guys with whom I only talked to over the phone, explaining my discontent with shallow men, and that I was not looking for anything other than a friendship. I made many male friends with whom I had great long conversations with, but the conversations never sufficed their ongoing curiosity of what many said to be "the incredible woman" behind the voice. I would try to explain and prepare them for the outcome that had become all too familiar to me in situations as such. I figured times were different, and media had evolved in such a way that speaking to people one had never met, had become a new acceptable way of establishing different forms of relationships. The advantage for me was that a guy could now see pictures and determine his comfort level. The guys would say I can see what you look like and I don't have a problem, believing this, I had agreed to meet a few.

One guy was extremely arrogant and appeared to be self-centered, but we had formed a great online conversation that spanned off and on for many months.

After much convincing, I agreed to meet him at an eatery in the small town of Ambler. I figured all would go well since there was no attraction, at least on my part, and I was not looking for more than a friend.

We met up a few days later, I arrived first and we spoke on the phone as I directed him right to where I was seated. I instantly noticed that familiar look of bewilderment, but had come to learn it held no true determination of one's final perception and feelings toward me. I made a mental note of it in the back of my mind, but figured that I would allow time to tell. He sat down and began to talk; the first thing he said was, "Wow, you are not bad." He became interested in learning all that happened to me. We sat and talked, and I denied the signs of my instincts, allowing myself to be comfortable and thought positive, because the conversation was going good. We laughed, he flirted a bit and maintained good eye contact, therefore in my opinion, all was well. He informed me he had to go, which I was already aware that he could not stay long, he hugged me and that was that.

Later that day he called, and it was then I knew my instincts were right. He stated it was a shame what happened, and he could understand how difficult it could be for a man to take to me; that although I had a beautiful heart, it would never be enough for a man in today's times. He was very forward by saying it would be hard for him not to look past my scars, that he had a reputation to uphold, and he felt bad I was not what he thought, because he really liked me.

What happened was enough for me not to meet anyone else no matter how much they tried to convince me differently, but I continued to do so with a few others, all with the same outcome. Through my desperation I would ultimately pay the price for what I settled for and tolerated, but I did not care. Again the thought that anything was better than being alone, and facing the fear of not having a man in my life seemed to overpower me. I would soon learn, however, that nothing is as it seems, at the point where I was most weak, God was building me stronger than ever.

CHAPTER 22

A Safe Place

MONTHS INTO LIVING AT the apartment on Germantown Avenue, there were problems with the unit we lived in, ranging from leaks that often flooded the floors and damaged the carpets. Almost two years later, the problems with the apartment worsened. The leaks that had never been fixed, created further structural damage to the walls, electrical issues proved a safety hazard for the children, and an uncontrollable infestation were among other growing issues that we endured.

The lack in care and concern began with a leak of the air conditioner in my bedroom. It was an old unit installed before we moved in. After many attempts to inform management of the imposing health concerns from mold growing from the saturation of the carpeting, I began to realize I may have rented property from potential slum lords. The realtor company was in transition of managers. Lisa, the woman who was the manager when I moved in, left stating issues with the owners that she had gotten tired of putting up with. When I saw that all of the good staff were leaving, it made me think there were difficult days ahead.

Almost three months passed when the matter regarding the leak and vile smelling mold had been addressed. In between failed communication with the mother of the owner, acting as the temporary manager until Lisa was replaced, I began researching how to handle further matters with landlords neglecting their responsibilities. I began to learn a lot about tenant landlord law, and began to gather information about the issues in my apartment that could potentially serve as evidence should the matter need to be disputed in court. I took pictures and communicated through written letters, and sent them certified mail. I had informed the office countless times that I was pregnant, had a toddler and a child with asthma, but nothing seemed of urgent concern, as the issues worsen.

My kids and I moved into the small living room, where we lived for a month, because the rooms were filled with the rancid smell of mold. Eventually a new manager was hired and of no comparison to the former manager, he was an arrogant African American man, who appeared to look down upon the tenants. He spoke very proper, and conducted himself as if he had the essence of a business man, but came across as unknowledgeable and unapproachable. When I initially met him, I reached out my hand to shake his, which he refused. From then on, my experiences with the new manager were anything but pleasant.

After the issue with the mold, there was the issue with the worsening leaks in both the bathroom and kitchen and infestation with mice and suspected rats. Since we lived on the ground level, inches from the building's dumpster and feet from an abandoned shack, there were constant sightings of wildlife, such as raccoons and possums. After discovering large droppings in the living room, kitchen, and in many of our things, including the baby's bottles and clothing, my complaints and requests for service became more frequent. All the while I was continuing to document and send certified written letters. I then began researching more and more and attended a tenant rights workshop. One thing I prided myself on was if I did not know something, given the time to research, I soon became an expert. I began to call agencies that I learned handled matters as such. The more I searched the more I became an expert in my own defense.

In the winter of 2013, it seemed to snow every other day. It was the major winter storm on Friday, February 14, that caused everyone in the building to suffer greatly because management refused to plow and remove the mounting snow from the previous storms that had accumulated so many inches of snow. The conditions prevented people from moving their vehicles and getting on and off the property.

One day, weeks after having Kiye, I had gone out to my car and slipped, injuring myself badly. My injuries were severe enough that I had to seek medical attention, leaving with my arm in a sling because of damage to my shoulder. Soon after, I sued the company. In conjunction to the law suit, I began reaching out to many of the city's bureaucracies that handled matters regarding tenant and landlord issues. I reached out to the city's License and Inspection (L&I) to make formal complaints and reports about the neglected repairs and conditions of my apartment. After about three months of waiting for management to oblige to L&I's demands, and after the allotted time given to the landlord passed, without any repairs having been made, the only infringement was that the company had to pay a fine.

I sought services from the Tenant Union Representative Network(TURN), and found that after completing a course on tenants' rights, the instructor was the only helpful resource during the entire battle I had with the landlord. One of the key pieces to successfully winning a case, TURN informed me of, was proof that there was not a valid Housing Inspection license for the property. This type of license permits a landlord to collect rent and prohibits them from evicting without. In order for one to be issued, the property must be free from any major L&I code violations, the property had over twenty dated years back.

From the program, I learned how to look to see if my landlord had this important license, among other pertinent legal filings, that through my own investigation, I discovered my landlord was in breach of. I was excited when I realized I had significant leverage over my landlord. I immediately went on the city's site to see if the building in fact had a valid Housing Inspection License, and to my surprise it did not, the building was without a valid license since 2011.

This put me in a great position to demand the issues with my unit be fixed, but I learned to never tell my left hand what the right hand was doing. Instead, I continued to research the law, and learned how to legally withhold my rent, since they had been illegally collecting it since I moved in. I discovered they owed taxes on the property, and was in debt with the water department.

For months I became obsessed with building a case against my landlord. I kept track of the time they were without a license, while withholding rent and demanding they fix the problems in my unit. I began informing other tenants with all of the information I came across, in hopes of getting support in efforts to band together to become a stronger unit to stand up against management, but many were afraid of being evicted. Even when I informed the tenants of their rights, many wanted to do something but chose to remain silent. I had one side kick who together we stood up to management, and did not tolerate the disrespect we received in return.

There was no way I was going to be silent, I had fought so hard to live independently after relying on shelters and the help from others, that all I knew how to do was fight. Management was not going to get away with the things I discovered through my investigations that tenants were not aware of. The other tenant and I became very close. Together, we opened up an escrow account to withhold our rent, and stood against the heat when the fire eventually broke.

I began to write higher offices, such as the Mayor, the Office of Inspector General, and all of the media news stations. One station appeared to be interested, but as I explained my story to a producer, she refused to take it. I went to City Hall to make formal complaints and to present my findings, but it was then, that I quickly learned who I was up against. None of the tenants had ever met the actual landlord, we only dealt with managers. I learned he was a high power lawyer in Philadelphia, which could possibly explain why it appeared that when I mentioned the name, no one seemed willing to help. I learned he had major clout in the city, and was affiliated with the news station that refused to cover the story to expose the deplorable conditions my children and I were subjected to. I had no money to just up and move, and attempted to withstand what I was going through until my father retired, which he planned to give me his house, and move to Florida. The problem was that he would not be retiring until November, which was more than nine months away.

The latest I would actually have access to the property would have been March of the following year.

I reached out to agency after agency in the city, but was constantly turned away because my situation had not reached the point to where I was facing an eviction. I did not understand, I was trying to prevent the latter. I continued to write and send letters to management, who began to retaliate toward me for contacting the city, and for informing the tenants of their rights to withhold rent for an invalid license.

In April of 2014, I went into the office with receipt of creating an escrow account with April's rent. Upon going into the office to deliver the receipt and to inform the manager my reasons for withholding rent, he then proceeded to threaten eviction, which I did not know was illegal at the time. Persuaded by fear of being kicked out, I paid April's rent. When I updated the representative from TURN who I frequently contacted to get advice, he instructed me that I was within my rights to withheld and I should not have paid. From then on, I continued to withhold up until July of that year.

All the while matters worsened and management became more belligerent toward me for not faltering to their threats. The manager said to me once, "Do you know who I work for? A lawyer! We evict at least ten tenants a month. You better quit while you are ahead." Unmoved by his threats, I continued to document and compile evidence that began to mount. Then one day in July while running a hot shower, the ceiling suddenly collapsed. I instinctively sensed something was about to happen in enough time to push my one-year-old son Caiden out of the bathroom, but could not get out in time before the entire bathroom ceiling fell on top of me, injuring me badly. I went to the hospital and informed management who did not seem to care about what happened to me. It was almost a week before someone from maintenance came to remove the pile of debris and repaired the ceiling.

I again attempted to contact city officials. I had been communicating with representatives from the local city council. I spoke to a few who stated they could help, but everything they instructed me to do, I had already done. I was growing more and more anxious that my family would be again without a home. I began to make my fears and concerns known with these city constitutes, who I was sure were in the position to make things happen to improve my situation. Instead, I got no resources and or support.

I had been speaking with a constituent of the council persons office, who after sharing with him what I was going through, who I was and what I was doing with my life, the conversation grew as he shared with me how he had overcome adversity, but had made a name for himself in mayor ways. He told me how impressed he was with me and all of my accomplishments, stating I was the kind of person their office was looking for to sit on a community board. I became excited of the possibilities and thankful for the opportunity the conversation appeared to present. He gave me his contact info and told me to keep him updated.

The next time I called to inform him of the ceiling falling, the lack of response from management and the fear of returning to a shelter, his response was unthoughtful and insensitive. I will never forget what he said to me, "Just go into a shelter and let them help you." I am sure he believed he was giving me the best advice, but after sharing with him my history with chronic homelessness, I realized he did not understand how devastating his words were to me. In that moment, I felt unimportant and hopeless. At that point, as days passed, I realized that going back into a shelter was becoming my only option.

I was beginning to see how landlords had more authority than the law indicated. It appeared they could do what they wanted and easily get away with it. There appeared to be no real repercussions by the city. What I experienced made me fight even harder, not only for myself but seeing that tenants living in other properties owned by the same landlord were also being victimized. I went to another property owned by the landlord to speak with tenants hoping to find out if others outside of my apartment complex were enduring the same issues. I then learned of the horrible conditions, unfair and insensitive practices of the landlord.

What I came to realize was that most of the tenants occupying the landlord's many ran down and deplorable properties, appeared to have similarities. They were mostly black, impoverished people living on some kind of a fixed income. I learned that many tenants had not been screened during the interviewing process, which allowed for many to bring with them all kinds of drama. Drama and concerns that should have posed as red flags, disqualifying one for rental. However, it would be the overlooking of such things, that would potentially be the cause for unforeseen evictions.

I did however receive a response from an unwanted agency, that of DHS. A case worked called and began asking me questions, caring little about my pressing housing issues, but treading for potential threats to the welfare of my children. My experience in the field of human services made me well aware of the social worker's intentions and I was familiar with the procedures. The conversation was brief, but blunt, asking for all of the kids' names and birth dates and my plan. Knowing who I was talking to, I knew I had to tell her that my plans were in motion to leave. Although there was nothing about my situation that lead her to believe the kids were in imminent danger, being neglected or mistreated, I knew there was a possibility she would call again to check on the status. If at that point nothing had changed, and the kids were still living in what had become inhabitable conditions that posed as an issue of safety, they were coming to take my kids. The social worker eluded to this fact by concluding the conversation with "You can stay and deal with the situation, but the children cannot."

I chose to take no chances and immediately called Keyonnee Thalia, the social worker at the shelter program of Philadelphia, to see if space was available for my family. We had been discussing the possibilities of this reality, and when it became definite, it was a matter of figuring a good time to enter. I was scared and extremely upset that I was putting Keyan through this again, along with a toddler and an infant. I was however grateful the program was willing to take us in and again be very supportive.

Since moving close to its' headquarters, I resumed communication with Rachael and was grateful for the support and resources they aided me with during the time I lived at the apartment. Rachael and Keyonnee basically ran Interfaith together after many budget cuts that affected staff and services. However, the level of care, service, and support from the two made the program appear to be ran by an army.

They became extremely supportive, empathetic and advocated many times on my behalf. What I loved and appreciated most about Rachael was that she understood. She understood the faults of the system and worked hard to change the perceptions of homelessness. She treated clients with the upmost respect and there was never the feeling of judgment, even when one's actions constantly brought them to seek the program's services. Rachael understood that the broken system plus a family's lack of recourse, because of the broken system equated to reasons for homelessness.

There were situations when I needed assistance with paying a month's rent, or clothing and diapers for the baby, whatever the need, Rachael and Keyonnee were there. When I was not working after obtaining my Master's degree, Rachael hired me as a parenting counselor for the women in the program. It was as much rewarding for me as it was helpful and therapeutic for the families. I was just starting out and the opportunity allowed me to gain experience.

Whether an alumni or current client, the program served more like a family than a program, where clients received support whenever there was a need. Its doors opened, welcoming all who entered with the same comfort and assurance as a loved one's warm embrace. Both Rachael and Keyonnee were aware of my countless struggles and the difficulties I faced with trying to fight the system.

I had come to realize throughout all of my struggles with the system, it was either black or white, with no accommodations for shades of grey. Either I had to be disabled or not, there was no in between for being successful and disabled. I understood and appreciated that there is a system intended to help the most destitute and underserved, but not everyone in need of assistance are uneducated, mentally and physically incapable or suffers from an addiction. It appeared through my experiences, that if my circumstances were specific to any of these impairments, then I would have had ample services available to me. It was frustrating, and I could see Rachael understood and agreed with my frustrations, which made me feel her efforts, concern and care for me were all genuine.

Keyonnee was the epitome of compassion and empathy. Her propensity to love and care for others caused her to shed her role as a professional and sit Indian style with someone suffering and take on their pain. Keyonnee's laidback, blunt, and "keep it real" approach showed she was able to relate. She became protective of me and the kids, because on many levels she understood my suffering. Her smile, beautiful spirit, infectious laugh and care for us, made me feel blessed to have had an angle on my side.

On August 1, 2014, the children and I moved into the shelter program. When I had given my notice to vacate the property, after I filed the personal injury suit for the ceiling collapsing, ironically I received notice of an eviction. Dealing with being injured, going into a shelter and being sued, took its toll on me. For the first couple of weeks I was an emotional wreck.

The shelter program in Philadelphia ran much differently than the program in Ambler. The program was six to nine months, with the goals of finding clients some form of housing, usually transitional. My goal was to wait out the time until my dad retired and the house became available for us to move into.

In my mind, I had convinced myself I could handle what was yet to come, considering I had already gone through so much, but had no idea the struggles that were yet to come. Keyan spent a month away with his father, so it was good he did not have to be thrust into the craziness. Time passed and Keyan was at an age where he could understand what was going on, and that we no longer had a home. It broke me that my children had to go through so much and I felt to blame for making them suffer because I had to suffer and because my life was so difficult. I felt like a failure as a mother, for not being able to provide for my children and feared Keyan being mentally damaged by such a traumatic experience. It had in fact changed him, and he struggled to cope with the constant instabilities of having to uproot and migrate every so often.

Ambler shelter was much easier for me physically, only having to navigate between three churches. The families were pleasant, with no issues that made living among one another problematic. The program in Philadelphia rotated through a number of churches. The first church we stayed at was a Quaker church. My children and I entered during the remaining two weeks of stay. We again had our own space that was converted into a room, and given metal transferrable cots and mats. Families in the shelter learned to claim their mattresses by putting their names on them using tape, to prevent having to share ones that others slept on. Initially there was a total of three families, but over the course of months, it fluctuated between four to five being housed by the program.

There was a particular woman in the program with her two sons and her husband with whom I was drawn to. She was young, in her mid-twenties, but physically she appeared much older. In many ways, she reminded me of my mother. Here mannerism, the way she carried herself and idiosyncrasies I recognized in my mother growing up. Immediately when I moved in she introduced herself as Tanya. I was briefly informed of Tanya by another mother who just moved out as I was moving in. I had gotten close to the woman and her son, and as I got to know her over time, I observed that she was overly sensitive to children because of her own traumas. Therefore, when she constantly told me about her issues with the way Tanya chastised and parented her children, I knew in part, she was reacting to her trauma. Nonetheless, I was not the kind of person to allow someone else's opinion of another to influence mine. In the shelter, my strategy was to stay far from drama and to be a comfort to others as I was hoping for the same during such a difficult time.

It was not long before Tanya and I established a connection. Despite the fact I began to recognize that she had many of the same personality defects that I found difficult to deal with in my mother, I befriended Tanya, Eventually however, I struggled with Tanya in the same ways I did with my mother. She spoke of never getting along with girls, that her husband and her mother were her only friends. Once becoming friends with Tanya it became evident that her unstable moods, irrationality and many times aggressive behaviors were the cause for unsuccessful relationships. I felt intimidated and forced to comply with her demands, just to prevent her from blowing up and getting upset.

It was not only Tanya, there was another woman, Belinda whose personality and parenting proved to be challenging. Her family consisted of her, her common law husband, and their two kids. They failed to discipline their son whose behaviors mirrored the aggression and inappropriate language of both his parents. I was surprised and a bit concern when Belinda's family returned to the program, after being dismissed for whatever reasons. Belinda was in the parenting group I facilitated when I worked for the program and she was not pleased with my analysis about her parenting at its conclusion. I felt she had a grudge toward me and I expected being in the program with her would not be easy.

Dealing with both Tanya and Belinda proved to be traumatic for me. With Tanya I experienced several situations that lead to arguments, in which she failed to take accountability for her and her children's actions. We had long talks, she invited me to her church and I availed myself to her in many ways as a friend, that I later realized made me susceptible to her manipulation and vindictiveness. I found myself resulting to old habits of going out of my way to please her, just to be on her good side, not realizing that no one stayed on her good side for long.

Moving from church to church proved to be difficult both physically and emotionally. During my stay in the shelter, we stayed at a total of nine churches. I was truly grateful for the majority of them that went out of their way to accommodate me, but it was still hard. I struggled in ways I had never before. Again I was not living I was existing. One of the conditions of the program was that each morning, the families had to be out of the churches by seven in the morning, and in by six thirty in the evenings for dinner. Having an infant, a toddler and getting myself together made it nearly impossible to be out on time. I got up sometimes four in the morning just to get everyone dressed and ready.

In the grueling winter, it became difficult to walk in snow while carrying my baby, and painful to use my hands in the fidget cold. My fingers cracked, blistered, swelled and bled, and in the hot summer, my legs swelled and I nearly sweat to death. Being on my feet more than I normally would, caused me to experience many strained muscles in my foot, making caring for my kids that more difficult.

Each church was different; one of the necessary accommodations that was not always available was a shower. Even when there was one, with so many people using it, it either proved to be an issue of availability or cleanliness. Not everyone practiced the same hygienic procedures, many did not clean up behind themselves or their children, which left the responsibility to the next person in line to clean up. There was a common case of "it wasn't me" when it came to explaining sometimes trifling conditions of bathrooms and washing areas.

Many times, I found myself taking on the task that no one admitted to or wanted to clean. I wanted to assure that we as a group did not leave a church in such a way, to me it was a matter of respect. When a shower was available, it was an appreciated comfort, a luxury, and when a shower was not available, I kept a small basinet, which I run with water to wash the babies. I would have Keyan wash in a secluded corner of the room, and I washed at night when all of the kids slept. Others bathed at program's day center, but I did not feel comfortable washing myself or my children in such a common area that was available to so many people.

Keyan returned at the end of the summer, I was relieved to have help, but was mindful not to put too much pressure on him, Keyan was still a child and after a few months I could see how being without a place to call home, and the conditions of the shelter was beginning to affect him. I could see that Keyan was affected by witnessing the ill treatment from mainly Tanya, filling Keyan with anger and helplessness over not being able to protect his mother. Keyan has always been very protective of me, and it was hard for him to watch others disrespect me. Keyan became afraid and upset because he could not defend his mother against adults who appeared as Giants. One of the biggest challenges of being in the shelter was dealing with the ways the others parented their children, which caused much frustration, and lead to heated confrontations, that ended with me being threaten and harassed by Tanya and physically assaulted by Belinda.

Dealing with ignorance and disrespect from both, not only trauma-tized me, but also Keyan.

After so long, Keyan had gone from being a single child, getting lots of attention to an older brother of two in a year. Then suddenly found himself surrounded by kids with whom he constantly had to share his space with, it all was a lot to handle. Keyan became dis-tant and withdrawn, and his self-esteem suffered, being in such a situation.

The strong bond that we had, began to weaken as I became consumed with exhaustion, hopelessness and depression. Keyan was also experiencing difficulties in school with being homeless, his behavior in class became defiant and he experienced being bullied and teased by classmates. For the first two years, Keyan walked to school with my nephew who lived with us for a while at the apart-ment, but living in the shelter and having to be out so early, I began dropping Keyan off daily. When I had Keyan I dreaded the day when he was old enough, and in public settings being faced with scrutiny because I am his mother. As soon as Keyan was cognizant of the fact that I looked different, I wasted no time explaining to him in ways he could understand. I also feared as he got older, he would lose under-standing and resent me for the negative attention drawn to him.

When Keyan started school, I let my father accompany him on his first day, I was grateful my father wanted to have the honor; as much as I wanted to share in the special moment, I was more consid-erate of my child's feelings. I knew how the children would perceive me, and was more concerned with Keyan's ability to emotionally handle the reactions of other kids, therefore determining it was best to make the situation less awkward and difficult for him. Whenever I had to take Keyan into school to attend a meeting or escort him to his class, I would walk Keyan to a certain point and allow him to go the rest of the way, remaining out of sight of his peers. We then found times to talk together, discussing his feelings, and answering any questions. As Keyan got older, I realized the importance of keep-ing my emotions hidden and intact to prevent Keyan from feeling he had to protect me by withholding his feelings.

I remember a time when Keyan was in first grade and asked me to wait while he stood in line to go into school. As soon as we both approached the single line made up of his classmates, the children quickly began to point, stare and make faces. I saw that their reactions affected Keyan, but at even the age of six, he had to prove to be strong, by hiding his embarrassment with a smile. He glanced at me and I mouthed "are you ok" he replied "I'm ok mommy." Instead, Keyan handled the situation well by answering kid's questions, while looking at me, and I assured him that it was okay to explain. When the line of kids disappeared through the doorway, I walked away and let out a loud cry.

I knew it was imperative that I demonstrate for my son strength, so he too would learn to courageously cope with the many years of people's cruelty and lack of understanding that was yet to come. I began naming feelings that I saw he struggled with such as shame and embarrassment he felt being seen with me. Although it broke my heart that my son was feeling as such, I knew he was no different than any other human being, and particularly he was a child who was not responsible, nor could he control such feelings.

Through the years, having an open and honest line of communication has helped Keyan to become more comfortable with introducing me as his mother and being tolerant to others' ignorance. Despite my feelings, I push through them and we have learned to face the hard truths together. I have given Keyan coping tools, things to say to people when they questioned or say mean things. I have always reminded him to have compassion for people because they do not understand. I have taught Keyan the importance of perception, that others do not always see things the way he does. I have shared with Keyan, that although people find if shocking and difficult in the beginning, once they see that I am no threat, and that I am a normal human being who just looks different, they then become comfortable. I have pointed out this truth many times with Keyan's classmates, many of whom showed excitement, by walking up to me to give me hugs, after first feeling afraid.

Enduring the shelter together was a humbling experience for us both, and despite the difficulties Keyan faced, I saw true resilience in him. There were times when I could not hold it together, although I tried Keyan sensed when there was something wrong; he would then take my hand and pray with me. I saved every dime I could, but there were times when I wanted to treat Keyan by taking him out, or buy him something special to cheer him up, Keyan would say, "Mom, I don't need anything, you need to save your money." I pointed out how blessed he was seeing that other children in the program did not have all Keyan did; children whose parents struggled to show their children respect, affection, consideration, and struggled to emotionally connect, which I explained to Keyan why it was difficult to get along with some of the kids in the program. With this new found empathy, Keyan than became more understanding, considerate and compassionate with other kids. It was impressive to see that in the face of such adversity, Keyan utilized and resulted to the information within him to cope and care for people.

Seeing that we both were struggling greatly, for me I realized it was not the time to falter; I had three little boys to protect and remain strong for. Therefore, Keyan and I began to see the programs' therapist. Being in the field of mental health, sitting and having someone to unload to was rejuvenating, but going through such a tough situation made having someone to talk to even more necessary. I found myself in a numb place; I was tired, angry and after fighting for so long, I began to lose sight of what I was fighting for.

I was struggling with the feeling that God did not care about what I was going through. I was going through so much and felt He was becoming more and more distant. Being in a place where I saw suffering daily made me lose hope for myself. I saw how many were complacent and expecting of whatever came their way, but I was too stubborn to. One of the things I discovered about myself in therapy, was that I was in a tug of war with wanting to give up or to fight. I was tired of fighting and giving up appeared to relieve my anxiety and stress, but fighting for what God entitled me to was in my DNA. I was designed to fight, and although it was incessant, it was all I knew how to do. It has been what has kept me alive, thriving and having overcome so many obstacles.

I pitied myself and realized that my weakened faith was a result of unrealistic expectations I had of God. I wanted God to pity me too. Seeing that I was in distress, I expected Him to make my life easier and give me the things I felt I deserved, and when it did not happen, I began to believe He did not care for me. I also learned I was struggling with a major internal conflict, Justice vs. Injustice. When things were unjust, I felt victimized, but reluctant to be helpless, I fought toward justice. However, many times while in sight of that justice, I subconsciously looked to sabotage it to find myself back in a place of injustice, where I had become more comfortable, and where everything that happened to me was bigger, which caused me to feel like I had no control.

I also dealt with the strained relationships with both my mom and my dad. Being in such a situation, I felt I had no support. I was constantly arguing with my dad for his lack of support and empathy. He was tired of me being so needy, and I felt I needed him more than ever. I just wanted him to understand what I was going through and he could not.

I went to my mother's house most times during the day since I had no job and no place to go with two babies. I did not like spending my time at the program's "day center" where other families in the program spent their time, just hanging out until it was time to return to the church.

Belinda and her children often left the place in disarray and there always appeared to be issues with regards to the way she parented her kids, which one day the tension finally reached a point that lead to a heated confrontation. Caiden was going through a biting phase which was typical developmentally for his age, but other parents were teaching their children to be aggressive with any child who was aggressive with them, regardless of the intent. Both Tanya and Belinda followed this principle. I ended up having two separate altercations with both.

First was with Tanya. Caiden kept biting her son, which after rationally trying to confront Tanya about my son's injury, her defensive attitude caused me to blow my top with her. I was irritated that she became indignant with my one-year-old who knew no better, when her five year old previously pushed Caiden into a brick wall causing a large contusion on his head which required medical attention. Tanya justified and minimized that event, but got in my face about my son biting hers, after he had been constantly picking on my child. I believed my one-year-old had had enough and bit him. In retaliation toward me for blowing up at her, Tanya left several messages on my phone, saying horrible things about me. She continued her verbal abuse by taking to social media and added more salt to the wounds she had already created. I was not surprised by her comments about my appearance, nor was I phased by them. What hurt the most was her saying "that is why your own mother and father don't want nothing to do with you. No one cares about you, you should just go kill yourself, do them a favor and die." Thinking we were friends, I had confided in her about what I was going through with my parents. She then went a step further to messaging me on social media, threatening Keyan – our boys attended the same school. She wrote that she instructed her oldest son to beat Keyan up.

She accused me of being jealous of her and wanting her husband, that no one would ever want me because I was ugly, and continued to say nasty things about my children.

It became apparent to me by the things Tanya said, that she was in fact envious and jealous of me. I had the things she wanted, she would always ask to borrow my stuff. When others complimented my children being well dressed and having good behaviors, she found smart things to say or rolled her eyes. When I thought about all of the hurtful things she said to me, I realized they were aspects of myself Tanya wished were true about herself.

Tanya envied that I was educated, kind, gentle, and got along well with the other families, volunteers and staff. She even envied the way her own children took to me. I played with and showed her children affection and attention, and she resented the fact. I felt bad for the two boys. I always took very good care of my children, even in such circumstances, they never wanted for anything, and no one could ever tell we were without. They were well mannered, temperament and groomed. My mother taught me to "never look like the hell that you're going through." I always handled my business!

One day I confronted Belinda about how she parented her children, because at that point it affected the way my child interacted with them. Her daughter was aggressive with Caiden, and he in turn pulled a chunk of hair out of her head. Belinda, was very intimidating in size, but I wanted her to know I was in no way intimidated by her, and continued to voice my opinion when she continued to disrespect me. What resulted was Belinda lunging and assaulting me. I was in fear for my safety considering I still had to reside with her.

It had gotten to the point where everything became too overwhelming. I had not been around so much drama, and was the reason I had always been cautious of the females I associated myself with, but in this situation I had no choice. It appeared I was surrounded around people with concerning mental health issues and I felt I was the only sane one. I had to travel from one church to another and could not escape the insanity. This was nothing new, because I felt this way about people my entire life, my mother, family, men. I had reached a boiling point and felt the level of my anger rise to where it eventually exploded on the least likely person I would have imagined—my mother.

I did not want to spend so much time at my mother's house, but had nowhere else to go. At the time, I could only tolerate my mother while not in her presence; I had always felt my mother did not respect me and still saw me as a child. Spending so much time there, I noticed how my mother would say things, without considering how her comments and judgment made me feel. Comments such as, "If you did not have these kids, you would not be struggling as you are." I began to feel like she was taking pleasure in my downfall. Her insensitive comments infuriated me to a point that one day I let out all of the anger I had pent up.

I told my mom I resented her for not being there for me during many tough times. I emphasized that I had taken care of her when it was her job to take care of me. To add salt to the wound, I shouted at her, saying, "It is your fault I have struggled. It is your fault I got burned!" I was angry that I was in a position where I needed my mom and it appeared she sought pleasure in tearing me down. I knew my mom was still struggling with aspects of her addiction, but

I had no more sympathy, I said some things to her and about her to her face I knew were not me, my rage had assumed my identity and I lost my composure.

In therapy, I gained incredible and profound insight about myself; and how to finally express the feeling I have denied myself without guilt. All my life, I believed I had to live according to others expectations and protect people's feelings by hiding my emotions. In doing so, I neglected, hurt and was unfair to myself. My feelings, reactions, and thoughts are a part of me, and learning that allowed me not to be so hard on myself. When I exploded on my mother, I did not feel remorse or anything negative. I knew the way I spoke to her was disrespectful, and had been the first time I ever stepped outside of character, but it also was the first time I had ever expressed years of anger and resentment that I denied myself to feel.

While in the program, I won the eviction against the landlord. My hard work paid off in such tremendously. I was commended for collecting such strong evidence and standing up to a powerful force; someone who used his professional power to take advantage of so many helpless people. Worse, he prided himself for taking away people's shelter. His mistake was that he "typed" me, assuming that I too was powerless because of my circumstances.

I stood before a very callus and unflinching judge, who was said to be no nonsense, and who was also known to rule in the favor of landlords. I presented my evidence and stood inexperienced and alone, against the vicious seasoned lawyers he sent on his behalf. This experience taught me that the truth always prevails no matter how good one may be in contorting it. When the judge stated that I owed nothing and told the plaintiff they should be ashamed of their practices, I broke down and cried. Through my sobbing, I told the judge, "Thank you! You don't know the misery they put my family through." I believe a part of his tough exterior was softened. Before my case was called, I along with a number of others who accompanied me for support, sat for hours, watching other similar cases unfold. In that time, I witnessed how the judge rushed along their cases; and appeared crass and intolerable to mostly the defendants (the tenants). However, with me, in that moment, he allowed me the time to exhale. It was the first time in two years I was able to do so.

While still in the shelter, I again found myself fighting the same eviction as the lawyer appealed in a higher court, this time in the Court of Common Plea. It was the first time I came face to face with my former mysterious landlord. After losing the first time, he illegally prohibited me from obtaining my belongings, and denied me the return of my security deposit. In the end however, I again came out as a winner! Thanks to an incredible lawyer, Michele Cohen from the Legal Help Center in Philadelphia, who was impressed by my tenacity and thoroughness to gather such evidence, took the case, and together we won the appeal. I also won two personal injury cases against him, one for the slip and fall in the winter when management neglected to maintain the property, and the second for the ceiling collapsing.

In March of 2015, my family moved into my dad's house, after he retired, and brought a beautiful house in Florida. It seemed surreal that I had made it so far, considering all I had gone through. I look back at times and still cannot believe I made it through another traumatic time in my life.

While in the shelter I participated in a workshop offered through the shelter program. My personality shined so bright, that it landed me a job with an amazing program, through the Child welfare system. It is amazing how life comes full circle. I was now working within the very system that cared for my brothers and I when we were younger. Tabor Northern Community Partners provides case management services for families involved with DHS. I was blessed to use my personal experiences along with my compassion for human suffering to help families. My work with the Community Umbrella Agency (CUA) allowed me to be recognized by DHS as a valuable employee, which was the highlight of my time with Tabor.

CHAPTER 23

Pain Made Me Brave

I WAS EXTREMELY LONELY and had again convinced myself all I needed was good conversation to pass the time away, and was not interested in meeting anyone, so I thought. I was checking messages on a popular site, as I then came across one from a guy, which I responded to, that turned into a four -hour messaging conversation.

He introduced himself as Gary and started out by telling me how courageous he thought I was and how the mini bio I had written about myself made him cry. He said he had never met anyone so strong before. From then on, Gary called me every day asking me how I was, starting the day with "Have a blessed and wonderful day." Gary messaged me all of the time before we exchanged phone numbers, which he then called every chance he had, just to say he was thinking of me. I did believe he was coming on a bit strong considering we had just met, but I loved the feeling of being thought of. Gary had a persona that made me feel I was the only woman he was interested in, in conjunction with saying all of the right things a vulnerable, and needy woman wanted to hear.

By the time I met Gary, I was at a point in my life where I was fearful of spending the rest of it alone. None of the previous relationships worked out, and I was heading into my fourth relationship hoping this time would be better. Gary and I began hanging out all of the time, I had a car and some money in the bank, so we went out and had fun on my dime. When I met Gary, I instantly found him to be extremely attractive and really thought this time I had found the one. The more I got to know Gary, there were things that refuted my belief, but I was tired of my intuitions getting in the way trying to steal what little happiness and excitement there was to enjoy, even if they had dire consequences in the end. In the beginning, things are always good, and that was what I at least wanted to experience considering how disappointing my life had become.

There were clear signs in the beginning that sound the alarm, but that I hit like a snooze button to shut off. Being in graduate school and studying clinical psychology, as well as recognizing the signs in my own struggles, I detected Gary had much internal conflict. By the way Gary shared some of the stories of his life and the mental state he appeared to be in some days, I could see things that concerned me. Again I dismissed the signs, because I felt I had no right to judge a person with whom I did not know very well. Gary began telling me how difficult it was for him to find a job, and spoke very candidly about the failed relationships, which included the one that ended around the time we met. In the few weeks we hung out together, I found myself assuming that "fixer" role. We had gone out to eat, and I convinced Gary to put in an application at the restaurant. I encouraged him to ask if they were hiring and to apply. When the manager gave Gary an application and offered him an interview on the spot, Gary was impressed and thanked me the entire night for giving him the confidence to speak up.

Throughout our conversations and during the times when we hung out, it was just fun, Gary was energetic and lively and knew how to have a good time, which I believed helped me to get out of my reclusive shell. I had never had such a time with someone before, but what I came to realize was that the good times were always at my expense. Before Gary secured a job, much time had passed and I wanted to express to him how much I appreciated him, how I was there for him and that I accepted Gary as he was. I put money inside of a card and gave it to him as a way to help until Gary found a job. I also knew it was the perfect opportunity to implement my ploy to get Gary to see me as someone he would be foolish to pass up on.

The more Gary thanked me for being so caring and supportive, the more certain I was that Gary was now invested in me.

What I did not know was that I was setting myself up to be a casualty of my own plot. Months past and we seemed to grow closer and closer, still hanging out and seeing each other every chance we had. I became comfortable with the idea of letting him meet Keyan, since I noticed we both were growing fonder of each other. Gary connected well with Keyan, but the real determination was whether Keyan connected with him, and he did. One night while on the phone, Gary told me how much he liked me and asked if I would be his girlfriend. I was shocked by the advance, but I was flattered and said yes, and just like that we went from friends to dating.

Gary introduced me to his family by inviting me to a gathering, where I went with Erica. Christmas Eve, I invited Gary to spend Christmas with my family. I had designed two musically inspired posters, among other things. Everything was moving so fast, but I did not care I wanted it to work; it had to, because I could not keep failing at finding love. I liked to believe I was selective in who I introduced to my family, I tried to pull the wool over their eyes many times, but I knew they saw the same things I saw, especially Josh. We were so much alike that I could tell the truth behind the smile and the accepting handshakes he exchanged. My brother's non judgment and understanding of me, kept Josh from telling me what he knew I was not in a place to hear.

Valentine's Day 2012, I had gone out of my way and bought Gary expensive cologne, and clothing. I surprised Gary with the gifts by planting them in his room at his parents' home, while he was away. I noticed that Gary was going through a lot and I found him during a rough time in his life. I wanted to lift his spirits, but also buy Gary's heart. For Gary's birthday, I found and paid for a photo shoot for head shots that would inspire him to pursue his interest as a singer. It was clear I was spoiling Gary, and in my efforts I was trying to convince him I was the one, but I was doing more harm than good.

Once into the relationship, I began to notice more about Gary, that rang the alarm even louder. He was into social media, and from the looks of it, Gary appeared to be very popular. I noticed he had an increasing number of female friends, but I thought nothing of it considering Gary made me feel I was the only one he was interested in.

Gary introduced me to his best friend at the time. He spoke so highly of their relationship, but also expressed disappointment in him for not understanding Gary's choice to be with someone who looked like me. Gary told me that when he showed his friend a picture of me, his friend told him I looked like a ghoulish character from the Harry Potter films. Gary went on to say how he constantly had to defend his choice to be with me.

I in no way ever sensed or believed Gary would lie about such things, but I in fact learned at least the comment supposedly made by his friend was untrue. About a month into the relationship, I had come to learn Gary was involved with another woman, via social media. When I learned of the conversations on his messaging, and saw the woman calling him, I wrote the number down and called. It was confirmed that they had been talking for almost as long as we had been, and further information from the woman crushed me.

I also took down his best friend's number in his phone to find out what I could about Gary that he was not telling. In the conversation, I confronted the friend about the insensitive comments he had made about me, which he denied. He said Gary was the one who actually made the comments, among other ones that were shocking to hear. Gary apparently told his friend that he had planned to see how far he could take things with me, implying his plans to take advantage of my kindness, considering how I had gone out of my way for him. Gary's own friend told me to be watchful of him; that he had issues with honesty and being loyal to one woman. Gary was four years younger than me, but his charming and mature personality made him appear much older. He had this Casanova way about him that was very convincing. Little did I know it was a ruse, and would soon learn Gary had the same effect on many unsuspecting women.

When I confronted Gary about the woman and the comments he claimed his best friend made, I was devastated by the deception, and my feelings were extremely hurt. Gary apologized about the woman, claiming she was no one, and defended the messages by saying he was not sure of his feeling for me, and was keeping his options open if things did not work between us. Gary professed however he was happy and it took this situation for him to realize he did not want to lose me. Gary then went on to talk about his and traumas that explained a lot about his behaviors and demeanor. We spent the night talking about things I could hear were extremely difficult for him to speak about, as they were difficult to hear and unimaginable for me to fathom. I believed as a result, my compassion and sympathy for Gary outweighed my anger and feelings of betrayal.

Then there was the way Gary acted and interacted with me that led me to suspect he was not actually as comfortable as he led on. Whenever we got together, the first thing I did was show my excitement with affection. I would run to Gary to give him a hug, but he never hugged me back, even after we were well into our relationship.

When we became more intimate with each other, Gary became avoidant, by barely touching me. I confronted him, looking for the opportunity to discuss any discomfort he was feeling with aspects of my body, that I knew to be difficult for a man to embrace. Gary denied and called me insecure, but assured me I had no reason to be. Gary then rationalized there were certain aspects of a woman's body he liked more than others, and that none of my concerns were concerns to him. Gary always told me I was perfect to him, but every time we were intimate, I felt more and more unattractive and undesirable. I began to feel it was a routine; despite feeling used and uncomfortable, I dismissed it all and went with the flow.

Eventually Gary admitted to the difficulties of adjusting, and feeling uncomfortable, but this confession came after I had to constantly plead with him to tell me the truth. I knew it was not that I was insecure, by this time in my life, I had become very much comfortable in my skin, and had come to a place where I felt and saw the beauty in myself. However, being with Gary began to eat away at that confidence.

Almost two years into the relationship, things went from good to bad. Gary constantly spoke to women on social media, having cyber relationships and sometimes meeting these women. I confronted him constantly poring my heart out about how he was hurting me, but Gary could not and would not stop. Through my snooping, I saw that he constantly told women how physically beautiful they were, but never said the same to me. I sometimes read lascivious conversations between Gary and other woman, feeling betrayed and disgusted at the same time. I began to see that everything he claimed he was not, he was. Gary would say over and over that looks meant nothing, how he could get any beautiful woman he wanted, but that being with an attractive woman was not what made him happy, but that I made him happy.

Gary constantly friended women of the same kind on social media. The more revealing and voluptuous their bodies were, the more he lusted after and further perused them. I became a vigilante, obsessed with accessing and prying through his phone, and social media pages to see what he was hiding.

We eventually moved in together, at night while Gary slept, I went into his phone, using my technological skills to break passwords and codes to discover what he thought he was clever enough to hide. I retrieved women's numbers, and confronted them. This became an obsession that I engaged in for most of the four years we were together. I had to have spoken to more women than I can count during that time. I began to do it so much, that I became immune to the betrayal, but had never gotten use to the pain it caused each and every time I spoke to a woman.

The women I spoke with many times knew of me and did not care. Many cursed me out, laughed at me, and continued to talk to Gary. Many appeared hurt and surprised when they learned about me, after being in what they believed was a relationship with Gary. A handful of women at different times throughout the relationship would recite the same story, telling me how Gary told them he did not want to be with me, because I was unattractive and not his type. They then told me Gary cheated on me with them, because the woman looked better, and could appeal to him sexually. They said things about me that only Gary would have known, which always left me feeling humiliated, and played. I could not stand that so much deceit was sexually based, and so many women prided themselves believing they were better, because of what they could do for a man sexually. Most often the men who cheated on me went after the women who only had such an advantage.

Seeing the pain Gary was causing me, Gary only denied, rationalized and manipulated, which caused me to truly believe I was crazy. Gary somehow convinced me that what was happening was not really happening. Gary then blamed me for the things he had done. Gary rationalized his online actions and downplayed my feelings by pointing out they were only women he talked to online.

There were many accounts of women claiming to have had physical encounters with Gary, and through their accounts I suspected reason to believe them. Gary manipulated me into believing his version, which I allowed myself to, thinking he would not go as far as physically cheating. Becoming accustomed to Gary's habits, I believed that he only went as far as talking to women, but the truth was, I really did not know. I was not ready to face the truth either way. I had been doing so much to collect the truth, that once I found it, and caught Gary in lies after lies, I did nothing with the information. There were empty threats to leave, but I did nothing. I did not hold Gary accountable, so fearful that the repercussions would backfire on me and Gary found just cause to leave, despite the fact he had continued to betray me. Time after time Gary began to realize he could do what he wanted and I would not do anything about it. For a while, I was so hung up on Gary's looks, that I failed to see his faulty character.

We did share many good moments together in the beginning, and spent most of the relationship trying to get back to that place, but the truth was, it was all a mirage. Gary showed me the version of himself that he wanted me to see, but a person can only hide who they are for so long. Eventually the truth came out and when it did, I should have believed and took heed that Gary was not right for me.

I began to see how shallow Gary was, his idealism of love was based on lust and beauty. Gary broke down once admitting to treating me as he did, as a result of having been hurt by an older woman with whom Gary really loved, but who cheated and left him for her ex. For the first year, Gary was consumed with grief over this relationship, and when I asked why he was so hung up over a woman who clearly did not respect him, he kept referencing to her appearance and how beautiful she was. For the first year and a half, Gary was still talking to and trying to pursue his ex. I felt my issues were with these women, when in fact they were with me.

As time passed, the relationship worsened. Not only was Gary continuing to talk to women, but now that we lived together, he was not playing his part. I had made it easy and comfortable for Gary, because I was responsible for everything. Not only did Gary talk to women behind my back, he also habitually lied to me, stole from me and had shown little to no respect for me.

When we moved into the apartment in Germantown after completing the shelter program, I had a significant amount of money from a car accident settlement, that was meant to be a safety net. I was using Josh's account to hold the money, and he allowed me to use his debit card. At some point Gary got hold of the pin number, and for months, he had been dipping into the account without my knowledge. At the time Gary had a job, so when he was making big purchases, I assumed that he was saving his money. Then one day my brother called upset claiming I had over drafted his account and he owed over five hundred dollars. I felt horrible that Josh was upset with me and I did not know why. The last I checked my balance, I had a lot of money, so I assumed it had to be a mistake. Josh kept accusing me and I kept denying, because I truly knew I had not spent so much money.

I began to think of how it could have happened, I never suspected Gary because I never thought Gary would take anything from me, but something told me to confront him, and when I did, to my horror, Gary admitted to watching me enter my pin and took the card during times when I was unaware. Over the course of about four months, Gary had stolen the seven grand I had remaining in the account. Gary bought himself expensive sneakers, clothing, and put rims on the Impala I had given him when I bought a new car. Gary had even met a woman at a strip club, going occasionally, showering her with dollars of my money.

I could not believe it! What was more of a disbelief was that after about a month of breaking things off with Gary, I easily forgave and welcomed him back. I believed Gary's cries and convincing words of how sorry he was. Left to pick up the pieces of my life Gary shattered, I slowly put them together with little expectations of Gary to help repair the damage he caused. Gary promised to never do the things he had done again, but it was only a matter of time before he did.

In April of 2012, I learned we were expecting our first child together. I was very excited when I learned I was pregnant and so was Gary. I was approaching my last semester in obtaining my Master's degree, and faced with the physical demands of being pregnant. I was determined however to push through; I was almost at the finish line and I was not stopping for anything. I told my doctor I had to deliver, what I found out was another boy, before the start of my last semester, which was a week after the new year. God was in agreement that I had come too far and worked too hard to quite, that Caiden came on the target date, which was New Year's morning of 2013. The next week I was in class and finished my last semester. Graduating meant that much more to me, knowing all I had gone through again to obtain it.

I decided to resign from my job at the college, because my body had really gone through so much while pregnant. I was blessed that again my family was there to support me. My sister had been living with me at the time, and my mom was much more of a positive support this time around. I was hoping having a baby would cause Gary to see he had a beautiful family and would clean up his act. Instead things continued to worsen.

Again dealing with postpartum depression after having Caiden, and feeling overwhelmed by Gary's constant disrespectful antics, I was a time bomb ticking, but finding out Gary was still disrespecting me even days after his first child was born, was the spark that lit the fuse. I went off on him. I became physical with Gary, and my sister had to hold me back. I discovered that while I was giving birth, Gary was again talking to some woman and I lost it. I had built up so much anger and resentment because he continued to disrespect me and would not stop. Gary was always sorry, and often tried to smooth over the pain caused. While I was pregnant Gary even went as far as proposing to me; although I accepted, nothing could make right the things Gary had done and the misery he was causing me.

In April of 2013, I found that I was again pregnant, and in December of 2013, we had another boy named Kiye. I'm sure my family was shaking their heads, but everyone again was supportive of me and never said what I knew they were thinking. Each of my children's births were interesting experiences. Keyan took too long to come into the world, Caiden came right on time, and Kiye came two weeks before his due date.

My greatest fear was to experience true labor. With Keyan I experienced hours of contractions that were painful enough to kill me. I remember the doctor sending me back home when I was sure I was in labor, by the severity of the pains, but they were still too far apart. The doctor told me that I would know for sure when I was in labor, determined when I was no longer calm and able to speak rationally. Sure enough when I returned, I was in active labor, and yelled out every expletive I could think of, while at the same time apologizing to my parents for talking out of character. I skipped the torture with Caiden, because my labor had to be induced and I was already drugged up before the contractions began.

However, with Kiye, I woke up December 23, 2013, and realized I was experiencing sudden pains, but thought nothing of it at first. Then by midmorning, I suspected I was in labor, because the contractions were more frequent and stronger. I went to the doctor and she stated I was only 1 centimeter dilated. I was sure by her measurement, I still had a long time before I would go into labor. By that evening, I was in active labor. I was cleaning the apartment and finished wrapping the few gifts in preparation for Christmas. I was alone with Keyan, Caiden, and my nephew Quadir.

Here and there, I stopped to allow for contractions to subside, before they began to hit consistently every few minutes. Not knowing what was happening to me, the boys laughed and made fun of the poses I learned to help ease the pain. I was sure I was not in labor earlier that day, but could not understand why I was experiencing contractions so severe. When the pain shot through my body like a lightning bolt, I knew I was in labor and that the baby was coming soon. I frantically called Gary, who was at work, and then Josh, hoping that one of them would get to me as quickly as possible. The pain worsened and by the time Gary came, I was exhausted, lethargic, and certain I was going to die.

Gary comforted and encouraged me to hold on to make it to the car. By the time we made it to the top level of about five steps leading from my apartment to the building's entrance, I knew I could not go any further.

"He's coming, Gary! I gotta sit down, I can't move!"

Panicked, Gary shouted, "You can do it, you can't have the baby out in the hallway!"

At the same time, Joshua entered and saw me screaming in the small stairwell. He asked me why I had not called an ambulance instead of him. My reply was, "I am in too much pain to think straight." While on the phone with the dispatcher, Josh was relaying the questions from the other end, but it was all too much. Suddenly I felt this huge urge to push. I was so afraid, and within seconds, my water broke soaking my pants. I told both Josh and Gary, "I gotta push! The baby is coming now!"

They both yelled out in unison, "No! Don't push!!"

I could see the fright in Joshua's eyes and could hear the panic in both their voices, as they scurried to find linens of any kind, to prepare for the baby. The baby was coming then and there, and with one big push, Kiye effortlessly slipped from beneath me as Gary swooped under like a pro football player just in time to catch his son. Josh who had never changed a diaper before, aided in the delivery of his nephew. Even Keyan and Quadir played a role by bringing blankets and towels to cover the baby. There to witness me push the baby out, Keyan stood with a look of stunned disbelief, and simply said, "So that is where babies come from."

Josh still on the phone with the dispatcher, who heard everything that took place, continued to relay through Josh a series of questions to assure there were no complications with the baby. In seconds, several paramedics rushed in to attend to both Kiye and I. We were taken to the hospital and the way they pried Kiye from my arms, once we arrived, made me fear that something happened to him because of the nature of delivery. In about an hour we were reunited. I believe that experience created such an affectionate bond, because Kiye still continues to cling to me, the way he did when his tiny body first touched mine.

By the time I had Kiye, I became disappointed with myself. Gary's mother was very angry with me when I had Caiden to the point that she did not believe he was Gary's. I remember her trying to tell me that Gary was not mature enough to have children, but I was blinded by who I believed Gary to be, that it would be much later when I understood what his mother meant.

Having such beautiful children gave me so much joy, I had my three kings. I realized how ignorant people were when I had Keyan and then the two boys. I constantly got (and still do) surprised reactions when people see my children, many often outright ask, "Is he your son? Are they your children? They are handsome." What they are not saying, is they are shocked someone with my appearance could have such good looking kids, as if they were supposed to be born looking like me.

With each of my boys, I knew the time would come when their eyes would see me the same as the world, and that I had to be prepared to answer and explain why mommy looked different. It broke my heart to see that although my boys mirrored my image, they were still very much different than me. They had the same perfect fingers, nails, feet, toes and facial features as everyone else, and their inability to relate to me physically, made me feel like an outsider among my own children. I coped with this insight, by always making sure I exposed the truth that I hid from others, so as to bridge any gaps related to my physicality that have the potential to make my children feel discomfort toward me, which I know is what often separates me from people.

I understood the importance of educating my children about diversity, after seeing how so many parents did not. Explaining to Keyan what happened to me, how people responded to me and how I coped with it, allowed for the opportunity to have many discussions about differences in people. I had always wished parents had the same conversations with their children, instead of discouraging their curiosity.

Children's brutal honesty is the sharpest, as soon as their faces gets a hold of mine, it sticks. Unlike adults, children do not hold back. A child looking with fright may tug at their parent and say, "Look at her face!" or "What happened to that lady's face?" or "Look at that lady, she looks like a monster." The parent may then sneak a peek, turn to the child and quietly say, "It's not nice to stare." Or yell at their child loud enough so that I can hear them supposedly teaching their child politeness. Experiencing this all of my life showed me the importance of teaching my children how to be sensitive from a very early age.

When Keyan inquired about someone who looked different, we talked about it, I explained as best I could what I knew about what appeared to be the person's difference. We then found ways to relate the conversation to my difference. This was a process for many years until Keyan felt comfortable around people with differences. There was a young man in a wheel chair, who attended the same church, and became a good friend while we were there. Keyan was four at the time and when he first noticed him, Keyan pointed toward the young man, and said, "Mommy, look at his wheels!" I thought Keyan was going to ask why the young man was in a wheelchair, but I believed he had lights attached to the wheels that created an effect when they spun. Keyan never questioned about the young man at any time, just called him his friend and said he liked going to church to see him.

Then there was John, a man who was homeless, who Keyan really took to emotionally, I believe because of our own personal experiences of being without. We always talked about how God wanted us to help and give to people in need regardless of how little we had, or why they were in need. Every time we drove and stopped for the light at the intersection on Adams and Roosevelt Boulevard, Keyan would ask if I had money to give to John. Keyan insisted that I give the money to him to give to John. The traffic light at the intersection was long, so it allowed us some time to talk with John. Keyan would give him the money and at the same time, sparked a conversation that continued over the course throughout the years every time we stopped at the light. Keyan was surprised to learn that John was a very nice guy, which he was. We learned a lot about John, that he was humble, proud, and always wore a rich man's smile.

I believed if I taught my child about adversity, then he would become sensitive to others which, would lessen their plight. Some people believe that turning away or ignoring is being respectful and considerate, when in fact it adds to the weight of rejection. I have learned to confront a situation where a child openly questions, and tell the parent it is okay their child is asking: assuring the parent that their child is supposed to. When the child sees me smiling and using language that helps them understand in a tender, tone they then feel comfortable. The parent will usually smile and say "thank you," admitting to feeling embarrassed by their child's remark. I would encourage the parent to find ways to educate their child instead of teaching them to look away, that is when they become ignorant.

I credit my mother for many of the great qualities I possess as a mother. From my mother I learned to put my children first, making sure their needs are met and never be too proud to seek help when I am unable to do so; and to make sure they are always a reflection of me. If I was lacking, I made sure my children never did. Putting both the love and fear of God in their hearts, as a moral compass to navigate a treacherous world.

I exhibited many great qualities as a mother, but I also am a product of my environment. Therefore, I have to be aware of those unhealthy and ineffective characteristics I also possess, and put constant effort in working to be a better mother. It is much easier said than done, especially being a single mother. I have even more respect for my mother, because she raised six children on her own without help. I have a deeper level of understanding for how easy it can be to become frustrated, overwhelmed and angry for having to carry so much responsibility alone. Having to be pulled 24-7 in different directions to satisfy individual constant needs, has been very humbling. Seeing how my mother was faced with the same challenges, while dealing with much more, has made me understand and relate to the disparity felt at times while doing so alone. When I am at my wits, end I still have to remember they are children who still have not developed an understanding of the things we as parents sometimes expect for them to know. Much of the pain a mother feels raising children as a single parent, comes from the resentment felt for the man selected to conceive with, when she is suddenly left alone to play both the role of the mother and the father. It is hard to separate the emotions, while having to maintain a relationship when the father is still involved in some way. For me, it is important because I know that as much as I can do, I cannot be the male figure my boys need to fully understand who they are.

One of the greatest skills taught by my mother, which I have in turn instilled in my children is the ability to be independent and self-sufficient. As soon as my children were able to talk and manipulate things with their hands, I encouraged and pushed them to learn to do for themselves. I adopted the same mentality my mother had when teaching me that "there is no such thing as you can't." I teach my boys to always put their effort in trying, and teaching them the importance of knowing when to ask for help. It is for me especially important to teach this philosophy to my boys, so they will grow up and not become dependent completely on others, especially women.

Even after having two children, the condition of our relationship continued on a spiraling downfall. Gary began turning off the ringer to his phone. He even bought additional phones in attempts to hide his deceit, but no matter what he did to be deceptive, I eventually found out. I bought spyware and installed it on Gary's phone so I could see where he was, and how frequently he spoke to women, as well as to read actual text messages between Gary and other women in real time.

I was sure I was crazy, and the need to always provide proof was how I kept sane. Even when faced with the truth he still denied. Gary always found the perfect excuse, and manipulated me into doubting what I knew was sound truth, or made me feel guilty for seeking out the truth. Nothing was ever his fault, and I somehow always felt I was to blame.

Gary waited for the kids and I to be fast asleep in bed, before sitting on the couch in the next room whispering and telling another woman he loved her. I began to feel unattractive and began to resent social media. I looked at the types of women Gary was pursuing on social sites, feeling inadequate that I did not have the type of body he most desired or the physical appearance. I strongly resented women for making it so easy for men to lust after them. The phenomenon of selfies and sexting lead me to believe finding a man the traditional way was unlikely. Why would a man want a wholesome woman, when most women used their looks and used sex to attract men. If I had ever felt finding someone genuine was difficult before, trying to compete with beauty and sex in today's way of meeting, made finding someone that more hopeless.

Seeing how Gary spend so many hours, becoming consumed with all forms of social media, the feelings of resentment made me stop using it. Seeing how obsessed with sexual images of women and lust, made me resent being intimate with him, I just did not feel good about myself and secure as a woman. I felt although he was physically with me, Gary was imagining himself being with anyone but me.

I noticed how Gary had taken down pictures with me in them, appearing to be a single father, as he had indicated in many of his profiles. This lead me to believe Gary was ashamed of me. When we went out in public, Gary would always walk off in his own direction, which made me feel he did not want to be seen with me. There were a few times, while alone, with me not far behind, Gary would talk to women and find time to exchange numbers; or talk to women on social media he knowingly and unknowingly knew I knew; it was embarrassing when I found out. Again I confronted Gary, expressing my feelings, which he simply denied and blamed on my insecurities. Still I stayed. For four years I stayed and dealt with the disrespect, lack of affection and emotional neglect.

As time went on, my eyes widened to the many truths about not only Gary, but about myself as well. I had come to see so many of his issues revolved around the things that happened to him in his life, and that Gary did not receive help to learn how to cope with. I had also come to see how Gary's perceptions were negatively developed by many influences that were significant to him. I realized that as much as I was doing for him, the more I prevented Gary from being responsible for himself. I had found myself again in a codependent relationship, just as I had been in all of my relationships, which mirrored the codependent relationship I had with my mom, and the emotionally unavailable relationship I had with my father.

I had learned through enabling, how not to hold others accountable for their actions and in many ways, had become dependent on these codependent relationships, because they allowed me to feel needed. I was just as unhealthy as they, because I could not see my worth or place in another's life without the dysfunction.

Being in a codependent relationship, I allowed the negative behavior, attitude and treatment by supporting men and making it easy for the dysfunction to continue. In each of my relationships, I recognized the pattern of romanticizing, and excusing other's behaviors, because I wanted to see the good in everyone. I could not separate the spirit from the behavior, not realizing that people are to be held accountable for their actions and behaviors. More importantly, in both is vital information about who that man is, and how he has learned to treat a woman.

Once I saw Gary in his truth, I became more empathetic, and tried to be supportive, now understanding that many of his issues were manifested in a deep rooted deficit within himself. There is nothing more demonstrative than a man who is unaware that a sickness breads inside of him. When I saw how vulnerable and lost Gary actually was, I wanted to help protect him, seeing he did not have that support close to him. Therefore, I began to rationalize, justify and tolerated the unacceptable things Gary did. I felt compelled to be there for him, believing his behaviors were a result of things Gary struggled with, that had plausible justifications, and were not behaviors he intentionally chose to demonstrate.

At the same time, even when I clearly saw that Gary struggled with who he was and who he wanted to be, I selfishly thought of myself and decided I rather put up with all I had, and accept the little he offered, all so I would not have to face being alone. There were times when Gary clearly said that he knew he was not ready for a relationship because he had never truly lived life on his own; I cried, begged and manipulated Gary into staying with me. We kept up this unhealthy and dysfunction for four years, until things began to negatively affected me and the children, forcing me to take a hard look at the truth I was trying hard to avoid in Gary and in myself.

Gary moved into the house my dad turned over to me. It was against my better judgment considering all I had gone through with him and the fact that Gary had not weathered the storm while living in the shelter with us. I knew having Gary with us in the shelter would have caused further frustration, therefore before we moved from the apartment, I told him the program was only for women and children. However, when things eventually became better, I allowed him back into our lives.

While in therapy at the shelter, I expressed how I wanted better, but too fearful to be alone, so I decided to continue with the insanity of the relationship. We attended couple's therapy for a few sessions, and then Gary attempted individual therapy, but nothing worked because I came to realize he did not want to and was not ready to face his problems. Shortly after, I realized it was a mistake. I picked up where I had left off, by assuming most of the responsibilities, and once again made it easy for Gary to be complacent; even more disappointing, was I had not spoken up when I should have. On my income, I handled everything and it was a matter of time before I knew everything would again collapse.

I was alone to care for the kids much of the time, running the house, and feeling alone in general. Gary brought with him the same issues that caused me pain throughout the relationship, but this time, I had changed. Once in counseling, the therapist asked me one simple question that had a profound effect on me, "Tanisha, tell me what are your needs, wants and desires?" A question that saddened me because I had no answer to.

All of my life, I had been concerned with everyone else, I had put everyone first, and denied myself what I wanted because I felt undeserving. I had neglected my needs, believing I was not worthy, and believing I did not have the right to have desires, because I did not have an attractive physical appearance. In essence, I saw for the first time, how I had denied myself the right to be human. Although so many hurt me, I too had shown injustice and maltreatment toward myself.

The therapist always ended each session by saying, "Be good to you!" Every time she said it, I resented the statement, but would come to realize I did so because I did not know how to do what appeared to be such a simple task. God truly works in mysterious ways, because he knew the truth in my heart, that I really wanted to be good to me, but had never been shown how to do so. He knew I wanted to be free from the self-inflicted pain, but too fearful to escape the only sense of safety I had come to know. The truth was, I felt safe in my pain, because I could not see past it. I continued to pray, asking God to strengthen my will to accept the things that I could not, and have the courage to live as He intended.

I began to resent myself for settling and allowing the things I had for so long. I resented that Gary's life was what it was, and that he deeply struggled with so much, and because of this fact, he truly did not have a chance to grow into the person he desperately tried hard to be. I was grateful that we found each other, but resentful of the issues that prevented us from being healthy together. I knew deep within Gary truly loved me, and so did I. I was resentful of the way the world molded Gary to believe he could not be content with such a true and powerful love, because of its form. His eyes had been trained to see attraction as a disillusion, which unfortunately caused Gary to struggle greatly with accepting me.

I somehow naïvely believed the strong love we had for each other would help us to overcome the issues affecting our relationship. In this codependent relationship I condoned and excused behaviors out of what I misconstrued as love, loyalty and empathy, but was in fact enabling. I made it easy for Gary not to be accountable for his actions and behaviors. After so many years I realized Gary's struggles, affected his ability to be affectionate, and emotionally cognizant with not only me, but with his boys. I witnessed how Gary's deep seeded pain, and undeveloped self, made it difficult for him to grow as a man. He owned the pain he caused, and knew where it resonated from, but lacked the confidence to cope and move past many of the painful events in his life.

I wanted to be the one Gary knew loved him for who he was, even though it all had become too much to handle. I struggled with guilt that I no longer had the patience to deal with him, knowing that without me, Gary felt even more alone. I saw that Gary wanted better for himself, to be a better partner, and a father. It broke my heart to see that the way he felt about himself did not match who he wanted to be. I did so much to assist Gary and encourage him, but my efforts only depleted the strength I needed for myself and for my children.

Gary constantly sought out countless women, because he needed the constant validation, which never suffice the emptiness Gary felt. We both came from similar brokenness, and had adversities that created great insecurities, feelings of isolation and loneliness. These commonalities I believed had the potential to create a deeper connection.

The problem was that I found myself working harder to help Gary, than he wanted to help himself. His apologies or explanations of his actions and behavior were always in the form of soliloquies, that many times were encrypted ways of saying I love you, but I am comfortable with who I am. Gary constantly placed blame on those who rightfully deserved to be, but I tried to get Gary to see that in doing so, he lost the ability to see his own power, over those who affected his life so greatly. I became frustrated and lacked empathy with the excuses Gary made for not moving forward, and realized these feelings and judgment came from my own bias. I could only see how I refused to make excuses over the things that happened in my life, and struggled to understand why Gary just could not be as strong.

Gary desperately wanted to step out of the shadows of those who had forsaken him, to become his own man, but without the tools to do so, he instead assumed their identities, affecting me and his children the same ways he had been affected. Gary's issues began to consume me to the point where I lost myself in his pain. When Gary began to sink into a hopeless depression so did I.

I knew how to duck and dodge when life threw its curve balls, but Gary did not. He came into the relationship having no real life experiences, or ways to cope with its injustice. I beat myself up a lot over this fact, knowing that when I suffered, so did those in my life, and I had begun to notice it was too much for Gary to handle. I wanted to shield Gary from any difficulties once I recognized he did not have many coping skills. I realized I was causing myself immense amount of stress trying to do for Gary the things he needed to do for himself; even more selfishly on my part, for his lack of effort to become who I wanted him to be. My inconsistency made things more confusing. One day I wanted Gary to step up, the next I was making it convenient for him not to.

I tried to make Gary stop doing the things that irritated me, and made me feel most uncomfortable. I realized his need to talk to random women on the internet was more than a disrespectful act but, an attempt to stroke his ego, because his true self was too insecure. I rationalized, while at the same time, tried effortlessly to stop the lying and constant deception, by attempting to control Gary and the situations, until finally after years of the same thing and little change, I had had enough. The insanity of four years left me doubting myself, feeling as if I was losing it. I became extremely angry, resentful and bitter. I suddenly, thought of all of the failed relationships in my life, how I allowed myself to be hurt, and how I was tired of men not valuing me.

For most of the relationship, communication became scant between Gary and me, until we just stopped communicating altogether. His personality became extremely difficult and impossible to rationalize with, that I felt it was best to cease communication, just to avoid arguing with someone who believed they were always right or who always felt attacked; I felt invisible. Gary spent all of his time talking to random women, failing to give me attention, but instead blamed me for the lack of affection and attention I no longer showed him; which I felt he was undeserving of, for the ways he treated me.

We lived in the same house, but I never felt more alone. For the first year of living together, I dealt with the constant lying, what I considered to be cheating, manipulation, and denial from Gary. I then continued to compromise in so many ways just to make him happy, while never having any of my needs met. The relationship was definitely one-sided and it became all about him. It all began to affect me to where my personality changed drastically.

I was always either crying or enraged and acting on that rage. I took my frustration out on the kids, by yelling and screaming at them and neglected myself. I would lock myself in my room, unavailing myself to my boys. I stopped caring about my personal hygiene and lost interest in everything and everyone. I became anxious to the point of feeling I could not breath most of the time, and paranoid whenever Gary had his phone in his hand, especially at night, when he waited to pursue women.

We began to verbally fight all of the time. We did not fight fair, attacking each other in ways we knew would shed blood emotionally and mentally. I stumped around and yelled, which felt good to get my rage and frustration out, but hurt me knowing that my actions were affecting the children. I just could not stop! Everything Gary did and said made me resent and dislike him to where I could not contain my rage.

As soon as we moved into the house, I told Gary I no longer was going to put up with him, I basically was running the house and taking care of the kids alone; although fearful of raising two small children so close in age alone, I knew I could do it by myself. I resented Gary for not being a better father, for being undependable, and for not showing me the respect I deserved. I mostly resented myself for believing I could not do better, and for thinking I would never find better, therefore staying in the dysfunction. I knew Gary had a lot going on that love alone was not enough to heal. I just wished Gary trusted the judgment of others who saw how special he was, when he was unable to see it in himself. There was much I admired about Gary's truth, he was smart, talented, humorous, hardworking and stronger than he knew.

I own my share of the blame. I hurt Gary as well, I took advantage of his vulnerability, I judged, criticized, belittled and emasculated him. I dominated him, and controlled Gary because I did not trust him. The fact that we had become toxic toward each other, and the fact that I no longer recognized the person I worked so hard to become, made me realize what I did not want to admit. It was an unhealthy relationship and I knew I had to let go. I had come to love Gary very much, I believe in part because of his pain, but knew I had come to love myself more, and needed to treat myself better.

The lies I told myself were very powerful. By believing in these fallacies, I inflicted far greater pain on myself than pain inflicted from others. For most of my life I was the antagonist in my own demise, and saw that I had to become the hero I needed to save myself from myself. I knew I had been entangled in a web of false perceptions of what it meant to be truly happy and fulfilled. My whole life I had learned I needed a man to be complete and happy, and was learning each day during that year, true fulfillment and joy had to come from loving and caring for myself. I was determined to break the chains that held particularly the woman in my family captive for generations. I became motivated to break free!

An interesting fact that I have observed about people, in dysfunctional and unhealthy relationships, is according to a universal truth. Many people look for love, could very well have it, but cannot recognize it, so they disregard that person, to go on to the next, still cannot find it and the insanity continues. This happens because many do not truly know what they are looking for, because they have not found it within themselves first, to then know what to look for in others.

What I had come to realize about myself and the reasons I sought after what I believed was love in the kinds of men I experienced, was that it was is impossible to give someone all of myself, when the reason for choosing them was to fulfill a part of myself that was broken and insecure. I had to continue to learn who I was, in order to know what I wanted from others. I then noticed an ugly truth – that I taught others how to treat me, based on how I treated and valued myself. If I did not love and respect myself, then how could I expect others to? For me, being broken and tied up was not the time to be venturing out to find anything to superficially fill my void. Breaking the emotional and mental strongholds that affected my self-esteem, required knowing who I am and having the courage to stand against who I was not. I had become bound by strongholds that restricted me from living authentically, that they created shifts in who I truly was and who I was meant to be. These two aspects were never meant to be incongruent.

I found myself needing Gary to support me when everything suddenly went wrong. The tipping point in the relationship was what I considered to be the greatest deceit of all. Gary dishonored the agreement we made before we moved into the house. We agreed to claim each of the boys on our income taxes, however Gary breeched the agreement, and filed both boys without my knowledge. It was January of 2015, I had had enough and asked Gary to prepare to leave once he got his return. I found out about his return weeks after my car broke down, and I found myself sitting at home desperately trying to find a means to get it fixed. Some time passed, and I had not still found a solution; things were looking grim to the point where I realized I would have to resign from my job at Tabor, because I did not have a means to get the kids to daycare and myself to work. Neither were far from where I lived, but physically it would have been difficult traveling with two toddlers.

Over the course of two weeks, Gary witnessed my desperation with trying to find a way to get to work and offered no support or care to help me. His car was in the shop, so he traveled to and from on the bus. About a week later, I had aversely given Tabor notice to resign, some days later, I was going through mail, and came across something with Gary's name on it; I felt it and realized the envelop contained a card. Something told me to open it, and when I did it was a debit card from his job.

Something again tugged at me to see if I could gain access to his account. I had his social security number and date of birth, I was surprised that was all I needed to hear his balance over the automated service. I did not trust Gary regarding anything, particularly money, because he was always so secretive. I was able to hear his balance and last transactions, which I almost lost my breath when it stated that Gary had about ten thousand dollars in his account. I was frozen with disbelief.

Gary had been staying with his parents after I asked him to leave because of a previous situation. I called him asking about the money, in which he nonchalantly said he claimed both the kids on his income taxes and had done so, because I told Gary I no longer wanted to be with him, which his excuse was that he needed to take care of himself. I was beyond enraged, Gary knew how important having a vehicle was for me, and had the money to get the car fixed. Gary saw how frantic I was over losing my ability to work, and allowed me to let go of the very thing that held my life together in so many ways. I saw his disregard, and cruelty as him shaking hands with the devil just out of spite.

When I checked his balance, I heard major transactions towards getting his car fixed, clothes and a pair of two hundred-dollar sneakers. When I confronted Gary, he rushed over to retrieve his card, angered that I had invaded his privacy by opening his mail. We yelled back and forth at each other, I was beyond irrational and doused his clothes and two hundred-dollar sneakers with bleach before throwing all his stuff outside in the trash. I then took a picture of the front and back of the card, using it online to make several purchases of food and household necessities, I needed to hold me and the boys over, before Gary found out. When he did, he cursed me out for using his card without his permission.

The boys and I were confined to the house for three months, I begged and pleaded with Gary to give me half of what he had, so that I could attempt to get my job back. Gary gave me money here and there, but it was not enough to sustain the three months we were without, before receiving the final settlement money from the case involving my former landlord, in which I used to buy a car.

Once again, I was faced with true hardship as a single mother who struggled physically and financially with the demands of caring for my two small boys, and maintaining everything on my own, including the bills Gary refused to assist me with he no longer lived with us. His constant manipulative argument became "since you don't want me to live there, I am not obligated to help you, with anything other than what I give you for the boys, whatever you go through is not my problem if it's not concerning my kids." This included times when I got notices of utilities being shut off, or when I just needed extra because every dime I had went to the house and caring for the kids, while Gary stayed with his parents rent free and had no other financial obligations. To add insult to injury, Gary often criticized me for always asking for money, telling me I needed to find a job and to stop being so dependent on him. This storm by far was the greatest, because for two years, I would face its turbulence alone.

Seeing how in many ways he added to the ciaos, I found myself in a situation where I would again pick up the pieces of my life. It was during this time of being completely down, out and again facing potential homelessness, that I had to get myself together, because my efforts to allow the ciaos to continue was ruining me and my life.

I found myself choosing to step into my lifelong fear of being without a man, to I realized I enjoyed being without the drama even more. I believed the love I was looking for could be found in a man, but I would come to learn what I was searching for must first come from God and then shown to myself. I always felt in my spirit, God trying to draw me closer to Him, and I appreciate that He allowed me the time to realize with Him was where my void could only be filled.

Ending the relationship was difficult, because I really wanted it to work, in part to prove that I was the one in control of my life. It was also because the desire of my heart was to be married and for my children to have two healthy parents. I had moments where I blamed myself for the direction my life went in, because of this relationship. I felt I could have avoided being hurt, by ending it the many times God gave me clear signs leading to a way out. Once I dealt with myself and my ulterior motives for holding onto this relationship as long as I had, it was easy to relinquish the control for wanting Gary to get himself together. We will forever have a special relationship, but one that is now different. I continue to hold onto hope that we can get to a healthy place of parenting together for our children and build a friendship where trust can be facilitated from healing and forgiveness. I have now set boundaries for what I will and will not allow into mine and my children's lives. I will be there for Gary, to support him, but he now knows it will only be when he chooses to help himself.

What I am grateful for, are the hard lessons these experiences have taught me, one that opened my eyes to the ways I have allowed men in the past to hurt me. The pain felt was great enough, that I never want to experience any like it again, by compromising myself. This pain allowed me to seek, love and comfort from within. I now look in the mirror without shame and pain staring back at me from what I allowed myself to go through when in these relationships.

Not just with this relationship, but there were turn of events during this time that changed my perception of success. These changes have, for the first time in my life, caused me to step into areas of my greatest fears, discovering, that once in them, there was nothing to fear once I learned to truly trust God.

Johnathan, a man of great wisdom and a beautiful soul, who I became good friends with while at Tabor; comforted me many days while sharing with him my fears, once said to me, "You must call fear out, so that it has nowhere to hide inside of you. You have to stop holding the struggles of your life inside of you and in your heart. You have to stop allowing fear to weigh you down. You have to be in control of it, by holding fear in your hand so that you can dump it when you're done with it." In doing so, I realized the only thing that was in the way of true success and happiness was me. I had to believe that God knew what was best for me than I did for myself. My true test has been letting go and accepting God's purpose for my life whether it differ from the idea of success I defined for myself.

For so long I looked to God to do in my life what I wanted, and in the time I determined. In the mist of my own self, I at times lost sight of His infinite power, unconditional love, everlasting commitment and the fact that He is omnipresent. In coming to terms with these facts, the more humble I have learned to become while dealing with the plights, pains, rejections, injustices and hardships in my life. I learned to see God profoundly and more realistically through the ways He shows Himself in my circumstances.

CHAPTER 24

Through it All I Conquered

BEFORE I WAS GIVEN life, God made me a conqueror with a purpose, and with such a powerful motive came great suffering. To suffer is to know God. To experience life in all of its ambiguity with faith and dignity, is discovering the precious gift of finding ourselves simultaneously. I have experienced the darkness and ugliness of suffering, but have also experienced the resiliency only suffering can produce.

I am grateful to God for having this great strength amidst great pain, and knowing that even while feeling the greatest discomfort, my strength is never depleted. God has built me strong enough to sustain, and knowing this gives me more strength and courage to live each day as it comes. It is the constant effort of being humble and having acceptance that quiets the loudness of negativity telling me to just give up, and having faith that sharpens my daggers to fight my way through injustice.

Having faith is to walk in pitch black darkness, with the confidence in knowing that my steps have been ordered. Confidence is knowing that even if I had nothing seemingly of value, my worth is greater than the sum of a man who has everything. Forgiveness is having the capacity to love, as if I have been loved by the world, when in fact I have been ridiculed, ignored, rejected and mistreated. It can only be the beating of a heart kissed by God himself that loves so passionately in response to great pain.

By rising above the ashes, unaffected from the flames that tried to destroy me, I became destined to conqueror whatever obstacles in place to asunder me from my purpose.

Blessings come in many forms and as a result of many circumstances. What happened to me was a tragedy, but what I found from it was beauty. Like the raging flames of the burning bush, in which God revealed Himself to Moses, He did the same through the flames that disfigured my body. The bush burned and burned, but did not change its form, the phoenix arose from the ashes unscathed, and my spirit refused to die.

Surviving this great event, set the foundation for the rest of my life's traumas and hardships. Years of tolerating indescribable pain, gave me the patience to endure. Self-awareness along with my personal experiences have given me profound insights into the suffering of others; and therefore allows me to reach many in ways that others are unable to.

What has made me more than a conqueror is having to push beyond my human capacities while fighting, and experiencing moments when both my faith and strength felt depleted, but knew that both are what got me through. When the pain proved too palpable, God's healing hands preserved me. When others determined me unworthy, God loved me more. When man could not relate, God showed me it was not their place to.

There have been times when God has charted my path and taken the wheel, while at other times, He has sat in the passenger seat, along for the ride as a quiet support, while I drove haphazardly down roads that took me off course. Nonetheless He has always been with me. In the darkest and most lonely places I have dwelt in my suffering, God was there collecting my tears and hardening them into incredible strength. I have learned, to be content with what I have been given, it is the perfect example of humility, which is most pleasing to God. In my most challenging times, I have learned that God will provide abundant peace in the trepidation in which I dwell, if I just surrender and trust Him.

God surpassed the human capacity to understand, empathize, accept and love me, when I was the most vulnerable. When many people judged and denied me the human experience to feel, God saw my humanness and did not expect anything more. When I felt the deepest of pain, He held me close. Regardless of time, he allowed respites in my pain, knowing that time was his determination, and that I would eventually get to where I needed to be. In all of the times I have found myself stagnant, alone and weary, God encouraged me.

The true nature of my heart is to love. All that I have gone through has had the potential to harden and mold my heart, instead love softened and expanded it. Through my suffering, I have been given incredible insight as to what it means to be human. Experiencing so much has allowed me to meet people in great capacities. Having love, faith and strength in my heart, has made the weight of my cross bearable.

God has shown me his love, and presence in ways by the many angles he presented throughout my life. Whether it was something as simple as a warm glance, a smile, a comforting hug, or words of wisdom and encouragement when my spirit needed recharging. He especially put into place those permanent pillars who refused to give up on me, when I wanted to give up on myself. For so long I had come to see myself as undeserving of help. As strong as I was, I also realized I was weak without allowing others to love and support me. I thought that by asking for or accepting help, I was being a burden to others, but by denying it when it was given, meant I was depriving myself and rejecting God. I was so fearful of being judged that I turned many people away, until I began contributing to my loneliness, and found myself alone when I no longer wanted to be, which I then only had myself to blame. I realized my pride was crippling my growth and was a form of self-neglect. Working on trusting people is something I still struggle with. However, the more I have put myself out there and seeing that people do care and are willing to be there, has helped strengthen my trust in others.

I came to realize through my suffering, I gained compassion to meet people's emotional needs. My suffering made me sensitive to the plight of others, having built up the tolerance from the weight of my own cross. Through encouragement, I learned to take from the strength I use while dealing with my own struggles to give to others in need. It is what has made me relatable, trustworthy and sensitive to what people are going though. I have always made strides to be the friend I wanted to have. I think what people find compelling about me as a confident, is that I am a good listener, but this came with much growth over time. For so long I wanted to always "fix" people's problems, because I could truly relate to their pain; and because I had this belief that everyone needs someone.

When others are in need, I give wholeheartedly, because God says we are to do so without judgment. Knowing what it feels like to be in need, when I see there is one, I get the greatest reward from meeting it. Seeing God through my suffering has taught me never to reject what appears invaluable, because it is in that very situation, where I gain profound insight and appreciation for the human experience, and God's perfect love.

Out of my adversity came forgiveness; because God's love for me is endless, I have the propensity to forgive. In all of the stories I have shared, I have come to forgive the many who have wronged and hurt me. What I have come to understand is that forgiveness should be something easily given to our foes, even when it takes everything within us to give. When we do so, we show them God's love, which then God shows us his grace. Not only have I learned to forgive others, but in doing so I have learned to forgive myself, at which point, I experienced true self love. Forgiveness is the most meaningful to me, because it has the key to unlocking and freeing oneself from the bondage of pain. Those who I have found it most difficult to forgive, I realized, were in the greatest need of love.

I have always shown my mother grace, despite justifiable anger and resentment, but because of them, I struggled to forgive her. It constantly pressed upon my spirit, but the distrust and pain, kept me from believing she was deserving of it. It was not until I was dealing with similar situations my mother had been dealing with for so long, such as experiencing true rejection, deep loneliness and true humility, it was then I realized just how much we were one in the same; more importantly just how much I needed my mother more than anyone else.

God would have it that the only person I could turn to for comfort was my mother, because in many ways, she understood what I was going through. For many years, I did not want to deal with her because of all that she was. I was too involved in separating myself from her, because I did not have time or the patience to tolerate my mother, many times in her weakest moments. I convinced myself that I had to remove myself from my mom to prevent being sucked into her misery. I judged and criticized her lack of effort to be better and get it together; and thought the situations my mom found herself in were results of her own doings, therefore her consequences were nothing to concern myself with. I had my own life, my own issues. I treated my mother no different than the church, many family members and supposed friends, who all at some point in her life lacked patience, empathy, compassion, and did not have the time to deal with the two headed monster which is mental health and addiction.

For so long, I held forgiveness from my mother, but it was during times while experiencing deep disparity, that she showed me nothing but love, and constantly encouraged me. It was during these times that I was proud to have such a strong woman as a mother. When I wanted to believe that giving up was the best option, again my mother lent me her strength as she had done so many times before.

I cannot imagine the strength it took for my mother to hold on during times when she was at her worse, but she did. It was of no coincidence God gave us to each other, it is because of my mother that I came into my strength; it is because of my mother that I learned to preserver. It is because of my mother that I learned to fight and that I am capable. It is because of her, that I recognized my own strength. I think of all the times my mother could have easily gave up, but hung on to God's word, which has always strengthened me to do the same. What I struggled to do, God facilitates with ease. The greatest feeling is knowing that one day, when my mother closes her eyes, I will have peace and have lived without any regrets.

Even with my father, although there is much healing that needs to happen, my love for him is immeasurable. My father has a beautiful heart and his efforts and intentions have always spoke to the depths of his love for me.

What has allowed me to love both my parents unconditionally and no longer with fault, is the understanding and acceptance that they did the best with what they had. Both came from places where love was scarce, and the fact they gave it abundantly to their children, speaks volumes to their true character. Although what they had to parent with was flawed and resulted from pain, out of their painful imperfectness, emerged love.

Out of much dysfunction, pain and poverty came invincible strength, patience, love, and loyalty. I consider myself extremely blessed to have come from a family that is the true definition of strength and perseverance. I am who I am because of these experiences.

I have learned from what I observed and experienced to be better and do better with my children. To forgive my parents is to forgive myself for repeating similar mistakes. Adopting many of their negative ways in my own parenting, has allowed me to have a deeper sense of understanding and compassion for them both.

I am most grateful for the lessons learned from the men who have entered my life. Were it not for these experiences, I would not have a reason to teach my sons differently. With each of my boys, I hoped for a girl, but God knew what was best for me, and for them. Through my sons, I have experienced unconditional love, and acceptance; because I am their mother, they will have experienced affection, God's love, nurturance of their individuality, sensitivity, and have a true understanding of beauty. I have taught Keyan to value a woman, to respect and honor her. To look for her truth in the ways she presents herself. She has to be driven, have moral integrity, but more importantly, she needs to have love and respect for herself. I emphasized having respect for women, especially when faced with women who do not respect themselves.

I have talked with Keyan about the many ways men knowingly and unknowingly degrade and disrespect women. We have had honest dialogue, when he has presented questions related to things he has heard and seen. For the protection of my child, I always forbid him from watching media that depict women in demoralizing ways, because I did not want him to learn by watching, the wrong ways to view women. However, knowing that Keyan would at some point have to make decisions on his own, I knew the importance of planting the seed of information to help Keyan make good decisions. I have told him, although many things and situations he will become exposed to have become socially acceptable, and considered harmless in the ways women are viewed, treated and what women allow based on social expectations, he could be seeking pleasure, excitement and fulfillment in unhealthy ways. I have informed Keyan that many women may have experienced some form of abuse or exploitation, that has damaged her esteem so greatly, that she has created a false self, one that appears to be beautiful, confident and alluring to men. A woman may appear confident, love and enjoy the negative ways she attracts attention, but she is really acting out, because of painful traumas she may have experienced. It is my prayer that when my boys become men, they will influence their generation to appreciate and accept all aspects of beauty, even in its less appealing form.

I have come to realize the things I lacked were not the true determination of my success. I have come to accept that if I have not succeeded in the expectations of the world, I am still successful because I have kept true to holding on to all of the things granted to me by God. Obtaining self-actualization through my adversities has been the greatest success. Self-actualization has allowed me to see the things in myself that prevented me from living in my truth and according to my purpose. As a speaker, I have always given people motivation and inspiration. Oftentimes, I felt ineffective and a hypocrite. My words encouraged people through their struggles, while I felt helpless and lost in mine.

What I realized was holding me back from living with purpose and according to my truth, was being bound by strongholds that significantly affected my self-perception, therefore holding me captive. I also allowed the fears from my life's experiences and the perceptions of others to keep me stagnant. I realized that once I began weeding out the bad and aggressively took charge to break from bondage, then and only then, would I come to see myself the way God does. I had to learn to believe what God sees in me is authentic, in order to experience freedom and have the audacity to just be who I am.

In my life, I had been bound by chains linked from my own fears and doubts, and entangled from knots made from other people's fears, doubts, expectations, judgments and criticisms of me. I eventually became enslaved to the choices I made and the circumstances as a result of them. For most of my life, I tried to fulfill the expectations of others and allowed their judgments and opinions to define me, resulting in afflictions and persecution from myself toward myself.

The negative perceptions I believed to be true about myself were in fact erroneous, untrue and highly deceptive. They filtered into my psyche, infected my mind and corrupted my way of thinking. My thinking caused me to see myself incorrectly and deceptively, which affected the way I saw the world as it pertained to my place in it. My perception of there being all good and safe in the world had become shattered by the reality that the world is flawed, painful, deceitful and unjust. I had learned to push pain so deep down into my subconscious as a protective mechanism.

The traumas in my life came with the implication that I was a powerless victim of my circumstances. With this sense of powerlessness, my faulty belief system led me to believe that I did not have the ability to change my circumstances, which lead to placing blame elsewhere. It was once I conceptualized spiritually, the bigger picture of my spiritual role, that I then gained power to break the holds of my negative thinking.

Breaking free from the things that held me captive, from my breakthrough, required taping into my inner strength. I allowed my circumstances to dictate my fate. I had given up all of my power, eventually developing the mindset that my circumstances were bigger than my ability to take control. So what did I find myself doing? Considering giving in and giving up. I was so tempted to give up the fight, not realizing that within my armor was the propensity to win. I had to come to realize no one will ever be able to fulfill my life, because I have everything inside of me to do it. I was designed to win, because God created me to be a warrior. Through my suffering, I have learned the title does not come without the promise of having to fight. It is a part of God's plan I fight, suffer and struggle. God says suffering provides the sufferer with an opportunity to realize

God's love and forgiveness when he is well again, understanding that God has "ransomed" him from an impending death (Job 33:24). The truth was always easy to see, it shined so bright, until that light began to slowly dim by what I manufactured to be my truth, making it eventually difficult to see my truth during the times when I found myself in complete darkness.

God had given me an indestructible armor, but I did not know it. I had everything I needed to break the strongholds and set myself free. I had a flaming torch to light my path out of darkness. One of my favorite quotes is 2 Corinthians 10:4: "The weapons we fight with are not the weapons of the world. On contrary, they have divine power to demolish strongholds." It was not until I had experienced the freedom of coming undone, that I was able to see myself outside of my experiences and in my true light. Once in that light I had formed a broader, transparent and healthy perception of myself. I eventually learned suffering and struggling are prerequisites to success!

Breaking negative ties that kept me bound, required great courage and faith. Most importantly, I learned it did not mean that I had to always be strong. I believed that every situation, strength was superior and weakness was inferior. What provided me great comfort was learning, God actually preferred that I operated in weakness, because it allowed God to demonstrate who He is. In my weakness and suffering was when I had to learn to rely on Him solely, so as to remember that it was Him and only Him who gave me strength. Courage is nothing but bold faith, and has given me the adrenaline to propel through adversity. Faith is the assurance that God will see me through the process, even though I cannot always see what is happening while I am going through.

What I had come to realize about myself was, someone or something may have caused the pain, but I then gave the pain a breeding place inside of me, cultivating and nurturing the hurt instead of healing it. I had to learn to see each situation for what they were, and come to understand spiritually, the bigger picture. God has allowed for this insight not to pain me, but to teach me, because what I am destined for I cannot reach while in bondage. In this truth I had to learn that I must expose to myself the vulnerability that I hide. I had to stand in the mirror unclothed and stare honestly at my raw truth, regardless of how painful it was to see. If I could not stand the sight of myself, then how could I expect others to? I had to show myself to myself, subtracting any adornments, revealing the parts of myself that I have gone to great lengths to conceal and deceive. I needed to rescue the child I locked away. I had come to understand that many of my struggles developed in my earlier stages of life. Therefore, revisiting those experiences were vital to moving into a healthy future. I discovered I held the key to unlocking the deadbolts that had me weighed down and bound as an adult. My inner child had the answers to my most complex problems, and she has been the sacred keeper of my truth.

My faulty belief system and negative thinking patterns, affected my judgment to make good and healthy decisions. My thinking controlled how I felt and then resulted in the outcome from my actions. I learned to tell myself that I am beautiful, and actually feel that way. I evolved to admire and adore myself. I can see in myself what many are unable to, and my confidence now reflects my high esteem.

There is a subliminal contradiction in the long running campaign to celebrate and improve a women's self-esteem and confidence by telling her to love and embrace her true beauty. Mix messages play out as such: one massage says, "Embrace the woman that you are and all of your imperfections." Then cuts to another message that says, "If you want to be beautiful and not feel embarrassed by even the most subtle flaws, that may not even be noticeable, then here's how."

There is huge emphasis on the idea of being perfect, and many women do not feel comfortable being anything less. The new trends are bigger everything. The more pain a woman endures to be sexually desirable and socially relevant, the better she will feel about herself. With these messages, she then goes out into the world with a skewed perception of what beauty is, feeling good with her new false confidence and then tells a young girl struggling with body image that she is beautiful just as she is.

I am extremely blessed with the confidence in knowing that I am physically beautiful despite what the world sees and thinks of me. Coming into this acceptance means more to me than anything, because at a point in my life, I could not see myself coming into this acceptance. Over time, I pushed myself to stand firm in wearing my difference, and I must say in my diva voice "I wear it well!"

I love the time I spend doing my hair and putting on my makeup. I have a ritual. During my alone time to prep myself for the day in my bathroom, I do so while in my undergarments, I put on some "hype" music and I begin. Dressing in less allows me to be visually conscious of my body, and to see every aspect of it. The time allows me to glance at the tapestry of scars that overtime, I have grown to love the sight of. I then stand in my full-length mirror and really observe my body with pride. I thank God for the process, and am proud of myself for getting to this point.

The sight of myself gives me the same confidence as a very attractive woman, because to me I have worked exceedingly hard for the right to feel as such. I have come to understand the importance of feeling good about myself and truly loving me, knowing that as soon as I take a step outside my door the world's view of me quickly contradicts the image I see.

There are times when I walk pass building windows or something that reflects my entire image, and in that moment, I can see what people see, the severity of my disfigurement, the deformities and the limp I walk with. In that moment I realize just how badly I was injured, and understand people's fears and avoidance. I then feel both shame and pity trying to slip in, but as the moment passes, I concentrate on the beauty I feel for myself despite my reflections' truth. Knowing how easy it is to get caught up in how the world views me, I have to remind myself daily that I am beautiful. My confidence has been birth in knowing I AM BEAUTIFUL because God says I am! It took me a long time to see my truth, but now that I do, I no longer focus on others' opinions, because they have not a clue what it took for me to finally come into acceptance. I worked hard learning to love myself and will never allow anyone to ever make me believe differently. I continue to focus and maintain confidence, by disowning anything that is not in agreement with what God sees in me and with what I believe to be true about myself.

When I learned to break free from the things that held me back from living according to my truth, I realized that much of the loneliness was necessary. I had come to learn my solo journey was one that required an intimate relationship alone with myself. God could not perform the work in me unless he had my undivided attention; constantly finding myself in uncomfortable and lonely situations, was a part of the process. For many, spending time alone is painful and scary because they are forced to face their greatest critic and advisory—themselves. As for me, spending time alone helped me to become more and more comfortable with myself. I eventually learned I could not look to others to give me what I had not first found within myself.

I have learned that real love, must first come from me. Once I learned to love myself, I was no longer desperate to search for it in a man. I have come to find acceptance with the likeliness of not having someone to share my life with, and for the first time I feel at ease in knowing that I will be okay. The world we live in has drastically changed. It has become more superficial, self-serving, and shallow. Its eyes have become tainted with lust and vanity. Even still, I remain optimistic that God has not forgotten the desires of my heart. I am human and there are times when I feel like I am missing out, and the loneliness from the absence of meaningful relationships with people on most days is truly felt; but my commitment to loving and putting myself first, now supersedes the urge to compromise myself. Regardless if someone enters my life or not, the time in this space has given me time to focus on what is most important, taking care of myself, and living according to my truth.

I realized self-love easily attracts love from others. Once I freed myself to love myself, I was then able to do so from a healthy, and organic place. In valuing myself, I teach others how to treat me, by no longer expecting anything less than what I now know I deserve. I realized that love is contagious, when people see the love I have for myself, they fall in love with my truth as well. Looking at myself from a healthier view, I have come to realize that all of the things the world told me about myself were both true and untrue. It all depended on my perception.

I have come to see and understand my growth is a process. During this process it is important to set and have realistic expectations of myself. I have learned to show myself kindness, love and grace. In the past, I judged and then assigned value to myself according to others' perceptions of me. My focus had become so much on what others were doing, that I deemed myself a failure when I could not emulate their success. It has taken me much time to come to understand that what God has for me individually is unique, and I am successful! I am not running this race for no one other than for myself, and my destiny is the finish line; staying in the right lane, and having a clear understanding that I am where God intended for me to be. Along my journey, I have come across people running the same race, but at different speeds; it was God's way of showing me I am never alone. I have learned that it is better to compare myself to my former self because I then have proof the grass is greener on the other side.

What makes me more than a conqueror is having the courage to stand on the peeks of my fears. Once I made the decision to confront my greatest fear, I was released! Being free from mental strongholds, has allowed me to be at war with myself no more, simply because I have learned to change my thoughts. Freedom from emotional strongholds is acknowledging my feelings, understand they are a part of me, but making the choice to no longer allow them to consume me.

Not having arrived at my destiny, my life is still streaming, but I have come to find peace within the progress of the process. This is why I have learned to focus on the progress and no longer the problem, which I have to be conscious of daily. I have learned that progress is space in between time. When I look at who I was, I see pain, but when I look at who I have become, I see Progress! Happiness is contingent upon knowing that perfection does not exist, and progress is all that can be measured. I know I am deserving of the promise God has for my life. I know that because of who I am, I will forever be faced with difficulties, insecurities, suffering, setbacks and pain. It is God's everlasting love and favor that reminds me I am More Than A Conqueror; which then gives me the strength and determination to walk in my purpose, boldly and courageously. No longer will I be turned away by fear, but now will stand firmly, knowing with everything I have gone through in my life and whatever is yet to come, God continues to favor me.

He said to her, "Daughter, your faith has healed you.
Go in peace and be free from your suffering."
(Mark 5:34)

Family reuniting after foster care

First Christmas

Josh and I

Neem and I

Mom and Dad holding Keyan

Rismary and I - 11th grad prom

Caiden and Kiye

Keyan and I

Younger Rasheen and Mom

Tysheen, Mark, I, Hakiem, Mom, Keyan,
Erica, Joshua, and Quadir

Sister and I

My cousin Aisha

This is me in the hospital in high school

Me speaking at a woman's event

ABOUT THE AUTHOR

SEVERELY BURNED IN A house fire at only six months old, Tanisha Carter suffered from multiple degrees of burns over 98 percent of her body, resulting in extensive scarring, and facial disfigurement. After her heart stopped twice, doctors lost hope, but God knew Tanisha's purpose was great! Surpassing the statistical odds of someone sustaining injuries so grave, Tanisha lives to share her testimony of how God favored her. Tanisha is a native of Philadelphia and is a graduate of Chestnut Hill College, where she received both a bachelor's in Communications in 2005, and a master's degree in Clinical and Counseling Psychology in 2013. Tanisha has been sharing her story since the age of eleven as a motivational and inspirational speaker. Tanisha has appeared as a featured guest on talk shows and shared her story internationally. Faced with countless struggles and adversities, such as abuse, discrimination, and intermittent homelessness with her three boys, Tanisha held on to her spirituality to see her through hard and unjust times, while never losing sight of her purpose to be a model of strength for others. Tanisha epitomizes determination and resiliency; and has found personal success through her consciousness to live authentically. Having spent some of her childhood in the foster care system, Tanisha's proudest moment was working in the child welfare system, and being recognized by the Department of Human Services (DHS) for her outstanding work with children and families. Tanisha is also an artist, who enjoys graphic design and oil painting. Tanisha is currently working on Authentic Gems, a youth personal development program, emphasizing on character building, self-esteem and self-image.